Strong NGOs and Weak States

Over the past decade, the Democratic Republic of the Congo (DR Congo) and South Africa have attracted global attention for high rates of sexual and gender-based violence. Why is it that courts in eastern DR Congo prioritize gender crimes despite considerable logistical challenges, while courts in South Africa, home to a far stronger legal infrastructure and human rights record, have struggled to provide justice to victims of similar crimes? Lake shows that state fragility in DR Congo has created openings for human rights nongovernmental organizations (NGOs) to influence legal processes in ways that have proved impossible in countries like South Africa, where the state is stronger. Yet exploiting opportunities presented by state fragility to pursue narrow human rights goals invites a host of new challenges. *Strong NGOs and Weak States* documents the promises and pitfalls of human rights and rule of law advocacy undertaken by NGOs in strong and weak states alike.

Milli Lake is an assistant professor at the London School of Economics' International Relations Department. Her work focuses on human rights, violence, and state-building in weak, developing, and post-conflict states.

Strong NGOs and Weak States

Pursuing Gender Justice in the Democratic Republic of the Congo and South Africa

Milli Lake

London School of Economics

CAMBRIDGE
UNIVERSITY PRESS

University Printing House, Cambridge CB2 8BS, United Kingdom

One Liberty Plaza, 20th Floor, New York, NY 10006, USA

477 Williamstown Road, Port Melbourne, VIC 3207, Australia

314-321, 3rd Floor, Plot 3, Splendor Forum, Jasola District Centre, New Delhi - 110025, India

79 Anson Road, #06-04/06, Singapore 079906

Cambridge University Press is part of the University of Cambridge.

It furthers the University's mission by disseminating knowledge in the pursuit of education, learning and research at the highest international levels of excellence.

www.cambridge.org
Information on this title: www.cambridge.org/9781108419376
DOI: 10.1017/9781108297745

First published 2018

A catalogue record for this publication is available from the British Library

ISBN 978-1-108-41937-6 Hardback
ISBN 978-1-108-41058-8 Paperback

Contents

Illustrations

Preface

In July 2009, I was invited to participate in a conference on human rights and gender violence in Goma, a city in the eastern Democratic Republic of the Congo (DR Congo). The organizers had asked me to speak about justice and human rights in the aftermath of the Rwandan genocide. As I was preparing for my talk, Jacqueline, the conference organizer, told me: "One day, the victims of war here in Congo can be like those in Rwanda. Our people will see justice for the violence committed against them."[1] With these words in mind, I took my place at the podium and addressed the women and men in the audience on the evolution of international justice and the merits of prosecuting human rights violations. The participants listened patiently.

When I finished speaking, Jacqueline turned to the audience members and invited them to share their experiences with me. One by one, the forty-five conference participants, all victims of unthinkable human rights violations, described their experiences. In turn, they shared graphic details of how they had been raped and sexually tortured. Some told me how they felt when they witnessed the murders of their loved ones. Others spoke of being forced to commit unspeakable harms against their partners or family members. Many showed me their wounds, recounting acts of physical and psychological torture. The participants explained how they had traveled from Walikale to the relative safety of Goma on foot, with only the clothes they were wearing, searching for a secure place to rest. On their arrival in Goma, many found refuge at a hospital renowned for its work with victims of gender violence. From there, a local NGO had recruited them to participate in the conference.

The conference participants received my rather abstract discussion of human rights and the rule of law with incredible generosity. Some asked questions and offered opinions. Yet, as the conference progressed,

---

[1] Jacqueline, DR Congo, July 18, 2009. For the purpose of confidentiality, all interviewees are referred to by first name pseudonyms throughout the text. Where direct quotations are used, interview dates are cited using footnotes.

members of the group expressed more concern about how they could access medical care, clean clothes, food for their children, and a secure place to live, rather than how to achieve justice for human rights atrocities. Some spoke about their desires for education and skills-based training. Above all, they told me, they wanted to live somewhere they did not have to fear violence and death.

It was too much, during the conference, to try to reconcile this collection of wants and needs with the ideas that first brought me to work in the field of human rights. Compared to the very real and practical concerns the conference participants faced, the idea that a strong and impartial justice system, grounded in the rule of law, could form the building blocks for the kind of society these individuals wanted to live in seemed abstract and remote. Despite my initial skepticism regarding legal capacity building following this encounter, over the years I have watched increasing numbers of victims and witnesses to sexual assault report crimes committed against them to local authorities and testify against perpetrators of human rights abuses in courts of law. In small villages, with no courtroom or police presence to speak of, I have observed innovative and groundbreaking human rights decisions that draw from some of the most complex contemporary human rights instruments. I have watched war criminals receive prison sentences for their roles in mass atrocities. And throughout this, many victims of violence have continued to express a desire for formal legal justice for crimes committed against them.

Criminal trials for human rights violations in eastern DR Congo provoke a number of questions. In a country whose government struggles to control more than a fraction of its territory, where do the ad hoc courts handing down judgments in remote Congolese villages derive their authority? How are cases selected and how are judicial decisions enforced? Who are the judges handing down these indictments and where did they develop their extraordinary knowledge of human rights and international criminal law? Finally, what do these trials mean for the landscape of violence in eastern DR Congo and the development of state infrastructure and the rule of law?

Understanding how to build the rule of law in fragile states is a challenge that has plagued scholars, donors, and development practitioners all over the world. From Afghanistan to Iraq, Rwanda to Sierra Leone, individuals and organizations in countries transitioning to peace have worked hard to build confidence in formal legal mechanisms as venues for resolving disputes between competing factions and coalitions. Many international organizations have devoted considerable resources to these ends, often focusing their efforts on legal capacity building and rule of law development.

In this book, I focus specifically on the pursuit of justice for sexual and gender-based violence. The successes and failures of advocacy and legal aid efforts in eastern DR Congo are brought into greater relief when compared with the pursuit of justice for sexual and gender-based crimes in another country in which I have conducted research: South Africa. South Africa has attracted similar magnitudes of international attention for its high rates of sexual assault and violent crime. South Africa is also recognized as a regional human rights leader on the African continent, with far greater resources at its disposal to deal with emerging challenges than many of its northern neighbors. Yet activists in South Africa have faced seemingly insurmountable obstacles in their efforts to improve legal accountability for gendered offenses, despite a great many domestic and international human rights organizations working toward this goal.

Since 2006, I have sought to better understand the relative successes and failures of rule of law development and human rights advocacy, and have examined the intended – and unintended – consequences of human rights programming. Questions about the successes and shortcomings of efforts to build the rule of law prove particularly illuminating in DR Congo and South Africa, where the respective successes and failures in each case dramatically challenge preconceived expectations. This book, therefore, analyzes how and why human rights practitioners in eastern DR Congo have succeeded in ensuring that specific Congolese courts give high priority to sexual and gender-based violence, whereas similarly situated in South Africa have remained resistant to efforts to improve gender justice.

Over the past decade of research on rule of law and human rights advocacy in sub-Saharan Africa, I have heard countless stories of violent crime from the perspectives of both perpetrators and survivors of violence. I have observed armed groups, militias, and social movements form and dissolve. I have watched territory fall from government control, symbolically and literally, and have witnessed many victims of devastating violence rebuild their lives after personal, political, and sexual attacks. While this project began as an effort to understand the intersection of gender advocacy, law, human rights, and state-building amid violence, it evolved into an analysis of the complex and often unanticipated ways that state strength and weakness have shaped efforts to promote human rights. I use in-depth case studies of gender violence advocacy in eastern DR Congo and South Africa's Western Cape to explore the challenges *and* opportunities that emerge for human rights activists working at the peripheries of the state and in some of the world's most challenged courts.

Acknowledgments

The communities featured in this book have witnessed far too many foreigners arriving to ask questions, and leaving, often never to return. Few have seen long-term improvements result from the millions of dollars of development aid that has been poured into the projects around them. Fewer still have anything to show for the community consultations, needs assessments, or research projects undertaken in their names. Yet each of the individuals I encountered over the course of my research was patient and accommodating.

It is an understatement to say that the project would not have been possible without their extraordinary generosity. I cannot thank most of the individuals who supported me by name, but special recognition is certainly due to Prisca Bwihangane, Innocent Cokola, Guy Mackongo, Richard Malengule, Henri Mashagiro, Passy Mubalama, Ilot Muthaka, Elysée Sindayigaya, James Songa, and Amani Matabaro Tom. In DR Congo, I would also like to thank Sofia Candeias, Natasha Carleton, Beau Davis, Pablo Kambale Ivanda, Abraham Leno, Desirée Lwambo, Jo Lusi, Emmanuel De Merode, Timo Mueller, Myriam Raymond Jetté, Cornelia Schneider, and Patrick Sikuli, for supporting me in various capacities, and at crucial moments of my research. Lina, Nadine, and Clarisse accompanied me to more trials than I can count. Jessie and her family kindly took me in and provided wonderful company with whom to wait out M23's occupation of Goma. Agnes and Dina always found room for me in Kigali, even when I showed up entirely unannounced. I was very fortunate to spend many weeks in the early periods of my dissertation working in Rwanda with Theoneste Bizimana, Batya Friedman, Zoe Khan, Freddy Mutanguha, Joseph Nkurunziza, Bob and Betty Utter, and Daisy Yoo. These trips gave me the opportunity to get many of the logistical arrangements for my fieldwork in place.

At the University of Washington (UW), I benefited from the guidance of many more friends and colleagues. James Long, George Lovell, Joel Ngugi, Arzoo Osanloo, and Aseem Prakash deserve special mention for the support and assistance they gave me as this project came to fruition as

my doctoral dissertation. Rachel Cichowski, Mary Kay Gugerty, Jamie
Mayerfeld, and Lynn Thomas provided critical support and mentorship,
as well as invaluable feedback on my dissertation research. And Margaret
Levi served as an informal mentor throughout graduate school and
beyond, providing analytic clarity, political engagement, tireless energy,
and personal encouragement and friendship. I am honored to have
worked so closely with her over the years. Bob and Margaret also contributed generous financial support to parts of this project in the form of
the Kaplan Levi Civic Engagement Grant. Finally, this project never
would have come to life without the unwavering support of my dissertation supervisors, Michael McCann and Joel Migdal. Michael began shaping this project, and contributing to my professional and intellectual
development, before I even entered graduate school. I am so grateful for
the time, patience, and intellectual energy he has devoted to it – and to
me – over the years. Joel's constructive advice and relentless kindness kept
me inspired, grounded, and excited about my research trajectory.
Together, Joel and Michael allowed me to think creatively about my
project in ways that few others would have permitted, pushing me to
embrace complexity and clarity simultaneously, to ask difficult questions,
and to reject easy answers. I hope I can always carry their insights with me,
and do justice to their mentorship in my future work.

In Seattle, I am also grateful to my graduate school friends and collea-
gues, who made the early stages of my research possible. I thank Hind
Ahmed Zaki, Yoav Duman, Emily Gade, Anne Greenleaf, Aaron Erlich,
Filiz Khamaran, Hyo Won Lee, Sijeong Lim, Meredith Loken, Mary
Anne Madeira, Kirstine Taylor, and Hadar Sharvit. Outside of academia,
Amanda Bhuket, Melanie Gouby, Nadine Lusi, Rachel Niehuus, and
Julie Norman taught me to think – and to live – differently. I am not sure
I could guess how many cumulative hours I spent writing early drafts of
these chapters next to Amanda Clayton, from Seattle, to Vegas, to Lamu,
to Rutshuru, to Nashville, to Berlin, and back to Seattle. And Daniel
Berliner has consistently provided careful suggestions, theoretical clarity,
endless patience, and the very best company. The generosity, grace, and
humor with which he has tolerated my many unconventional life choices
are things I will never take for granted.

Since leaving Seattle, I have been fortunate to spend time at Freie
Universität, the University of Minnesota, Arizona State University, and
the London School of Economics. Tanja Börzel, Thomas Risse, James
Ron, and Kathryn Sikkink profoundly influenced my work, long before
I knew any of them in person. Since our first encounters they have been
incredibly generous with their time, attention, and feedback, and this
book is far stronger for each of them. I am especially indebted to

Kathryn for keeping me focused on the motivations underpinning my research, and inspiring me to hold myself accountable to every word on every page. At ASU, I am indebted to Cameron Thies for providing me with such a supportive environment to prepare this manuscript. In my time at ASU, I also benefited (directly and from afar) from input, support, and friendship from Alex Braithwaite, Jason Bruner, Geoff Dancy, Chris Farris, Faten Ghosn, Magda Hinajosa, Miki Kittleson, Steven Landis, Babak Rezaeedaryakenari, Sarah Shair Rosenfeld, A. J. Simmons, George Thomas, Carolyn Warner, Ryan Welch, Holly Williamson, Thorin Wright, and Reed Wood. Perhaps most memorably, I am grateful to the Four Corners Conflict Network; Jess Braithwaite and Erica Chenoweth remain sources of immense inspiration. I miss Will Moore's commentary all the time.

I feel very lucky to have had an extended committee of scholars and friends who have provided me with feedback, guidance, and invaluable professional advice. In particular, I thank Séverine Autesserre, Dara Cohen, Kate Cowcher, Maria Eriksson Baaz, Amelia Hoover Green, Cyanne Loyle, Leonie Newhouse, Rachael Pierotti, Laura Seay, Anastasia Shesterinina, Susan Thomson, Aili Mari Tripp, Judith Verweijen, and Elisabeth Wood, who have shaped my thinking and shared helpful comments, contributions, and critiques along the way.

In addition to the Kaplan Levi Civic Engagement Grant, much of the research presented here was supported by the US Institute for Peace (USIP)'s Jennings Randolph Peace Fellowship. I am also grateful for financial support from the University of Washington's Graduate School Chester Fritz Fellowship and Graduate School Presidential Dissertation Fellowship. Parts of the manuscript draw from research supported by the International Law and Policy Institute through its project: "Preventing Sexual and Gender-Based Violence in the Great Lakes Region," commissioned by Norad, the Norwegian Agency for Development Cooperation. At Cambridge University Press, I thank Lew Bateman, John Haslam, and Claire Sissen, as well as Colleen Jankovic and two anonymous reviewers for their thoughtful comments on the manuscript. And I thank Nephtaly Abassa, Emily Gemar, Anissa Haddadi, and Shantel Marekera for their passionate and meticulous research assistance.

Finally, in London, I am indebted to my new academic community. Kirsten Ainley, Kristin Bakke, Megan Black, Cathy Boone, Alex Hartman, Livia Schubinger, Aisling Swaine, Peter Trubowitz, Lisa Vanhala, and others have already made my research stronger. And I am grateful to be back among my family (Lakes, Mackinnons, Rentons, etc.), who taught me to see politics everywhere, and to model feminist love in its shadow.

Researching human rights, gender violence, and civil conflict firsthand forces a different relationship with the world. It exposes the violence of patriarchal power, and, in doing so, demands its rejection and disman-tling in every corner. Because expressions of patriarchal power every-where are sustained by its reproduction anywhere, researching violence requires living differently. And so the field of violence and human rights research is populated by extraordinary and uncompromising women. Women who refuse to participate. They push the field forward, and are changed by the work that they do. I am thankful for them every day. Marie Berry, Kate Cronin Furman, Alma David, Sarah Dreier, Roxani Krystalli, Chloe Lewis, Devorah Manekin, Sarah Parkinson, and many more. This book is dedicated to extraordinary and uncompromising women.

Translation of Key Foreign Terms

Terms translated from French, except where indicated:

Arbre de paix	Peace tree
Arrangement à l'amiable	Amicable arrangement
Assesseurs indigènes	Customary judges
Auditorat militaire	Military prosecutor
Auditeur supérieur	Chief prosecutor
Avocats Sans Frontières	Lawyers without Borders
Baraza (Swahili)	Council of elders
Bourgmestre	Mayor
Chef coutumier	Customary chief
Chef de quartier	Chief of the quarter
Chef de village	Village chief
Chefferies	Chiefdoms
Conseil des sages	Council of elders
Cour de paix	Peace court
Dôte	Dowry/bridewealth
Génocidaires	Perpetrators of genocide
Indaba (Zulu)	Business (referring to a meeting of elders)
La Ligue pour la Protection de l'Enfance Noire	League for the Protection of Black Children
Lobola (Xhosa)	Bridewealth
Maire de la ville	Town mayor
Mutins	Mutiny
Mwami (Swahili)	Chief
Nyumbakumi	Head of ten houses
Procureur général	Chief prosecutor
Sensibilisation	Sensitization
Tribunal de centre	Central court
Tribunal de chefferie	Court of the chiefdom

Tribunal de grande instance	High court
Tribunal de secteur/collectivité	Sector court
Tribunal de territoire	Territorial court
Tribunal indigène	Customary court
Tribunal militaire de garnison	Military garrison court
Tribunaux de paix	Court of the peace
Tribunaux européens	European court
Ukuthwala (Xhosa)	Bride capture
Zone rurale	Rural zone
Zone urbaine	Urban zone

Acronyms for armed actors referenced in this book:[1]

AFDL	(Alliance des Forces Démocratiques pour la Libération du Congo-Zaïre): Democratic Alliance for the Liberation of Congo
CNDP	(Congrès National pour la Défense du Peuple): National Congress for the Defense of the People
FAR	(Forces Armées Rwandais): Armed Forces of Rwanda (pre-1994)
FARDC	(Forces Armées de la République Démocratique du Congo): Armed Forces of the Democratic Republic of the Congo
FAZ	(Forces Armées Zaïroises): Armed Forces of Zaire
FDLR	(Forces Démocratiques de Libération du Rwanda): Democratic Forces for the Liberation of Rwanda
FRF	(Forces Républicaines Fédéralistes): Federalist Republican Forces
MLC	(Mouvement de Libération du Congo): Movement for the Liberation of Congo
MONUSCO	(Mission de l'Organisation des Nations Unies en République Démocratique du Congo): United Nations Organization Mission in the Democratic Republic of the Congo
PNC	(Police Nationale Congolaise): Congolese National Police Force
RCD	(Rassemblement Congolais pour la Démocratie): Rally for Congolese Democracy

---

[1] This is not a complete list of armed actors in eastern DR Congo. These acronyms refer to groups discussed in this text. For a more complete list, see www.irinnews.org/report/89494/drc-who-s-who-among-armed-groups-in-the-east.

RPA   (Armée Patriotique Rwandaise): Rwandan Patriotic
                       Army
RPF   (Front Patriotique Rwandais): Rwandan Patriotic
                       Front

Maps

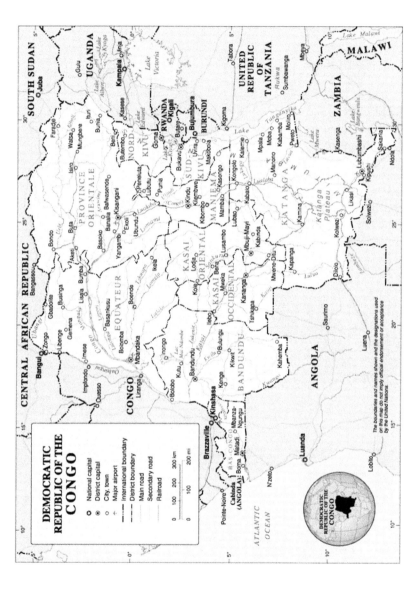

1 Democratic Republic of Congo, Map No. 4007 Rev. 11, May 2016, United Nations (http://www.un.org/Depts/Cartographic/map/profile/drcongo.pdf). Reproduced with permission from the United Nations Publications Board.

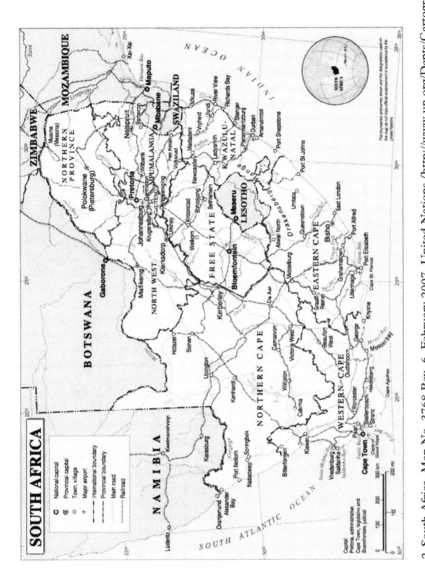

2 South Africa, Map No. 3768 Rev. 6, February 2007, United Nations (http://www.un.org/Depts/Cartographic/map/profile/southafr.pdf). Reproduced with permission from the United Nations Publications Board.

Part I

1   Law in Unforeseen Places

Introduction

Makeshift Justice

In 2006, in a small town in the Equateur Province of the Democratic Republic of the Congo (DR Congo) – nearly 1,000 miles northeast of Kinshasa and 3,000 miles north of Johannesburg – a military judge handed down life sentences to 7 Congolese soldiers for the mass rape of civilian women in the town of Songo Mboyo.[1] The soldiers, former rebels who had been integrated into the Congolese national army, had mutinied after not receiving pay promised to them by their commanders. They caused havoc through the town, looting houses and assaulting men, women, and children. In war-torn DR Congo, such incidents were not uncommon within the armed forces. However, the trial that followed broke new ground in both Congolese history and international criminal law. Despite the fact that DR Congo's laws lacked strong protections against rape at the time, the decision combined elements of the Congolese Penal Code with international human rights protections to arrive at one of the most innovative human rights rulings concerning rape as a crime against humanity that the world had ever seen. The judgment also made DR Congo one of the first countries in the world to utilize the Rome Statute of the International Criminal Court to prosecute international crimes through its domestic courts. The judge ordered the accused to pay $5,000–10,000 USD in compensation to each of the victims and their families.[2]

This landmark human rights decision was produced despite seemingly insurmountable challenges facing the Congolese justice system. At the time, DR Congo's annual budget was insufficient to cover judicial salaries for even one month of the year, meaning that many Congolese state employees and law enforcement officials rarely received the compensation

[1] Tribunal Militaire de Garnison de Mbandaka. RMP 154/PEN/SHOF/05 / RP 084 / 2005 (April 12, 2006).
[2] Ibid.

they were owed. Moreover, magistrates and military judges received little human rights training as part of their formal legal education, especially not in the complex areas of international criminal law invoked in the 2006 judgment. While most towns lack a functioning courtroom, court buildings that do exist typically lack electricity, computers, the Internet, office equipment, or filing space (International Bar Association 2009). Since most courts, police stations, and prosecutors lack any budget whatsoever to carry out their duties, activities like investigating cases or keeping judicial records typically occur either on an informal basis (paid for by victims or other stakeholders) or not at all. Yet, in spite of these challenges, courts in DR Congo's eastern provinces have been incredibly active on specific human rights issues. Most notably, since the landmark 2006 judgment, local courts have produced an extraordinary number of judicial decisions convicting perpetrators of sexual and gender-based violence for their roles in mass atrocities and ordinary sexual offenses.[3] Judges and prosecutors have relied heavily on international human rights instruments to do so.

Attention to sexual and gender-based violence has not been restricted to DR Congo's military courts. In recent years, sexual and gender-based violence has also garnered attention in the civilian justice system. Poor record keeping makes precise figures very difficult to obtain; however, a United Nations Development Programme (UNDP) monitoring project reports that for 5,042 gender violence cases reported to the police in three Congolese provinces from 2010 to 2011, 76.6 percent (3,866 in total) were transferred to the prosecutor's office for investigation. These figures stand in stark contrast to statistics from many other countries. In a study of six European and commonwealth countries, for example, only thirty-five percent of all rape cases reported to police made it as far as the prosecutor's office (Daly and Bouhours 2010).[4]

---

[3] The term "gender-based violence" refers to any form of violence (physical or psychological) that is rooted in structural gender inequalities or results from power imbalances based on traditional gender roles. While this project focused predominantly on judicial responses to systematic and widespread sexual violence, human rights practitioners often employ the term "gender violence" rather than "rape" or "sexual violence" in order to encompass myriad forms of violence. For this reason, I use the term "gender-based violence" to include sexual and nonsexual gender-based crimes. Where I use the term "sexual violence," I refer explicitly to violence of a sexual nature. The term "ordinary" sexual offense is used to refer to any sexual offense committed or criminalized under the ordinary civilian or military penal codes, rather than those offenses that constitute international crimes. My use of these terms is discussed more fully later in this chapter.

[4] See Kelly, Lovett, and Regan (2006); Koss et al. (2004); and Lonsway and Archambault (2012) for comparable statistics in the United States and the United Kingdom. While legal processes in both civilian and military courts were riddled with many of the usual challenges faced in severely under-resourced legal systems, elements of legal practice, particularly in cases dealt with by specialized police units, exemplified fairly remarkable gender sensitivity.

For lack of a functioning courtroom in close proximity to the site of the mutiny, the landmark Songo Mboyo ruling was handed down in a makeshift courtroom in the shade of a line of trees. Many such rulings have since been delivered in similar locations: in equatorial towns, dense forests, and remote hillside villages almost entirely inaccessible by road. Yet, time and time again, these decisions have invoked cutting-edge human rights provisions, drawing from a large body of international human rights law and the most innovative international jurisprudence. Of even greater surprise in a country renowned for its egregious human rights violations, collapsed state apparatus, and dilapidated judicial infrastructure, victims of gender violence have turned to Congolese courts in increasing numbers to resolve their grievances.

This book compares the surprisingly progressive response to gender-based violence from courts in DR Congo's eastern provinces to the legal response in another country, South Africa, where human rights advocates have called attention to similarly shocking incidence of gender-based violence, but this time against the backdrop of a legal system that emerged from its political transition as a human rights leader. Like DR Congo, South Africa has attracted considerable international attention for its extraordinarily high rates of sexual crimes. Yet South Africa's institutional response has differed notably from eastern DR Congo's. Analyzing the treatment of sexual and gender-based crimes by courts in a fragile and under-resourced state against their treatment in a very different – and more robust – institutional setting brings this book's central questions into greater relief.

A Point of Comparison

South Africa, like DR Congo, has frequently been referred to as "the worst place in the world to be a woman" (Abrahams 2013; Faul 2013; Snodgrass 2015). Despite avid global attention to the country's so-called rape crisis, South Africa's courts have been notably silent – even hostile – toward widespread gender violence, which remains notoriously difficult to prosecute. Some reports suggest that fewer than five percent of reported sexual offenses ever make it to South Africa's courts, and those few cases that do go to trial rarely result in conviction (Human Rights Watch 2011). In addition, in stark contravention of South African law, the victim's prior sexual conduct and other characteristics have too often been permitted as mitigating circumstances in investigation and sentencing to suggest that the victim provoked the attack.

These facts are particularly startling given that South Africa's courts are endowed with considerably greater resources and far more institutionalized human rights protections than those of DR Congo. Following the end of apartheid, South Africa was hailed as a regional human rights leader by virtue of its progressive record on a variety of human rights concerns. In 2007, South Africa passed exemplary legislation criminalizing sexual and gender-based offenses, and its domestic legal protections against rape are among the strongest in the world. Moreover, the country is home to one of the world's most influential women's rights movements. Yet survivors of sexual violence in South Africa have faced immense difficulties in securing justice for crimes committed against them. Given that domestic and transnational human rights advocates in both countries have campaigned tirelessly for gender justice, why have their efforts in eastern DR Congo resulted in an emerging culture of legal accountability and increasing numbers of gender-sensitive rulings (despite an institutional environment that would seemingly obstruct the effective pursuit of criminal justice), while the efforts of activists in South Africa have met endless barriers? Strong domestic human rights coalitions in South Africa, who have robust links to global donors, have failed to exert real influence over formal institutional processes, police responsiveness to gender violence cases, courtroom practices, or judicial decisions.

In both countries, rape and sexual violence are notoriously widespread. Both South Africa and DR Congo have been described as the "rape capitals" of the world by media and humanitarian outlets (Wilkinson 2014). Reports suggest that one in every three women will be subject to nonconsensual sex in her lifetime (Thomson Reuters Foundation 2011; United Nations Office of Drugs and Crime 2014). In a South African study from 2007, one in four men admitted to an act of rape (Jewkes et al. 2011), and a similar study involving men in eastern DR Congo arrived at a comparable figure (Sonke Gender Justice Network 2012). In South Africa and DR Congo, reports of sexual attacks on men, as well as public assaults on men and women, the sexual mutilation of young children and newborn babies (both male and female), and brutal gang rapes of civilians have attracted domestic and international media attention and condemnation. While government representatives have acknowledged so-called rape epidemics in the respective countries, and have introduced policies and legislative reforms designed to mitigate violence and facilitate prospects for criminal accountability, influential political elites in *both* countries have appeared reluctant to sincerely engage with this threat to social order and gender security. Given these fairly comparable responses from political elites, why have local courts in eastern DR Congo diverged so dramatically from those in South Africa in their legal responses?

The Argument: Human Rights Advocacy and Openings Created by State Fragility

The argument I advance in this book is that state fragility in eastern DR Congo has created opportunities for non-state actors to shape the human rights practices of local courts in ways that have proved impossible in environments with stronger institutional capacity and better-respected state sovereignty. Opportunity structures created by state fragility in DR Congo have enabled both domestic and international NGOs and human rights practitioners to exert considerable influence over judicial processes at multiple levels of governance, most notably at the level of local courts. Put differently, state weakness has allowed human rights practitioners to bypass the central state in order to assume selective responsibility over legal practice in ways that prove impossible in stronger state environments. A coalition of NGOs and other non-state actors have thus been able to ensure that courts and prosecutors give high priority to certain human rights issues – in this case, the prosecution of sexual and gender-based violence – to a greater extent than have similarly situated activists in South Africa.

Activities undertaken by external actors in eastern DR Congo have led to striking advancements in the legal system's capacity to hold perpetrators of gender-based crimes criminally accountable for their actions. These include steady increases in rates of convictions for sexual and gender-based offenses in courts across the east, as well as a growing willingness among some victims to turn to the legal system for support. Many judges and prosecutors have also adopted increasingly progressive and gender-sensitive legal reasoning in their decisions and arguments, and legal practitioners have engaged in considerable efforts to afford the protections required by law to victims and witnesses throughout the legal process. Gender violence activists and human rights NGOs in eastern DR Congo have thus met greater successes on a range of indicators than have their counterparts in South Africa.

However, the successes of NGOs and other non-state actors in promoting justice for gender-based crimes through local courts in eastern DR Congo have not come without a price. Indeed, capitalizing on state fragility to advance gender justice has introduced a host of new challenges. For example, a singular focus on securing convictions for gender-based crimes has meant that the rights of defendants, and the enforcement and implementation of legal decisions, have sometimes been overlooked in favor of bolstering prosecutorial capacity. Emphasizing gender violence over other pressing human rights concerns has created perverse incentives for legal practitioners and human rights organizations, such that other violent crimes persist with impunity.

Finally, victim-centered processes are most evident in cases targeted by NGO interventions or supported by NGO legal teams, while others vary considerably in their treatment. The extent to which victim-sensitive practices are likely to generate future spillover effects elsewhere in the legal system remains an open question.

In order to elucidate the intended and unintended consequences of using opportunities created by weak state capacity to advance specific human rights agendas, this book is divided into two parts. Part I outlines the ways in which state weakness in eastern DR Congo has created opportunities for human rights advocates to shape judicial approaches toward sexual and gender-based violence in accordance with international human rights norms. Part I also shows how a very different institutional environment in South Africa has stymied possibilities for similar legal developments, given the state's demonstrable resistance to gender justice. Part II explores the contradictions and complexities that arise from a singular international focus on bolstering legal capacity for sexual and gender-based violence, exploring the repercussions of targeted human rights interventions that circumvent the juridical authority of weak states.

This book draws its definition of opportunity structures from the literature on social movements and legal mobilization. Kitschelt (1986: 58) defines opportunity structures as specific configurations of resources, institutional arrangements, and historical precedents for social mobilization that facilitate or constrain certain actions and behaviors. The term has typically been used to describe tactics employed by social movements, whereby coalitions of actors take advantage of certain political structures, regime types, or environments, in order to promote particular political agendas. While some have defined a political structure's "openness" according to its regime's responsiveness to its electorate (Eisinger 1973), others have examined opportunities for advancing human rights claims that arise from changes in procedural rules (Alter and Vargas 2000), institutional context (Bloodgood, Tremblay-Boire, and Prakash 2013; Noonan 1995; Wilson and Cordero 2006), political climate (Hilson 2002; Ramirez 2012), and new possibilities for resource mobilization (Byrne 2013; McCarthy and Zald 1977).

For Eisinger (1973), an open opportunity structure involves a government that provides opportunities for formal representation of diverse segments of its population, and that allows those constituencies to influence government policy. While Eisinger was writing about opportunities in Western democratic systems, the broad concept of open and closed political structures has traveled to other political and institutional contexts. Scholars working on political transition, for example, have employed the term "political opportunity structures" to refer to how changes in political structure or regime type might create new opportunities for political reform or minority inclusion (Berry 2015, 2018; Noonan 1995; Ramirez 2012; Tripp 2010). A similarly well-developed literature on legal opportunity structures emphasizes the extent to which changes in laws, processes, and structures can alter human rights strategies, create possibilities for new forms of legal mobilization, or lay the foundations for more progressive social justice outcomes, decisions, or judicial reasoning in courts (Cichowski 2007; Vanhala 2012; Wilson and Cordero 2006).

I interpret the openness of the political opportunity structure in eastern DR Congo (and, at times, in transitional South Africa) fairly broadly. In eastern DR Congo, the political opportunity structure has remained "open" in the sense that the institutional configurations created by state fragility have generated opportunities for non-state actors to advance their agendas through multiple institutional channels. Not only has state fragility permitted unprecedented access to local and national political structures by human rights organizations but, as discussed in Chapter 3, the heavy reliance on aid distributed by international agencies, combined with other empirical realities of weak statehood, has meant that courts are heavily incentivized to respond to the agendas of external stakeholders. This openness across a variety of dimensions has enabled organizations, including NGOs, foreign governments, international agencies, and others, to exert influence over national policy and its implementation in the eastern provinces. These dynamics illuminate the institutional context from which gender-progressive legal practices and reasoning have emerged. Sometimes organizations have worked in collaboration with one another to promote these goals, and sometimes they have acted independently.[5]

Openings created by state fragility, which allow organizations working on sexual and gender-based violence to exert influence over legal processes, arise from both "empirical" and "juridical" dimensions of state

---

[5] In this sense, the phenomenon I describe differs significantly from the social movements described in sociology literature. The literature presents social movements as collective, rational decision-makers that mobilize their followers and promote their causes with the best available strategies given their limited cognitive and material resources (McCarthy and Zald 1977; Oberschall 1995). While a social movement is typically understood as a bottom-up movement that gains salience at a specific moment in history, the phenomenon I outline involves a broad coalition of actors often employing top-down strategies guided by global human rights scripts. This loose coalition of actors sometimes works toward similar goals and objectives but is not necessarily unified by a single agenda or approach. Global efforts to overcome sexual and gender-based violence, and their particular manifestations in South Africa and DR Congo, are discussed at greater length in Chapter 3.

fragility (Jackson and Rosberg 1982; M. Lake 2014). First, a general lack of oversight and capacity on the part of the central state has meant that well-resourced human rights NGOs have, in effect, been able to assume direct responsibility for one of the most fundamental functions of govern-ance: the administration of justice. They have also been able to shape law and policy at national and local levels and through formal and informal channels. Second, the international designation of DR Congo as a "weak" or "fragile" state has channeled attention and resource flows toward state capacity building, as well as provided a justification for non-state actors to intervene in matters usually under the jurisdiction of a sovereign govern-ment, which would not be possible in a stronger state environment.[6]

To elaborate, when states are described as weak or fragile, that description often reflects an empirical reality in which NGOs, religious groups, and/or civil society organizations have assumed some of the basic functions of governance (Lund 2006; Mampilly 2011; Menkhaus 2007). Since the central state in DR Congo has remained absent from the organization and regulation of local communities for a number of decades, as in other weak state settings a variety of non-state actors have stepped in to perform governance activities. The empirical realities of weak statehood in eastern DR Congo have thus meant that domestic civil society organizations, sometimes in partnership with international and humanitarian agencies, often function as the de facto legitimate authorities: they make decisions about policy, employ per-sonnel, and manage institutions in ways that could not occur in stronger state settings (Büscher and Vlassenroot 2010; Seay 2009; Trefon 2011). The de facto assumption of power by these diverse sets of actors has created opportunities for non-state actors to enter and influence judicial processes, engaging in tasks normally reserved for sovereign governments.

"Juridical" dimensions of state fragility have also created opportunities for human rights advocacy. Jackson and Rosberg (1982) suggest that the formal recognition of sovereign states (known as juridical statehood) facilitates actions and resource flows from other states and members of the international community. Similarly, state fragility can be recognized both formally (for instance, by UN Security Council Resolutions), and informally (through failed states indices and the discursive frames employed by development practitioners and other key actors).[7] When

---

[6] See Caplan (2006), Chesterman (2005), Donais (2009), and Zaum (2006) for discussions of international actors promoting norms of human rights, good governance, and state-building in weak or post-conflict states.

[7] See Autesserre (2009, 2010, 2012) for further discussion of the discursive frames applied to DR Congo's (post)-conflict identity.

ascribed by international representatives, terms such as "fragile," "(post-) conflict," or "failed" statehood perform similar functions, channeling international funding toward specific aspects of state development and justifying continued intrusions on national sovereignty.[8] The formal *and* informal recognition of state weakness has facilitated resource flows toward post-conflict reconstruction in eastern DR Congo and directed attention toward state-building and justice sector reform. State fragility has also been used to direct international attention toward widespread sexual and gender-based violence, with DR Congo identified as one of eight priority countries by the Action Against Sexual Violence in Conflict Network under the UN's Special Representative on Sexual Violence in Conflict.[9]

Perhaps the most important formal recognition of DR Congo's state fragility was the establishment of the United Nations Organization Mission in the Democratic Republic of the Congo (MONUC, now MONUSCO) in July 1999, following the Lusaka Ceasefire Agreement. MONUSCO is the largest peacekeeping mission in UN history. The UN Security Council legitimized its interventions by identifying state weakness, ongoing conflict, violations of international law, and attacks on the territorial integrity of the state by armed groups, to justify and expand its mission.[10] The mandate included: the protection of civilians under threat of physical violence; the disarmament, demobilization, repatriation, and reintegration of armed groups; and the provision of technical assistance to rebuild infrastructure in the eastern provinces. Using Chapter VII of the UN Charter, the UN provided formal recognition – grounded in international law – of the Congolese state's inability to provide these basic public goods to its population.

In 2002, the International Criminal Court (ICC) in The Hague also formally recognized the magnitude of the crimes taking place in DR Congo's eastern provinces, and the Congolese state's incompetence to deal with these crimes domestically. Preliminary ICC investigations established that war crimes and crimes against humanity had almost

[8] In cases such as Somalia, Haiti, and Afghanistan, the international community has invoked state weakness, sometimes through the language of the responsibility to protect, to provide moral or legal justifications for intrusions on national sovereignty by UN peacekeeping missions, NATO, or international occupations. In other cases, state weakness has been invoked to justify a more subtle sharing of sovereignty such as international support provided to government ministries and agencies (Krasner 1999).
[9] See the Office of the Special Representative of the Secretary-General on Sexual Violence in Conflict. www.un.org/sexualviolenceinconflict/about-us/about-the-office/.
[10] United Nations Security Council (1999a and 1999b). In 2012, MONUC became MONUSCO, the United Nations Organization Stabilization Mission to the Democratic Republic of Congo, or the Mission de l'Organisation des Nations Unies pour la stabilisation en Republique democratique du Congo.

certainly occurred. Under international law, such crimes are considered so egregious that they warrant "international concern" and the international community as a whole is implicated in accountability. In 2004, the Prosecutor of the ICC formally opened an investigation in DR Congo following a referral from DR Congo's government. The investigation was opened on the grounds that DR Congo's justice system was ill equipped to conduct investigations domestically (International Criminal Court 2004). These rulings drew international media attention to the scale and gravity of crimes in eastern DR Congo, and prompted a number of NGOs to incorporate judicial capacity building and ICC outreach in DR Congo into their program objectives. The dispatch of the largest UN deployment in history, combined with the ICC investigations and DR Congo's frequent appearances at the bottom of failed states and development indices, has reinforced the idea that DR Congo is a fragile state with a weak infrastructure. The language of state fragility has thus served to justify intrusions on Congolese state sovereignty, and interventions into affairs that elsewhere would fall to the responsibility of sovereign governments' ministries.

Instead of hindering judicial developments, these two dimensions of state fragility – the "empirical" and the "juridical" – have allowed external actors (NGOs, UN agencies and other non-state actors involved in state capacity building and justice sector reform) to directly intervene in the work of target courts across the east. As such, these actors have been able to direct justice sector activities toward issues the international donor community deems "urgent priorities," namely: gender justice. In a 2014 program report, the United Nations Development Program noted that its support for mobile courts in eastern DR Congo fell under its mandate to improve women's access to justice and the prosecution of gender crimes. The United Nations Development Program therefore required that the courts hear a prespecified quota of gender cases as an explicit condition of its financial and logistical support (United Nations Development Programme 2014: 9). Counterintuitively, therefore, state fragility in eastern DR Congo has facilitated, rather than obstructed, aspects of human rights advocacy, particularly legal attention to gender violence.

In stark contrast, a comparatively stronger central state and a well-resourced judiciary in the case of South Africa has meant that activists have struggled to overcome deeply institutionalized political resistance to gender reform, as well as conservative attitudes that pervade the courts and obstruct possibilities of legal accountability for gender-based crimes. The South African state, while under-resourced in some areas, exhibits gargantuan capabilities when compared to DR Congo's. While the collapse of the apartheid regime in South Africa in 1994 – and the country's subsequent transition to democracy – created moments of opportunity, the institutional openings available to NGOs in eastern DR Congo have proved absent or short-lived in South Africa, largely because of the country's more centralized and robustly entrenched state apparatus.

After the collapse of apartheid in 1994, a number of entry points opened for domestic and international actors to influence the domestic human rights regime. Human rights activists, who were at the forefront of anti-apartheid activism, were able to exert considerable influence over the human rights policies and practices adopted by the nascent democratic state. In this brief window, South Africa became internationally renowned for its human rights commitments and practices. Yet, in the years since South Africa's democratic transition, human rights activists have found it increasingly difficult to access and influence the agendas of political elites. First, the gap has considerably widened between the priorities of domestic and international human rights activists and those of South Africa's political elite. Indeed, the post-2009 political elite has articulated increasing hostility toward the internationally acclaimed human rights ideals espoused in the Mandela/Mbeki era.[11] Second, as the capacity of the transitional South African state has grown and stabilized, contemporary political elites no longer feel as beholden to the domestic and international human rights organizations that were pivotal to the struggle against apartheid.[12] Finally, South Africa's postapartheid reputation as a stable Weberian democracy with a rapidly growing economy has meant that the prevailing norms of what Stephen Krasner terms "Westphalian sovereignty" have been respected (Krasner 1999). As a result, international actors have refrained from intervening in matters under the jurisdiction of the sovereign South African state. Simply put, the South African government is deemed capable – and therefore responsible – for governing within its own territory. This includes making its own decisions over where to expend resources and how to prosecute criminal offenses. To use Eisinger's language, political and legal opportunity structures in South Africa have, over time, become increasingly "closed."

---

[11] See Gumede (2008) and Mangcu (2009) for a discussion of the rise of populist politics in South Africa and a rejection of what has been perceived as neocolonial human rights politics.

[12] See Hilson (2002) for a discussion of the ways in which social movements have utilized opportunity structures created by institutional changes to shape legal outcomes elsewhere.

Transnational Human Rights Advocacy: Expectations from the Literature

The relationship between state capacity and human rights advocacy in eastern DR Congo and South Africa's Western Cape counters the expectations of many human rights scholars. Many predict that institutional legacies best explain human rights successes and failures (VonDoepp 2009; Weingast 2010; Widner 2001). Characteristics such as an independent judiciary (Lupu 2013; Skaar 2011; Trochev 2010), strong human rights laws (Keith 2002), and high rule of law (Apodaca 2004; Carothers 2006) have often been invoked to explain the likelihood that domestic courts will adopt and enforce international human rights protections. These arguments are intuitive: regimes in which certain rights and political freedoms are already entrenched should be more likely to respect and promote emerging international norms, and should also possess institutionalized mechanisms through which new international human rights protections can be implemented or incorporated into domestic practice.

Yet DR Congo is not the only fragile state in which courts have behaved unexpectedly. In Afghanistan, Liberia, Somalia, and South Sudan, courts have periodically delivered surprising (albeit extremely limited) legal victories to female victims of domestic violence in recent years, despite domestic institutional environments that would appear hostile to such developments (Buss et al. 2014; Massoud 2006; Motley 2014; United Nations Development Program 2012). In the aftermath of the civil wars in Liberia, Rwanda, Sierra Leone, and Timor Leste, local courts were also active on particular human rights issues, despite almost entirely decimated domestic legal systems. Small and often under-resourced district courts in Timor Leste, for instance, indicted perpetrators of international crimes (Cohen 2002; United Nations Development Programme 2014a). In the mid-2000s, magistrates' courts in Sierra Leone and Liberia began to deal with gender offenses for the first time, in environments where such issues had previously fallen to customary authorities. In Liberia, legal authorities became active in reducing pretrial detention rates and protecting the rights of defendants. Institutional explanations such as those summarized earlier explain broad trends but they prove unable to account for human rights developments that occur in weak state settings. Moreover, they remain entirely ill equipped to explain why some weak states exhibit stronger human rights performances in certain spheres than states with more effective institutional capacity.

Literatures on NGOs and transnational advocacy networks have proved somewhat more successful at explaining why human rights advancements occur in certain contexts and at particular historical moments. Hafner-Burton and Tsutsui (2005), Murdie and Peksen (2014), Neumayer (2005), and Simmons (2009) each find evidence that a proliferation of NGOs or international nongovernmental organizations (INGOs) in a given country increases the likelihood that international human rights treaties or laws will improve human rights practices in the domestic sphere. Many have also analyzed the powerful role of transnational advocacy networks in this context. Keck and Sikkink (1998) famously argued that strong links between local and transnational organizations lead to increased pressure on offending regimes to improve policies and practices. Where transnational activist networks are present, pressure can be levied simultaneously by domestic actors and from abroad, leading to an increased likelihood of positive human rights outcomes in issue areas prioritized by transnational networks.

However, this body of work similarly falls short of explaining the surprisingly divergent outcomes in eastern DR Congo and South Africa's Western Cape. Much of the research on NGOs and human rights assumes that the larger the domestic NGO network in a given context, the more successful domestic activists will be in influencing a state's institutional procedures, policies, and behavior. Outside of political science, scholars have drawn similar conclusions. Sally Merry (2006) finds evidence that advocacy around international human rights issues is likely to be far more effective when it is supported by a robust homegrown domestic human rights movement whose actors are well positioned to "translate" international human rights norms into local practice. Yet, as the foregoing discussion demonstrates, this has not been the case in the South African and Congolese experiences. Despite an incredibly active domestic movement around sexual and gender-based violence and strong transnational linkages in South Africa, versus a glaring absence of a transnationally networked movement in eastern DR Congo prior to 2006, we see that the practical implementation of gender-progressive human rights law in some domestic courts has been significantly *more* effective in DR Congo.[13]

Even scholars who look closely at the implementation of laws rather than the introduction of new laws or policies have a tendency to assume that, where state capacity is weak, we would observe a "decoupling"

---

[13] While there were a large number of local grassroots human rights organizations working on gender issues across DR Congo prior to 2006, some of which were even funded by international stakeholders, these organizations were often working on isolated issues on a fairly ad hoc basis. A broad-based coalition of local women's rights and gender violence activists – or anything resembling a broad-based and transnationally connected movement like the one observed in South Africa – was missing in DR Congo until the 2000s.

between law and practice (Meyer et al. 1997). Scholars in sociology's World Society school, for example, have powerfully argued that even if international actors are successful at promoting policy reform at the level of the central government, the weaker the state, the *less* likely it is that such reforms will result in genuine human rights advancements at the local level. Instead, we should expect a decoupling between law and practice in weak state settings. These findings have been echoed in recent studies from Risse, Ropp, and Sikkink (2013) and Risse (2011). Like many before them, each of these authors reaches the conclusion that state capacity exists as a powerful scope condition for the effective diffusion of international human rights law, and state fragility would ultimately serve as a strong and direct impediment to local implementation.

I argue that these earlier approaches miss the unique ways that state fragility might facilitate elements of human rights advocacy at various levels of governance, by allowing domestic and international human rights organizations local entry points through which to directly shape and influence the work of courts and legal institutions. In eastern DR Congo, domestic and international NGOs have been able to oversee the implementation of human rights law and policy in local courts and ensure victim-sensitive judicial responses in ways that proved impossible in South Africa. Such efforts have been important and consequential: training and resources have dramatically improved the collection of evidence in sensitive sexual assault cases. Sensitization programs have been crucial to overturning "rape myths" that previously overshadowed investigations and compromised the respect shown to victims by police and law enforcement practitioners. Knowledge of new laws and cutting-edge legal principles relating to gender violence, as well as increasing expertise in international human rights law, has made it uncommon for judges and prosecutors across the east to consider a victim's sexual history or attire as relevant to the subject of consent, to engage in questioning that might further traumatize the victim, or to use personal characteristics as grounds to question the credibility of his/her testimony.

However, while state fragility has created unique opportunities for human rights activists to influence specific activities within local courts, it also presents challenges. Since external attention has been directed predominantly toward bolstering legal accountability through prosecution and conviction, other important human rights efforts – such as protecting the rights of defendants, and implementing and enforcing decisions once rendered – have been treated as low priority. International donors' frequent emphasis on a single human rights issue (gender violence), and one particular response (criminal prosecution), is worthy of careful scrutiny. So too are the ways that external actors and international organizations have assumed direct responsibility over tasks normally reserved for government actors. Human rights gains at the peripheries of the state thus manifest as Janus-faced. Taking advantage of state fragility to advance a singular human rights agenda has made consequential human rights innovations possible; yet state fragility can prevent these gains from spilling over into other areas. And, indeed, activists working in such contexts continue to face tremendous challenges.Opportunity structures created by state fragility provoke inevitable questions about the value, longevity, and sustainability of human rights gains that circumvent the usual channels. Part II of this book returns to these challenges, weighing them against the hard-fought victories Congolese gender rights activists have won in local courts.

Gender Violence: A Note on Terminology

Given a glaring lack of consensus over definitions of rape, consent, or forced sex, it is useful to clarify these terms as they are employed in this manuscript. The term "gender-based violence" was introduced by the United Nations in the 1993 Declaration on the Elimination of all Forms of Discrimination against Women and became widely used at the turn of the twenty-first century. "Gender violence" is used as an umbrella term to refer to any form of violence (physical or psychological) that is rooted in structural gender inequalities or that results from power disparities based on gender roles. Such violence may include rape, sexual assault, relationship violence in heterosexual and same-sex partnerships, sexual harassment, degrading treatment, or verbal abuse. In its broadest sense, it can also encompass economic violence used by one individual over another by virtue of that person's gender identity (such as the withholding of child support on the basis that it is the job of the mother to provide for her children).

Gender violence may be perpetrated by men or women. The term "gender-based violence" largely superseded the terms "violence against women" and "sexual violence" in human rights discourse to reflect the idea that both men *and* women may be victims of gender violence, and that violence stemming from gender inequities may go beyond violence of a sexual or even a physical nature. The term retains at its core the sentiment that certain types of violence target groups or individuals specifically on the basis of either their sex and/or their socially constructed gender roles, and serve to reinforce or exploit traditional gender identities.

In this book, I am primarily concerned with judicial responses to *sexual* violence – that is, violence of a sexualized nature, including rape, assault, sexual mutilation, and unwanted intercourse. When I use the terms "gender violence" and "sexual and gender-based violence," I refer more broadly to advocacy efforts that encompass myriad forms of sexual and nonsexual gendered harm. Despite the book's primary focus on sexual crimes, for several reasons I rely more heavily on more expansive terminology when discussing general themes and broad trends. This is because laws in DR Congo and South Africa have adopted expansive definitions of rape and sexual violence and legislation and advocacy efforts in both countries typically utilize the term "gender violence" rather than "sexual violence." Moreover, the project occasionally encompasses cases involving other forms of nonsexual gender violence such as physical or economic abuse. Thus, when speaking in general terms, I typically default to using "gender-based violence" or "sexual and gender-based violence," which I employ interchangeably. Where I use the term "sexual violence" in isolation, I refer exclusively to acts of violence of a sexual nature.

Comparing Gender Justice in Eastern DR Congo and South Africa's Western Cape

At first glance, South Africa's Western Cape and DR Congo's eastern provinces may seem like an unlikely comparison. Yet, despite the differences between them, there are a number of meaningful similarities. First, and most importantly, in recent years DR Congo and South Africa have arguably attracted more international attention for their high levels of sexual and gender-based violence than any other country in the world. Second, both countries underwent dramatic political transitions in the early to mid-1990s: South Africa transitioned from apartheid to democratic rule in 1994, and, in 1997, DR Congo transitioned from Zaire to the Democratic Republic of the Congo following the removal of the country's longtime autocrat, Mobutu Sese Seko. While South Africa's transition to democracy was relatively peaceful, the events of the mid-1990s in DR Congo prompted two regional wars, involving nine African countries. Since each country emerged from periods of extreme violence and repression in the 1990s, both are considered "transitional" or "post-conflict" (International Center for Transitional Justice 2015).

Whereas eastern DR Congo has been the site of two major regional conflicts and one of the largest humanitarian peacekeeping missions in history, South Africa was, until fairly recently, widely hailed as sub-Saharan Africa's most stable and prosperous democracy. Nevertheless, in spite of the stark differences in the types of violence experienced in each country during the 1990s and beyond, the transitional or post-conflict designation illuminates some important parallels. Particularly for many of the countries' poorest and most vulnerable civilians, the hardships of daily life can be strikingly similar. The lived realities for some inhabitants of the high-crime townships of Khayelitsha and Gugulethu, for example, where the bulk of my South African research was carried out – bears some resemblance to those faced in eastern DR Congo. Many inhabitants live in poorly constructed makeshift houses on dirt roads, with no access to toilets or running water. In addition to serious public health concerns, many South Africans fear threats to their personal security in the form of robbery, violence, or assault. High-level corruption, as well as the misuse of public funds by local officials, is frequently reported in South African media outlets (De Swardt and Uwimana 2013; *The Economist* 2014). Furthermore, many residents of the Western Cape and the eastern Congolese provinces live far below the poverty line, subsisting on extremely low wages and struggling to make ends meet for themselves and their families, while fellow citizens enjoy immense wealth.[14]

When compared with DR Congo, the South African state nevertheless boasts a wealth of resources and capabilities. Moreover, the South African government has hardly been resistant to diverting its resources toward public goods. A full 3.5 percent of the country's GDP is spent on state pensions and child welfare, and such grants are distributed promptly and effectively (Ferguson 2013).[15] The state's public health service is available free of charge to all South Africans, and provides relatively high-quality medical care (Coetzee et al. 2004; Ridde and Morestin 2011). A range of other social services and benefits – including unemployment and disability allowances – places South Africa closer to the Organisation for Economic Co-operation and Development (OECD) countries in terms of social spending than most other non-OECD countries.

Yet, despite all of this, for many South Africans, especially those living in remote rural locations or densely populated urban areas, the presence of the state can remain unfelt, and its image glaringly absent from day-to-day life. Individuals and communities may benefit enormously in ways that they take for granted (through welfare assistance and free medical care), but nevertheless live in environments characterized by insecurity and abject poverty. Government statistics indicate that approximately 18 million South Africans lack access to basic sanitation, including

---

[14] The percentage of inhabitants in DR Congo subsisting below the poverty line is far larger than in South Africa.

[15] State pensions in South Africa compare fairly well with OECD countries, with a maximum state pension of approximately $1,400 USD per year in South Africa, compared with $12,500 in the United Kingdom. While the disparity between these figures is quite large, when compared to an average annual salary of $11,000 USD in South Africa and $52,000 in the United Kingdom, these figures are more comparable. Source: OECD/ILO 2013: http://stats.oecd.org/Index.aspx?DataSetCode=SOCX_AGG.

running water or toilet facilities in their homes (Government of South Africa 2010). Up to 500,000 people in Cape Town lack access to basic sanitation, and in the nearby township of Khayelitsha, as many as 500 may share the use of a single public toilet (Social Justice Coalition 2014). Municipal elections in 2011 were dominated by disputes over sanitation and public toilets, after councils across the country installed makeshift toilets in the open air with no walls to shelter users from public view (Smith 2014). This has compounded security challenges for the poorest South Africans, as a significant number of sexual assaults occur while individuals are en route to or from public toilets. As a result, some residents may resort to relieving themselves using plastic bags in the home, rather than risking the walk to an open-air toilet by the roadside at night. In high-crime neighborhoods, police are rarely seen. This means that the material assistance distributed by the state is overshadowed by the state's notable absence in other areas. Even in the country's wealthiest neighborhoods, security remains an ongoing challenge, with those who can afford to typically employing the services of private security firms rather than leaving their security in the hands of the national police. While there are certainly unique challenges facing the individuals and families affected by DR Congo's wars, and there are a number of privileges (such as free health care and social security benefits) afforded to South Africans that Congolese citizens cannot access, the day-to-day hardships experienced by the poorest residents in each country are not as different as state-based indicators might lead us to expect.

Finally, it is worth reiterating that all of the dimensions on which the Congolese and South African contexts differ are the very same dimensions that would lead us to expect South Africa's judicial response to widespread reported gender violence to be far more effective than DR Congo's. Its weak state capacity, dilapidated judicial infrastructure, ongoing civil conflict, and the lack of a strong domestic gender violence movement prior to 2006 make DR Congo a *least* likely case for international human rights principles to be incorporated and implemented by domestic courts. South Africa, on the other hand, appears to promise a far greater likelihood of successful human rights outcomes. Given far more sustained domestic activism around sexual violence in South Africa, as well as strong transnational networks linking preexisting South African NGOs with global donors and advocacy movements, such as the Open Society Foundation, the Gates Foundation, the MacArthur Foundation, the Coalition for the International Criminal Court, and many others, the existing literature would lead us to expect gender advocacy to have been more effective in influencing both policy and practice within South Africa's legal system. Yet South African NGOs have been unable to hold the government to account, or to ensure adequate implementation of existing gender rights reforms. By representing two extremes, the South African and Congolese examples acutely expose the shortcomings of preexisting scholarship on this topic.

Since DR Congo and South Africa display striking similarity on some variables – such as their prevalence of violence, social stigma toward sexual crimes, international and domestic attention to gender violence, and pervasive human rights advocacy – and key differences on others, the comparison is an illuminating way to better disentangle how human rights advocacy and intervention plays out in different institutional environments (Anckar 2008; George and Bennett 2005; Gerring 2004; Lieberman 2009; Ragin 2014). I use the townships of Khayelitsha and Gugulethu in South Africa to explore the treatment of sexual and gender-based crimes by courts in a site of high crime and sustained advocacy. In DR Congo, I exclusively focus on the Kivus. While rates of gender violence are high across DR Congo (Demographic and Health Survey 2014; Peterman, Palermo, and Bredenkamp 2011), the Kivus are unique in that they have been the focal point of international attention, outreach, and intervention. The arguments made in this book, therefore, are expected to generalize to environments where the international community has directed attention toward improving human rights outcomes in particular issue areas. The arguments do *not* easily travel to other Congolese provinces, since the majority of these have received little external attention or support. Similar dynamics – and similar outcomes – can be observed to a lesser extent in Maniema and Ituri, which in recent years have received increasing levels of international attention. But, while gendered crimes are far from absent elsewhere in the country, international stakeholders have devoted few resources toward interventions in other provinces, and thus the dynamics I observe in the Kivus are absent.

Contributions to Existing Literatures

This project contributes to a number of broad debates about the conditions under which human rights advocacy is most likely to affect change in domestic legal systems. There has been a great deal of research in recent years on governance and public service provision in areas of limited statehood. However, the ways in which different institutional environments might shape the activities and outcomes brought about by human rights activists has been understudied in the political science literature. Few scholars have taken seriously how state absence – or what Börzel and Risse (2013) refer to as "low" consolidated statehood – may lead to *more* effective human rights promotion, diffusion, and implementation in specific contexts. This book explores the opportunities born out of state fragility, as well as the limitations accompanying human rights activities that bypass the central state.

Governance, External Intervention, and State (Un)Making

In addition to the literature on transnational human rights advocacy and its domestic implementation, this book's findings also contribute to scholarly knowledge of governance and security. In response to pervasive insecurity, Jeffrey Herbst and Greg Mills have famously argued that the Congolese state simply "does not exist," stating in various forums that "there is no such thing as [the] Congo" (Herbst and Mills 2003, 2013).

Yet despite DR Congo's prominence on various failed states' indices, many aspects of local governance prevail (Kabemba 2001; Mampilly 2011; Raeymaekers 2005; Seay 2009; Trefon et al. 2011). Scholars increasingly agree that even the most complex elements of governance do not always dissipate in areas of limited statehood. Moreover, governance is not always effective, even in sites of apparent state strength (Holzgrefe and Keohane 2003; Krasner 2004a; Lake and Fariss 2014; Menkhaus 2007; Nojumi, Barfield, and Thier 2008; Raeymaekers, Menkhaus, and Vlassenroot 2008; Risse 2011). Timothy Mitchell notes that "through the language of legal practice, the architecture of public buildings, the wearing of military uniforms, or the marking out and policing of frontiers," states everywhere generate and are generated by structural effects that reinforce and reproduce their legitimacy and authority (Mitchell 1999: 81). Yet many scholars have shown that, in a variety of state contexts, the state is typically only *one* source of regulatory authority (Lund 2006; Mampilly 2011; Menkhaus 2007; Migdal 2001; Schlichte and Migdal 2005; Raeymaekers et al. 2008; Risse 2011; Seay 2009). Further, a variety of non-state actors, including religious organizations, NGOs, and armed groups, deploy the "language of stateness" to legitimize their claims to authority (Hoffman and Verweijen 2013).[16]

Many scholars thus take issue with what they perceive to be a simplistic rejection by Herbst and Mills of the Congolese state, which draws from a strictly Weberian notion of what the Westphalian state *should* look like (Vogel 2013). Vogel and others have pointed out that, in fact, the Congolese state is extremely visible to the vast majority of Congolese

---

[16] Some of the ideas in this section draw from research presented by Kasper Hoffman and Judith Verweijen at the Workshop on Armed Forces and Conflict Dynamics in the Great Lakes Region, Kampala, October 28–30, 2013.

civilians. In spite of its governance failures, state agents can be seen across the east in large numbers, regulating the lives of ordinary civilians and demanding illicit taxes for traveling to market, purchasing property, importing goods, or simply subsisting. Additionally, agents of the state can be seen looting, stealing, or inflicting physical harm. In South Africa – a country that boasts a far stronger state bureaucracy, infrastructure, and institutional safety net to any outside observer – the state can seem strikingly *in*visible to many of its residents. Although South African citizens are recipients of public services such as pensions and health care, outside of urban centers, South Africans rarely encounter visual symbols of the state in their daily lives. Moreover, where they might expect the state to offer protections from very particular forms of harm, it is nowhere to be found.

This research, therefore, reveals the many different ways in which a seemingly capable state in South Africa fails to achieve what Bourdieu (1994: 12) describes as the "effect of universality." While the comparatively weak Congolese state appears to many of its citizens as an ever-present symbol of domination (in the form of uniformed public officials extracting illicit taxes from the population at every turn), for better or worse, the South African state falls short of conjuring any perception of dominance for many of its inhabitants. Further, as feminist scholarship has consistently emphasized, state presence and capacity do not equate to security (Tickner 1992; Towns 2010; Tripp, Ferree, and Ewig 2013). Rather, *in*security can manifest in myriad forms, and those at risk of gendered (or other forms) of harm find themselves no more secure in South Africa than in DR Congo, despite a more robust state apparatus. This book illuminates what different manifestations of state strength and capacity mean for the lived realities of ordinary citizens, and reveals how these contrasting realities differently affect the work of NGOs and other non-state human rights actors.

In addition to deconstructing dominant paradigms of state strength and security, this book also explores conceptualizations of governance and sovereignty. Governance is almost always the product of a complex *sharing* of sovereignty (Krasner 1999). In transitional settings, these governance activities may be performed by a multitude of domestic and international actors. In this sense, governance activities themselves reveal little about the strength or weakness of the state (Berger and Lake 2018). Whereas some victims of violence in eastern DR Congo benefit from increased access to what appear to be state-led justice institutions, for example, the reality is that the activities of these institutions are pioneered by a coalition of state and non-state partners.

State fragmentation has ambiguous implications for the exercise of capacity building. Drawing on Foucault, Hoffman and Verweijen describe the various ways in which the Congolese state is made and unmade through performative, epistemological, discursive, and material practices (Hoffman and Verweijen 2013). They suggest that, where armed groups appropriate the performance and symbolism of stateness by reproducing government titles and command structures, wearing military uniforms, and establishing parallel systems of bureaucracy and governance that mimic state infrastructure, they are simultaneously reproducing the myth of the state while *undermining* its de facto legitimacy and authority by challenging its monopoly on violence and its right to govern.

In the same ways that armed groups, community militias, and civil society service providers have engaged in state mimicry in eastern DR Congo, NGOs and international organizations have similarly sought to reproduce the institutions of the state through supporting local legal institutions and a "mobile court" program embedded within the Congolese military and civilian justice systems that is, in practice, NGO led and funded. The state mimicry of NGOs facilitating traveling ad-hoc state courts reinforces the *idea* of the state, while simultaneously undermining or calling into question its competence, authority and capacity to govern. Indeed, one of the biggest critiques Herbst and Mills made of the international community's response to state collapse in eastern DR Congo is that donors continue to support the "myth" of the existing government, by propping it up with a reported $27 billion USD in aid money since 2000 (making the Congolese state the biggest recipient of aid after Afghanistan (Herbst and Mills 2013)). As yet, we know little about the long-term effects of such assistance.

There is no question that activities rooted in bolstering the capacity of the legal system to adequately respond to gender-based violence in eastern DR Congo have resulted in some unambiguously positive outcomes. These include alerting potential perpetrators of violence to the possibility of legal accountability for gender-based crimes (resulting in the potential for deterrence or socialization); the provision of support, attention, and material assistance to victims and witnesses of violence; and the creation of heightened awareness of gender-related power imbalances among domestic and international audiences. However, other repercussions prove less clear-cut. Interventions raise a number of questions – both normative and empirical – about the legitimacy, sustainability, and long-term consequences of human rights and transitional justice activities that are pioneered by external actors in environments of extreme state fragility. Scholars working in other contexts have suggested that the involvement of international actors in micro-level governance activities in weak states serves not to build capacity, but to further relieve the state of its responsibilities to provide basic goods and services to its citizens (Gary 1996). The proliferation of non-state actors ready to fund and promote governance activities reduces incentives for the central government to reinvest its own time and resources in developing a functional state apparatus, and potentially risks bolstering the capacity of illicit or predatory "state" actors.

Through an examination into externally-led rule of law reform, this project scrutinizes the various ways in which international stakeholders participate in state "making" and "unmaking." The extent to which NGOs and other external actors in eastern DR Congo contribute to supporting and strengthening existing state structures, rather than simply engaging in the same types of state mimicry as the host of other actors competing for power, authority, and influence in the shadow of the Congolese state, remains an open question. Do human rights and rule of law programs contribute to the consolidation of state power? Do they reify a mythicized abstraction of the Weberian state that fails to reflect local realities? Or do they undermine the building or making of that state altogether, by reproducing hollow institutions without sufficient consideration for their relationships with preexisting structures of power and governance?

This book cannot answer these questions empirically, but Part II grapples with these debates. While the study identifies a number of opportunities that emerge from conditions of state fragility, it also identifies some of the challenges and shortcomings of exploiting openings created by state weakness to advance a singular human rights agenda. These questions resonate far beyond DR Congo and South Africa. In countries across the world, legal capacity-building programs seek to influence the content of new laws, provide legal representation to victims of crime, provide training to lawyers and judges, and assist in the management of national budgets. Similarly, humanitarian organizations provide food and medical supplies to local organizations, NGOs train teachers and health care professionals, and international agencies engage in water sanitation programs and advise ministries and government representatives on the management of national budgets, conservation efforts, energy consumption, and the building of domestic transportation and communications infrastructures. Given that such projects are often more elaborate and far-reaching in weaker state contexts,[17]

[17] See the American Bar Association Rule of Law Initiative; the International Bar Association Human Rights Institute; and the United Nations Development Program, for examples. American Bar Association. 2011. "Reflections on ABA ROLI's Efforts to Combat the Rape Crisis in War-Torn Eastern Congo." ABA Rule of Law Initiative (DR Congo). June. www.americanbar.org/advocacy/rule_of_law/where_we_work/afric a/democratic_republic_congo/news/news_drc_reflections_aba_roli_efforts_to_combat_ the_rape_ crisis_0611.html; International Bar Association. 2015. "Training and Capacity Building".www.ibanet.org/Human_Rights_Institute/About_the_HRI/HRI_A ctivities/Training-and-Capacity-Building.aspx; UnitedNations Development Program.

a close analysis of how they are realized in different institutional settings deepens our understanding of the relationship between the overarching objectives and the practical realities of rule of law, security and capacity-building.

Repercussions for Violence and the Rule of Law

Finally, this book unveils insights into the extent to which legal remedies prove able to deliver on other promises made by human rights activists. In recent decades, scholars and practitioners have increasingly turned to the rule of law as a "cure-all" for many of the ailments of the developing world. Legal capacity-building initiatives in weak or fragile states have been considered a cornerstone of state-building, stability, peace, and economic development (Carothers 2006; Rodrik, Subramanian, and Trebbi 2002; Thies 2004; Weingast 1997). This logic has guided the funding priorities of major international donors, who have heavily invested in projects devoted to building and strengthening legal institutions. One of this book's central conclusions relates to the various tensions that emerge when external actors become deeply involved in the domestic authority structures of states, promoting new development priorities and disrupting existing patterns of behavior. While some of the developments that emerge may appear normatively "positive" – in this case, victims of violence have new avenues of recourse for crimes committed against them – they may also recall tired memories of colonial occupation. In bringing new and potentially emancipatory ideas and structures to previously marginalized populations, human rights practitioners have been accused of reproducing the "civilizing mission" of colonial rule, through reinventing dispute resolution and regulating sexual behavior, while failing to give careful thought to their interventions.[18] Such actions have the potential to leave legal systems in a worse state of disrepair than they were found (Comaroff 2001; Mamdani 2001; Massoud 2013).

The extent to which legal remedies – particularly those implemented somewhat half-heartedly – can "rescue" fragile states raises a number of red flags for many socio-legal scholars, especially those working in deeply

---

2014. "Evaluation of UNDP's Support to Mobile Courts in DRC, Sierra Leone and Somalia." www.undp.org/content/undp/en/home/librarypage/crisis-prevention-and-recovery/evaluation-of-undp-ssupport-to-mobile-courts-in-drc-sierra-leo.html.

[18] In DR Congo, a variety of laws, policies and programs, including the foundation of La Ligue pour la Protection de l'Enfance Noire, sought to regulate sexual relationships and maternal health care on extreme levels. Interventions by the Belgian Ligue into how mothers breastfed their children and how soon after birth married couples should resume sexual relations have led Nancy Hunt to argue that Europeans intervened "more substantially and on a wider scale in maternal and infant health [in Congo] than any other colonial power in sub-Saharan Africa" (Hunt 1988: 402).

divided postcolonial or post-conflict societies. An important concern that has proved salient in both the Congolese and South African cases is that legal remedies will only be able to do so much, given the broad range of other political and socioeconomic injustices affecting impoverished or otherwise marginalized communities.

This powerful critique derives from questioning the utility of law as an instrument to dismantle systemic injustice or oppression. Law played a powerful role in the construction of the colonial and apartheid state apparatus. Both the apartheid state in South Africa, and Congo under Belgian rule, were characterized by intrusive and far-reaching laws and policies that sought to regulate many aspects of public and private life. In South Africa, the Group Areas Act of 1950 and the Immorality Act of 1927 strictly governed where and with whom black South Africans could live and travel (Artz and Smythe 2007: 6; Dixon and Van der Spuy 2004). In DR Congo, a variety of laws, policies, and programs sought to regulate colonial relationships, criminalize "uncivilized" behaviors, and alter social and political structures on extreme levels.

Given the history of legal regulation of the public and private lives of individuals and communities under colonial rule in Africa, it is not surprising that activists have often turned to legal avenues to redress historical injustices. Transitions to democracy and independence in both countries, but particularly in South Africa, have thus been characterized by a heavy focus on the reform of instruments of state regulation as the solution to a variety of social problems. However, given this focus, others remain skeptical of the extent to which legal remedies are able to promise genuine social change. Since the law has frequently been leveraged by the state to exact violence on civilian populations, many worry that strengthening legal institutions serves the purpose of further entrenching the power of ruling elites vis-à-vis their citizens, rather than offering avenues for emancipation or rights-claiming. Skeptics thus critique the law as the "master's tool," asserting that the same political weapons that were leveraged to build systems of oppression can never satisfactorily be reformed to dismantle them (Lorde 1984). Others note that selective rights-granting or rights-claiming can lead to new and unexpected forms of violence or injustice (Smith 2015). In such instances, legal "order" may serve to fuel rather than to mitigate various forms of political violence (Comaroff and Comaroff 2006; Englund 2006; Goluboff 2007; Massoud 2013; McCann 2006; Merry 2000; Rosenberg 1991; Scheingold 2004; Smith 2016).

Tracing high-profile cases that have traveled through eastern DR Congo's military courts, for instance, indeed revealed that apparent human rights victories in landmark cases against high-profile figures have sometimes been used as a means to dispense with potential dissidents and troublemakers, or to broker deals between armed groups and elites (Lake 2017). In these ways, selective accountability serves to build and entrench the power of conflict-era elites. These dynamics are reproduced in civilian trials, as those with power, money, or influence can deflect legal attention, while poorer individuals or ethnic or political outsiders may be disproportionately targeted or scapegoated for crimes they did not commit. These facts often escape the attention of external rule of law specialists who are not always familiar with local conflicts and often single-mindedly focus on securing convictions in order to meet specific program goals within short-term funding cycles.

While some of these questions exclusively pertain to the role of the law in its capacity to redress human rights violations, many others raised in this study remain pertinent for a broad range of international interventions in fragile states and elsewhere. Humanitarian initiatives, international development agencies, and NGOs are engaged in a broad range of governance activities around the world. Activities range from the direct provision of public goods such as immunizations, urgent care, and the distribution of food aid; to the development of local economies through microfinance initiatives, small business loans, and training programs; to the setting up of schools, vocational training, and educational scholarships; to drafting laws, advising on government policy, and lobbying for the protection of conservation sites or vulnerable or minority populations. Such activities provoke questions concerning the extent to which the types of activities undertaken by external actors offer genuine opportunities for emancipation for marginalized individuals, populations, and issue areas.

This book thus represents an attempt to examine the realities of human rights governance and advocacy in an environment where juridical statehood is weak or lacking. It also represents an inquiry into what happens when similarly situated human rights advocates (local and transnational) are confronted with strikingly different institutional contexts in which to carry out their work. South Africa and DR Congo demonstrate that, under certain circumstances, particular forms of state fragility can create short-term opportunities for non-state human rights actors to influence institutional policy and practice, as well as human rights outcomes, in a variety of consequential ways. Yet it also exposes myriad unique challenges that accompany human rights gains won at the margins of a centralized state apparatus.

Chapter Outline

The primary objective of this study is to document how and why advocacy and outreach around human rights and the rule of law can succeed in improving aspects of criminal justice reform in some extremely fragile states, yet fail dramatically in contexts that would appear more receptive to human rights advocacy efforts. This project also unveils insights into the longer-term consequences of promotion of the rule of law in different institutional settings, highlighting the challenges that can result from bypassing the central state in the pursuit of emancipatory human rights agendas. The analysis was primarily concerned with the question of why local courts in eastern DR Congo have been able to offer some form of (albeit imperfect) accountability to victims of violence, while courts in South Africa have appeared to flounder in the same endeavor. Yet the conclusions that emerge touch on issues far beyond these central questions, directing much-needed attention toward the politics of transnational advocacy movements, rule of law promotion, and state-building in weak or post-conflict states.

This manuscript thus proceeds in two parts. Part I explains divergent gender justice outcomes in contexts of differing institutional capacity, whereas Part II examines the repercussions and unintended consequences of external human rights interventions that exploit openings created by state fragility. Chapter 2 provides background on the two cases and discusses the ethics and practicalities of carrying out research in volatile and challenging research environments. Chapter 3 analyzes the development of state policy and practice with regard to gender violence in DR Congo and South Africa, explaining the introduction of exemplary gender violence laws in both countries, as well as countless national strategies and policies designed to address rising levels of violence. Chapter 3 also considers the consequences of policy reforms at the level of the central state and what they mean for systemic change in the two respective cases.

Chapter 4 departs from state policy and practice to consider the activities of regional courts in the eastern DR Congo and the Western Cape, examining the interests and priorities of actors outside of central state institutions who are implicated in the local realization of gender justice. These actors include judges, police, prosecutors, bar associations, civil society organizations, transnational advocacy movements, foreign donors, and local, regional, and international organizations. Chapter 4 presents crucial evidence in support of the core argument of this book, demonstrating how international and domestic human rights activists in eastern DR Congo have taken advantage of openings created by state fragility to exert direct influence over judicial processes in local courts, resulting in the gender-sensitive patterns observed. It is notable that decisions produced without NGO assistance vary significantly in their compliance with gender violence law, even in Goma and Bukavu's courts.

In South Africa; however, very few of the judgements analyzed demonstrated compliance with the law. Gender advocacy efforts by similarly situated actors have been stymied by deeply institutionalized patterns of behavior and entrenched conservative attitudes toward gender issues that pervade the country's legal system and obstruct possibilities for gender justice.

Chapter 5 examines why some victims of violence in eastern DR Congo have turned to formal institutional mechanisms in the aftermath of sexual violence (even in an environment where rape is heavily stigmatized and the state has consistently failed to deliver even the most basic of services to its citizens), while similarly situated victims in South Africa have often proved reluctant to do so. In order to secure indictments for rape and gender violence, victims and witnesses need to be willing to participate in trials. Without them, trials would not move forward and legal systems would collapse. Yet, throughout much of the world, sexual violence is deeply stigmatized. Victims are often reluctant to speak about their experiences due to the shame that such crimes bring to themselves and their families (Brouwer et al. 2009; Bunting 1993; Merry 2006). As a result, in many cases, victims of gendered violence are compelled to keep silent, and are thus often unwilling to seek justice or to participate in legal proceedings. Evidence from interviews with victims of violence and their acquaintances and allies presented in Chapter 5 suggests that advocacy and outreach in eastern DR Congo has been somewhat successful in overcoming the stigmatization felt by rape victims in specific cases and locales, and incentivizing participation in legal processes. The interviews also reveal that some victims of violence have been able to use the language of legal accountability to reject customary approaches to justice that they felt left them with few options. Victims of violence in the Western Cape, however, encounter few of the incentives or motivations that have encouraged victims in eastern DR Congo to pursue and participate in legal processes.

While Part I explores how and why local Congolese and South African courts have responded to widespread sexual and gender-based violence in such dramatically different ways, Part II turns its attention to the consequences of human rights interventions for violence and the rule of law in weak state environments. Chapter 6 draws from interviews with victims of violence in eastern DR Congo, in an effort to understand what criminal prosecutions have meant for the individuals they are most immediately intended to benefit. Chapter 6 further examines how participants in legal processes have experienced their first interactions with state law. Despite overwhelming disappointment in the legal process in many cases, many interviewees reflect positively on their decisions to pursue legal remedy, highlighting the importance of receiving formal state recognition for the violence committed against them. The purported value of legal recognition, however, should not be considered in isolation from the many moments when the legal process dismally failed them.

Chapter 7, the final substantive chapter of this book, reflects on the broader relationship between legal justice, gender violence, and efforts to build the rule of law. This chapter does not draw from empirical data, but instead raises a number of questions, policy implications, and unintended consequences that emerge from human rights advocacy and capacity building that occur in contexts of ongoing state fragility and weakness.

The chapter highlights three key repercussions that derive from exploiting opportunities created by state fragility to promote a singular human rights agenda. First, the prioritization of gender violence to the exclusion of other issues by international donors has created a series of perverse incentives for individuals and organizations. From 2006 to 2015, the period over which the research for this book was conducted, there was a common perception among human rights and development organizations in eastern DR Congo that programs must have a sexual violence component to their work in order to receive international funding. In some instances, this led organizations to abandon other important development programs, and in others, it led to an inflation of rape statistics in efforts to attract additional international funding (Douma and Hilhorst 2012; Heaton 2013). Further, the disproportionately high number of rape cases in the east, as compared to other categories of crimes, suggested that rape was the only crime taken seriously by NGOs and the law. This perception does little to overcome entrenched impunity in other areas.

In addition to a singular focus on sexual and gender-based violence, the top-down nature of international development aid has invariably led NGOs to focus on activities that can be easily quantified, measured, and reported back to donors as evidence of successful programming. For this reason, legal capacity-building organizations often prioritized arrests, criminal trials, and convictions over slower-burning and far more challenging obstacles to justice, such as overcoming political interference in the legal system.

Chapter 7 thus also explores the ways in which internationally supported gender violence programming has, until recently, overlooked local dynamics of power. In their efforts to secure convictions and prosecutions, practitioners involved in legal capacity building have tended to focus on cases that local elites are least likely to obstruct. Thus, prosecutions are often defined by preexisting hierarchies of power, with lower-ranking officers or already marginalized individuals facing the full force of the law (or, worse, scapegoated for crimes they did not necessarily commit), while those with more power remain protected from prosecution. These dynamics have played out in both the civilian and military justice systems.

Third, drawing from the preceding discussions, Chapter 7 poses a question about whether interventions by international organizations serve to undermine rather than bolster the capacity of the state over the long term. The chapter situates critiques of the "NGO industrial complex" in the context of the many positive externalities and opportunities that have arisen from accountability efforts, returning to a comparison with advocacy efforts in the Western Cape.

2 Researching Violence, Law, and Human Rights in South Africa's Western Cape and DR Congo's Eastern Provinces

Introduction

One evening, in a bar on the shores of Lake Kivu, a colleague introduced me to a public relations (PR) officer from an international human rights organization. Over a glass of wine, the PR officer told me about her grueling day, which had involved photographing and interviewing a twelve-year-old rape victim for her organization's new campaign on wartime sexual violence. The day had been frustrating, she explained, not because the story was tragic – although it was. The day had been frustrating because it was her last day filming, and the girl's story was not quite tragic enough. She told me she had wanted someone younger, and more helpless. Someone who would really move the American public to donate money.

This anecdote was not altogether surprising; I had heard similarly flippant remarks from others, particularly those accustomed to flitting between one war zone and the next. In both South Africa and the DR Congo, researchers, journalists, and campaign staff arrive in search of stories from vulnerable individuals – especially from victims of sexual assault. Many arrive seeking stories of the worst forms of brutality and harm.

In the United States and much of Europe, stringent regulations protect vulnerable populations in their interactions with researchers and journals. While university ethics review boards attempt to moderate the risks posed to academic research subjects, their procedures are often ill suited to environments of ongoing war or violence, where states command little authority or relevance, or where literacy levels are low. This means it is often the responsibility of individual researchers to weigh the value of their research against the risks posed to interviewees, as well as the many complex power imbalances inherent within interviewer–interviewee interactions (Bouka 2015; Cronin-Furman and Lake 2018; Mitchell 2013; Wood 2006).

Nevertheless, the perspectives of the intended beneficiaries of legal aid and gender justice are integral to understanding how law works for those intended to gain from it. And far too many policy interventions in sub-Saharan Africa have failed to take seriously the reflections and responses of those individuals and communities they most affect. I did not want to replicate the tendency to erase and obscure the voices of target recipients.

Given these concerns, I made a number of trade-offs and calculations throughout the course of my research. Where possible, I took the decision to rely heavily on careful firsthand research conducted by other scholars. In South Africa, for example, a number of excellent studies have already featured in-depth interviews with victims of gender-based violence. I felt it irresponsible to replicate similar interviews for the sake of academic propriety. For relevant sections of this book, therefore, I draw heavily on work carried out with victims of violence by Rachel Jewkes, Dee Smythe, Lisa Vetten, and their coauthors, supplementing their research with my own formal interviews and informal conversations with counselors, health workers, family members, community support workers, lawyers, church groups, and first responders. In a very few instances, I also conducted my own interviews with victims of violence. In eastern DR Congo, there was less existing research to draw from. At the time I commenced my research, access to law and justice had been relatively understudied. I thus took the decision to interview a carefully selected sample of individuals affected by violence and involved, in some capacity, in the pursuit of legal remedy.

This chapter discusses many of the challenges I encountered researching sensitive human rights issues in volatile or high-crime environments, as well as how these challenges affected and informed my research. It describes decisions I took in the field and prior to leaving, as well as how the particularities of each site shaped the research I undertook. It begins, however, with an overview of the key characteristics of sexual and gender-based violence in each site and a discussion of why I selected these sites for my research. After discussing the similarities and differences between the scale and nature of violence in each site, I summarize my own research approach.

The Scale and Nature of Violence in DR Congo and South Africa

Feminist scholars of international relations have repeatedly commented on the ways in which conventional understandings of both "stateness" and "security" obscure the specific concerns of women, children, minorities, or otherwise marginalized groups (Baer 1999; Butler 1990; MacKinnon 2006b; Tickner 1997; Tickner and Sjoberg 2011; Tripp, Ferree, and Ewig 2013; Towns 2010). These populations may remain vulnerable in very particular ways even when a state is deemed strong or secure by conventional measures. Although South Africa is one of the world's most rapidly industrializing democracies (World Economic

Forum 2012), state-centric measures of security and development typically tell us little about the insecurities faced by the country's most vulnerable inhabitants, nor about the fate of women and men at risk of specifically gendered harms. While DR Congo and South Africa differ significantly on a number of metrics, there are nevertheless a number of informative parallels between the nature and prevalence of gendered violence in each site. These parallels are important for understanding responses to violence in each site, as well as for their role in exposing the deeply gendered assumptions embedded within mainstream security discourse and notions of statehood.

In addition to numerous similarities, citizens of eastern DR Congo face a number of *distinct* security concerns, stemming from the country's twenty-year war, which do not affect citizens of South Africa. Some men, women, and children have experienced sexual torture related to the war, or other explicitly gendered conflict violence (Cohen 2016; Meger 2010). Yet, in reality, only some of the gendered violence that affects Congolese civilians in the east is a direct product of the war. Much of the violence perpetrated in both public and private spheres resembles the day-to-day violence that afflicts women and men across the country, and elsewhere around the world. To attribute the scale and nature of gendered violence in eastern DR Congo exclusively to the war is theoretically and empirically misinformed. Instead, teasing out the particular forms of violence that are indirectly related to or exacerbated by conflict in eastern DR Congo, from the high rates of intimate partner violence and civilian abuse that are pervasive in South Africa and elsewhere, illuminates the analogous experiences of women and men in both research sites. Studying institutional responses to sexual violence necessitates carefully contextualizing the distinct forms of harm and vulnerability that are present in each case.

DR Congo

The forms of gendered harm felt by women and men in DR Congo and South Africa exhibit a number of similarities, as well as some clear differences. One of the most obvious differences is the presence of ongoing conflict in the DR Congo's eastern provinces. Many scholars attribute this violence to the mass displacement that followed Rwanda's genocide and civil war in the early 1990s. In the aftermath of the Rwandan genocide, Rwanda's unity government feared reprisals from Hutu refugees who had fled Rwanda after the victory of the Rwandan Patriotic Front (RPF) and were living in refugee camps along the Rwanda–Zaire border. Unconvinced that the Congolese government was taking the necessary measures to curb the threat of another genocide, in 1996 a rebel group led by Laurent Désiré Kabila and backed by Rwandan and Ugandan forces led a march on Kinshasa to overthrow President Mobutu Sese Seko. Not long after this group, the Alliance des Forces Démocratiques pour la Libération du Congo-Zaïre (AFDL), took power, Kabila dismissed his Rwandan chief of staff, James Kabarebe, and ordered all Rwandan and Ugandan troops to leave the country. This move angered Kabila's former Rwandan and Ugandan allies, who assumed they could count on Kabila's support. In response, a movement known as the Rassemblement Congolais pour la Démocratie (RCD) emerged in the city of Goma to protect the interests of Congolese Tutsis in the eastern provinces. The Rwandan-backed RCD, supported by the Ugandan-backed Mouvement de Libération du Congo (MLC) and a coalition of local armed groups, launched an assault on government forces, instigating a five-year war that involved nine African countries. Kabila was assassinated in Kinshasa 2001, and succeeded in office by his son, Joseph.

While the war officially ended in 2003, and elections won by Kabila in 2006 and 2011, fighting has continued to destabilize the eastern provinces. The RCD officially became a political party in 2003; however, former RCD affiliates have periodically defected from the national army to create new insurgencies – most notably in the form of the Tutsi-dominated Congrès National pour la Défense du Peuple (CNDP) and, later, the M23. During their height, both the CNDP and the M23 controlled sizeable territories in North Kivu. In addition to the periodic resurrection of RCD elements, dozens of other fragmented and localized armed groups, including various Mai Mai self-defense militias, and the Forces Démocratiques de Libération du Rwanda (FDLR, a group largely comprised of so-called Hutu *génocidaires* who fled Rwanda in 1994) continue to control sizeable territories in the Kivus. These groups engage in continued negotiations and armed struggles over land, mining sites, administrative positions, access to infrastructures, and local authority.

Both during the war and in the years since its apparent conclusion, violence against civilians has been pervasive. The FDLR, in particular, numbering approximately 8,000 troops after the war officially ended, has been notorious for brutal acts of torture and sexual assault inflicted on local populations. The Congolese government, in partnership with MONUSCO, attempted to incentivize FDLR combatants to repatriate to Rwanda. Given the stigmatization in Rwanda at the time of anyone associated with the *Interhamwe*, many preferred to remain in DR Congo, prompting the Congolese government to launch an offensive, *Umoja Wetu*, against the FDLR in 2008. The FDLR ramped up its hostilities to coincide with the offensive, abducting civilian hostages to use as human shields and executing them when the FDLR's headquarters in Kibua were attacked

(US Department of State 2009: 161). Such atrocities were not uncommon; in 2009 alone, the FDLR was accused of burning the village of Mianga to the ground and murdering forty-one villagers, including the village chief. The FDLR has routinely been implicated in the abduction of sex slaves, the rape, mutilation, and torture of men, women, and children, and the burning of thousands of houses across the Kivus.

While violence perpetrated by the FDLR has received the most notoriety and attention, other armed groups have been implicated in similarly grave atrocities. Myriad armed groups have exacted violence against civilians, engaged in pillage and predation, or abducted men, women and children for sexual exploitation, labor or to deploy in combat (Baaz, Stearns, and Verweijen 2013). Mass rapes and opportunistic assaults have been perpetrated with alarming frequency. Multiple integrations, defections, and reintegrations into the Congolese national army have meant that FARDC forces, as well as Congolese police officers and even armed civilians, have been responsible for committing acts of violence against unarmed civilian populations over the years since the war's formal conclusion. A culture of impunity exacerbated by weak statehood has meant that the postwar period in the Kivus has been characterized by protracted insecurity and cyclical outbreaks of low-intensity conflict. A variety of different armed actors have resorted to increasingly violent behaviors in order to secure positions of influence, or to call attention to their political struggles (Autesserre 2012; Human Rights Watch 2012).

In addition to contributing to violence perpetrated by armed groups, decades of exploitative relationships between those in positions of power and some of DR Congo's most impoverished and vulnerable men have contributed to what many have termed a crisis of masculinity. Scholars and activists have interpreted the violence employed by soldiers, police officers, and ordinary civilians as a means of regaining a sense of power and control (Baaz et al. 2010; Baaz and Stern 2011; Sonke Gender Justice Network 2012). This logic, combined with a long-standing societal tolerance for nonconsensual sex, has compounded problems of sexual and gender-based violence perpetrated in the context of the conflict, as well as in the home. While the vast majority of media attention to gender-based violence in eastern DR Congo has focused on the war, familial violence, violence in churches and schools, and other forms of nonconsensual sex are equally widespread.

Reliable statistics on the prevalence of rape and sexual violence are notoriously difficult to obtain, since the vast majority of incidents goes unreported. Still, a number of researchers have made efforts to arrive at reliable statistics that take into account reporting challenges and poor infrastructure. For example, a Demographic and Health Survey carried out among households in eleven Congolese provinces in 2007 found that almost ten percent of women reported that their first sexual encounter was against their will (Demographic and Health Survey 2007), with sixteen percent reporting sex against their will at some point in their lives. A separate survey – a randomized household survey conducted in sixty-seven villages in three eastern provinces in 2010 – placed this figure much higher, finding that 39.7 percent of women interviewed (and 23.6 percent of men) had experienced sexual violence at some point in their lives (Johnson et al. 2010). The 2014 Demographic and Health Survey found that twenty-seven percent of women between the ages of fifteen and forty-nine reported that they had experienced sexual violence at some point in their lives (Demographic and Health Survey 2014).

In addition to random and opportunistic rapes perpetrated by soldiers and civilians, sexual violence has also been systematically employed as a weapon of war by a number of armed groups operating in the eastern provinces, including the government forces. Although rape has been used as an instrument of conflict for centuries to terrorize populations, torture or punish civilians, reward soldiers, and, in extreme cases, physically and psychologically prevent women from procreating, many have commented that its use as a targeted military strategy in DR Congo's wars has been unmatched in recent conflicts (Meger 2010, 2011).

Surveys in DR Congo have reported varying responses to questions about wartime rape. For example, in Kirsten Johnson and her colleagues' 2010 household survey conducted in the eastern provinces, of the 39.9 percent of respondents who reported they had experienced sexual or gender-based violence at some point in their lives, 74.3 percent of women (and 64.5 percent of men) reported that the rape or sexual assault they experienced was conflict-related, while only thirty-one percent attributed violence to an intimate partner (Johnson et al. 2010: 557).[1] Susan Bartels and her colleagues (2013) support the claim that the majority of sexual assaults is perpetrated by armed combatants. However, the 2007 Demographic and Health Survey revealed the frequency of *civilian* rather than military rape. In their countrywide analyses, Peterman, Palermo, and Bredenkamp (2011) found that approximately twice the number of women who admitted a history of rape reported that they had experienced sexual violence at the hands of a partner (221 per every 1,000 women of reproductive age, compared to only 121 reporting any history of rape). Further, rates of rape and intimate partner violence in North and South Kivu were comparable to many other parts of the country, including those where conflict is no longer endemic. This suggests that the ongoing conflict in the east has not necessarily played a formative role in

---

[1] Respondents were asked whether they or their household members had been beaten, shot, seriously injured, sexually assaulted, raped, abducted, had violent amputations, or been subjected to forced labor by combatants during the past sixteen years (Johnson et al. 2010).

shaping the scale or nature of violence there. While North and South Kivu experienced some of the highest rates of sexual violence, reporting in Equateur, Kasai, Bandudu, and Maniema was also high, and even higher when accounting for other forms of intimate partner violence (Peterman, Palermo, and Bredenkamp 2011: 1064).[2]

International organizations and government agencies such as the Ministry of Gender, MONUSCO, the United Nations Population Fund (UNFPA) have also devoted considerable time and resources to monitoring and documenting a variety of health- and population-related statistics, including incidents of sexual and gender-based violence. Under United Nations Security Council Resolution (UNSCR) 1960 on Women, Peace and Security, the UN Security Council mandated the improvement of data collection and analysis of incidents, trends, and patterns of rape and other forms of sexual violence.[3] UN Action supported the monitoring, analysis and reporting arrangements (MARA) in four priority countries, including DR Congo, and attempted to systematize MONUSCO's approach to the collection of sexual violence statistics (MONUSCO 2014; MONUSCO and UN-OHCHR 2014: 19). MARA has built on efforts already underway by other UN agencies and government ministries, as well as local organizations and health clinics. For example, in its analysis of data collected from health care centers in seven provinces in 2011 and 2012, UNFPA found that fifty-seven percent of all reported rapes or sexual assaults were perpetrated by strangers, with only forty-three percent perpetrated by assailants known to the victim (UNFPA 2013). The vast majority of all attacks (eighty-two percent) was committed by perpetrators wearing civilian clothes. Moreover, the UNFPA study showed that only twenty-three percent of cases registered affected displaced persons; the majority of victims – even in the high-conflict provinces of North and South Kivu – were not displaced by the conflict, but remained within their domestic environments. The average age of victims in all provinces and all studies was under thirty. The Ministry of Gender (MinGenre) has engaged in similar efforts at data collection in collaboration with the UNFPA's Data and Mapping Project, collating sexual violence reporting statistics from health centers across the country (MinGenre 2013).

It is important to take into account the reporting challenges associated with these various figures. While many victims of violence face incentives to hide the incidents from their families and communities, they are more

[2] North Kivu scored slightly higher than other provinces in respondents answering that they had experienced a history of rape, but similar to other provinces with regard to intimate partner violence.
[3] UNSCR 1960 on Women, Peace and Security. Adopted by the Security Council at its 6453rd meeting on December 16, 2010, S/RES/1960.

likely to come forward to report a sexual assault if they become pregnant, need medical attention, contract HIV/AIDS, or have been abandoned by family members. Since rapes by soldiers are more likely to be violent, such cases might motivate increased reporting, particularly in medical facilities. Where rape and sexual assault are committed within the context of a partnership, and particularly where they do not result in visible physical harm, we likely know far less about them.

In spite of these barriers, qualitative and quantitative data suggest that a considerable proportion of all sexual and gender-based violence occurs not on the battlefield, but in the context of interpersonal relationships – between couples, neighbors, family members, students and teachers, or in other familiar settings. It is incorrect to assume that wartime rape is the most prevalent form of violence.[4] However, it is also necessary to recognize that civil conflict can compound and heighten problems of non-conflict violence, leading to its escalation in all spheres of life (Clark et al. 2010; Cockburn 2004; Horn et al. 2014; Wolfe 2014).

South Africa

Like DR Congo, the vast majority of gender-based violence in South Africa takes place in the context of intimate partner relationships (Dunkle et al. 2004). Yet South Africa has also received considerable media attention, both domestically and internationally, to its high rates of opportunistic, brutal, and public sexual assaults. These assaults are more common in high-crime urban settings, although they have been common in rural areas as well (Human Rights Watch 1995, 1997, 2001, 2011).

South African health researchers have engaged in various efforts over the years to determine the prevalence of rape. Early efforts revealed that four percent of women nationwide had been forced to have sex against their will, and seven percent of women who had ever had sex had been either forced or persuaded (Department of Health 1998). Drawing from specialized sexual violence data collected in the Eastern Cape, Mpumalanga, and Northern Province, Jewkes and Abrahams (2002: 1232) found that, for all incidents of rape reported across the three provinces, forty-three percent were committed by strangers, twenty-one percent by acquaintances, nine percent in school, nine percent by relatives, eight percent by partners, and eleven percent by others (Jewkes and Abrahams 2002). Other studies found that rapes are

---

[4] See Cohen et al. (2013) and Cohen (2016) for further discussion of this point in other conflict environments. It is also incorrect to assume, as Cohen (2013) makes clear, that the rape and sexual violence perpetrated in DR Congo is characteristic of violence in all conflict environments. In fact, there is considerable variation in the types of violence employed by armed actors both within and across conflicts.

far more likely over the weekend, particularly between the hours of 6:00 PM and 10:00 PM, when people had been drinking and were most commonly perpetrated in open spaces such as fields (thirty-one percent), in the rapist's home (twenty-nine percent), or in the victim's home (fourteen percent) (Jewkes and Abrahams 2002; Swart et al. 2000). Early studies suggested high rates of gang rape and stranger rape as compared to intimate partner violence. This presumably derives from the fact that incidents of stranger rape, and assaults resulting in severe physical injury or requiring urgent medical attention, are reported with greater frequency than sexual assaults perpetrated in the home or leaving no outwardly visible trace.

More recent studies that often adopt more nuanced or careful approaches to data collection paint a slightly different picture. In 2014, the Western Cape Gender-Based Violence Indicators Study (GBVI) revealed that thirty nine-percent of all women surveyed had experienced some form of gender-based violence in their lifetime, and the same proportion of men in the household survey admitted to perpetrating violence. Forty-four percent of the women who had experienced some form of gender violence had experienced violence at the hands of an intimate partner: Forty percent of this violence was emotional, twenty-five percent was physical but nonsexual, thirteen percent was economic, and thirteen percent was sexual (Gender Links 2015). A further seven percent of all women surveyed reported that they had experienced rape at the hands of a non-partner, and six percent reported that they had experienced other forms of non-partner sexual harassment.[5]

The most recent Demographic and Health Survey in South Africa (South Africa Department of Health 2017) included anumber of questions on sexual and gender-based violence. The survey is one of the few nationally representative studies. It revealed that twenty-one percent of ever-partnered women had experienced some form of physical violence at the hands of a partner at some point in their lifetime, whereas six percent of ever-partnered women had experienced sexual violence at the hands of a partner at some point in their lifetime. The survey did not pose questions on non-partnered violence. Interestingly, the Western Cape reported among the lowest rates of sexual violence of all the South African provinces, with Northwest Province reporting the highest (South Africa Department of Health 2017).

This research raises a number of questions about the prevalence and reporting of sexual and gender-based violence in South Africa. The South African Police Service (SAPS) itself has estimated that only 2.8 percent of all rapes that occur in the country are ever reported to police or to health

[5] The definition of sexual harassment in the survey included both physical and verbal harassment and the survey data do not differentiate between physical and nonphysical harassment (Gender Links 2015: 52).

care professionals (South African Police Service 2014). More recent studies, including the Western Cape GBVI Study, place this figure much lower, with the Western Cape GBVI Study suggesting that only 1.6 percent of all women who had ever experienced rape reported the incident to the police, and 2.6 percent of all those experiencing other forms of nonsexual physical violence (Gender Links 2015: 54). In 2014, South African Police Service (SAPS) National Crime Statistics reported 43,219 incidents of rape that were reported to the police across the country from 2013 to 2014 (South African Police Service 2014). These figures show a decrease in the number of reported rapes of about six percent from previous years, and a decrease in the number of reported sexual assaults by five percent from previous years. However, like DR Congo, the vast majority of rapes goes unreported, and those that take place in the context of intimate partnerships or by assailants known to the victims are among the least likely to be reported to police. Survey respondents may also be unwilling to admit to intimate partner violence, even in the context of anonymous surveys. It remains perpetually unclear, therefore, whether low or varied rates across different surveys indicate varying rates of violence; variation in reporting; or variation in the survey instruments employed and how questions are posed to respondents.

To correct or corroborate reporting bias and fill in gaps in existing research, Jewkes and colleagues (2011) have attempted to assess the prevalence of rape through surveys with male rather than female respondents. Through a survey of 1,686 men, Jewkes and colleagues found that thirty-three percent of respondents admitted to raping or attempting to rape a woman, whether an intimate partner, stranger, or acquaintance. Almost half of the thirty-three percent said they had either participated in a gang rape or assisted in a rape, and more than half reported having been violent on multiple occasions. The survey revealed that men admitting to rape did not significantly differ from others according to age or educational attainment, but were more likely to be cohabiting with an intimate partner, less likely to be married, and more likely to have multiple sexual partners. Moreover, there were some differences in the gender attitudes held by those admitting to rape, who were generally more adversarial in their views about women. Reported motivations usually related to anger or a sense of sexual entitlement.

Given underreporting, qualitative work has sought to fill gaps in scholarly knowledge. In this context, researchers have highlighted the significance of nonviolent coercion in marital or seemingly consensual relationships. Coercion may include implicit or explicit threats of physical violence, locking the door until a woman agrees to sex, or threatening economic insecurity if a woman does not do as her partner wishes. Coercion may also be persuasive, with boyfriends or partners using phrases such as "sex strengthens our love," or "in relationships people must make sacrifices" (Wood, Lambert, and Jewkes 2007: 288). Understanding the ways coercion can function within relationships nuances how we understand responses to questions about forced sex, consent and non-consent. Jewkes and colleagues (1999, 2011) have observed that coercion should be interpreted according to a culture of male sexual entitlement, which has been reinforced over time through various social and cultural institutions. A study in the Eastern Cape (Jewkes et al. 1999) revealed that seventy-nine percent of female survey respondents believed that if a man paid *lobola* (bridewealth) for his wife, she was obligated to satisfy his sexual needs whenever he demanded. A further sixty percent reported that they did not believe that a married woman could refuse sex with her husband. Additionally, the belief that if a girl accepts a boyfriend's proposal to "love" or to be in a relationship, then she is obliged to have sex whenever her boyfriend wants, is prevalent among young South African women. Often sexual intercourse is expected in return for a combination of gifts, money, or being taken out (Wood and Jewkes 1997, 1998). A woman or girl's refusal to have sex undermines this informal contract and challenges dominant norms about male sexual entitlement. These beliefs remain prevalent among youth across South Africa, in both rural and urban areas, and parallel attitudes are reported in similar studies in eastern DR Congo (see, e.g., Sonke Gender Justice Network 2012).

Sexual Entitlement and Transactional Approaches to Sex

Many scholars have written about the transactional approaches to sexual interaction that characterize male–female relationships in societies around the world. In both South Africa and DR Congo, women entering into romantic partnerships can face deeply gendered expectations vis-à-vis their relationship roles. Men may be expected to bear the costs of gifts, clothes, meals, and other items for their female partners. In return, women are often expected to satisfy their partners' romantic needs and desires, while deprioritizing their own (Biddlecom 2007). Many (but not all) of my female interviewees and acquaintances portrayed their romantic relationships in this way when the subject arose. Despite social taboos concerning sex before marriage, women often entered into relationships with an understanding that they were obliged to fulfill their partners' sexual needs, whether or not they wanted to do so. In order to fulfill their roles in the partnership, many unmarried, partnered (and often younger) female interviewees in both research contexts upheld that they must consent to sex whenever their partners wished because they were the recipients of clothes, school fees, or other gifts. Among married women, many communicated an understanding that consent to intercourse was given upon entering into the marriage, and not obtained for each sexual encounter.[6] In their study of transactional sex in a South African township, Wood, Lambert, and Jewkes (2007: 293) note: "Sexual consent and sharing beer went hand in hand. A woman who drank and who did not subsequently fulfill her sexual obligation was effectively thought of as having committed theft, and this was humiliating to the man who funded her 'enjoyment.'"

These dynamics are further complicated by a widely held social expectation in both research sites for women to demonstrate that they are not promiscuous. Marriage customs and rituals around the world capture ideas about promiscuity differently, intersecting with consent in potentially challenging ways. One Congolese marriage ritual, for instance, involves a performance of capture: the woman is expected to flee from her partner on her wedding night and feign a show of resistance while the groom engages in her pursuit.[7] In South Africa, the practice of *ukuthwala* (bride capture) displays similar elements, wherein the bride is captured by her prospective groom and his party and taken to be married, sometimes in secret. Versions of this ritual, practiced around the world, are intended to demonstrate that the bride is pure and chaste, and does not exhibit unwanted characteristics of sexual desire, depravity, or promiscuity. In the words of one interviewee, such practices inevitably lead to the "performance of rape being normalized in the context of marriage."[8]

If a woman consents to sex too readily, she might be perceived as "easy" or "promiscuous," which is undesirable to many men. As a result, women and girls in DR Congo and South Africa – as in many other places around the world – face social pressure to resist sexual advances, at least at first, even in the context of genuinely consensual interactions. In her study of sexual consent in the Transkei, Marston (2005: 79) observes similar patterns of behavior. She writes: "if women are expected to resist sex, then being coerced is the socially 'correct' way to consent to sex."

This has led to a widespread perception among many men that saying "no" to sexual intercourse really means "yes." This perception extends far

---

[6] Interview. Francine. DR Congo. April 26, 2013. For a discussion of transactional sex across sub-Saharan Africa, see Cole and Thomas (2009).

[7] Field Notes; Informal Conversation. Lynette, Public Health Practitioner. DR Congo. July 7, 2012. In reference to a Bembe marriage ritual. Similar performative marriage rituals and practices are found in Rwanda, Ethiopia, and South Africa, as well as elsewhere around the world (Woodrow Wilson Center 2013; Yarbrough 2013).

[8] Interview. Lynette, Public Health Practitioner. DR Congo, July 7, 2012. Note that, in spite of social norms that function to normalize rape in the context of some romantic relationships, there is widespread societal intolerance toward accusations of rape in other contexts. Smith (2018) discusses vigilante violence in response to rape accusations, including a notorious incident in KwaMashu, in KwaZulu-Natal.

beyond DR Congo and South Africa, to communities across Europe and the United States (Muehlenhard and Hollabaugh 1988). It leads many men (and some women) to claim difficulty in understanding the nuances of sexual consent, particularly in legal terms. To compound these dynamics, many men (and women) in both DR Congo and South Africa share the opinion that "not taking no for an answer" demonstrates a man's love for a woman. If the suitor were to give up, it might signal that he was not interested or committed to his female partner. Wood and colleagues (2007: 292) quote a young man who articulated this sentiment: "I'm talking about gentle force, holding her hands and lying on top of her and kissing her, and then I do my thing. I can call it forced sex [not rape] because I'm trying to be romantic. You are not rushing to penetrate, you are rushing to put her in the mood."

These attitudes are crucial for understanding dynamics of violence and consent in South Africa, and are captured in the fact that the Xhosa language uses different words for rape committed by strangers and by partners (Wood et al. 2007).[9] This linguistic distinction hints at the sociocultural approaches underpinning consent and coercion within and outside relationship contexts. For instance, *ukulala ngekani* (to sleep with by force) or *ukunyanzela* (to force) are each used to describe unwanted intercourse within sexual partnerships, whereas *ukudlwengula* refers to forced sex by a non-partner or stranger (Wood et al. 2007: 277). Many men (and some legal practitioners and even judges) do not believe that a woman has been forced or coerced into sex if physical violence has not been used. Thus, accusations of rape that revolve around implicit coercion are often rejected both by society at large and by those in law enforcement infrastructures such as police, prosecutors, and judges.

Despite the fact that intimate partner violence likely constitutes the most pervasive form of sexual assault in both sites, it is the practice of gang rape, or "jack-rolling," that has received unprecedented media attention. In the townships of Khayelitsha and Gugulethu, reports of women abducted at gunpoint or knifepoint while they were waiting for buses, walking home from school, using public restrooms, and other such activities were not uncommon. Across the country, the phenomenon of "corrective rape" has been used to target individuals with ambiguous sexualities, those who challenge conventional gender norms, and women who are thought to dress too provocatively (Human Rights Watch 2011; Lock Swarr 2012). One interviewee captured a common sentiment:

Women here in South Africa want to be Western. They wear Western clothes, like short, short skirts. When a man sees that, he has to do something about it. He has

---

[9] The following paragraphs draw from Wood et al. (2007).

to teach her that that is not an African way to dress. By wearing those clothes she tells him that she wants to have sex.[10]

Criminologists have argued that motivations toward gang rape differ from motivations toward single-perpetrator rape, since gang rape can involve male bonding through watching and taking turns (Cohen 2013; Cohen et al. 2013; Holmstrom and Burgess 1980). In South Africa, this has taken on the additional dimension of "teaching" women lessons about how to behave and conform to gender norms (HRW 2011).

In addition to teaching women lessons, rape in South Africa cannot be delinked from a broader culture of rising levels of violent crime. One nurse interviewed by Wood and Jewkes in an early study (1998: 18) claimed:

Ngangelizwe [neighborhood] is very bad, it's better now but it was dirty, full of running water, full of plastic, the gutters are open, and it is congested. You have seen the housing, full of over-crowding, dagga smoking people there don't have the money to pay the rent sometimes. They want a TV, so they go and steal and buy dagga and smoke in gangs, they go about in the streets and if they see a girl they catch her and rape her.

Many interviewees referenced a culture of entitlement – "taking what's yours," "taking what you want," or taking what people think society "owes" them to compensate for past injustices – as the primary reason that rape is so widespread. In Jewkes and colleagues' 2011 study, men who had engaged in acts of rape were more inclined to present themselves as victims, expressing that they had not attained what they felt they deserved or were owed from life. The rhetoric of entitlement has also been invoked by soldiers in eastern DR Congo. When they have been in the bush for extended periods of time, many soldiers report that when they see a woman, they are entitled to take her by force, as compensation for all the work they have done fighting for their country or their armed group (Baaz et al. 2010; Baaz and Stern 2008).

Research also shows that men who have been exposed to trauma in their early years, or who suffer from low self-esteem, seek validation and positive reinforcement from peers who engage in physically aggressive behavior. The physical expression of power through (often sexualized) violence represents what Jewkes and colleagues refer to as "exaggerated masculinity" (2011), which allows young males to exert dominance and control in ways that they cannot do in other areas of their lives. I return to the ways in which patriarchal gender hierarchies have been reinforced in the household and in local and national politics in Chapter 4.

[10] Field Notes. Khosi, Human Rights Technician. South Africa, March 17, 2013.

Historical Legacies of Violence

Decades of state-sponsored or state-sanctioned violence in South Africa and eastern DR Congo have resulted in a climate in which physical violence has been normalized as a response to dispute or discord (Bourgois 2001; Godoy 2006 for discussions of this phenomenon in other contexts). Commanding respect, obedience, or authority through the physical expression of force or violence was an everyday feature of colonial and apartheid regimes. The subjugation of black men under apartheid (and similarly in the Belgian Congo) created what Wood (2005) and others have referred to as a crisis of masculinity (Walker 2005). In South Africa and elsewhere, scholars have used this trope to refer to a sociopolitical environment wherein the systematic disenfranchisement of generations of working-class men, profoundly disadvantaged by the migrant labor economy, meant that the family domain became the primary sphere to assert power and dominance and to reclaim a waning sense of masculinity. The use of force against those less powerful, in the context of sociopolitical interaction or in the home, is thus unsurprising. Neither is it surprising that sexually coercive or violent behavior has remained inextricably bound up with postcolonial and postapartheid constructions of masculinity.[11]

Given disparities in survey instruments and reporting mechanisms, as well as stigma surrounding sexual violence reporting, it is difficult to

---

[11] Wood and Jewkes, in their interviews with young men in 1998, note that: "Multiple sexual partners, by all accounts virtually universal among boys, seemed to be an important defining feature of 'being a man'" (Wood and Jewkes 1998: 20). They also find that men typically express a strong need to control where their girlfriends are: "From the narratives it is clear that many men had expectations that their girlfriend should wait in her home for them to visit, and not finding her there would lead them to conclude that she was seeing another man" (23). Yet underlying discourses of machismo and control was a strong sense of vulnerability. "Acquiring girlfriends in the first place was obviously a preoccupying issue for the boys. In particular, male informants who came from much poorer backgrounds as well as those who were still at school expressed their vulnerability over girls preferring wealthy partners with cars, who were said to enable them to 'boast' and compete with other girls. Thus one of the poorer boys complained that since he came from a home that was 'hungry' and 'full of damp,' he had 'no status' among women; another commented that it made him 'feel bad' that girls were interested in rich men, adding 'I know that one day they will realize that that's not love because love is what you feel on the inside'" (25). Some groups have attempted to address the association between inadequacy and the need to present a heightened masculinity to the outside world. For instance, in circumcision school, elders "actively spoke against the physical abuse of women as being 'unmanly.' Thus here boys were provided with alternative constructions of masculinity to those prevalent in the streets, ones which were said to emphasize respect for others and non-violence. Initiates were told that beating women, using violence to force respect, fighting with knives, drinking excessively and having large numbers of partners were among the behaviors of 'boys' and not men" (41). However, Wood and Jewkes found that, in the longer term, most reverted to pre-circumcision ways after receiving such trainings.

conjure a full picture of the scale and nature of sexual and gender-based crimes. What we can glean from existing research; however, is that, despite the two countries' differences, many women and girls in eastern DR Congo and South Africa, and some men and boys, face similar threats of gendered violence, and equivalent barriers to reporting. The scale and nature of violence and insecurity felt by those I was working with, as well as the parallels between the types of gendered violence experienced across the two research sites, profoundly shaped the direction of my research. Importantly, the nature of gendered harm faced by women (and some men) across DR Congo and South Africa, and the ways in which threats to gender security have structured reporting, investigation and prosecution, made a comparison of the evolution of the legal and institutional responses to violence in the two sites particularly illuminating. The fact that legal responses in eastern DR Congo have often transcended deeply entrenched sociocultural gender norms concerning male entitlement and transactional sex, which have continued to constrain legal responses in South Africa, provided the basis of my puzzle. The ways in which similarities and differences between the dynamics of violence in each site structured my research approach is the subject of the next section.

Conducting Research on Law and Violence: The Kivus and the Western Cape

Both South Africa and DR Congo have been sites of intense and targeted advocacy over the past decade, in which international attention has been directed toward sexual and gender-based crimes. The fact that advocacy efforts in each site have been similar, but have engendered such divergent institutional responses, makes their side-by-side analysis informative.

Since I sought to understand how efforts to promote legal accountability for violent sexual crimes have been experienced differently across the two research sites, it was necessary to immerse myself, to the extent possible, in the processes and interactions through which law and violence have been produced over time. It was beyond the scope of this project to fully explore subnational variation. Instead, I focus on DR Congo's eastern provinces and South Africa's Western Cape over the past two decades as sites of some of the most targeted domestic and international gender advocacy. Relatedly, North and South Kivu and the Western Cape each house important justice sector institutions and large numbers of domestic and international NGOs.

The research that informed this book was carried out over multiple trips to both countries between 2008 and 2016. Between May 2012 and October 2013, I conducted approximately thirteen months of field research, eleven of which were spent in the eastern provinces of DR Congo and two in South Africa. I undertook subsequent research trips to DR Congo in 2013, 2014, and 2016, and I conducted supplementary archival research using South African court documents in 2016 and 2017. This research built on prior visits to both countries in my earlier academic and professional work, as well as many follow-up skype, email, and phone conversations in both countries.

Although I have undertaken a number of research trips to South Africa, I spent the majority of my in-country research time in the eastern Congolese provinces of North and South Kivu. The decision to focus my research efforts in eastern DR Congo was informed by a variety of factors. Most importantly, for all the development aid that has been devoted to legal capacity building in eastern DR Congo, at the time of my research there was no systematic record of cases heard by the Congolese legal system and no easy access to judgements or decisions.[12] Many judgments were never written up, and many of those that were had been handwritten and were only available in hard copy. Collecting reliable data therefore meant traveling to each court in person to examine court records and to obtain documents, as well as to monitor and observe proceedings firsthand. To supplement my legal analysis, I spent extended periods of time observing the activities of legal aid clinics, police stations, courts, and NGOs.

In the Western Cape, on the other hand, a large body of existing research was, at the project's inception, already devoted to the treatment of sexual and gender-based violence by the country's justice system. I was able to draw from research carried out by the Women's Legal Centre, as well as by Lillian Artz, Rachel Jewkes, Lisa Vetten, and Dee Smythe, among others (e.g., Artz 2003; Artz and Smythe 2005, 2007, 2008; Jewkes et al. 2009). To complement existing scholarship, I undertook original in-country fieldwork in the Western Cape in 2013 to analyze the legal treatment of sexual and gender-based violence in two courts: Khayelitsha Magistrates Court and the High Court of Western Cape. This research, discussed more fully in what follows, built on in-depth archival analysis of South African court documents, police records, and case files, as well as prior visits and ongoing communications with various South African scholars, legal practitioners, and human rights activists.

---

[12] In 2013, to my knowledge I was the first person, for example, to compile a comprehensive list of war crimes and crimes against humanity investigations and trials in the Kivu provinces. Since I carried out this work, the International Center for Transitional Justice has compiled a similar database; however, this work had not been undertaken when I was collecting my data. Avocats Sans Frontières has conducted periodic analysis of the domestic prosecutions of international crimes in DR Congo, but these efforts have focused on legal analyses rather than a comprehensive survey of cases.

The arguments presented here are thus drawn from 193 formal in-depth interviews conducted over the past eight years, as well as countless informational interviews, conversations, and participant observations in both countries. Informally, my knowledge of the subject matter has been informed by approximately 150 supplementary interviews I have undertaken on related subject matters in association with other projects. For this book, I collected and analyzed approximately 400 judgments and case files from Congolese and South African courts.

The Ethics of Interviewing Amidst Violence

An issue that warrants careful attention here is my interaction and engagement with victims of violence. In order to develop a holistic and accurate portrayal of the repercussions of legal accountability and human rights advocacy, it was necessary to incorporate the perspectives of those most affected by violence into my analysis. In addition to specifically gendered harms, however, the legacies of war and apartheid meant that many of my interviewees and interlocutors had also experienced other forms of state and non-state violence firsthand.

One of the central questions my research sought to answer was how legal outreach, accountability efforts and access to justice programming have been implemented in DR Congo and South Africa respectively. Answering this question required understanding how victims of violence have responded to legal interventions and to prospects and opportunities (or lack thereof) for formal justice. This includes how they assessed the options available to them in the aftermath of gender-based assault and why they chose – or rejected – courts or formal legal processes as avenues of redress. I was also concerned with understanding how victims of violence interacted with formal law enforcement mechanisms in both countries, and how the work of domestic and international human rights advocates shaped these interactions.

In both sites, although more so in DR Congo, I encountered individuals in urgent need of medical attention or protection. I met women and men who had been gang raped by soldiers and had nowhere safe to seek shelter. I met young children who were pregnant, HIV positive, and rejected by their families. I frequently met women who had been robbed of all their worldly possessions and separated from their families, who asked me for advice and guidance on what they should do next.

Many scholars and researchers have battled with the ethical dilemmas associated with interviewing vulnerable populations (Clark 2007; Cronin-Furman and Lake 2018; Fujii 2012; Wood 2006). The question of when and how to incorporate the perspectives of vulnerable or violence-affected individuals and communities is especially troubling for academic researchers, given that the benefits of academic research are rarely – if ever – visible to interviewees. Where benefits do exist, academic studies do not typically result in the much-needed food distribution, financial aid, or medical care that follow research missions undertaken by aid agencies. It was difficult to alert potential interviewees – particularly in rural parts of eastern DR Congo where education levels were low – to the difference between the kind of scholarly research I was undertaking, and the outreach and development assistance provided by the humanitarian and NGO communities they were accustomed to seeing. For some, the mere presence of a white woman in their village generated hopes of development assistance. And although vulnerable populations have frequently been photographed for human rights campaign materials (Graham 2014) or questioned by aid organizations about their needs and experiences (in the documentation of human rights abuses or the design of aid distribution programs), few have witnessed tangible improvements to their lives as a result of these interactions.

These dynamics presented a sequence of ethical dilemmas. I was not confident that my informed consent process could fully persuade prospective interviewees facing extraordinary hardship that speaking to me would not result in material benefit. My ethics review board at the University of Washington prevented me from compensating my interviewees financially for their time. I worried that some victims of violence might consent to speak to me, not because they understood something about my research and were genuinely willing to assist me, but because they believed, despite my assurances to the contrary, that assistance of some form might result (Cronin-Furman and Lake 2018).

I weighed these questions carefully. I did not wish to write the perspectives of the intended beneficiaries of legal aid and gender advocacy programs out of my scholarship. And indeed, any satisfactory analysis of how law and legal accountability work in practice necessitates a bottom-up approach that centers the experiences of those most marginalized by existing injustices. Yet I did not wish to create expectations, raise false hopes, exacerbate insecurities, or place any additional burdens on those facing hardship or harm.

In the Western Cape I was fortunate enough to be able to draw from outstanding research conducted by a number of South African scholars. Given the quality, sensitivity, and rigor of this work, in order to augment my understanding of victims' experiences with the legal system I needed to conduct only a small number of my own interviews with individuals who had interacted with legal institutions after experiencing violence. In eastern DR Congo, preexisting firsthand scholarship on the experiences of victims of violence with the law was less readily available; in order to answer my questions well, I needed to rely more heavily on firsthand research. I approached interviewing victims of violence and participants in legal processes carefully. I was fortunate enough to work with a number of excellent and incredibly sensitive local research partners who did their best to identify potential challenges in advance of my interviews and to ensure that my interviewees understood as much as possible about the nature of my research before they agreed to meet with me. I made every effort not to interview minors, and I was careful not to interact with anyone who would be endangered in any way by meeting with me.[13]

In addition to the danger of raising expectations in my research, I was also concerned about trauma and revictimization. While my focus was always on the legal process, and not on the incident of violence, many interviewees volunteered to recount their histories to me, which were always painful to hear and must have been incredibly painful to tell. I stopped my interviews whenever interviewees appeared visibly distressed by the subject matter, and I employed various strategies to ensure that my research did not raise false expectations or inconvenience my research participants in any way. Despite these precautions, I was still constantly forced to reflect on whether the value of my research outweighed the time and emotional investment required of those who were generous enough to share their stories with me. The perspectives of these interviewees, and further details of the decisions I made surrounding them, are discussed in Chapter 5 and in Appendix B.

DR Congo

In DR Congo, the Kivus represent a crucial case for any study of legal and advocacy responses to gender violence. The country's eastern most provinces have been the focus of considerable international attention since the war broke out in 1996. Additionally, the civilian and military courts in the provinces of North and South Kivu have produced the vast majority of sexual and gender-based violence rulings across the country. Given that international and domestic attention and advocacy around sexual and gender-based violence has been focused on North and South Kivu, this is perhaps unsurprising. However, in order to fully

[13] On various occasions, I was in situations where minors requested interviews with me and I agreed. I do not generally cite from these interviews, although they have informed my broader understanding of accountability and barriers to justice. I have conducted many interviews with minors outside the context of this project, including in the context of a USAID-funded project that focused on child prostitution. This project drew predominantly from the experiences and testimonies of girls aged between eleven and eighteen.

understand *how* and *why* activists have been effective in directing the attention of local courts toward sexual and gender-based crimes, it was necessary to scrutinize the local courts that have been responsible for producing these decisions.

Most of my work was carried out in the provincial capitals of Goma and Bukavu where the judicial institutions of North and South Kivu are headquartered. However, my research also involved extended travel to remote rural locations to observe trials, collect decisions, and conduct interviews. I interviewed lawyers, prosecutors, military and civilian judges, police officers, representatives from domestic and international NGOs, international organizations, members of local civil society groups, members of the Congolese national army, defendants in human rights trials, members of armed groups, and victims of violence who had attempted to access formal justice mechanisms. In addition to interview data, I monitored military and civilian court cases from their points of entry into the legal system, observed a large number of criminal trials, and traced a subset of legal processes involving gender violence since 2006. I conducted interviews in French and English and, where necessary, I relied on the assistance of interpreters to translate from local languages such as Kinande, Kiswahili, Kinyarwanda, Lingala, and Moshi. I supplemented interview and observational data with the collection of court cases and analyses of legal processes.

Eleven months of research allowed me to become familiar with the aspects of "everyday" life relevant to my research. My immersion in day-to-day life in the Kivus also enabled me to build relationships and develop trust. Combining different research techniques proved critical for my understanding and interpretation of the data I collected. For example, given the deeply unpredictable nature of conducting research in eastern DR Congo, I was constantly forced to reevaluate my approach and to reassess what kind of data were needed, which methods were appropriate for answering which questions, and what would be possible given the evolving security situation. Two incidents in the early phases of my research profoundly affected my research approach and the subsequent decisions I made in the field. In stark contrast to the formal record keeping that is standard practice in South Africa, courts in eastern DR Congo typically lack the technological capacity to record activities and keep track of cases. Thus, the simple task of knowing how many gender violence cases courts in Goma had heard in one year (or in comparison to years prior) was a momentous undertaking. I spent a period of many weeks in December 2012 and January 2013 copying out pencil-written court records from dusty brown binders into an Excel spreadsheet. Simply obtaining statistics for one court in one year took approximately two weeks of work. It rapidly became clear that collating records for just one court going back to 2006 would eat up almost all my time in the field. This would not even offer me comparative statistics from courts in other locations. After taking a break for reflection, I began observing court cases at Goma's central prison. Many of the cases were appeals from the previous year, and thus should have shown up in my meticulously collected spreadsheet of cases from 2012. Yet only three of the eleven cases I observed that week appeared in my records. I went back to the Tribunal de Grande Instance to consult the binders. Upon finding no records, I asked the clerk why the cases didn't appear. "*C'est comme ça ici* [that's just how it is here]," he said, laughing at me. "Do you see computers here? No. We have nothing. I write the cases here myself. I write everything. But sometimes it is the job of Maître Olivier to write, sometimes others. We are now transferring to an online system. I will enter these cases now." It became abundantly clear that any effort to collect court statistics would mean very little in the end. Even provided unlimited resources and capacity to collect comparative statistics from select years for specific courts, this exchange shook my confidence in the data's reliability. If the numbers I recorded bore little relevance to the cases heard in courtrooms, then comparative records would do little good. What information would I be able to glean from them? It was clear that my insights would need to come from other sources. Information pertaining to the justice system's response to sexual and gender-based violence would instead emerge from observation and conversation. This too would take time, but my extended immersion in the Congolese legal system provided me with the necessary tools with which to make informed assessments and analyses of these data and would allow me to incorporate an understanding of how the positionality of my interviewees might affect the information they were giving me.

M23's takeover of Goma in November 2012 further shifted my research plan. When the rebels entered the city, they liberated Goma's central prison, Munzenze, which served as the primary prison for the Petit Nord (the southern territories of North Kivu). Almost every conviction that I had analyzed as part of my research in North Kivu to date had resulted in a sentence at Munzenze. After the prison liberation, rumors circulated that the approximately 1,500 inmates were gone. Having spent a great deal of time at Goma's central prison, I headed to Munzenze, harboring hopes of meeting with the director to find out what had happened. I arrived to find the place eerily deserted. The barracks outside, normally occupied by hundreds of officers from the Police Nationale Congolaise (PNC) and the national army (the Forces Armées de la République Démocratique du Congo – FARDC), were empty. Old clothes were strewn across the floor, and a few onlookers watched me curiously as I picked my way

through the razor wire fence erected around the prison. It became immediately clear that I would meet neither the director nor any returned
prisoners. In the director's office, prison records filled the room – not
filed in boxes along the walls as they had been previously, but in shredded,
ripped, and burnt paper strewn across the floor.

Figure 1 Outside Munzenze Prison. Goma, DR Congo. November 28,
2012. © Milli Lake.

It wasn't clear if the office had been intentionally ransacked, or if this was
just the result of 1,500 individuals making a very quick getaway. Shortly after
this visit, I met with the country director of a legal capacity-building organization. "Everything we've worked for, everything we've built over the past six
years is destroyed," the country director informed me, unable to hide his
despair. "We've seen these kinds of shifts in power time and time again in
eastern Congo," he added. "You start everything over again. That's how it
works." With new forces in charge of the city, the rules had changed again.[14]
   I was to be reminded of this fact time and time again over the coming
months. When I next visited the Auditorat Militaire, they didn't have
chairs left to sit on. When I visited the police seven months later on my last

[14] Field Notes. Stephan, Country Director. DR Congo. November 28, 2012; January 12,
2013.

visit to the station before I left Goma, no one had replaced the vehicles that were stolen in the M23 occupation. The police and the courts were going about their business, going through the motions, but insurgents had looted all their possessions. All case files, records, documents, modes of transport, power cords, and chairs were stolen, burnt, or destroyed. One military judge laughed as we stood together in his office. "Look," he said, pointing at an Internet outlet in the wall. "The United Nations pays every month for our Internet, but we have no Internet cable and no computer! What good is this?"[15] Working in Goma during this specific time period bolstered my appreciation of what it meant to build legal institutions in the midst of ongoing violence and insecurity.

While the law prescribes a Tribunal de Paix to be located in each territory and a district court (TGI) in each major provincial city, in practice the picture is more murky. In North Kivu, TGIs are located in Goma, Beni, and Butembo. In South Kivu, in Bukavu (Kavumu) and Uvira.[16] At the time of my research, the lower courts in Lubero, Rutshuru, Masisi, and Walikale were functioning to some degree, and a lower court in Nyirangongo was not functioning at all. In South Kivu, lower courts in Mwenga, Kalehe, Idjwi, and Fizi were occasionally operational, but none was functional on a day-to-day basis.

In part by design and in part by necessity, I focused the majority of my research in courts where NGOs and legal aid programs were most active. Indeed, my arguments remain most applicable to those courts – and indeed the specific cases – that have been the targets of attention and advocacy. I do not expect gender-progressive practices to spill over to courts that have little contact with legal capacity-building initiatives. Since my arguments rest on the premise that NGOs exert considerable influence over legal processes in areas of state fragility and weakness in ways that prove impossible in stronger state settings, I expected their influence to be largely unfelt in locales where NGOs have only limited presence.

In order to evaluate these arguments in full, I visited courts and police stations with varying degrees of functionality, and varying degrees of support and attention from NGOs. In each location, I conducted personal interviews with relevant local personnel, observed proceedings (where courts were open or in session), and secured court documents and police records (where available). In North Kivu, the court in Rutshuru was under M23 control for almost the entire period of my initial research. When I visited courts, prosecutors, and police stations in Rutshuru territory, I liaised with M23's bureaucracy rather than with representatives of the Congolese state. M23 did

---

[15] Interview and Field Notes. Safari. Military Judge. May 23, 2013.

[16] In 2014, the Décret d'organisation judiciaire n°14/015 du 08 mai 2014 fixant les siéges et les ressort des Tribunaux de Grande Instance reorganized the jurisdiction of the Tribunaux de Paix and Grande Instance, creating a number of new courts.

not grant me access to court or police records. Even still, my interviews and observations there were deeply illuminating.

Political insecurity and ongoing conflict made safe, reliable access to field sites and data extremely difficult. Each trip to a new village required careful weighing of the intellectual payoff versus threats to personal safety. For example, in 2012–2013, I decided against travel to Beni and Butembo. At that time, the roads between Goma and Beni were occupied by armed groups, including M23, FDLR, and Mai Mai, making safe passage uncertain. Two colleagues who made the trip by road described it as "extremely risky" upon their return. Armed groups stopped them on multiple occasions, and they elected to fly back via commercial airplane so as not to risk their luck again. While I could have traveled to Beni by road through Rwanda and Uganda, or taken domestic flights, these options were too time-consuming, costly, or unpredictable to be productive for my purposes.

On other occasions, I had to cancel scheduled visits to courts in Walikale and Shabunda, since they could not safely be reached by road. M23 was rapidly gaining territory at the time of my scheduled visits, and the only way to reach either site was by UN flight. Since NGO workers and journalists were beginning to discuss possibilities of evacuation, I was forced to think carefully about my role as an unaffiliated researcher. Not being an employee of an international organization meant that I would have to make my own choices about when and how to leave, rather than having evacuation protocols decided for me. I ultimately decided that the logistical challenges of negotiating evacuation under such circumstances (and the potential resources that might be needed) outweighed the presumed benefits, particularly since the British and American embassies declined to assist individuals traveling under such precarious political circumstances. In other instances, however, I traveled with NGO escorts, UN convoys, humanitarian flights, or private cars to occupied territory or hard-to-reach locations, in order to visit courts, observe mobile court proceedings, and conduct interviews across the provinces.

Undertaking these calculations on a daily basis attuned me to the ways that insecurity crept into even the most banal life decisions: for the legal practitioners working in the courts I was studying; for the police and NGOs to whom cases were initially reported; for the local colleagues, drivers, and interlocutors facilitating my work; and for victims of violence.

I was most successful in collecting and analyzing written judgments from Goma and Bukavu, although still not without significant challenges. Even in Goma, many prison, police, and court records were destroyed in the M23 occupation in 2012. For those records that were not destroyed, many decisions and judgments across both provinces were never recorded or written down; others were handwritten, with missing or incomplete pages, or barely legible. I collected as many judgments and case files as I was able to dating back to 2006. Of 149 written decisions, 106 were from the civilian courts and 33 were from the military courts. Complete case files included first-instance rulings, as well as cases that had gone to appeal. The rest of my analysis was observational and interview-based.

Figure 2 Filing Office, Munzenze Prison. Goma, DR Congo. November 28, 2012. © Milli Lake.

For the same reasons that I faced challenges accessing certain courts, so too did NGOs engaged in legal capacity building. Courts in Beni, Butembo, Masisi, Mwenga, Walikale, and other hard-to-reach locations were not, therefore, hubs for the kinds of intensive and targeted NGO advocacy as those in Goma and Bukavu, and their proceedings typically reflected more conservative gender attitudes than the more easily accessible institutions. With the exception of a few fairly high-profile mobile court hearings, the more remote the court or police station, the less likely its proceedings were to exhibit the protections described in Chapter 1. Further discussion of this variation is presented in Chapters 4 and 5.

South Africa

My work in South Africa was, predictably, very different. South Africa, transitioned from a brutally oppressive apartheid regime to one of the world's most respected and admired democracies in the early to mid-1990s.

I selected the Western Cape as my primary field site for a number of reasons. In both DR Congo and South Africa, I elected to spend an extended period of time in one place, in order to become familiar with local responses to violence, the inner workings of the justice system, and the ways in which legal accountability has been felt by those most affected by violence. The townships of Gugulethu and Khayelitsha in the Western Cape are, like the eastern provinces of DR Congo, among the more insecure areas of the country. Crime rates in general are high according to national averages, and sexual and gender-based violence is widespread (South African Police Service 2014, 2015).[17]

Moreover, like Goma and Bukavu, Gugulethu and Khayelitsha are fairly densely populated. Their close proximity to the legislative capital of Cape Town, which houses some of the wealthiest neighborhoods in the country, means that large disparities in wealth are highly visible. Yet Cape Town, like the provincial capitals of Goma and Bukavu, is home to a strong and well-connected advocacy movement working on a wide array of gender issues. A large number of domestic, regional, and international human rights and legal advocacy organizations are headquartered in Cape Town, and many of them focus resources and attention on the nearby townships of Gugulethu and Khayelitsha. In addition, there are a number of grassroots human rights organizations, civil society groups, and church groups based in Khayelitsha and Gugulethu themselves working on issues of gender violence.

In many ways, the availability of formal data in South Africa made research there less challenging. Yet extraordinarily high levels of violence and the climate of fear in which many South Africans go about their daily activities rivaled anything I observed in eastern DR Congo. In DR Congo, I spent time in refugee camps, in rebel-held territories, and with victims of brutal human rights abuses. While Congolese civilians often seemed weary, but accepting in their attitudes toward the risk of violence, it was rare to encounter the sustained sense of unease that was widespread among many urban working South Africans. In Khayelitsha, I heard stories from medical practitioners of girls being gang raped, tied up in trashcans, and left for days after getting into taxi-buses.[18] I heard stories of carjackings and of friends of friends who ran out of gas on the freeway and were raped or stabbed before they had

---

[17] Although the most recent Gender Links survey rates sexual violence in the Western Cape lower than other provinces, rates are still high overall, and SAPS data identify the Western Cape as having one of the highest crime rates in the country.

[18] Interview. Anathi, Consellor. South Africa. March 15, 2013; Interview. Phumzile, Program Officer. South Africa. March 15, 2013.

a chance to call the police.[19] I saw medical and forensics teams sweeping local neighborhoods in their reportedly routine clean-up after the alcohol-fueled violence that was expected to follow payday. Everyone had a story. I met countless people who warned of the dangers of using public toilets after dark. Despite the fact that there were few other options given that most Khayelitsha residents do not have toilets or running water in their homes, women would rarely venture the few steps to the community toilet, because this – many told me – meant they would surely be raped.[20] Despite multiple trips to South Africa over the years, I have always found it incredibly difficult to assess the extent to which stories like these reflect the lived realities faced by the townships' ordinary residents, or the extent to which stories of streets rife with crime are legacies of deeply racialized paranoia. Apartheid's scars are especially sorely felt in the Western Cape, which is home to the country's largest white population. The province remains deeply segregated, and relations between whites, blacks, coloreds, and other populations (Nigerians, Zimbabweans, and Indians) are often characterized by division and mistrust.

Segregation and fear in the Western Cape has deep roots. The Native Land Act of 1913, which formed the basis for the apartheid-era "home-lands" or *bantustans*, confined South Africa's eighty percent nonwhite population to only thirteen percent of the country's land. Moreover, the land on which blacks and coloreds were permitted to live was heavily regulated and, while living conditions in white South Africa grew to resemble the high standards enjoyed by citizens of Western Europe, living conditions on the homelands were characterized by poverty, poor sanitation, overcrowding, and insufficient food, clean water, and necessary public services. A series of laws was passed that exacerbated conditions in the homelands and made life for nonwhite South Africans incredibly challenging. In 1950, after the 1948 election of South Africa's National Party, the Group Areas Act reinforced and expanded the jurisdiction of the Native Land Act, and precipitated the forced removal of blacks from urban centers to the homelands. The Population Registration Act strengthened the country's existing pass laws, which restricted the movement of nonwhite South Africans and required passbooks to be carried by any nonwhite South African traveling outside of his/her homeland to work, or between one homeland and another. The Separate Amenities Act and the Native Labor Act of 1953 enshrined the color bar in law. These laws restricted jobs by race and prohibited the use of "white-only"

[19] Field Notes. South Africa. March and April 2017; Informal Conversation. Khozi. Human Rights Technician. South Africa. March 17, 2013.
[20] Field Notes. South Africa. March 2017. Informal Conversation. Thembele and Nikelwa, Community Activists. South Africa. March 2, 2017.

transportation, post offices, schools, and restaurants by nonwhites, even for those working as domestic or urban laborers in white-only cities and neighborhoods (Meredith 1988). Any South African found to be in violation of these restrictions was subject to the full force of the law. Beatings, physical and verbal abuse, torture, and other assaults on non-whites were an everyday occurrence. In addition to extraordinarily high levels of opportunistic violence against black and colored populations, state-sponsored, extralegal assassinations, as well as targeted lynchings by vigilantes, not only persisted with impunity between 1948 and 1991, but were actively supported by South Africa's apartheid government against those perceived to be resisting apartheid rule or demonstrating organized or ad hoc opposition to legal segregation (Motlhabi 1988). Moreover, South African security forces coordinated targeted offensives against border states thought to harbor members of the political opposition (defined as terrorists by the apartheid state). Particularly notable was South Africa's 1978 bombing of Angola, in which more than 700 South Africans thought to be affiliated with the antiapartheid opposition movement were killed (South African Truth and Reconciliation Commission 1997).

The widespread violence, brutality, torture, and subjugation inflicted upon nonwhite South Africans have, predictably, had devastating repercussions. Following the country's transition to democracy in 1994, a great deal of fear and mistrust remained on both sides. Many whites had, since birth, been warned about the perceived dangers of black majority rule, and had been fed unrelenting propaganda about the innate criminality and violence of black South Africans. The racist portrayal of black South Africans as inherently violent has proved a sensitive issue in the postapartheid era, particularly when media attention has focused on high crime rates. Moreover, deeply racialized fear of black violence has meant that many whites remain afraid of traveling in traditionally nonwhite areas. It can be challenging to disentangle everyday reports of rising crime from racist propaganda propagated and manufactured by apartheid apologists (Moffett 2006).

However, the stories of violence I describe here rarely came from white South Africans, or from those living behind security systems in gated communities. Instead, they were first- or secondhand accounts from ordinary citizens and first responders living in some of the poorest neighborhoods in the country. Conducting research in health clinics, police stations, and hospitals meant that these stories were undoubtedly some of the worst. Nevertheless, working in townships in the Western Cape, home to some of the highest crime rates and starkest inequality in the world, alerted me to the many parallels, as well as the contrasts, with day-to-day security in eastern DR Congo.

Research in the Western Cape necessitated a number of methodological and epistemological decisions that never arose in DR Congo. First and foremost, unlike eastern DR Congo, in South Africa it proved extremely difficult to assess personal risk, leading to calculations that would have significant repercussions for the research I could conduct. As a white foreigner, the extent to which I was prepared to conduct research from "behind closed windows" was a constant negotiation and renegotiation. Many white South Africans do not travel to Khayelitsha or Gugulethu, and appear to believe that doing so ensures violent assault. Many others, including those involved in advocacy or nonprofit work relating to housing, sanitation, violence, and other pressing social issues, travel to their project sites in taxis and leave before dark, echoing warnings against the use of public transport, walking, or even driving through certain neighborhoods. Others still professed that traveling around the Western Cape was no more dangerous than travel in any major city, and any expressions to the contrary were simply the product of highly racialized legacies of apartheid and a historical belief that black or colored neighborhoods are rife with violence. In order to understand what law and lawlessness looked like for victims of gender violence in South Africa, it was necessary to move – physically and mentally – beyond the narratives promoted and described in urban centers. Doing so meant that I was constantly forced to weigh legitimate warnings for personal safety against a determination not to be intimidated by racist and classist paranoia.

Thus, while I conducted many informative interviews in the administrative and legislative capitals of Cape Town and Johannesburg, much of my research in South Africa occurred in the townships of Gugulethu and Khayelitsha. There, I interviewed judges, police officers, civil society activists, health workers, counselors, and victims of violence. I visited courts, hospitals, community centers, and police stations, and I traveled around in cars, on foot, and by public transport. Even for a short time, occupying the spaces and routines that my research subjects occupied, rather than arriving and leaving by car, allowed me some insight into the knowns and unknowns that shape and define the regulation of violent crime for ordinary Khayelitsha residents. Firsthand knowledge of the impact and implementation of national and local policies and institutions, as well as knowledge of the day-to-day challenges faced by local activists and transnational human rights organizations, was critical for answering the questions central to my research. In both South Africa and DR Congo, I learned far more from these accidental, unplanned, and everyday encounters and interactions than from my formal data collection efforts (Coffey 1999; Schatz 2009; Soss 2006; Wedeen 2010).

My research in South Africa was not, however, characterized by the immersion and time that I spent in DR Congo. Although I spent two months conducting original research in South Africa, I relied far more heavily on archival documents and preexisting scholarship. In addition to data held by the South African Police Service (SAPS) and National Prosecuting Authority (NPA), I conducted interviews and spent time in district courts, magistrates' courts, specialized sexual offenses courts, and the High Court in the Western Cape. I interviewed and corresponded with a number of stakeholders, including NGOs and researchers that have been monitoring the legal treatment of sexual and gender-based violence cases for more than a decade. Finally, I collected and analyzed 219 first-instance and appeals decisions from Khayelitsha Magistrates' Court and the High Court of Western Cape between 2006 and 2014, focusing on key moments for gender reform (for instance, prior to and following the passage of the 2007 Sexual Offences Act). Due to the sheer volume of decisions available compared to eastern DR Congo, I chose to focus on two courts in particular: Khayelitsha's District and Magistrates' Courts and the Western Cape High Court.

I chose these courts as two courts serving areas of high crime that have attracted targeted attention for high rates of sexual and gender-based violence. Khayelitsha Magistrates' Court serves a poor, predominantly working-class, black and colored population, whereas the High Court is situated in an extremely affluent part of downtown Cape Town. The median annual income of Khayelitsha according to 2011 census data was approximately $445 USD per working adult per year (R6,000 per capita). Employment is approximately fifty percent of the adult population, and more than fifty percent fail to achieve a secondary education (Seekings 2013). Khayelitsha is comprised of approximately ninety percent black South Africans, eight percent colored, and less than one percent white and Indian.

In South Africa, rape and sexual offenses cases are heard by both High Courts and Magistrates' Courts as the courts of first instance. South Africa has nine High Court divisions – one in each of the nine provinces, with local seats in Bhisho, Mthatha and Port Elizabeth, Johannesburg, Durban, Thohoyandou, and Lephalale (South Africa Department of Justice and Constitutional Development 2016). Below the High Courts sit the Regional Magistrates' Courts (which deal with criminal cases) and the District Magistrates' Courts (which deal with criminal and civil cases).

The Western Cape houses fifty-six District Magistrates' Courts, many with attached Regional Magistrates' Courts that deal with more serious cases than the District Courts (South African Government 2013). District Courts can hear civil and criminal cases carrying sentences up to a maximum of three years, or a maximum fine of R100,000 (or approximately $7,000

USD, South Africa 2007. Criminal Law Sentencing Amendment Act. No 38). With a few exceptions, Regional Magistrates' Courts can impose a maximum sentence of fifteen years, or fines up to R300,000. For crimes of murder or rape, however, Regional Magistrates' Courts may impose life sentences; and for armed robbery or stealing a motor vehicle, they may impose sentences up to twenty years (South Africa 2007). In practice, where complexities in a particular case emerge, Magistrates' Courts can often refer rape and sexual offense cases to the High Courts as the court of first instance. Specialized sexual offenses courts and children's courts are also housed at select Magistrates' Courts, and are, in theory, equipped with expertise and resources to prosecute sexual offenses. The sexual offenses courts can impose life sentences for rape and other sexual offenses. The Western Cape High Court is the first court of appeal for cases heard by all of Western Cape's Magistrates' Courts and sexual offenses courts. The Supreme Court of Appeal hears appeals for any cases heard by the Western Cape High Court as the court of first instance.

Of the 219 decisions I analyzed, 150 were first-instance decisions. One hundred and twenty-nine of these were heard by the Western Cape High Court as the court of first instance, and 21 were heard by the Magistrates' Court. Sixty-nine were appeals from lower courts heard by the Western Cape High Court. Ultimately, while I conducted field-work in Khayelitsha, I spent less time analyzing the judgments produced by the Khayelitsha Magistrates' Court because these lacked written explanations of the legal reasoning. I thus drew from accompanying documentation in the Magistrates' Court case files, and supplemented my archival analysis with observation and interviews in the legal institutions based there. As Wynberg was the site of the country's first specialized sexual offenses court, I also conducted a limited number of interviews there.

Both Khayelitsha and Gugulethu are hubs for grassroots campaigning and mobilization around gender violence, as well as housing a number of national gender justice organizations and programs. Interviewees in the Western Cape therefore included prosecutors, registrars, clerks, judges, police, investigators, defense counsel, community organizers and representatives from local NGOs, civil society groups, and legal aid organizations.

Conclusion

Fluid boundaries between conflict-related sexual violence, opportunistic violence, and violence within interpersonal relationships make it difficult to gage the prevalence or pervasiveness of gendered harms. Further, a lack of clarity over what constitutes sexual consent makes measuring sexual violence notoriously challenging. Nevertheless, in both North and South Kivu and in the Western Cape, various distinct forms of sexual and gender-based violence affect large numbers of women and men. Insight into the ways in which proximity to violence shaped both my own research practices and the day-to-day experiences of many of the communities I was working with offers important context for the evidence presented in this book.

Qualitative, embedded, and contextually situated research has sometimes been criticized for its perceived lack of generalizability. However, detailed and careful analysis of particular cases affords researchers new insights into the micro processes through which legal outcomes are constituted. My embedded approach allowed me to scrutinize the lived realities of apparent legal advancements as they have been experienced by those most directly affected, illuminating those innovations that have been welcomed by their intended beneficiaries, as well as those that have created new tensions. While this chapter calls attention to the many ethical challenges associated with conducting research with and among populations affected by violence, it nevertheless emphasizes the importance of centering the experiences of those whose perspectives might otherwise be marginalized. Given that many existing studies of human rights diffusion and law reform focus on fairly narrow indicators of legal implementation, or otherwise dismiss so-called failed states altogether, they risk missing the nuanced ways in which local courts and other actors and entities in weak or war-torn countries engage with internationally promoted human rights practices. Furthermore, they risk erasing the distinct ways in which women, in particular, experience violence, insecurity, law, and the state. Given that building the rule of law relies on establishing public confidence and trust in legal institutions, foregrounding the perspectives of the law's intended "recipients" is integral to any careful analysis of how rule of law and state-building work in differing institutional settings.

Although this project was not without its limitations, its embedded approach offers scholars of international relations a window into the politics of human rights advocacy and state-building that travels far beyond the particular sites of study. Indeed, NGOs have certainly been presented with similar types of opportunity structures elsewhere. The stories presented in this book caution, once again, against binary approaches to concepts such as "war" and "peace," "security" and "insecurity," and "state strength" and "state weakness," which are not generally equipped to encompass complex lived realities. The conclusion to this book touches on this project's significance for other issue areas and in environments similarly dominated by external advocacy around law and state-building.

3   Explaining State-Level Policy and Practice

Introduction

Despite striking differences in how laws have been implemented in DR Congo and South Africa, the legislative and policy frameworks governing the prosecution of gender-based violence in each country are remarkably similar. This chapter provides an overview of national and international responses to sexual and gender-based violence in DR Congo and South Africa, as well as details of relevant legal instruments and national policy frameworks. It explores how and why legislative and executive elites in DR Congo and South Africa have adopted such similar gender-sensitive legislation and policy platforms on the national stage, before moving on to examine in Chapter 4 why similar legislative frameworks have resulted in such different implementation outcomes.

Throughout this book, I show that state fragility creates opportunities for certain types of human rights diffusion that are absent in states with stronger overall infrastructure and capacity. Empirical and juridical state fragility in DR Congo has, with varying effects, allowed activists to direct targeted legal attention toward sexual and gender-based violence. The reluctance of South African political elites to take gender violence seriously, on the other hand, combined with better-established, far reaching, and globally respected state capacity, has introduced barriers for gender activists in their efforts to improve legal accountability through South Africa's courts.

At the time the research and writing for this book was undertaken, DR Congo's political infrastructure was typically characterized by its crippling fragility and weakness, whereas South Africa was hailed as an example of relative political stability and strength. This dichotomy has not always been as stark. This chapter documents the ways in which the Congo wars and South Africa's transition to democracy in the mid-1990s created openings and opportunity structures in *both* countries that allowed domestic and transnational human rights actors to promote gender-inclusive policy platforms.

A burgeoning body of scholarship theorizes the opportunities that can emerge from political transition and conflict, which can disrupt and fundamentally reorder gender relations (Berry and Lake 2017a, Tripp 2015). Demographic, social, and economic shifts can lead to changes in the labor force, propelling women's increased engagement in political and economic spheres. War, state collapse, and other political shifts can also create institutional disjunctures, allowing space for international norms to take root domestically as constitutions are rewritten, legal systems reformed and restructured, and institutions rebuilt.

In South Africa, strong linkages between the women's rights movement and the antiapartheid activists who later came to comprise South Africa's postapartheid governing elite meant that domestic gender experts were uniquely positioned to influence law and policy in apartheid's aftermath. As a result, South Africa's formal legal framework for prosecuting rape and sexual violence is among the strongest in the world. In DR Congo, gender activists in partnership with international experts played similarly crucial roles in shaping new domestic laws. In the war and postwar period, and in DR Congo's transition to democracy in 2006, Congolese gender activists, with international stakeholders, intervened heavily in the state's governance activities, and in the process and content of institutional reform. In both countries, the gender experts involved in legal reform were connected to a growing global feminist movement and drew from transnational discussions to ensure that the formal laws and policies that were enacted were at the cutting edge of feminist legal discourse. This chapter discusses the introduction of these laws and the policy programs accompanying them, whereas the subsequent chapter analyzes how new laws and policies came to be implemented so differently in each case.

To provide context for the passage of new laws, I first offer a discussion of the international and domestic legal frameworks governing sexual and gender-based violence. The chapter then documents the actors that have propelled (and in some cases resisted) the passage and implementation of gender-sensitive law and policy reform, and how and why each country's laws and policies have taken the forms that they have. For additional context, Appendix C (DR Congo) and Appendix D (South Africa) summarize the respective structures of the two legal systems and criminal justice processes.

The Evolution of Gender-Related Law and Policy in DR Congo and South Africa

The International Legal Framework

Gender-based legal reform in DR Congo and South Africa cannot be delinked from broader international trends to strengthen protections for victims of physical and structural gendered harms. Prior to the conflicts in

Central Africa and the former Yugoslav republics in the early 1990s, sexual and gender-based violence was almost entirely overlooked in international law and humanitarian relief work. International and domestic institutions had failed to take seriously the ways in which women are disproportionately affected by conflict, and sexual crimes in war were sorely underreported and poorly investigated. Ignoring rape as a war crime perpetuated a culture of impunity that devalued women and enabled soldiers and civilians to treat women as "spoils of war" (Enloe 2000). Yet, following the scale and brutality of sexual assaults in Bosnia and Rwanda in the early 1990s, the unique plight of women in conflict attracted international attention, and feminists and human rights activists capitalized on this momentum to push the issue to the forefront of the international agenda.

Consequently, sexual violence committed in wartime is increasingly approached – legally and discursively – in three overarching categories: as a targeted military strategy, as an opportunistic crime committed in the context of war, and as an act of ordinary criminal violence. In practice, these boundaries are more fluid than rigid distinctions allow. When civilian and combatant identities are not clear cut, or when the climate of impunity that undergirds war fosters an environment of rising crime more generally, rape committed as an opportunistic crime by armed combatants, for instance, can be hard to distinguish from an ordinary criminal offense. Similarly, rape committed as a targeted military strategy can be perpetrated alongside opportunistic sexual violence (Baaz and Stern 2008). Nevertheless, the classification of rape as an instrument of conflict was an important development in international criminal law, and represented a milestone in recognizing and classifying some of the many gendered ways in which civilians can be victimized in conflict.

In the mid- to late 1990s, women's rights advocates thus used the attention directed towards sexual violence in conflict situations to advocate for the criminalization of rape as a weapon of war under international law, and to promote shifts in the treatment of violence against women more generally. The Furundžija and Kunarac cases of the International Criminal Tribunal for the former Yugoslavia (ICTY) brought the first international criminal prosecutions of rape and sexual enslavement as crimes against humanity in 1998.[1] In the same year, the International Criminal Tribunal for Rwanda (ICTR) became the first court to establish rape as a crime of genocide in the case of the *Prosecutor* v. *Jean-Paul Akayesu*.[2] Against this

---

[1] International Criminal Tribunal for the Former Yugoslavia. 1998. Prosecutor v. Furundžija, ICTY Case No. IT-95-17/1-T; and Prosecutor v. Kunarac, ICTY Case No. IT- 96–23/1-T and IT-96–23-T.

[2] International Criminal Tribunal for Rwanda. 1998. Prosecutor v. Jean-Paul Akayesu. Case No. ICTR-96-4-T, September 2, 1998.

backdrop, proponents of the International Criminal Court (ICC) made a concerted effort in 1998 to draw explicit attention to victims of gender violence, and to the unique plight of women in conflict, expanding the legal definition of rape to codify the protections enshrined in the ICTR and ICTY case law. Arguably, the sensitive treatment of this issue by the ICC has influenced the legal and discursive treatment of rape in a number of domestic legal systems. The ICC's Rules and Procedures of Evidence (RPE) includes special provisions for the treatment of victims of gender violence in the collection of evidence on sexual crimes (International Criminal Court 2002b). Rule 16 of the RPE notes that the Registrar is responsible for: "Taking gender-sensitive measures to facilitate the participation of victims of sexual violence at all stages of the proceedings" (International Criminal Court 2002b, Rule 16, 1 (d)). Rule 17, 2 (a) specifies that the Victims and Witnesses Unit shall: "provide [victims] with adequate protective and security measures and formulating long- and short-term plans for their protection" (ii); "assist them in obtaining medical, psychological and other appropriate assistance" (iii); and "make available to the Court and the parties training in issues of trauma, sexual violence, security and confidentiality" (iv). Rule 18 (c) notes that administrative and technical assistance must be available for witnesses and victims who appear before the court.

The Rome Statute's Elements of Crimes expands the definition of rape beyond the limited notion of penile-vaginal penetration that still exists in most contemporary criminal codes (International Criminal Court 2002a). The definition in the Elements of Crimes is as follows:

1. The perpetrator invaded the body of a person by conduct resulting in penetration, however slight, of any part of the body of the victim or of the perpetrator with a sexual organ, or of the anal or genital opening of the victim with any object or any other part of the body.

2. The invasion was committed by force, or by threat of force or coercion, such as that caused by fear of violence, duress, detention, psychological oppression or abuse of power, against such person or another person, or by taking advantage of a coercive environment, or the invasion was committed against a person incapable of giving genuine consent. (International Criminal Court 2002a)

The scope of this definition is important for a number of reasons. First, it was the first codified definition of sexual violence as a war crime and a crime against humanity. Second, in many countries there is little possibility of prosecuting rape without penile penetration. Cases where penetration involves sharp instruments that cause serious physical damage, for example, are often charged as sexual assaults. Since rape usually carries a far higher sentence than sexual assault (twenty years, compared to five years in DR Congo, for example), prosecuting rapes perpetrated with "any object or any other part of the body" is significant. Third, the Statute precludes the possibility of a defense based upon the nominal consent of the victim in a conflict environment. The Elements of Crimes states that a person may be incapable of giving genuine consent if affected by natural, induced, or age-related incapacity, or by a "coercive environment." The presence of armed conflict can be sufficient evidence of a coercive environment. Finally, the Rome Statute definition is the first definition of rape to explicitly assert that the concept of "invasion" is broad enough to be gender-neutral, leading to the criminalization of rape against men and boys for the first time in a number of countries where the definition has been adopted. The explicit reference to penetration of any orifice by any object or part of the body also allows for the possibility that rapes can be committed by women.

Both DR Congo and South Africa have incorporated elements of this legal framework into their domestic laws. And even countries that have not ratified the Rome Statute have been influenced by its gender-progressive provisions. In India, for example, a country that had not ratified the Rome Statute and expressed stark opposition to the ICC, the Rome Statute has nevertheless contributed significantly to gender-based legal reform. Activists have drawn extensively from Rome Statute language and definitions of gender-based violence to shape the country's Sexual Assault Bill, passed into law in 2013. Article 375 of the Criminal Law Amendment Act reads:

A man is said to commit rape if he penetrates his penis to any extent into the vagina, mouth, urethra or anus of a women; inserts to any extent any object or a part of the body...into the vagina, urethra or anus of a woman; manipulates any part of the body of a woman so as to cause penetration into the vagina, urethra, anus or any part of body of such woman;.... applies his mouth to the vagina, urethra, anus of a woman (or makes her do so with him or with any other person" (Government of India 2013).[3]

The inclusion of Rome Statute language in India's definition of rape was the result of a sustained advocacy campaign spearheaded by India's National Commission for Women, and in conversation with women's groups across the country and transnational feminist networks.

The diffusion of the Rome Statute's gender protections can be situated in a long history of gender advocacy in the international system. The first international instrument to make reference to protections on the basis of gender was the 1948 Universal Declaration of Human Rights (UDHR).

[3] *The Gazette of India.* The Criminal Law Amendment Act. No. 13 of 2013. Article 375. http://indiacode.nic.in/acts-in-pdf/132013.pdf.

Article 2 of the UDHR reads: "Everyone is entitled to all the rights and freedoms set forth in this Declaration, without distinction of any kind, such as race, color, sex, language, religion, political or other opinion, national or social origin, property, birth or other status." Women's rights advocates such as Mandavi Mehtta and Eleanor Roosevelt fought hard for the inclusion of this provision, and for gender-neutral language in all UN documents. The wording of Article 2 was the outcome of a broader social movement advocating for the protection and promotion of women's rights by the international system. Other limited successes of this movement included the UN General Assembly's establishment of the Commission on the Status of Women (CSW) in 1946, tasked with preparing recommendations relating to urgent problems in the field of women's rights. In 1963, the CSW was tasked with drafting a declaration exclusively dedicated to the elimination of all forms of discrimination against women. That same year a special rapporteur was assigned to the issue of family planning, and the Committee on Economic, Social and Cultural Rights adopted a resolution on women in development, foregrounding the unique plight of women in areas of health, housing, poverty, and education.

In this period, the CSW elaborated the Convention on the Political Rights of Women (later adopted by the General Assembly in 1952), the Convention on the Nationality of Married Women (adopted by the General Assembly in 1957), the Convention on Consent to Marriage, Minimum Age for Marriage and Registration of Marriages (1962), and the Recommendation on Consent to Marriage, Minimum Age for Marriage and Registration of Marriages (1965).[4]

On December 5, 1963, the UN General Assembly adopted a resolution that pledged to combine the relevant international standards pertaining to the equal rights of men and women into a single legal instrument. This declaration – the Declaration on the Elimination of Discrimination against Women – was adopted by the UN General Assembly on November 7, 1967. While this declaration was nonbinding, it formed the basis for the Convention on the Elimination of All Forms of Discrimination against Women (CEDAW), which entered into force in 1979. The United Nations declared the period 1976–1985 the "Decade for Women" and CEDAW remains the core human rights treaty protecting women's rights on the international stage.[5]

---

[4] See "Short History of the CEDAW Convention" on UN Women for a brief history of the women's rights movement in the postwar period: www.un.org/womenwatch/daw/cedaw/history.htm. See also Bunch (1990), Ferree and Tripp (2006), and Fraser (2000).

[5] The Convention on the Elimination of All Forms of Discrimination against Women (CEDAW). 1979. Adopted by the United Nations General Assembly.

Although this period represented a focus on women's issues within the nascent UN system, these legal instruments did little to tackle systemic gender discrimination and marginalization head on, often adopting conservative language and following, rather than pioneering, social change. Additionally, UN instruments tended to focus on "women" specifically, rather than on a broad spectrum of gender-related issues. However, while these instruments did little in and of themselves to actively protect rights of women worldwide, many scholars have argued that they had an indirect effect on catalyzing, or at least reinforcing the work of activists advocating the protection, promotion, and entrenchment of women's rights in domestic legal systems (Cichowski 2007; Gray, Kittilson, and Sandholtz 2006; McBride, Mazur, and Lovenduski 2010; Montoya 2015; Simmons 2009; Tripp 2013; Zwingel 2012). They also created a focal point for a transnational network of women's rights activists, working to shape domestic and international law simultaneously.

The year 1993 saw the international community's first attempt to explicitly define gender-based violence in its 1993 Declaration on the Elimination of Violence Against Women.[6] The declaration notes:

For the purposes of this Declaration, the term "violence against women" means any act of gender-based violence that results in, or is likely to result in, physical, sexual or psychological harm or suffering to women, including threats of such acts, coercion or arbitrary deprivation of liberty, whether occurring in public or in private life (Art. 1).

Article 2 notes:

Violence against women shall be understood to encompass, but not be limited to, the following: (a) Physical, sexual and psychological violence occurring in the family, including battering, sexual abuse of female children in the household, dowry-related violence, marital rape, female genital mutilation and other traditional practices harmful to women, non-spousal violence and violence related to exploitation; (b) Physical, sexual and psychological violence occurring within the general community, including rape, sexual abuse, sexual harassment and intimidation at work, in educational institutions and elsewhere, trafficking in women and forced prostitution; (c) Physical, sexual and psychological violence perpetrated or condoned by the State, wherever it occurs.

Following the adoption of CEDAW in 1979, and the UN Declaration on Violence Against Women in 1993, a 1995 UN conference on women, known colloquially as the Beijing Conference, endorsed a "gender mainstreaming" approach to women's equality, calling on governments

[6] United Nations. 1993. Declaration on the Elimination of Violence against Women. www.un.org/documents/ga/res/48/a48r104.htm. 1995. Beijing Platform for Action. www.un.org/womenwatch/daw/beijing/platform/plat1.htm#statement

worldwide to foreground gender equality as an explicit and central part of their policy and planning. The Beijing Platform for Action represented an important milestone in emphasizing that gender violence results from historically unequal relations between men and women, which have prevented women's full advancement and undermined the pursuit of international peace and security.[7]

The UN's focus on gender issues facilitated the growth of a global women's rights movement that lent support to women's rights and gender activists in domestic political contexts, but that also began to exert direct pressure on governments to enact domestic legal reform. Gray, Kittilson, and Sandholtz (2006) note that CEDAW has had a powerful effect on sparking new debates about women's roles in politics and public life, as well as leading to the passage of new gender-sensitive legislation, the creation of women's rights commissions, and improvements in women's access to literacy, birth control, and employment. Courts all over the world have directly invoked CEDAW to uphold the legal equality of women and legislators and national courts have used CEDAW to push for tangible policy changes (Celik Levin 2004). Yet there remains considerable debate over the extent to which improvements in women's rights over the latter part of the twentieth century can be attributed in any direct way to CEDAW ratification or other international instruments. Many argue that CEDAW ratification itself has been motivated by changing domestic attitudes, beliefs, and policies toward women's rights issues in domestic country contexts. Others note that it was not necessarily the text of CEDAW itself, per se, that sparked policy changes, but the countless women's organizations and national and international dialogues that accompanied its creation (Tripp 2013).

Whether or not international instruments have precipitated or followed changing gender norms, women's rights – both in law and in practice – have been significantly strengthened in many countries over the past thirty years, and the UN has played a role in promoting and supporting these developments. The UN's growing emphasis on women in conflict has also spawned considerable repercussions for the domestic treatment of gender violence in a variety of conflict-affected states. In addition to the creation of a Special Representative of the United Nations' Secretary General on Sexual Violence in Conflict, a United Nations Special Rapporteur on Violence against Women, the introduction of UN Women, and the work of a variety of other UN agencies dedicated to women, peace, and security, United Nations Security Council Resolution

---

[7] United Nations. 1995. Fourth World Conference on Women. 4–15 September 1995, Beijing, China.

1325 (UNSC 1325) recognized the ways in which conflict disproportionately affects civilians, particularly women and children. The Resolution, which was passed in 2000, sought to emphasize the centrality of women in the prevention and resolution of conflicts and in peacebuilding, and to stress their equal participation in decision-making concerning conflict prevention and resolution and their efforts to maintain and promote peace and security.[8] UNSC 1325 further affirmed the urgent need to mainstream a gender perspective into peacekeeping operations and called for specialized training for all peacekeeping personnel on the protection of women and children in conflict situations, and the inclusion of women in positions of power in peacekeeping forces and host country administrations.

The UN Special Representative on Sexual Violence in Conflict serves as the United Nations' spokesperson and political advocate on conflict-related sexual violence. The office was established by Security Council Resolution 1888 in 2009 and the Special Representative also chairs the network UN Action against Sexual Violence in Conflict.[9] The core priorities of the office include: ending impunity for sexual violence in conflict by assisting national authorities in strengthening criminal accountability, responsiveness to survivors, and judicial capacity; protecting and empowering civilians who face sexual violence in conflict; mobilizing political ownership by fostering government engagement; increasing recognition of rape as a tactic and consequence of war; and harmonizing the UN's response to these issues through the Action against Sexual Violence in Conflict Network.[10] As one of the network's eight priority countries, DR Congo has received support and attention from thirteen UN agencies that amplify programming and advocacy on this issue.[11] The criminal justice priority, in particular, has been important in channeling funds toward legal capacity building and combating impunity for gender-based crimes in DR Congo.

[8] The United Nations Security Council. 2000. United Nations Security Council Resolution 1325 (S/RES/1325) on Women, Peace and Security. Adopted by the Security Council at its 4213th meeting, on 31 October 2000.
[9] The United Nations Security Council. 2009. United Nations Security Council Resolution 1888 (S/RES/1888) on Women, Peace and Security. Adopted by the Security Council at its 6195th meeting, on 30 September 2009.
[10] United Nations Special Representative on Sexual Violence in Conflict. 2015. "About the Office | Office of the Special Representative of the Secretary- General on Sexual Violence in Conflict." Action against Sexual Violence in Conflict Network. www.un.org/sexualvio lenceinconflict/about-us/about- the-office/.
[11] The Office of Special Representative on Sexual Violence in Conflict has eight priority countries, but works on eleven countries in total. These are Bosnia and Herzegovina, Central African Republic (CAR), Colombia, Cote d'Ivoire, Democratic Republic of Congo (DRC), Liberia, Mali, Somalia, South Sudan, Sudan, and Syria (United Nations Special Representative on Sexual Violence in Conflict).

Scholars have recently debated whether UNSC 1325 and other such efforts have succeeded in influencing or altering gendered dynamics in peacekeeping operations, questioning whether UNSC 1325 has been effectively implemented, and to what extent it creates the conditions for more likely and more sustainable peace (Karim and Beardsley 2016; Olsson and Gizelis 2015; Oudraat 2011; Willett 2010). Perhaps unsurprisingly, its effects have varied considerably from place to place. As early as 1996, the United Nations Children's Fund (UNICEF) reported that rates of child prostitution actually *increased* in sites where peacekeepers were present (UNICEF and Machel 1996). In spite of countless targeted efforts to combat pervasive discrimination and to increase the presence of women in peacekeeping missions, reports and allegations of abuses by peacekeeping forces, including rape and prostitution, remain widespread over a decade after UNSC 1325 was passed (Caplan 2012). In 2012 alone, Guardado and colleagues (2015) estimated that 58,000 women ages eighteen to thirty had engaged in transactional sex with United Nations Mission in Liberia (UNMIL) personnel, despite a strict UN ban on such relationships. MONUSCO in eastern DR Congo has been similarly implicated in a variety of such scandals (BBC News 2017). While MONUSCO has played an important role in supporting the legal system's capacity, its effects on protecting civilians from sexual and gender-based violence are uncertain.

Elite Politics and the Legal Framework Governing Gender Violence Prosecutions in DR Congo

Due to the scale and brutality of sexual crimes perpetrated in the Great Lakes region of Central Africa, sexual and gender-based violence in DR Congo's wars has received almost unprecedented international attention (Freedman 2015). Experts claim that anywhere between 200,000 to more than 1 million rapes have been committed over the duration of the conflict (Peterman, Palermo, and Bredenkamp 2011; United Nations Mapping Project 2009). DR Congo has consequently been referred to as "hell on earth" (Kirchner 2007), "the worst place in the world to be a woman" (IRIN 2008), and "the rape capital of the world" (UN News 2011). Although there is little consensus over whether the figures cited by journalists and NGOs explicitly refer to rapes committed as tactics of war (for example, as war crimes or as crimes against humanity), or to *any* rapes committed over the course of the conflict, eastern DR Congo's alleged "rape crisis" has drawn international and domestic attention. This attention has prompted shifts in national policy.

Since 2004, international and domestic responses to gender violence have underpinned the passage of a number of government reforms intended to facilitate the prosecution of rape and other forms of sexual and gender-based violence. New laws have raised DR Congo's age of sexual consent from fifteen to eighteen for both men and women, and have imported more expansive definitions of rape into the country's Penal Code.[12] Ministry of Justice reforms have supplemented and reorganized judicial budgets to divert important resources toward the new laws' implementation.

Accompanying the creation of the country's new constitution in 2006, the 2004–2007 justice sector reforms divided the Congolese court system into three jurisdictions (civil/criminal, military, and administrative). In 2008, the Conseil Supérieur de la Magistrature (CSM) was reinstated by law. The CSM theoretically assumes responsibility for recruiting, training and disciplining judges and magistrates, as well as many other tasks. In practice, it has lacked the budget or authority to carry out its basic functions.[13] The Congolese Penal Code and Congolese Military Code were revised to include new war crimes and crimes against humanity legislation, as well as a new law governing sexual violence.[14] Moreover, the 2006 Constitution explicitly includes articles protecting the rights of women, and prohibiting gender-based discrimination and sexual violence. Article 14 reads:

The public authorities see to the elimination of all forms of discrimination against women and ensure the protection and promotion of their rights. They take in all domains and most notably in the civil, political, economic, social and cultural domains, all appropriate measures in order to ensure the full realization of the potential of women and their full participation in the development of the nation. They take measures in order to fight all forms of violence against women in public and private life. Women are entitled to equitable representation in national, provincial and local institutions. The State guarantees the achievement of parity between men and women in said institutions. The law determines the conditions for the application of these rights (DR Congo 2006a, Art. 14).

Article 15 includes a provision prohibiting sexual violence as an instrument of conflict and displacement:

---

[12] See Loi No 06/018 de 2006 modifiant et complétant le Décret du 30 janvier 1940 portant Code Pénal Congolais (Law Amending the Congolese Penal Code).

[13] Art. 49, Loi organique n° 06/020 du 10 octobre 2006 portant statut des magistrats; Art. 20, Loi organique no 08/013 du 5 août 2008 portant organisation et fonctionnement du Conseil supérieur de la magistrature.

[14] See Loi No 06/18 de 2006 modifiant et complétant le Décret du 30 janvier 1940 portant Code Pénal Congolais (Law Amending the Congolese Penal Code); Loi No 06/019 de 2006 du 20 juillet 2006 modifiant et complétant le décret du 6 août 1959 portant Code de Procédure Pénale Congolais (2006 Law on Sexual Violence). See International Bar Association (2009) and Afrimap (2010) for a comprehensive discussion of legal reform in DR Congo in this period.

Public authorities are responsible for the elimination of sexual violence used as an instrument to destabilize and displace families. International treaties and agreements notwithstanding, any sexual violence committed against any person with the intention of destabilizing or displacing a family...is established as a crime against humanity punishable by law (DR Congo 2006a, Art. 15).

The passage of the 2009 law for the protection of children enshrined a number of additional gender-based rights and protections.[15] More recently, and generating some controversy over its content, DR Congo revised its family law, overturning many of the gender conservative provisions of the earlier Family Code. The new law establishes a formal basis for the applicability of customary law in marriage (e.g., Art. 340, 363, 367), establishes rights for both parties to appeal to a court of law in the case of a marital disagreement (Art. 449, 455, 460), and prohibits forced marriage and the marriage of minors (Art. 352).[16] It is worth noting that the 2016 Family Law involved a series of compromises, and preserves some significant gender imbalances, including retaining the provision that the husband is the head of the household (*"Le mari est le chef du ménage."* Art. 444).[17]

The 2006 Law on Sexual Violence, however, has been central to efforts to increase accountability for gender-based violence in both conflict and non-conflict spaces. The law has served a dual purpose. First, it has offered a comprehensive and gender-progressive definition of rape and sexual violence for prosecuting gender-based crimes through the civilian courts. Second, and equally important, it has provided a legal framework that practitioners can invoke in their broader treatment and interpretation of sexual and gender-based violence, even in the context of crimes tried through the military justice system or as international crimes. Drawing its definition of rape, and especially of penetration, directly from the Rome Statute, the law has sensitized legal practitioners to a new internationally recognized definition of rape that foregrounds the rights of victims and provides a more gender-sensitive and expansive interpretation of various sexual crimes. Notably, the 2006 law removed the possibility that judges could invoke aspects of the victim's character or prior sexual conduct as attenuating circumstances when judging the severity of the crime (DR Congo 2006b and DR Congo 2006c). See Art. 18 and 19 of the 1940 Penal Code (DR Congo 2004), which stipulates that sentences may be reduced as the judge

---

[15] Loi n° 09/001 du 10 janvier 2009 portant protection de l'enfant. Journal Officiel - Numéro spécial - 25 mai 2009. See also Loi N° 08/011 du 14 Juillet 2008 portant protection des droits des personnes vivant avec le VIH/SIDA et des personnes affectees.

[16] Loi N° 16/008 du 15 juillet 2016 modifiant et completant la loi N°87–010 du 1er aout 1987 portant code de la famille. See also Loi n° 15/013 du 1er août 2015 portant modalités d'application des droits de la femme et de la parité on women's rights and gender parity.

[17] ibid.

deems appropriate ("Les peines de servitude pénale et d'amende pourront être réduite dans la mesure déterminée par le juge"). Prior to the passage of the 2006 Sexual Violence Law, judges frequently invoked Art. 18 of the Penal Code in sexual violence cases.[18]

Explicitly recognizing the influence of international law, the preamble to the 2006 Sexual Violence Law reads:

Until now, Congolese criminal law did not contain the protections afforded by international law since 1946 to deter those, young and old, who violate international law, and international humanitarian law, thereby denying civilian populations the dignity of their humanity. Thus, this law amends and supplements the Congolese Criminal Code by incorporating the provisions of international humanitarian law that are relevant to sexual violence. It takes into account the protection of those most vulnerable, including women, children and men who are victims of sexual violence. In doing so, it contributes to redressing public morality, public order and the security of the country.[19]

The 2006 law provides clear definitions, that draw from feminist legal discourse and international best practice, of a range of sexual offenses, including assault, forced prostitution, harassment, sexual slavery, sexual mutilation, forced prostitution, forced pregnancy and the transmission of sexually transmitted diseases (DR Congo 2006b). The law defines rape as:

Any person who has committed a rape, using violence or serious threats of coercion against a person, either directly, or through a third party. Coercion can be construed as surprise, psychological pressure, taking advantage of a coercive environment, or the abuse of power against a person incapable of giving genuine consent:

a) Any man, regardless of age, who penetrates, however superficially, any part of a woman, regardless of her age;

b) Any man who penetrates, however superficially, the anus, mouth or any other orifice of the body of a woman, or of the anus or genital opening of a man, with a sexual organ, with any object, or with any other part of the body;

c) Any person who has inserted, however superficially, any other body part or any object into the vagina;

---

[18] See Human Rights Watch (2009: 28) for further discussion.

[19] DR Congo 2006b. Author's translation. ("Jusque là, le droit pénal congolais ne contenait pas toutes les incriminations que le droit international a érigées en infractions, comme un rempart dissuasif depuis 1946 contre ceux qui, petits et grands, violent le droit international, notamment humanitaire, reniant ainsi à la population civile la qualité et les valeurs d'humanité. Ainsi, la présente loi modifie et complète le Code pénal congolais par l'intégration des règles du droit international humanitaire relatives aux infractions de violences sexuelles. De ce fait, elle prend largement en compte la protection des personnes les plus vulnérables notamment les femmes, les enfants et les hommes victimes des infractions de violences sexuelles. Elle contribue ainsi au redressement de la moralité publique, de l'ordre public et de la sécurité dans le pays.")

d) Any person who forced a man or a woman to penetrate, however superficially, the anus, mouth or orifice of another person with any object, any sexual organ or any other part of his or her body.

———

Whosoever shall be convicted of rape shall be punished by a sentence of imprisonment of five to twenty years and fined no less than one hundred thousand Congolese francs. (DRC 2006b)

Like the Rome Statute, this definition overturns the common law definition of rape that is limited to penile to vaginal penetration. The 2006 definition includes penetration of any orifice by any object or any part of the body, and broadens the definition of rape such that it is gender neutral. It similarly lifts its understanding of consent from the Rome Statute, emphasizing that consent cannot be granted under conditions of coercion which itself is broadly construed.

In addition to expanding and clarifying the definitions of myriad gender-based crimes, a separate law modified the 1959 Criminal Procedure Code to enshrine expansive protections for victims (DR Congo 2006c). The law reads "In order to [combat impunity for sexual violence], certain provisions of the Criminal Procedure Code deserve to be amended in order to safeguard the dignity of the victim and to guarantee legal assistance (DR Congo 2006c)." The law further emphasizes the importance of criminal prosecution, and the need to protect the dignity and identity of victims in sexual offenses cases. The law necessitates that investigations must be initiated within one month of being referred to the relevant judicial authorities; judgments must be rendered within three months; and that victims have the right to representation by legal counsel (Art. 7, DR Congo 2006c). Similarly drawing its language and provisions from international best practice, and the Rome State's Rules and Procedures of Evidence, the law further stipulates that a doctor and psychologist must assess the victim to determine the appropriate care (Art. 14. DR Congo 2006c); that a victim's silence cannot be construed as consent (Art. 14: 1 and 2. DR Congo, 2006c); that evidence of a victim's prior sexual behavior cannot exonerate the accused from criminal liability (Art. 14: 3 and 4. DR Congo 2006c); and that the prosecutor must take the necessary measures to safeguard the security, physical and psychological well-being, dignity and respect for the privacy of the victims or any other person involved (Art. 74. DR Congo 2006c).

Despite the fact that the 2006 Law on Sexual Violence does not technically have jurisdiction in the military courts, in the absence of equal protections, or a strong definition of rape and other sexual offenses in the Military Penal Code, or in war crimes or crimes against humanity legislation, this law (together with the Rome Statute) has formed the basis for understanding, interpreting, and defining sexual and gender-based violence in both conflict and non-conflict settings, as well as in civilian and military courts, for many Congolese legal practitioners.

Due to the nature of DR Congo's conflict, provisions for prosecuting sexual and gender-based violence as war crimes and crimes against humanity have been especially important in overcoming impunity for conflict-related sexual violence, and in the broader pursuit of gender justice. In 2002, DR Congo introduced new war crimes and crimes against humanity legislation. Although these laws introduced sexual violence as an international crime, they retained a narrow definition of rape that has been criticized by women's rights and human rights groups. For example, the Military Penal Code of 2002 introduced rape as a crime against humanity in Article 169(7), but failed to define the crime. The article reads:

Any widespread or systematic attack that is knowingly launched against the Republic or against the civilian population also constitutes a crime against humanity and carries a sentence of death, whether committed in a time of peace or in a time of war, [including]: Rape, sexual slavery, forced prostitution, forced pregnancy, forced sterilization and other forms of sexual violence of comparable gravity. (DR Congo 2002a. Art. 169).

The wording of this law leaves the definition of rape vulnerable to a narrow interpretation, and the failure of the Military Penal Code to criminalize rape as a war crime has attracted criticism on similar grounds. The consequence of these shortcomings, however, is that an opening has been created for legal practitioners to look beyond the Military Penal Code to define rape, and often invoke the Rome Statute, or rely on definitions elaborated the 2006 Law on Sexual Violence.

Under Congolese law, military courts reserve sole jurisdiction over infractions of the Military Penal Code, or crimes committed by any agent of the state. Until 2013, military courts also held subject matter jurisdiction over any crime that could potentially constitute a war crime, crime against humanity or crime of genocide.[20] Civilian courts, on the other hand, retain jurisdiction over ordinary violations of the Congolese

---

[20] *Ordonnance/Loi portant institution d'un Code de Justice Militaire* No72/060 du 25 septembre 1972 (Art. 161). A 2013 law revised this jurisdiction, giving civilian courts jurisdiction over international crimes (see: the *Loi organique No13/011/B portant organisation, fonctionnement et competences des jurisdiction de l'ordre judiciaire*, or, in English, the Law on the Organization, Functioning and Jurisdiction of the Courts). Since it was slow to be implemented, this reform did not affect the research undertaken here, since the military courts retained de facto responsibility for international crimes until after the research was completed.

Penal Code, including any instance of rape or sexual violence perpetrated outside of the conflict, or where the accused is not an employee of the state security services. Civilian courts also hold jurisdiction over all civil law matters, including divorce and inheritance rights.[21]

In 2013, the *Loi organique* (No13/11/B) technically transferred subject matter jurisdiction for international crimes to the civilian courts. In reality, the military courts continued to prosecute international crimes throughout the duration of this research, due to logistical challenges associated with the transfer of cases. This has meant that most sexual and gender-based crimes committed in the context of the war, or by soldiers or police, have been prosecuted through DR Congo's military justice system, whereas the country's civilian courts have prosecuted all other gender offenses.

Due to jurisdictional confusion and the shortcomings of the Military Penal Code, lawyers and human rights groups have long urged DR Congo to incorporate the Rome Statute into domestic law through formal Rome Statute implementing legislation. In 2003, the Permanent Commission for Congolese Law Reform prepared draft legislation to implement the Rome Statute. The bill was submitted to the National Assembly in 2005. However, when the transitional parliament was dissolved in the 2006 transition to democracy, all pending bills expired (International Center for Transitional Justice 2010; Witte et al. 2011). A new draft implementation bill was presented to the parliament in 2007 and revised in 2010. It was finally approved by the parliament in September 2010, but was rejected in the National Assembly in June 2012. In June 2015, revised implementing legislation was presented to the parliament again. The Senate finally approved the law in December 2015, and it entered into force on December 31, 2015 (DR Congo 2015; Etinga 2015).

State Fragility and Opportunities for Law Reform in DR Congo

The road to gender-sensitive legal reform has not been without its obstacles, and gender activists have not always been wholly successful in their efforts to enshrine protections for victims of gendered harms in Congolese law. Nevertheless, the reforms described are significant. The 2006 Sexual Violence Law in particular is one of the most far-reaching pieces of sexual violence legislation in the world, in terms of the protections it affords to victims. Why has DR Congo been at the forefront

---

[21] In this regard, the 1987 Congolese Family Code was revised in 2016 (loi modifiant et completant la loi n°87-010 du 1er aout 1987 portant code de la famille). Until 2016, courts relied on the 1987 Family Code for many questions of women's and gender-based family rights.

of gender sensitive legal reform? And why have legislators incorporated such progressive and innovative reforms in some areas, while falling short in others? Law and policy developments in Kinshasa, which have significantly improved prospects for prosecuting rape and sexual violence, can be largely attributed to a coalition of domestic and international non-state actors in the aftermath of the Second Congo War. I argue that various features of state weakness in this period facilitated the passage of new laws and policies to support their implementation. Importantly, ongoing conflict, and demo-cratic transition in the presence of the largest ever UN peacekeeping mis-sion, created opportunities for domestic and international gender advocates to influence aspects of state policy and practice in ways that would not have been likely in a different institutional environment.

When the UN Security Council first established its mission in DR Congo, it recognized the need to assist in the protection of human rights in the country. In 2004, the UN Mission introduced a technical assistance / rule of law program under the umbrella of its newly created Rule of Law Section. The Rule of Law Section adopted a three-tiered approach to judicial capa-city building. This approach included supporting the legislative and execu-tive branches in coordinating strategic plans to build judicial capacity through legislation and judicial restructuring; the short and long term implementation of the strategic plan; and providing direct and immediate support and resources to courts themselves.[22] With material and logistical assistance from MONUC and the European Commission, a body entitled the Comité Mixte de la Justice (CMJ) was established under the auspices of the Congolese Ministry of Justice. This body, which was created and pre-sided over jointly by the European Commission and the Ministry of Justice, was responsible for overseeing justice sector reform (International Bar Association 2009: 25). Similarly, in 2006, the Groupe Mixte de Réflexion sur la Réforme et la Réorganisation de la Police was created to conduct a review of the challenges facing the Police Nationale Congolaise, and in 2008, introduced the Comité de Suivi de la Réforme de la Police. These initiatives have been supported by donors including UK Department for International Development (DfID), EUPOL, Deutsche Gesellschaft für Internationale Zusammenarbeit (German Agency for International Cooperation, GIZ), the United Nations Mission to the Democratic Republic of Congo (MONUC/MONUSCO), the United Nations Development Program (UNDP), and others.

MONUC also established the Comprehensive Strategy on Combating Sexual Violence in DR Congo and created a dedicated unit to coordinate

---

[22] See MONUC (https://monuc.unmissions.org/en/rule-law) and MONUSCO (https://monusco.unmissions.org/en/what-rule-law-section-mandate) for further details.

activities derived from this strategy. Additionally, a coalition of domestic and international stakeholders created the 2006 Pooled Fund on Sexual Violence, the Stabilization and Recovery Funding Facility, the Comité Provincial de Lutte Contre les Violences Sexuelles (CVPLS), and various other multi-donor, multi-stakeholder trust funds and initiatives. With support from MONUC and other UN bodies, the Ministry of Gender, Family and Children was established within the Congolese government and the National Strategy against Gender-Based Violence was introduced (DR Congo Ministere du genre, de la famille et de l'enfant 2009). Targeted advocacy meant that these policy initiatives coincided with the passage of the 2009 Law on the Protection of Children. Under the support of the UN Action against Sexual Violence in Conflict Network, on July 14, 2014, President Kabila appointed the Personal Representative on Sexual Violence and Child Recruitment, Jeanine Mabunda Lioko, who worked with the president and relevant UN agencies to oversee the launch of the armed forces action plan against sexual violence. On November 29, 2014, a ministerial order was issued to mark the creation of a national commission to oversee the plan's implementation (United Nations Special Representative on Sexual Violence in Conflict 2015b).[23]

The ministerial order that created the CMJ in 2004 included the provision that any "partner to development" (including international and domestic stakeholders) who wished to attend the meetings of the CMJ could do so. Thus, the proceedings of the committee were opened up to a variety of international and domestic actors and, importantly, foreign donors who exerted considerable influence over the committee's work. One of the committee's most relevant achievements since its establishment was the 2007 Action Plan, which identified forty-three projects divided into eleven programs and a "roadmap" to ensure visible and quick-impact activities. The committee and its roadmap received considerable financial and logistical support from MONUC, the United Nations Development Program (UNDP), the European Union, and various national governments. The UNDP is a particularly important contributor, having launched a $390 million USD governance program in DR Congo in 2008.[24] The United Nations Joint Human Rights Office

---

[23] Olive Lembe Kabila served as a figurehead for the "Je Dénonce" campaign in 2007 to encourage women to speak out against sexual violence that coincided with these efforts. The campaign, which was initiated in 2007 and was fairly active until 2011, was supported by various UN agencies and complements the work of other access to justice initiatives (Human Rights Watch 2009; Le Monde 2010).

[24] See IBA (2009) for further details of the CMJ's work and the involvement of external stakeholders in Congolese justice-sector reform.

(UNJHRO), the United Nations Development Program (UNDP), the European Union, and many other international agencies and organizations provide resources, logistics, and capacity-building support to implementing country-wide judicial reform programs.

The introduction of the Law on Sexual Violence in 2006, the development of new central policies concerning justice sector reform, and the direction of new funds toward justice activities at the central level can each be traced back, either directly or indirectly, to work mandated under or supported by MONUC's technical assistance programs. In addition, influential Congolese gender activists, in partnership with international NGOs, contributed to the wording of the 2006 Law on Sexual Violence through a series of consultations that drew from the Rome Statute and other international instruments and best practices. The crafting of the 2009 Law on the Protection of Children and 2016 Family Code were the result of similarly protracted dialogues, consultations and negotiations between national and international legal experts, advisors and civil society organizations.

In tandem with international organizations, agencies, and donors, local gender advocacy movements also contributed to gender reform. Existing organizations capitalized on new international attention to gender violence to promote their work, and new organizations emerged in response to heightened attention, new funding opportunities, and shifting global priorities. In the east, Umoja Wa Akina Mama Fizi (UWAFI, the United Women of Fizi) was established in 2000 to champion women's human rights and to raise the consciousness of women through education, training, research, and advocacy. Together with its sister organizations, Umoja wa Wanawake and Wakulima wa Kivu ya Kusini (UWAKI, Women Together and Growers of South Kivu), it emerged as an umbrella for approximately fifty-five women's community-based organizations in the east (Global Fund for Women 2007).

Panzi Hospital in Bukavu, and Heal Africa in Goma, were established in 1999 and 2005, respectively. In addition to other work, both hospitals developed considerable expertise in treating victims of conflict and non-conflict related sexual violence. Directors Dennis Mukwege and Jo Lusi and their staff have played influential roles on the national stage, contributing to sexual violence law reform, advising on national policy, and providing a link between international donors and grassroots organizations working on gender violence.[25]

---

[25] Before Heal Africa, Jo Lusi founded DOCS in 1994, an organization devoted to providing access to high quality medical care in eastern DR Congo. For more on the history of Heal Africa see www.healafrica.org/history. On Panzi, see www.panzifoundation.org/what-we-do/.

The Union des Femmes pour la Promotion et l'Education et Droit de l'Homme, established in 2003 in Lumbwe to promote women's rights; AFEDEM KIVU, created in 1999 with a focus on gender discrimination; Promotion et Appui aux Initiatives Féminines (PAIF), working since 1992 on facilitating women's political and social participation in public life; Solidarite des Femmmes Activistes pour la Defense des Droits Humains (SOFAD), working to research and campaign against sexual violence and provide counseling to survivors of gender violence; Fédération de Femmes pour la Paix et le Développement (FEPADE), created in 2002 with the mandate to improve the living conditions of local communities affected by the conflict and to support women and children – as well as many other localized and grassroots organizations and collectives – have been central to social and legal reform efforts.[26] Since the early 2000s, SOFAD has lobbied the government to deliver justice and embarked on gender-related legal reform (Global Fund for Women 2007). Organizations like PAIF have similarly pioneered local outreach to educate rural women on legal texts pertaining to women's rights, monitored cases of gender violence in local courts, and offered free legal assistance to women involved in gender violence cases. PAIF was also involved in providing socioeconomic support and medical assistance to victims of gender violence long before international organizations such as the American Bar Association (ABA) became active in this area.[27] They have been supported by International Alert and the Global Fund for Women since 2004.[28] In addition to organizations working explicitly on legal and social support, organizations such as Voix de Sans Voix ni Liberté (VOVOLIB) play important roles in socializing local populations toward issues of women's rights and economic empowerment. VOVOLIB, for example, manages a local radio station in order to "combat women's subjugation and marginalization due to deeply entrenched cultural norms," with the view to overcoming discrimination against women in customary institutions.[29] VOVOLIB was one of the earliest local organizations to lobby for the investigation into international crimes committed in DR Congo by the ICC (Human Rights Watch 2014). More

---

[26] See the websites of AFEDEM (www.afedem.org/?page_id=520), PAIF (www.paifrdc .org), and FEPADE (https://fepaderdc.wordpress.com) for more information.

[27] See http://sofadinternational.org/about.

[28] See the PAIF report at Global Fund for Women (https://grants.globalfundforwomen.org/ GFWSearch/index.php?id=7915) and International Alert (www.international-alert.org/ partner/solidarité-de-femmes-activistes-pour-la-défense-des-droits-humaines).

[29] See Radio Okapi (www.radiookapi.net/mot-cle/voix-de-sans-voix-ni-liberte). The Global Fund for Women provides an informative overview of local initiatives to promote women's legal rights prior to and immediately following the passage of the 2006 Law on Sexual Violence (https://grants.globalfundforwomen.org/GFWSearch/index.php?id=17041).

recently, Dynamique des Femmes Juristes (DFJ) and similar organizations across the provinces have played crucial roles in representing and supporting women in taking cases to court.

An emerging body of literature calls attention to the ways in which war can disrupt and fundamentally reorder gender relations in its aftermath, creating new opportunities for women and for grassroots organizing (Berry 2015, 2018; Berry and Lake 2017a; Tripp 2015). In this instance, the opportunity structures created by war and state collapse allowed for a powerful alliance between external actors interested in promoting women's rights across Africa, and grassroots gender activists. International actors were able to rely on preexisting women's advocacy and support networks, and domestic organizations were afforded external funding and new political platforms and opportunities. Prior to 2004, few international funds were available to support this kind of advocacy or to coordinate and target the efforts of different ad hoc programs spread across the country. Since the mid 2000s, the activities of these local organizations – particularly in the Kivus – have been harmonized toward a few overarching objectives, including the passage of news laws and national policy platforms for overcoming impunity for gender violence through legal channels, as well as providing support to victims of a variety of gendered harms.

DR Congo's consistent rankings at the bottom of various development and state failure indices, combined with the recognition of the Congolese state's need for urgent infrastructural assistance encapsulated in a number of UN Security Council resolutions, have prompted urgent development aid from a variety of major donors (including the European Union and the Belgian, Swedish, and British governments). This aid aims to support various aspects of state development, like the implementation of the 2007 Action Plan. The scale of international intervention in tasks normally reserved for domestic governments (such as passage of laws, control over budgets, and development of policy priorities), as well as the money poured into these enterprises, have been both justified and enabled by the empirical reality that the Congolese state had consistently proved itself unable to manage and oversee the activities of its own justice sector. Rising levels of violence and insecurity in DR Congo, and increasing media coverage of the prevalence of sexual and gender-based violence, combined with continuing incapacity of the Congolese state, created gaps that external stakeholders sought to fill. As a result, external gender consultants working with the UN Mission and other aid and development programs in DR Congo have been able to heavily influence the content and passage of new laws and important legal and judicial reforms. This is in spite of the fact that many political elites in Kinshasa retain conservative attitudes toward a variety of gender issues and, in some cases, have demonstrated little genuine commitment to the gender-progressive content of particular reforms. As will be discussed in later chapters, implementation has occurred despite the fact that political commitment in Kinshasa has waxed and waned (Freedman 2015).

Elite Politics and the Legal Framework Governing Gender Violence in South Africa

In December 2007, the South African government passed into law Act No. 32, the Sexual Offences and Related Matters Amendment Act (the Sexual Offences Act), amending the Criminal Procedures Act and broadening the legal definition of rape to include a range of sexual offenses (South Africa 2007). The new laws repealed the common law offense of rape that referred only to penile to vaginal penetration and replaced it with a new statutory offense of rape that covered all forms of sexual penetration without consent, irrespective of gender, orifice, or organ. The definition of penetration in the new Act is:

Penetration to any extent whatsoever by the genital organs of one person into or beyond the genital organs, anus, or mouth of another person; any other part of the body of one person or, any object including any part of the body of an animal into or beyond the genital organs or anus of another person.[30]

Reforms to the Criminal Procedures Act also introduced new practices pertaining to the management of sexual offenses by the police, forensic practitioners, and courts.

The 2007 legal reforms built on reforms introduced following South Africa's transition to democracy. In 1997, South Africa's Criminal Law Amendment Act introduced mandatory minimum sentences of ten years for rape in the case of a first offense, fifteen years for a second offense, and at least twenty years for a third or subsequent offense (Criminal Law Amendment Act 1997; Part III, Schedule II). For other sexual assault crimes, a first offender faced imprisonment for no less than five years; a second offender for no less than seven years; and a third or subsequent offender for no less than ten years (Part IV, Schedule II). Mandatory minimums did not apply in cases where the accused was younger than eighteen.

The 2007 Sexual Offences Act and related Criminal Law Amendment Act changed South Africa's age of consent to sixteen for both men and women (previously, the age of consent had been nineteen for boys and

[30] Sexual Offences Act, 32 of 2007. Available at: www.justice.gov.za/legislation/acts/2007–032.pdf. See also the Criminal Law Amendment Act of 1997: www.legislation.qld.gov.au/legisltn/acts/1997/97ac003.pdf.

sixteen for girls). The Act also adopted gender-neutral language so that both men and women, under the new law, could be either victims or perpetrators of rape. The law established the National Register of Sex Offenders, prohibiting people convicted of sexual offenses against children and/or people with mental disabilities from working with either of these two groups. Under the new law, rape victims were entitled to antiretroviral drugs to prevent them being infected with HIV and could demand mandatory HIV testing for the accused. Evidentiary issues characterizing the earlier law (such as the provision that previous sexual history of the victim could be used as attenuating circumstances in judging whether a rape had been committed), as well as the cautionary rule (which required the court to apply "caution" in judging the validity of the apparently "notoriously unreliable" victim testimony), were repealed (Artz and Smythe 2007). The 2007 law also introduced restrictions on the use of judicial discretion in sentencing, prohibiting judges from finding substantial compelling circumstances on account of the sexual history of the victim; an apparent lack of physical injury; the defendant's cultural or religious beliefs about rape; or any prior relationship between the victim and the accused.

The formal abolition of the cautionary rule built on case law from 1998, in which South Africa's Supreme Court of Appeal dismissed an appeal in the case of *S* v. *Jackson* on the grounds that the victim's testimony should be considered unreliable. In its judgment, the Supreme Court established new case law with regard to the cautionary rule that should, theoretically at least, be considered by lower courts in all subsequent cases. The court ruled:

The notion that women are habitually inclined to lie about being raped is of ancient origin . . . The fact is that such empirical research as has been done refutes the notion that women lie more easily or frequently than men, or that they are intrinsically unreliable witness . . . In my view, the cautionary rule in sexual assault cases is based on an irrational and outdated perception. It unjustly stereotypes complainants in sexual assault cases (overwhelmingly women) as particularly unreliable. In our system of law, the burden is on the State to prove the guilt of an accused beyond reasonable doubt – no more and no less. The evidence in a particular case may call for a cautionary approach, but that is a far cry from the application of a general cautionary rule.[31]

The 2007 law thus provides that "a court may not treat the evidence of a complainant in criminal proceedings involving the alleged commission of a sexual offence pending before that court, with caution, on account of the nature of the offence" (South Africa 2007, Section 60).

---

[31] South Africa Supreme Court of Appeal. *S* v. *Jackson*. March 20, 1998. (35/97)[1998] ZASCA13; 1998 (4)BCLR424 (SCA);[1998] 2AllSA267 (A). Some appeals decisions are available at: www.saflii.org/za/cases/ZASCA/1998/13.html.

The 2007 law also criminalized "compelled rape," meaning that any person who unlawfully and intentionally compels a third person, without their consent, to commit an act of sexual penetration with a complainant, without his or her consent, is punishable by law. This law was intended to allow individuals present at gang rapes to be charged with rape, whether or not they had directly participated in sexual acts. Like in DR Congo, rape carries a higher sentence than sexual assault, and therefore expanding the definition of what can be prosecuted as rape puts comparably grave offenses on an equal legal footing. The law also explicitly outlined a new legal definition of consent, which precluded the possibility of consent for any sexual act that resulted from physical or verbal intimidation, threats of violence to an individual or his/her loved ones or property, the threat of losing a job or failing a class, or any other abuse of authority. The law upheld that under no circumstances could consent be granted if an individual was asleep, unconscious, under the influence of drugs or alcohol, under the age of twelve, or possessing a mental disability.

Since 2007, South Africa's legal framework governing the prosecution of sexual and gender-based violence has been one of the most sophisticated in the world, drawing from some of the most innovative contemporary human rights reasoning and feminist jurisprudence. Like DR Congo, the legal definition of rape in South Africa and the provisions governing investigation, prosecution, and sentencing of the crime draw much of their language directly from the Rome Statute of the ICC. That means that the victim-sensitive definitions of rape used in the Rome Statute have made their way into domestic law and can be invoked directly by domestic courts through the Sexual Offences Act.

In addition, South Africa was one of the first countries in the world to implement the Rome Statute of the ICC into domestic law, meaning that the Rome Statute and its implementing legislation can also be invoked directly in South Africa's domestic legal system to prosecute sexual and gender-based violence as a war crime or a crime against humanity. No war crimes or crimes against humanity have been investigated in South Africa since the introduction of these laws, although the country's legal framework for addressing these crimes is strong should such crimes be brought before South African courts.

In addition to legislative reform, the South African government has introduced a number of other policies intended to address the prevalence of sexual and gender-based violence in the country. These include annual colloquia, conferences, *indabas*, and summits designed to "share experiences and practices on gender justice in africa to promote information and experience sharing" (Radebe 2012). The Commission for Gender Equality was established by law in 1996 with the mandate to transform society by "exposing gender discrimination in laws, policies and practices; advocating changes in sexist attitudes and gender stereotypes; and instilling respect for women's rights as human rights" (Commission for Gender Equality 1996). High-ranking government officials have delivered a number of speeches and policy platforms in order to publicly express their commitment to resolving this issue.

Work inspired by the Commission for Gender Equality includes the "Service Charter for Victims of Crime" (the Victims' Charter), a justice-promoting instrument that consolidates the rights of survivors of crime to access criminal justice services introduced in 1996. The Charter provides that all state departments that form part of the criminal justice system must treat victims with fairness and respect for their dignity and privacy, in order to avoid secondary victimization; victims should be attended to promptly and courteously and steps must be taken where necessary to prevent the victims from experiencing any type of inconvenience; victims must be provided with all information relating to the criminal justice process or proceedings in a language s/he understands; state departments must protect victims when their safety is threatened; as well as a host of other victim-centered protections.[32] In order to ensure the Victims' Charter was being upheld, in 2004, the "Minimum Service Standards for Victims of Crime" was developed to set out the duties of relevant government departments with respect to victims of crimes.

The "National Policy Guidelines on Sexual Offenses" were introduced in 1998 to codify and clarify the official duties of the police in dealing with victims of sexual assault. Building on the Victims' Charter, the policy guidelines state that victims of sexual assault must be treated with respect, empathy, and professionalism; that police must respond to reports immediately; that police must introduce themselves, explain their role, assist the victim confidentially, and privately request his/her details; assess whether the victim needs medical assistance; and finally open a docket, contact an investigating officer, and stay with the victim until the next step in the process has begun.

In 1995, the government established the Family Violence, Child Protection, and Sexual Offenses (FCS) Unit within the South African Police Service, and the National Council against Gender-Based Violence.[33] In 1992, the first specialized Sexual Offenses Court was introduced in Wynberg as part of a pilot to ensure that the criminal justice

---

[32] See the Victims' Charter (1996): www.justice.gov.za/vc/docs/vc/vc-eng.pdf.

[33] See the South African Police Service: www.saps.gov.za/org_profiles/core_function_com ponents/fcs/establish.htm. The FCS was restructured in 2004 and again in 2010, resulting in the recruitment of more than 1,000 new offices between 2010 and 2012 (Institute for Security Studies 2014).

system adequately attended to the unique problems facing rape victims in search of legal accountability (Sadan, Dikweni and Cassiem 2001). By 2003, twenty more Sexual Offences Courts were established, and by 2005, there were seventy-four specialized Sexual Offenses Courts across the country.[34] These bodies were tasked with setting up structures and building capacity to provide strategic leadership, coordination, and management of gender-based violence initiatives in South Africa and to ensure adequate enforcement of existing laws. The specialized courts have led a tumultuous existence. The fact that the Sexual Offenses Courts were better resourced than other courts was perceived to violate the constitutional right of other victims of crimes to equal protection from the law (Department of Justice and Constitutional Development 2013). In 2013, the government announced that it would reinstate the Sexual Offenses Courts in three phases: first, by revamping those courts already in existence; second, by establishing new courts in high-crime areas; and finally, by instating alternative models in rural areas.

Nevertheless, while the Sexual Offenses Courts have been somewhat effective in ensuring that the necessary expertise, skill, and experience are applied to sensitive sexual assaults, they are frequently under-resourced. Discussed at greater length in Chapter 4, some were disbanded and later reinstated, leading to jurisdictional confusion among practitioners and a lack of clarity for victims of crimes.

In the early 2000s, the National Prosecuting Authority institutionalized the Thuthuzela Care Centres, which are located in various hospitals throughout the country. The Thuthuzela Care Centres are known as "one-stop shops," where victims can report a case to medical practitioners and the police, as well as receive medical exams, give statements, and receive counseling and medical care. The centers are predominantly funded by the Department of Health, and are supplemented by various private donors. However, in recent years, their budgets have been dramatically cut. Some centers were closed down altogether, and others were forced to scale down their activities. Many reopened in 2013 with a new slew of reforms, but their status remains uncertain and under-resourced. In addition to various social programs on prevention, response, support, coordination, and communication, every year the Government of South Africa celebrates the global "Sixteen Days of Activism" campaign to mobilize awareness among communities for the unique challenges posed by violence against women.

[34] In 1999, with support from the Canadian Government, the pilot project was extended to other provinces. The Department of Justice drafted a blueprint for Sexual Offences Courts in South Africa, and a National Sexual Offences Task Team was created under the National Prosecuting Authority (South Africa Department of Justice and Constitutional Development 2013; Gillwald 1999).

Despite South Africa's proactive legal framework and a broad spectrum of seemingly impressive national policies, research shows that the government has, to a large extent, failed to uphold its own legislative and policy mandates. It has failed to sufficiently budget for the necessary implementation of new laws, provide training to educate or alert legal practitioners to the new protections, develop monitoring or evaluation mechanisms, or build the capacity of existing services. The failure to implement exemplary laws and mandates indicates a broad-based lack of commitment to gender-progressive national policy on the part of legislative and executive elites, and waning influence over law reform and policy implementation on the part of gender advocates. The few policies that have been introduced have been characterized by inconsistency and excessive delay. Poor infrastructure and weak service delivery have left the vast majority of sexual and gender-based violence victims without any recourse to the law.

Moreover, the countless speeches and policy platforms delivered by the government, especially those designed to "raise awareness," have frequently lacked substance. One interviewee commented: "It's like the government wants to show the world it's taking this issue seriously, but it has no real interest in doing what it takes to eradicate the culture of hostility towards these [gender violence] issues. It's like it's all icing, but they never actually put the time or money into these programs."[35] Even those policies that have redirected government funds toward specific policy objectives, such as the Thuthuzela Care Centres or the Sexual Offenses Courts, have often done so half-heartedly, providing insufficient funding to successfully roll out programs.[36] More often than not, funding has expired after short periods of time, meaning that programs are often terminated before they can demonstrate visible successes.

One example of the South African government's failure to deliver on its policy platform on this issue can be found in procedural recommendations made by a coalition of experts to the South African Law Reform Commission (SALRC) relating to the treatment of rape survivors in the criminal justice system and their right to legal representation. The SALRC acknowledged that a number of other adversarial jurisdictions provided for the representation of victims throughout the trial process, and that these were necessary for adequate implementation of the new Sexual Offences Act. The Commission agreed that representation was necessary to ensure that the victims' interests were adequately represented in court, since the current legal system was consistently failing, yet nevertheless ruled that providing legal representation

---

[35] Interview. Lauren, NGO director. South Africa, March 7, 2013.

[36] See South Africa Rape Crisis for further discussion of the weak implementation of South Africa's Sexual Offences Act. http://rapecrisis.org.za/rape-in-south-africa/#_ftn41.

to victims was both too radical and too costly (Artz and Smythe 2007). On this point, Artz and Smythe (2007: 13) note: "Legislating rights and protections for victims, without providing a mechanism for ensuring that they are implemented, has very little transformative effect."

Foregrounding Human Rights and Promoting Gender Justice in South Africa's Transition to Democracy

Why has the South African government adopted such exemplary and victim-sensitive legislation on the issue of sexual and gender-based violence, when it has exhibited minimal commitment to enforcing its laws and policies in practice?

South Africa's innovative legislative stance on this issue can be attributed in part to opportunities for law reform following the demise of the apartheid state in the mid-1990s (see Tripp 2010 for similar patterns in other African post-conflict contexts). Like in DR Congo, South African human rights organizations, with support from a broad coalition of international partners, played a significant role during the postapartheid period in shaping the legal apparatus of the newly democratic state. Initially, activists were able to situate rape law reform within the context of democratic transition, constitutionalism, and nurturing a culture of human rights. In the words of Rebecca Hodes, "this allowed the coalition to broaden the scope of the argument beyond just a piece of legislation, and to symbolically link rape law reform with democracy, constitutionalism and modernity" (Hodes 2011: 12).

With the collapse of the apartheid state came a broad-based commitment from domestic and international actors that the "new" South Africa should uphold all the basic rights and freedoms that the apartheid government denied. With this commitment came an inclusive agenda that sought to enshrine into law protections for all South Africans, regardless of race, ethnicity, age, religion, gender, sexuality, or any other distinguishing feature. Given the fairly sudden and ready availability of material resources and political capital to support human rights and democracy in general and gender rights in particular, South African gender activists were able to exert considerable influence over the laws and policies of the postapartheid state. Equipped with sophisticated knowledge of the vast array of human rights abuses committed throughout the world, the architects of the postapartheid state set out to ensure that groups that had experienced marginalization and persecution during the twentieth century – in South Africa and beyond – would be protected under South Africa's new constitution (Bois and Bois-Pedain 2008; Dubow 2012; Vos 2007).

The collapse of the already weakened apartheid government in 1994 thus created space for NGOs, international organizations, foreign donors, academics, civil society organizations, religious groups, and other nonstate actors to play a significant role in the construction of South Africa's new state apparatus.[37] South Africa's antiapartheid movement was propelled by a number of dedicated and internationally recognized human rights activists who were, at the time, embedded in highly organized domestic and transnational human rights networks. When the apartheid state collapsed, many leaders of the resistance movement, who were prominent human rights activists in their own right, took up positions within the postapartheid government. As such, the South African human rights organizations that had been integral to the resistance movement, which included prominent gender activists and their political spokespeople and allies, were able to imprint their own progressive human rights stamp on new national laws and policy. In the same way that political opportunity structures in DR Congo could be described as "open" by virtue of the gaps created following the end of the war and the establishment of the UN peacekeeping mission, the collapse of the apartheid government created similar openings that allowed domestic and international human rights advocates considerable influence in shaping the content of South Africa's new democracy.[38]

South African gender activists were so prominent and renowned during the country's transition to democracy that they played a critical role far beyond South Africa, shaping emerging gender norms on the global stage. Given the global attention afforded to South Africa's antiapartheid activists in the late 1980s and throughout the 1990s, many of the country's influential human rights activists gained a prominent voice in transnational human rights networks. South African feminists thus played a powerful role in shaping the evolution of global feminist discourse and spearheading an international conversation about gender-based crimes (Tripp 2013). These activists were also influential in the creation of the International Criminal Court, and played key roles in ensuring that this new international

---

[37] The Canadian Government, for example, in 1999 contributed 1 million Rand to support the South African Government in establishing 20 new Sexual Offences Courts, as well as witness cubicles with one–way glass, closed circuit television facilities and separate waiting rooms for victims and witnesses in sexual violence cases (Gillwald 1999).

[38] The types of opportunity structures here differ from the legal opportunity structures examined by Andersen (2009), Evans Case and Givens (2010), Vanhala (2012), and Wilson and Cordero (2006), who are predominantly concerned with procedural shifts that facilitate mobilization. However, some parallels can be drawn with the spaces created for social movements in these contexts, particularly as Vanhala (2012) and Anderson (2009) analyze in the context of environmental law and lesbian, gay, bisexual, and transgender (LGBT) law, respectively. See Epp (1998), Cichowski (2007), and Hilson (2002) on discursive shifts, legal opportunity structures, and the availability of new political allies.

body took gender-based crimes seriously (Hassim 2006). This collection of activists thus heavily shaped both national and international agendas, setting the tenor of the global conversation on a range of gender issues.

In the context of the opportunities created in wake of South Africa's democratic transition, a coalition of activists working together in a formalized collective since 1998 are often attributed with creating the architecture of the gender-sensitive legislative framework that now governs the prosecution of sexual and gender-based violence (Hodes 2011; Pithey et al. 1999). This coalition, which later became known as the Western Cape Consortium on Violence against Women, began its work with funding from the Open Society Foundation. In 1999, the Department of Justice's Law Reform Commission was tasked with investigating reform of South Africa's rape laws. As a result of ongoing advocacy and alliance building by the Western Cape Consortium, influential leaders within the women's movement were consulted at length on how to strengthen South Africa's laws and policies in this area. The result of this lengthy consultation was the proposed 2003 Sexual Offenses Bill. Although the 2003 Bill was never passed into law, it created the building blocks for later legal reform. A broad-based coalition in Johannesburg called the National Working Group on Sexual Offenses began to build on the work carried out by the Western Cape Consortium to lobby politicians and other stakeholders to expedite passage. Its goal was to promote "the development and implementation of legislation and policy that ensures that women and child survivors of sexual violence receive the optimal legal, medical and psycho-social support, treatment and care" (Hodes 2011: 5).[39] The work of the coalition ultimately resulted in the spectrum of legislative amendments and reforms that comprised the 2007 Sexual Offences Act and related legislation.

This coalition has remained active since the Sexual Offences Act was passed. However, its work has predominantly been restricted to state-level legislative and policy reform (Hassim 2006; Hunter 2010). In 2010, the United Nations Development Program (UNDP), the Open Democracy Advice Centre (ODAC), and the South African government's Department of Social Development undertook a "Victim Empowerment Feasibility Study" to identify key gaps in legislation. The idea was to identify the causes of women and children's disempowerment after sexual assault and work toward possible legislative remedies through a Victim's Empowerment Law.

In a similar vein, the "Road to Justice Project," spearheaded by the Rape Crisis Centre, developed a virtual tour of the criminal justice system that allowed the user to "see" inside a police station, a health facility, and

---

[39] See the National Working Group on the Sexual Offences Bill. 30 October 2005. Submission to the parliamentary Joint Ad-Hoc Committee on Socio-Economic Development.

a courtroom to gain some sense of the atmosphere of the journey toward justice (Rape Crisis Centre 2013). Other advocacy initiatives undertaken by members of the coalition include the Sexual Offenses Monitoring Project (SOAMP) of the University of Cape Town's Gender Health and Justice Research Unit (GHJRU), and the Shukumisa Campaign of the National Working Group on Sexual Offenses.

These initiatives have focused on influencing and shaping the government's national policy framework to improve the implementation of the 2007 Sexual Offences Act. Yet, because the movement consistently failed over time to establish a strong regional support base, its activities were, by design, restricted to lobbying national elites in urban centers. Efforts to link gender violence to broader democratic and constitutional values met declining success as the postapartheid state grew and stabilized. Some politicians, frustrated at adversarial tactics employed by the Western Cape coalition and other urban feminist elites, invoked anticolonial rhetoric to discredit the movement. Thus, the ability for activists to exert substantive influence over legislative and policy reform, and its local implementation, has waned over the years.

Theorizing Political Resistance to Gender Justice in Postapartheid South Africa

Many of the early legislative reforms in DR Congo and South Africa can be attributed to efforts by both domestic and international non-state actors who have capitalized on opportunities presented by weakened state infrastructure and political transition. In DR Congo, international organizations and NGOs, in partnership with a loose coalition of domestic human rights actors, used gaps created by state fragility and post-conflict democratic transition to influence the passage of new laws and evolving state policy and practice. In South Africa, domestic NGOs and women's rights coalitions have mobilized the interests of the broader human rights community to bring sexual and gender-based violence to the forefront of the domestic legal reforms that occurred following the end of apartheid.

Whereas in DR Congo state weakness has provided continued opportunities for relevant actors to contribute significantly to the implementation of these laws and policies through local institutions, in South Africa, as the government gained in strength and momentum, political elites became more resistant to the demands of gender activists. Many political elites have increasingly emphasized "traditional" African values, which they have constructed as an alternative to gender-progressive legislative reform. As the postapartheid state has matured, feminists and gender activists have found themselves increasingly excluded from national policy dialogue.

Unlike DR Congo, the South African government has both the financial and bureaucratic capacity to manage its own national priorities without external interference.[40] Because the issue of prosecuting sexual and gender-based violence has slipped further and further down the national agenda, feminist groups have had a difficult time pushing the government to treat any gender-related issue as an urgent priority, especially when confronted with the host of other pressing issues facing the administration. Periodically, and potentially to appease domestic or international pressure, African National Congress (ANC) elites have made token gestures in the form of speeches or new public policy platforms. However, cabinet members have demonstrated little genuine commitment to directing critical resources toward lasting reform.

The reasons for the South African government's reluctance to prioritize gender violence, even in spite of considerable international and domestic pressure, are complex. Many scholars have argued that the discourse around race has repeatedly served to stifle open scrutiny of the issue of gender violence (Baehr 2008; Moffett 2006). Under the apartheid regime, latent black criminality was often invoked by white elites as a form of social control to legitimize apartheid rule. Whites warned of the violence that would ensue should South Africa's black majority be given power to govern themselves (Comaroff and Comaroff 2006). Under apartheid and colonial occupation, the rhetorical association between black South Africans and criminality and violence is one that the ANC fought hard to overcome. The accusation that rape and sexual violence have escalated to unprecedented levels in South Africa since democratization is a claim that the postapartheid government has remained sensitive to. In response to allegations that rape in South Africa had reached unprecedented levels, in 2004 Thabo Mbeki stated:

The psychological residue of apartheid has produced a psychosis among some of us such that, to this day, they do not believe that our non-racial democracy will survive and succeed. They dare not allow themselves hope for the future, because they know that the pain of having it dashed, which they are convinced will happen, will be too great. So they look everywhere for evidence of decline, in order that they cannot be disappointed. Crime in our country provides them with the most dramatic evidence

---

[40] See the World Governance Indicators at https://datacatalog.worldbank.org/dataset/worldwide-governance-indicators for a comparison of state capacity across countries. In 2012, South Africa ranked seventy-seventh in the world on the "governance effectiveness" indicator. By way of comparison, South Africa's position is just below Italy and Turkey, and just above Mexico and Greece. It ranks significantly higher than most other African countries on governance effectiveness, as well as a range of other indicators, including rule of law and regulatory quality.

of that decline, the evidence that they are right to foresee a hopeless future for our country, the proof that sooner or later things will fall apart.[41]

Helen Moffett (2006) and others have argued that this sensitivity to the issue of violent crime has served to divert much-needed attention away from the issue of sexual violence and to obstruct a robust political and judicial response. This position is supported by the fact that attempts to address problems of widespread rape have often provoked denials by South African political elites, who have framed such accusations as racialized attacks on the competence of the postapartheid state. Black and white women's rights advocates, attempting to draw attention to the issue of widespread rape in South Africa, have been accused of reinforcing old apartheid stereotypes by portraying black South African men as a threat to social order (Moffett 2006). Individuals ranging from low-ranking law enforcement officials to high-ranking politicians (including current president Jacob Zuma, former president Thabo Mbeki, and others) have consistently dismissed domestic and international efforts to address what has been referred to as a "rape crisis." When Charlize Theron, a white South African actress, aired a commercial in collaboration with Cape Town's Rape Crisis Group to raise awareness of rape as a significant social problem, the commercial was almost immediately removed from the air by the Advertising Standards Authority (ASA). Thousands of complaints led the ASA to conclude that the commercial implied that all South African men were rapists and was therefore inappropriate for broadcast.[42] Despite the fact that black and colored South Africans have been at the forefront of the country's gender activism, many contemporary elites have nevertheless attempted to discredit the movement as predominantly white and urban, and therefore ill-equipped to represent the interests of "real" South Africans.

Yet, if this argument could fully account for the government's hostility toward gender violence, we would expect to see a similar reluctance toward engaging *any* issue involving violent crime, not only gender-based violence. On the contrary, in recent years in particular, government officials in South Africa have adopted a fairly tough rhetorical stance on rising crime rates. In addition, as this chapter has shown, public officials have hardly shied away from "talking tough" on sexual violence. The problem appears to lie not in a discursive avoidance of the issue, but instead in a reluctance to direct resources toward the deep-seated socioeconomic disparities that create the conditions for violent crime in general, and sexual and gender-based violence in particular (Dixon and Van der Spuy 2004). More likely,

---

[41] Thabo Mbeki, "When Is Good News Bad News," *ANC Today*, October 7, 2004, www.anc.org.za/ancdocs/anctoday/2004/at39.htm (quoted in Baehr 2008).

[42] "Real Men Don't Rape." Broadcast on April 17, 2009. Available at www.youtube.com/watch?v=hNjSDW0ktWE.

the current composition of the country's political administration does not share the gender-progressive stance of many of its political forbearers, and these shifting priorities are reflected in the implementation of national policy. The ways in which these priorities come to define the administration of justice and the work of regional courts is the subject of the next chapter.

Conclusion

Over the years, local authorities, colonial officials, national elites, religious organizations, and, most recently, domestic and international feminists and human rights advocates have sought to regulate sexual relationships. In spite of considerable political resistance among local and national elites in both countries, domestic and international coalitions of feminists and human rights activists were extremely successful in influencing national law and policy on a variety of gender-related issues. This influence can largely be explained through openings and opportunities created within each country's political system in the context of fairly dramatic political transitions. Precisely because it is so destructive, war, regime change and state collapse can topple existing sociopolitical hierarchies, creating opportunities for new norms, structures, and relationships to emerge (Berry 2018, Berry and Lake 2017a). The following chapters examine why new national laws and policies in each country have experienced such stark differences in implementation.

In spite of the fact that gender activists were at the forefront of democracy and human rights reform in South Africa, and were successful in shaping the evolution of gender norms on the world stage, gender activists have struggled to translate gender-sensitive law and policy into gender-sensitive practices in courts and by law enforcement officers. Instead, legal practice tends to reproduce conservative and patriarchal attitudes toward gender, minimizing, discrediting and devaluing the experiences of victims, and privileging male power. In DR Congo, however, whose domestic feminist movement was more dispersed and less globally networked than South Africa's, legislative changes that were introduced in roughly the same period as South Africa's have transformed legal practice in many courts across the east. Chapter 4 explores these divergent experiences through an examination of local justice sector institutions in eastern DR Congo and the Western Cape. A political administration with the capacity to direct and define state policy and its implementation in South Africa (and whose interests and priorities have diverged significantly from those of the influential gender activists of the 1990s), is contrasted with a weaker state apparatus in DR Congo, whose priorities continue to be shaped by the influence of non-state human rights actors. State capacity has thus significantly altered the local implementation of gender-progressive policy platforms in each case.

4   Local Justice Institutions and Opportunities Created by State Fragility

Introduction

New sexual offense laws have frequently been used in local courts in eastern DR Congo to uphold and protect the rights of victims in sexual and gender-based violence cases. Courts at both trial and appellate levels in South Africa, however, have rendered surprisingly conservative rulings with regard to sexual and gender-based violence, often in clear violation of South Africa's gender-progressive legislative framework. This chapter examines how and why justice institutions in eastern DR Congo have been responsive to legislative reforms, and have often been effective at implementing new legal protections in local courts, whereas courts in South Africa have continued to deliver judgments that fail to comply with new laws.

This chapter demonstrates that international and domestic human rights activists in eastern DR Congo have taken advantage of openings created by state fragility to exert influence over how local courts deal with sexual and gender-based violence cases. Non-state actors, including international organizations and NGOs have assumed direct responsibility over activities normally undertaken by government agencies, such as organizing and funding criminal trials. While South African human rights activists were able to exert considerable influence over new laws and policies during the country's transition to democracy, government enthusiasm for gender-based reforms has waned in the years since transition. A lack of commitment to local implementation on the part of political elites has meant that efforts by NGOs and gender activists in South Africa have been stymied. South Africa's criminal justice system continues to reflect deeply entrenched conservative attitudes toward a variety of gender issues, which have been reproduced within and throughout state bureaucracies, and by law enforcement officials, judges, and even prosecutors.

This chapter opens with a discussion of judgments produced by appellate and trial courts in South Africa and DR Congo. These judgments illustrate the striking differences in how the victim-sensitive legislation discussed in the previous chapter has been implemented in the two cases. This chapter moves on to consider the influence of non-state actors and advocacy movements over the workings of the criminal justice system. It considers the critical role that external (non-state) actors have played in training legal practitioners and assuming direct responsibility over the coordination of criminal trials in eastern DR Congo. These types of activities, which have significantly shaped criminal justice processes from victim support to judicial reasoning, are absent in South Africa, where gender activists have been consistently obstructed in their reform efforts. The chapter considers the actions and behaviors of stakeholders embedded within each country's local justice institutions, including judges, police officers, prosecutors, lawyers, magistrates, bar associations, civil society organizations, transnational advocacy movements, NGOs, human rights activists, foreign donors, and regional and international organizations.

Hostility toward Gender Issues in South Africa's Courts

On Monday, May 8, 2006, Jacob Zuma, the future president of South Africa, was acquitted of the rape of Fezeka Kuzwayo, the thirty-one-year-old daughter of a family friend, while she was visiting his Johannesburg home. In the controversial and high-profile case, both parties agreed on the basic sequence of events that had unfolded on the night of the alleged rape. The trial hinged not on whether Ms. Kuzwayo had genuinely consented to the act (which she adamantly denied), but on the question of malicious intent. Because the prosecution was unable to prove beyond reasonable doubt that Mr. Zuma had *intended* to commit an act of rape (and had not simply misconstrued the victim's allegedly flirtatious behavior as consent), Justice Van der Merwe of the Witwatersrand High Court concluded that Mr. Zuma could not be convicted.

The trial was riddled with controversy and provoked a heated response from a number of different constituents across South Africa. Three aspects of Justice Van der Merwe's decision in particular attracted severe and widespread criticism. First, Ms. Kuzwayo was extensively questioned on her sexual history, whereas the prior sexual conduct of the accused was deemed irrelevant. Second, the judgment highlighted an argument made by the defense that because the victim had attempted to file rape charges on previous occasions, her testimony could not be considered reliable.[1]

---

[1] The defense argued that the fact that she had reported rapes to the authorities previously demonstrated a history of vendetta against men and thus her testimony could not be considered reliable. The judge thought it pertinent to highlight this argument in his decision

Finally, the fact that the victim adorned a short skirt on the night of the attack was used by the defense to suggest that her behavior was flirtatious. While it is fairly well known to those who have been trained in investigating allegations of gender violence that victims of rape do not always behave in the ways the public might expect, Van der Merwe nevertheless questioned why Ms. Kuzwayo had not resisted the accused's advances. In his judgment, he noted:

> The complainant conceded that at the time of the alleged rape she weighed 85 kg and was 1,65 metres tall. She was thirty-one years of age. She accepted that the accused was at the time sixty-three years of age and weighed approximately 90 kilograms. It was suggested to her that she could have resisted easily and that she could have broken the hold the accused had on her two hands. She then explained that she did not pull her hands away because she did not move. She could not move as she froze at some point when she saw he was naked. The only thing she did and could do was to turn her head away and keep her eyes closed.[2]

Despite the fact that it is not uncommon for victims of sexual assault to remain silent due to the shock they experience in the face of nonconsensual advances, in his verdict Justice Van der Merwe nevertheless reiterated Ms. Kuzwayo's seeming lack of resistance. This is in spite of the fact that Ms. Kuzwayo clearly testified that she felt frozen and paralyzed in the moment. Justice Van der Merwe noted Ms. Kuzwayo's lack of resistance, and the fact that she wore no underwear, in the final judgment to discredit the victim's testimony and her professed lack of consent.

After the verdict, thousands of supporters of President Zuma gathered, calling Ms. Kuzwayo a whore and a bitch, and burning effigies of the victim.[3] Ms. Kuzwayo was placed in witness protection and later granted asylum in the Netherlands. While the public hostility toward Ms. Kuzwayo can be attributed to Mr. Zuma's political prominence, the *nature* of her treatment, both by the courts and by the public, was by no means unique to this case. Rapes and sexual assaults are notoriously difficult to prosecute in South Africa. Police frequently close cases immediately after they have been reported and without further investigation. One interviewee reported that, in what she referred to as cases of

because in two prior incidents the complainant had pursued charges of rape that were later dropped. The judge states: "From a motive point of view, Mr Kemp [defense counsel for Mr. Zuma] argued, it was necessary to investigate the two incidents to find out why the present incident is hotly pursued but the two others were not." High Court of South Africa Witwatersrand Local Division. 2006. *State v. Jacob Gedleyihlekisa Zuma.* 8 May, 2006.

[2] High Court of South Africa Witwatersrand Local Division. 2006. *State v. Jacob Gedleyihlekisa Zuma.* 8 May, 2006. Pg. 46

[3] For examples, see coverage at BBC News: http://news.bbc.co.uk/2/hi/africa/4708960.stm; News 24: www.news24.com/SouthAfrica/Archives/ZumaFiles/Zuma-protest-Burn-this-bitch-20060307; Mail & Guardian: http://mg.co.za/article/2006-03-21-timeline-of-the-jacob-zuma-rape-trial.

"complex" rape (including cases of partner rape or where alcohol was involved), police repeatedly inform victims that their forensic examination results are still pending, aiming to deter victims' desires to seek formal justice and push them to abandon the charges.[4] Because the bar to demonstrate a lack of consent beyond reasonable doubt in such cases is high, prosecutors and police would rather devote attention to cases that pose fewer evidentiary challenges.

Illustrative of these trends, a case involving the gang rape of nineteen-year-old "Buyisiwe" by eight men in 2005 was delayed twenty-three times. Eventually referred from the Tembisa Regional Court to the Supreme Court of Appeal due to excessive delay and frequent violation of procedure in the lower courts, the case continued to be postponed and was plagued by lost documents and faulty procedure in Johannesburg.[5] The case only eventually went to trial four years after it was first reported; nearly ten years later, the case was still ongoing. Cases that do not benefit from media attention and campaigning face an even greater likelihood of delay, or of falling through the cracks altogether (Bennett 2008).

In some cases, rather than delaying dockets in the hope of attrition, police may simply close cases that seem challenging. If they learn of any relationship between the victim and the accused; if alcohol has been involved; if the victim shows no visible signs of physical assault; or if the attack has taken place in a social environment such as at a bar or a party, police or investigators might themselves deem these "complex rapes," sharing the view that the victim was looking for sex and thus the act could not be considered "non-consensual." (Human Rights Watch 2001).

Because of a lack of confidence in the criminal justice system, as well as the social stigma surrounding sexual violence, Human Rights Watch and other organizations report that very few rapes that occur in South Africa are ever even reported to the police in the first place (Human Rights Watch 2011: 18; One in Nine Campaign 2007). Due to high rates of attrition, official South African Police Service (SAPS) statistics reveal that, among those cases that are reported, only twenty-two percent are ever finalized and only fourteen percent result in convictions (Women's Legal Centre and Rape Crisis Cape Town Trust 2013: 7).

For the few cases that do eventually reach the courts, the flaws identified in the Zuma judgment are wholly representative: the past conduct of the victim and any potentially flirtatious or outspoken behavior is routinely used to complicate issues of consent or to discredit victim testimony

---

[4] Informal conversation. Carline, Prosecutor. South Africa. 8 June 2017.
[5] Field notes, March 2013. See also *Mail & Guardian* (2009); One in Nine Campaign (2009); News 24 (2009).

in court, even though such practices directly conflict with South African law. The attitudes toward sexual consent expressed in the Zuma judgment reflect the gender-conservative attitudes and behaviors of a large number of state officials in South Africa, from police officers all the way to high-ranking politicians.[6]

Why have police and courts in South Africa remained so consistently hostile to legal accountability for widespread sexual violence? And why have national courts failed to implement the exemplary legislation introduced on the national stage – even at the appellate level? The judgment in the Zuma case is revealing. While we might expect lower-level courts in remote rural locations to be more tightly enmeshed in patriarchal or gender-conservative structures, practices, and ideas – and perhaps remain more isolated and distanced from emerging laws and best practices in urban centers – the Witwatersrand High Court that delivered the Zuma judgment is located in the center of Johannesburg, South Africa's capital city. Moreover, Justice Van der Merwe is a highly educated and prominent South African judge who has presided over a number of high-profile human rights cases.[7]

South Africa's postapartheid courts have a history of taking a strong stance on a range of human rights issues. Activists, legislators, and politicians went to considerable effort to promote equality, freedom, and the rights of groups and individuals through legal structures in the wake of apartheid. The government introduced legislation criminalizing all forms of discrimination, protecting the rights of women and minorities in the workplace, and providing access to reproductive health, including free and safe abortions. Indeed, in the same year that Justice Van der Merwe handed down his judgment in the Zuma case, the Witwatersrand High Court issued a number of innovative human rights decisions, including Justice Van der Merwe himself invoking constitutional protections for social and economic rights to uphold the right to housing for supposedly illegal occupants of a Johannesburg dwelling.

South Africa's courts have also demonstrated episodic sensitivity to gender rights. In 1997, South Africa's Supreme Court of Appeal delivered a groundbreaking ruling in a sexual violence case, confirming a lengthy sentence for three counts of rape, declaring:

---

[6] In response to the Zuma allegations, Julius Malema, the head of the ANC youth league, insinuated that rape victims in South Africa often enjoy the experience. He stated: "When a woman didn't enjoy it, she leaves early in the morning. Those who had a nice time will wait until the sun comes out, request breakfast and ask for taxi money." Afriknews: www .afrik-news.com/article15208.html.

[7] Justice Van der Merwe's most notable achievement was the trial of Eugene de Kock, the apartheid-era police commander, recently released on parole, who was originally sentenced to 212 years in prison for crimes against humanity, including torture and murder of ANC activists.

Women in this country are entitled to the protection of [their] rights. They have a legitimate claim to walk peacefully on the streets, to enjoy their shopping and their entertainment, to go and come from work, and to enjoy the peace and tranquility of their homes without the fear, the apprehension and the insecurity which constantly diminishes the quality and enjoyment of their lives ... The Courts are under a duty to send a clear message to the accused, to other potential rapists and to the community: We are determined to protect the equality, dignity and freedom of all women, and we shall show no mercy to those who seek to invade those rights.[8]

In 2005, the South African Constitutional Court issued a ruling declaring a constitutional right to same-sex marriage, making South Africa only the fifth country in the world to do so.[9] South Africa also boasts a strong record of women in parliament, ranking tenth in the world for gender parity in politics.[10]

These examples and many others paint South Africa as a regional human rights leader, applauded for its progressive stance on many human rights issues.[11] South Africa's domestic human rights record – and vocal support for gender equality – makes the country a likely case for the diffusion of gender-progressive laws and practices, particularly given its active grassroots women's rights movement. And given South Africa's resources, capacity, and high quality legal education, we would expect its appeals courts to exhibit compliance with the country's laws, if not best practice. Instead, gender violence cases are riddled with contradictions and violations vis-à-vis South African law.

---

[8] South Africa Supreme Court of Appeal. *S v. Chapman.* May 22, 1997. 345/96 [1997] ZASCA 45; 1997 (3) SA 341 (SCA); 1997.

[9] The ruling was based on Section 9 of the Constitution of South Africa, invoking the guarantee of equal rights and equal protection for all and the explicit prohibition on discrimination. The court ruled that South Africa had "a multitude of family formations that are evolving rapidly as society develops, so that it is inappropriate to entrench any particular form as the only socially and legally acceptable one." South Africa Constitutional Court. 2005. *Minister of Home Affairs and Another v Fourie and Another.* 1 December 2005. CCT 60/04. 2005. ZACC 19; 2006 (3) BCLR 355 (CC); 2006 (1) SA 524 (CC).

[10] South Africa has also legislated to promote women's rights in the workplace and access to reproductive health care, including safe and legal abortions. (Human Rights Watch 2001a). See also: Inter-parliamentary Union: www.ipu.org/wmn-e/c lassif.htm, IDEA: www.ipu.org/wmn-e/classif.htm.

[11] The South African Constitutional Court has arrived at a number of internationally acclaimed decisions involving the right to housing and the right to health, namely the 2002 decision demanding that the drug Nevaripine (a drug effective for reducing the transmission of HIV from mother to child) was made available at all South African hospitals. Furthermore, South Africa's equality courts have been proactive in the area of discrimination law. For further discussion, see Goldstone (2006) and the Center for the Study of Violence and Reconciliation (2001).

To supplement my qualitative research in the Western Cape, which included visits to courts, legal aid clinics, and one-stop-shops, as well as interviews with legal practitioners and other key stakeholders, I analyzed 219 case files from Western Cape courts over a period of eight years. These case files were drawn from the Khayelitsha Magistrates' Court and the Western Cape High Court. The Khayelitsha Magistrates' Court is the first-instance court for the vast majority of sexual and gender-based violence cases reported in the high-crime townships of Khayelitsha and Gugulethu. The Western Cape High Court also serves as the first-instance court for cases referred from the district and regional courts across the Western Cape, and serves as the appeals court for the province.

For both courts, I analyzed court processes before and after the passage of the 2007 Sexual Offences Act. While case files from the Khayelitsha Magistrates' Court included arrest warrants, police dockets, medical reports, and witness testimonies, they did not detail the legal reasoning behind the decisions. Therefore, I analyzed only twenty-one case files from the Khayelitsha Magistrates' Court, and supplemented this analysis with interviews and by spending time at the court in 2013. For the High Court, I analyzed 129 first-instance decisions and sixty-nine appeals decisions. My research assistant and I read through the High Court's charge sheets to identify and select all cases that involved sexual offense charges from the years 2005 (before the passage of the Sexual Offences Act), 2008 (just after its passage), and 2011 (four years after its passage). We requested and analyzed all sexual offense cases from these years. My research assistant conducted follow up fieldwork and interviews on two trips in 2017.

There was considerable variation in the treatment of rape and sexual offenses at the Western Cape High Court. While some case files suggested full knowledge and compliance with the law, a surprisingly high number of cases demonstrated either a complete lack of knowledge or disregard. Even at the appeal stages, judges declined to uphold mandatory minimum sentences, misdefined rape, and admitted character assassinations of the victim, as well as his/her prior sexual history, as evidence.

The weak diffusion of gender violence laws, and the limited effects of gender advocacy, can be observed in three principal areas. First, courts – even at the appellate level – often explicitly violated the provisions of the 2007 Sexual Violence Act. Second, and even more frequently, judges and legal practitioners subverted the *intent* of the 2007 law, applying judicial discretion to give benefit of doubt to the accused. While judges are legally *entitled* to judicial discretion, the frequency with which they employed this discretion to reduce sentences on the grounds that the rape did not seem serious, undermines the law's efforts to center the rights of victims.

Finally, advocacy efforts have largely failed to ensure that victims are treated with credibility and respect at the moment of reporting. Skepticism, character assassinations, and abuse instead characterize many victims' experiences of reporting. This treatment leads to high rates of attrition, and deters victims from seeking justice. Compounding these problems, police or prosecutorial staff intentionally lose, stall, or dismiss cases that appear too complex, or where they themselves do not believe the victim's story.

In the sections that follow, and drawing from three bodies of data (my in-country research; my analysis of 219 cases; and patterns revealed by archival and NGO analysis across the country), I demonstrate the areas in which South African gender activists have struggled to influence legal culture vis-à-vis sexual violence, or to ensure implementation of gender-based law reform through the country's courts.

South Africa's Sexual Offenses Laws in Court

One of the most visible failures of gender-based law reform is evidenced in the consistent (mis)application of rape laws in South Africa's courts. Notably, judges routinely invoke the legal discretion afforded to them under the law to disregard mandatory minimum sentencing guidelines, applying lenience in the vast majority of sexual violence cases analyzed.

The 1997 Criminal Law Amendment Act introduced mandatory minimum life sentences in cases of rape where the victim was raped more than once by the accused or by any co-perpetrator or accomplice; where the incident was perpetrated by a person who had been convicted of two or more offenses of rape; where the perpetrator was knowingly HIV positive; where the victim was a girl under the age of sixteen years; where the victim was a physically disabled woman rendered particularly vulnerable, or mentally ill, according to the Mental Health Act (Act No. 18 of 1973); or where grievous bodily harm was inflicted (South Africa 1997. Criminal Law Amendment Act, Part II, Schedule 2, Section 51). The same sentencing guidelines apply to aggravated compelled rape. In cases of rape that did not meet these categories, a first offense was punishable by at least ten years in prison, a second offense by at least fifteen years, and a third or subsequent offense by at least twenty years (South Africa 1997, Criminal Law Amendment Act. Part III, Schedule II). For other sexual assault crimes, a first offender faced imprisonment for no less than five years; a second offender for no less than seven years; and a third or subsequent offender for no less than ten years (Part IV, Schedule II). The law stipulates that mandatory minimums do not apply in cases where the accused is younger than eighteen.

The Criminal Law Amendment Act of 1997 permits courts to depart from the mandatory minimum sentences if they are "satisfied that substantial and compelling circumstances exist which justify the imposition of a lesser [sentence]" (South African Government 1997). In the context of any deviation, judges are required to clearly enter the substantial and compelling circumstances on the record of the proceedings in the imposition of a lesser sentence.

The 2007 reforms largely preserved these mandatory minimums, but offered new and more expansive definition of rape; clarified many of the provisions of the earlier Act; and restricted the grounds on which substantial or compelling circumstances could be applied. The 2007 Criminal Law Amendment Act clearly upholds that sentences *cannot* be reduced on grounds of the complainant's previous sexual history, an apparent lack of physical injury to the complainant, an accused person's cultural or religious beliefs about rape, or any relationship between the accused person and the complainant prior to the offense being committed (South Africa 2007, Criminal Law Sentencing Amendment Act, Section 51, 3(a)).

Yet judges frequently deviate from the prescribed minimum in sexual offense cases, often in direct contravention of these provisions. Most often, sentence reductions take the form of fairly abstract references to a lack of prior convictions on the part of the accused (a first offense) or the damaging consequences of imprisonment. In the case of *William Brown* v. *the State* (Case No. A458/2007, February 8, 2008), for example, the Western Cape High Court reduced the fifteen-year mandatory minimum sentence imposed by the lower court for a second offense of rape on the grounds that the first offense took place more than twenty years prior, and a sentence of fifteen years would likely have damaging repercussions for the appellant.[12] In the case of *The State* v. *Omar Genever, Riedewaan Hendricks, and M.I.* (Case No. SS77/2006, May 5, 2008), the judge ruled on appeal that the life sentences for rape awarded by the lower courts should be reduced due to the socioeconomic circumstances of the accused and the fact that one was under the influence of drugs.[13] Although such bases for sentence reductions are not explicitly prohibited (indeed, the law permits judges to take into account the character of the defendant and the impact on the community in exercising discretion), such consistent deviations privilege the potential damage caused to the

[12] Western Cape High Court. 2008. *William Brown v. the State*. Case No. A458/2007. South Africa. February 8, 2008.

[13] High Court of South Africa Cape of Good Hope Provincial Division. The *State v. Omar Genever, Riedewaan Hendricks M.I.* Case No. SS77/2006. South Africa. May 5, 2008.

accused over the victim's right to punitive legal remedy, even where guilt is established beyond reasonable doubt.

In their analysis of 175 high court decisions across the country since the passage of the 2007 Sexual Offences Act, the Women's Legal Centre found that these trends persist beyond the Western Cape. High courts set aside rape sentences altogether in approximately one in every four rape cases that went to appeal, showing flagrant disregard for the spirit of the law (Women's Legal Centre 2012). In the case of *Motlhakane* v. *S* in North West Province, for example, the defendant, Moses Silas Motlhakane, was convicted by the Schweizer Reinecke Regional Court of the rape of his twelve-year-old stepdaughter.[14] Mr. Motlhakane was accused of entering his stepdaughter's bedroom, removing her clothes, and forcing himself onto her while threatening to hurt her if she screamed. Applying the minimum sentence mandated by law for persons found guilty of raping a minor, the Schweizer Reinecke Regional Court sentenced Mr. Motlhakane to life imprisonment. However, on appeal, the High Court reversed the regional court's decision and, in spite of the minimum sentence of life imprisonment for rape cases involving victims under the age of sixteen, applied a sentence of twelve years. In the Motlhakane judgment, the High Court justified its decision in terms of the "destructive impact of unduly long sentences."[15] It pointed out that the appellant retains his "inherent worth and dignity," which must be considered in the process of determining an appropriate sentence.

Similarly, in the case of *Sangweni* v. *S*, a defendant convicted of raping a seven-year-old girl had his sentence reduced by the Kwazulu-Natal High Court at Pietermaritzburg from life imprisonment to eighteen years on the basis that the defendant was:

Thirty years old, and at the time of his arrest gainfully employed. He supported his family, which consisted of his brothers and one sister. He was the only breadwinner at the family homestead, and also a first offender, making him, in the words of the court, a strong candidate for "rehabilitation." (Women's Legal Centre 2012: 63)

While mandatory minimums should not be regarded as a gold standard of criminal justice reform (and can themselves have problematic ramifications), they exist as one of the few protections the law affords to victims of sexual and gender-based violence pursuing formal criminal justice. Already, sexual offenses are unique in the evidentiary burden placed on victims to *prove* that consent was not granted in order to establish guilt beyond reasonable doubt. Once such guilt has been established, frequent deviations from

---

[14] North Gauteng High Court, Pretoria. *Moses Silas Motlhakane v. The State*. Case No. A639/2008. South Africa. December 10, 2010.
[15] ibid.

mandatory minimum sentences, even on legally permissible grounds, violate the spirit, if not the letter, of the law. Such deviations deny sexual assault victims one of the very few protections the law is able to afford them.

But it is not only the spirit of the law that is frequently undermined in court. In many cases, judges violate the law's provisions directly. Despite the 2007 law's restrictions on judicial discretion in sentencing, lower and higher courts frequently referenced lack of physical injury, whether the victim was intoxicated, whether she failed to protest, or whether she encountered the accused in a nightclub or bar, to complicate questions of consent and to justify reduced sentences. Furthermore, where lesser sentences were applied, judges in lower courts almost never made clear their reasoning. Indeed, almost all of the convictions analyzed from the Khayelitsha Magistrates' Court, involving counts of rape after the passage of the 2007 Sexual Offences Act, resulted in sentences far less than the legally mandated ten years. The most common sentences for charges of rape were suspended sentences of five years or less (in approximately twenty percent of convictions) and correctional supervision instead of imprisonment (in approximately forty percent of convictions). Almost none of the sentences handed down by the Khayelitsha Magistrates' Court between 2005 and 2014 complied with minimum sentencing guidelines, and lengthy prison sentences were only awarded by the lower court in rape cases that also involved extreme physical violence. Even in cases of extreme violence, lower courts almost never awarded the life sentences mandated by the law. Yet, in none of the police records, court files, or judgments from Khayelitsha were substantial or compelling circumstances formally noted, and many interviewees confirmed that it was common for mandatory minimums to be disregarded altogether by lower courts.[16]

While deviation from sentencing guidelines was far more common in lower courts than in high courts, judges in rape and sexual assault cases in the high courts also frequently strayed from the minimum sentences mandated by law – both in first-instance decisions, and on appeal. In the case of *Allan Diedericks and Leonard Claasen* v. *the State*, for instance, the regional court found substantial and compelling circumstances to justify a lesser sentence in the gang rape of a twenty-nine-year-old woman. In stark contravention of the law (which, again, provides that sentences cannot be reduced on grounds of an apparent lack of physical injury to the complainant), the judge justified a lesser sentence on the grounds that the "appellant is a first offender; that intoxicating liquor played a role; and that the complainant had, fortunately, not suffered any

---

[16] Author's fieldnotes. South Africa, 2013; 2017.

serious injuries".[17] While the defendants appealed on the grounds that the eighteen-year and eight-year sentences were "shockingly and disturbingly inappropriate," the High Court judge noted: "I find no basis upon which the exercising of the sentencing discretion by the magistrate can be faulted".[18]

In addition to applying sentence reductions, a number of South African courts have mischaracterized the crime of rape. The 2007 Sexual Offences Act defines rape to include any act of penetration of any orifice by any object or part of the body. Despite the clarity of the law on this issue, decisions too often revert to a common law definition of rape – which is restricted to penile to vaginal penetration – in judging the severity of an offense, or whether or not an offense has been committed. Prior to the 2007 Sexual Offences Act, anal rape, for example, could not be prosecuted as a crime of rape since it does not involve penile to vaginal penetration. This means that prior to 2007, anal rape could only be tried as indecent assault and was therefore subject to a maximum five-year sentence for first offenders, rather than being subject to the mandatory minimums for rape (South Africa 1997, Part IV, Schedule 2, Section 51). Similarly, despite the fact that the law clearly specifies that rape constitutes penetration of any orifice, by any object or any part of the body, incidents of vaginal penetration that do not involve male sexual organs are frequently discounted as rapes. In the case of *Deon Raymond Larry* v. *the State*, for example, the accused was charged with sexual assault of an eighteen-year-old girl, for touching her breasts and forcing his hands into her vagina.[19] He was sentenced to three years.

While the decisions analyzed from the Western Cape High Court did not, in general, explicitly misdefine the crime of rape, judges nevertheless referred back to the common law definition in order to warrant sentencing reductions. Confusion was especially rife in cases that involved incidents of anal rape as well as penile to vaginal rape, and in cases involving multiple incidents where the initial incident took place prior to the passage of the 2007 law.

Courts have exploited confusion over the changed definition to justify reduced sentences. In the case of *Calwyn Uithaler* v. *the State* (Case No. A490/2013), the Western Cape High Court reduced a sentence of twenty-eight years to twenty years on the grounds that one of the acts of penetration was anal penetration.[20] The case involved two rapes that

---

[17] Western Cape High Court. 2010. *Allan Diedericks and Leonard Claasen v. the State*. Case No. A737/2010. South Africa. May 20, 2011.

[18] Ibid.

[19] Western Cape High Court. 2013. *Deon Raymond Larry v. the State*. Case No. A573/2013. South Africa. June 13, 2014.

[20] Western Cape High Court. 2013. *Calwyn Uithaler v. the State*. Case No. A490/2013. South Africa. February 10, 2014.

took place in early 2007. One was penile-to-vaginal rape and one was anal. Until May 2007, anal penetration did not constitute a crime of rape but could only be charged as indecent assault. Given that the incident was a gang rape involving two accused; that the complainant was bleeding and injured; and that penile-to-vaginal rape occurred in addition to anal rape, a mandatory minimum sentence of life was applicable even without the anal rape charge. Nevertheless, the High Court judge used the definitional confusion to further reduce the sentence, on the basis that he disagreed that two counts of rape (anal and vaginal) had occurred. Despite the fact that both courts confirmed that a violent gang rape was committed (warranting life sentence even under the pre-2007 legal framework), the fact that the lower court judge incorrectly cited the 2007 anal rape *as* rape motivated the High Court judge to apply leniency.

The case of *Llewellyn Carelse* v. *the State* (Case No. A748/2010) exploited similar definitional confusion.[21] The Western Cape High Court reduced a sentence of thirty years for the rape of a minor (a fifteen-year-old girl) to a sentence of eighteen years on the grounds that the lower court sentence was excessive; this was in spite of the fact that the victim had suffered multiple rapes by the accused, her uncle. The High Court similarly set aside the mandatory minimum sentence on the grounds that anal rapes that occurred prior to 2007 were not defined as rapes until the passage of the 2007 Sexual Offences Act in May 2007. Although the accused was found guilty of vaginal as well as anal rape of the complainant in January to March of 2008, subsequent to the passage of the 2007 Sexual Offences Act, the judge nevertheless ruled that the thirty-year sentence imposed by the lower court judge was excessive and in violation of the law, given that anal rape was not classified as rape at the time the first incident occurred. Note that the accused also perpetrated common law rape (against a minor) prior to 2007, so the decision to award a life sentence did not rest on the anal rape.

Analyses conducted by South African scholars and NGOs identify similar confusion over the definition of rape elsewhere in the country. In the case of *Allen* v. *S* (2010), a defendant was convicted and sentenced to twenty years' imprisonment for raping a twelve-year-old girl by inserting his fingers into her vagina and asking her to lick his penis. On appeal of the case in 2011, the North West High Court of Mafikeng showed reluctance to take this action seriously as a crime of rape. Judge Gura ruled:

---

[21] Western Cape High Court. *Llewellyn Carelse v. the State.* Case No. A748/2010. South Africa. May 9, 2011.

In my view, although the offence of rape is a serious violation and is also prevalent, this is not one of those worst rape cases which one can think of . . . All the appellant did was to insert his finger in the victim's private parts. Apart from that, she licked his private parts. There is clearly a marked disparity between the sentence which was imposed by the trial court and the sentence which this court would have imposed, had it been the trial court . . . Consequently, the appeal is upheld and the sentence of twenty-years is set aside and substituted with seven-years imprisonment.[22]

This is in stark contravention of the provisions of the 2007 Sexual Offences Act, which clearly defines rape as: "Penetration [by] any other part of the body of one person or, any object including any part of the body of an animal into or beyond the genital organs or anus of another person." (South Africa 2007). Post-2007, regional court judges have dismissed cases or applied lenient sentences even more frequently than higher courts, demonstrating their staunch commitment to a common law definition of rape.

In my analysis from the Western Cape, references to degrees of rape came up again and again. In the case of *Waterboer* v. *the State*, the judge cited the following two judgments:

In S v Abrahams 2002 (SACR 116 SCA, at 127), Cameron, JA (as he then was) held that:- " . . . some rapes are worse than others, and the life sentence ordained by the Legislature should be reserved for cases devoid of substantial factors compelling the conclusion that such a sentence is inappropriate and unjust.

As Davis, J stated in S v Swartz and Another:- "As controversial a proposition as this is bound to be, as not all murders carry the same moral blameworthiness, so, too, not all rapes deserve equal punishment. That is in no way to diminish the horror of rape; it is however to say that there is a difference even in the heart of darkness."[23]

Ultimately, the appeals judge in this case declined to reduce the sentence. However, he did so, not because the premise of the appeal was unreasonable, but because he did not concur with the assessment that the case was not one of the "worst" kinds of rapes. He noted:

Here is no suggestion that the personal circumstances of the Appellant were not properly considered. The main issue is whether the rape falls in one of those "worse categories" as mentioned in the Abrahams case . . . it is evident that the Appellant has a flagrant disregard for human dignity and physical integrity. He not only raped the first complainant, but used violent force against her and the second complainant. Moreover, what compounds the seriousness of this rape is that despite the physical trauma of the rape itself, the Appellant viciously

[22] North West High Court of Mafikeng. *Allen v. S.* Case No. A26/2010 ZANWHC2. South Africa. January 27, 2011.
[23] Western Cape High Court. 2011. *Waterboer v. the State.* Case. No. A193/10. South Africa. February 18, 2011.

stabbed the first complainant in her abdomen when an attempt was made to ward him off. The stab wound caused her to be hospitalised as she sustained internal injuries. A more serious and inhumane attack on a person that barely weighs 30 kg, as in this instance, is difficult to imagine. The contention therefore that this is not "rape of the most serious kind" is, in my view, untenable and can safely be rejected.[24]

This reasoning clearly gives the impression that mandatory sentences are only for the worst forms of rape. Sentencing in less "serious" cases are clearly taken to be at the judges' discretion.

These patterns are once again evident across the country. On appeal, high court judges frequently declared that the crimes before the court were not the "worst kind of rape" even when those cases involved children or the abuse of authority (Women's Legal Centre 2012: 14). Judges frequently referenced the victims' "lack of serious injuries" as a mitigating factor warranting a reduced sentence, despite the fact that the 2007 Criminal Law Amendment Act precludes the lack of physical injury as a basis for substantial or compelling circumstances warranting a reduced sentence. In *S* v *Ngada*, the Eastern Cape High Court reduced a sentence of twenty-three years to eighteen years in part because the swelling and bleeding the fifteen-year-old victim experienced did not constitute "serious enough injuries" to prove that the attack had resulted from force.[25]

In the case of *Sehlake* v. *S*, the North Gauteng High Court in Pretoria reduced a sentence of life imprisonment to just twelve years, despite the fact that the case involved a four-year-old victim.[26] The judge noted in his decision:

Rape is always a serious offence. It is particularly serious when the victim is so young. Nevertheless, in the present matter, the court is not dealing with the category of the worst rapes, and this should be considered in arriving at an appropriate sentence. The rape did not cause the complainant any serious injury.

Such rulings intimate that judges fundamentally disagree with the sentencing guidelines provided for by law. Given that, in this case, the victim was four years old, it mounts a fairly bold challenge to the law for the judge to suggest that the crime was not among the worst rapes and thus worthy of a lower sentence than the law deems appropriate for rape.

---

[24] Western Cape High Court. 2011. *Waterboer v. the State*. Case. No. A193/10. South Africa. February 18, 2011.

[25] Eastern Cape High Court. 2009. *S v Ngada*. ZA ECGHC Case No. 379/08. South Africa. March 16, 2009.

[26] North Gauteng High Court. 2008. *Sehlake v. S*. Case No. A977/08. South Africa. 2008.

Discrediting Victim Testimony

Despite being overturned in 1998[27] and formally outlawed in 2007, judges at all levels also continued to utilize the Cautionary Rule in cases involving sexual violence. The Cautionary Rule, which was standard practice for decades, encouraged judges to use caution with regard to the reliability of witness testimony in rape cases. Across the country, analysis of high court cases carried out by the Women's Legal Centre found that use of the Cautionary Rule was especially common in child rape cases, given the perception that children could not always be considered reliable witnesses by the court. The Women's Legal Centre found that high courts were most likely to affirm convictions in cases where the complainant's evidence could be corroborated by additional witnesses or medical testimony, or where the victim reported the rape quickly. Of the 175 cases the Women's Legal Centre analyzed, judges treated victims' testimony with caution to overturn twenty-three percent of rape convictions and to reduce sentences in an additional thirty-six percent of cases (Women's Legal Centre 2012: 14). Even in South Africa's Supreme Court of Appeal, such problems persist. In the case of *Van der Watt* v. *S*, the Supreme Court noted that the behavior of the complainant the day after the alleged incident was "inconsistent" with the story that she was raped:

The complainant woke up the following day and continued with her normal duties as if nothing had happened until she completed what was necessary. Nothing prevented her from leaving at the earliest available opportunity that morning to go and report her rape as she claims she intended to. (Women's Legal Centre 2012: 23)[28]

The research by the Women's Legal Centre demonstrates that victim testimony in rape cases continues to be treated with undue suspicion, even by South Africa's higher courts and even in spite of a legislative framework designed to explicitly prohibit and overcome prejudices toward victims of gender violence.

These trends were corroborated in my analysis of Western Cape decisions. In the case of *Athini Vumsindo* v. *the State*, the Western Cape High Court entirely set aside the Vumsindo's conviction on the grounds that the sitting judge did not consider the victim's testimony credible.[29] The 2007 Sexual Offences Act clearly states that "a court may not treat the evidence of

---

[27] South Africa Supreme Court of Appeal. 1998. *Jackson v. S.* Case No. 35/97. South Africa. March 20, 1998.

[28] South Africa Supreme Court of Appeal. 2010. *Van der Watt v. S.* Case No.488/09) ZA SCA 22; 3 All SA 434. South Africa. March 23, 2010.

[29] Western Cape High Court. 2010. *Athini Vumsindo v. the State.* Case No. A634/2010. South Africa. May 13, 2011.

a complainant ... involving the alleged commission of a sexual offence ... with caution, on account of the nature of the offence" (South Africa 2007, Section 60). The appeal decision nevertheless rested on the fact that the victim's testimony could not be considered reliable. The judge referenced the victim's earlier relationship with the accused, as well as inconsistency and delay in her testimony,[30] in spite of the fact that the psychological effects of rape are well known to lead to delays in reporting or to other unexpected behaviors (Burgess, Fehder, and Hartman 1995; Jordan 2004).

In 2010, the Western Cape High Court's judgment in the case of *Van Wyk* v. *the State* noted that "because the complainant was a single witness and was intoxicated at the time of the offence, her evidence must be approached with caution".[31] Ultimately, the court rejected the appeal and sided with the complainant. Nevertheless, this passage indicates that the cautionary rule continues to permeate judges' reasoning. In the case of *Damane* v. *the State* in 2012, the judge similarly cast doubt on the reliability of victim testimonies, resulting in the acquittal of the accused.[32] The judge acknowledged in his decision the shortcomings of the legal system with regard to the reliability of witness testimony, noting that "I am required to make a determination if the state has succeeded to prove its case beyond reasonable doubt ... it is a trite principle of our criminal justice system that the onus to prove the accused's guilt beyond reasonable doubt lies on the state. There is absolutely no onus on the accused to prove his innocence ... if doubt is found to exist, the accused is entitled to the benefit thereof, and ultimately, to his acquittal".[33] With these words, the judge highlights the tension between the abolition of the cautionary rule and the presumption of innocence. However, he continues to cast doubt on the victim's testimony by virtue of her identity. He comments:

A finding can be based on the evidence of a single witness, but that such evidence is *always* treated with caution [emphasis added] ... In a criminal matter a conviction will normally follow only if the evidence is substantially satisfactory in every material respect, or if there is corroboration ... All the complainants with regard to all the counts preferred against the accused are children. The evidence of a young child has been said to be unreliable because of the child's inexperience, imaginativeness and susceptibility to influence.[34]

This is in spite of the fact that, elsewhere in the judgment, the judge sympathizes with the defendant's claim that the victim presented herself

---

[30] Ibid.
[31] Western Cape High Court. 2010. *Van Wyk v. the State.* Case No. A372/09. South Africa. August 30, 2010.
[32] Western Cape High Court. 2012. *Damane v. the State.* Case No. SS 16/12. South Africa. December 4, 2012.
[33] Ibid.
[34] Ibid.

as older than sixteen and displayed immense maturity. In support of the claim that the witness may not be reliable, and also that she presented as an adult, the judge referenced "rumours and allegations that the complainant went about sleeping with married men. All these factors taken into account and cumulatively, could easily have led a person to believe that the complainant was older than what she in fact was." In the case of the other complainants, the judge used the fact that they did not report the incidents to persons in authority shortly after such incidents occurred or even to their parents to discredit their credibility as witnesses. Each of these moves raises the specter of the cautionary rule, while also considering the sexual history of one of the claimants to be relevant.

In the case of *The State* v. *Rashied Staggie and Randall Bosch*, the Western Cape High Court applied similar caution in interpreting the credibility of witness testimony.[35] In this case, two members of the Hard Livings Gang, known to the complainant, kidnapped and raped the said complainant when she was nineteen. They raped her as punishment for being a police informant. The judgment frequently referenced the past sexual behavior of the complainant, as well as her behavior after the assault and earlier rapes committed against her. In cross examination, she was questioned on her "practice of making rape charges for financial benefit from her earliest years." The judgment noted that this practice was her *modus videndi* and that she was not raped and her allegations were false. The judgment similarly noted that the complainant had used the word "sex" in place of the word "rape" in her testimony.[36] Although the judge ultimately found in favor of the complainant and upheld the lower court sentences against the two accused, the fact that the witness was allowed to be questioned so extensively on her prior sexual history and on previous sexual assaults committed against her contravenes the protections the Sexual Offences Act enshrines.

Attrition, Reporting, and the Treatment of Victims and Witnesses

Research consistently demonstrates that where cases concern statutory rape or rapes that occurred within the context of a relationship, prosecutors and police are less likely to prioritize the case (Vetten and Motelow 2004). This is not necessarily because prosecutors doubt the allegations made by the victim (although this also persists), but because they believe that a prosecution in such cases is more difficult. Prosecutors, police, and

---

[35] Western Cape High Court. 2002. *The State v. Rashied Staggie and Randall Bosch*. Case No. 131/2002. South Africa. January 28, 2003.
[36] Ibid.

investigators prefer to devote scarce resources to clear-cut or easily "winnable" cases. Further, prosecutors frequently commented that victims tend to withdraw cases involving intimate partner rapes, thus wasting prosecutors' time and resources.[37]

Among the most common factors impeding successful indictments are delays that lead to withdrawal and attrition. The lack of coordination between investigating officers and prosecutors in relation to securing evidence presents a significant problem in the lower courts, when cases are frequently dismissed due to lost or missing dockets, incomplete files, or a lack of necessary evidence that should have been collected at the investigative stage. Furthermore, forensic reports can frequently take months to return to investigative units, stalling cases sometimes indefinitely. Extremely heavy caseloads cause prosecutors to prioritize certain types of cases, and deprioritize those deemed less likely to result in convictions. Rape cases are often among the hardest to prosecute due to heavy evidentiary burdens; thus, these are most likely to be abandoned by prosecutors. Furthermore, heavy caseloads limit the time available to prosecutors to consult with witnesses and prepare for trial. The inevitable delays caused by these two factors lead victims and witnesses to lose confidence in the justice process, motivating them to withdraw cases or to not show up to testify. When it appears that a case is not going anywhere, witnesses are unlikely to feel that it is worth their time to participate. Without witness testimony, convictions in rape cases are extremely difficult to secure.

Finally, victims are notoriously ill-treated at each stage of the criminal justice process. From reporting cases to the police to being interviewed by prosecutors and cross-examined as witnesses, victims are asked about their prior sexual history, their relationship with the accused, what they were wearing at the time of the alleged assault, whether they had been drinking, and many other details often irrelevant to the case. Many of those interviewed made comments such as:

If you don't know your rights and the law – the police will treat you very badly. They will imply, or tell you directly that you wanted to be raped, or they will just laugh at you. Other times they cross-question you: "How did you like it? How did you enjoy it?"[38]

A health worker who accompanied victims of violence to the police noted: "Police in general think girls ask to be raped. In their interviews, they ask what she was wearing, whether she flirted with the boy before, etc."[39]

---

[37] Field notes, South Africa, 2013, 2017.
[38] Interview. Thembela, Community Activist. South Africa, March 6, 2013.
[39] Interview. Anathi, Counsellor. South Africa, March 15, 2013.

The vast majority of cases falls out of the criminal justice system at its very first stage – the reporting stage. A large body of literature has examined attrition in reporting rapes to the police (see, for example, Artz and Smythe 2007; Artz, Smythe, and Leggett 2004; Keehn et al. 2013; Vetten 2013; Vetten et al. 2008; Vetten and Motelow 2004). Reasons for rape case attrition in police stations include a failure to track down the accused or locate the victim; a lack of available evidence; a failure to collect evidence; a withdrawal by the victim; a private settlement reached between the victim and the accused; the docket being lost; or police delay. Vetten and colleagues (2008) note that, in their study of attrition in Gauteng, the victim could not be located after she had reported an incident in almost one in every three cases, thus creating a significant barrier to prosecution. In many of these cases, the inability to track down the victim after the case was reported was due to a failure on the part of the police to accurately record contact information. In almost half of the cases in Vetten and colleagues' study, a first witness statement was never taken. For the cases that proceeded to the prosecutor's office, twenty-two percent were disposed of by the trial courts before coming to trial on the basis of insufficient evidence or lack of witnesses. A further sixty percent of all cases that went to court resulted in the acquittal of the accused (Vetten et al. 2008: 51).

At each stage of the legal process, rape and sexual assault victims are forced to encounter their attackers in courtrooms and police stations. In the vast majority of South African courts, plaintiffs and accused share waiting rooms, toilet facilities, and cloakrooms. Thus, if the case reaches the trial stage, the experience of arriving to testify is often extremely traumatic.[40] Victims frequently recount stories of being threatened by the accused or by members of the accused's family in the court waiting room. In contravention of national policy on this issue, children and traumatized individuals are often cross-examined in busy courtrooms in front of large audiences. This experience often has the effect of retraumatizing victims of rape and sexual assault, again motivating attrition and withdrawal. Moreover, the law demands that victims under the age of eighteen testify using a microphone from an adjoining area, yet only a handful of courts in the country have installed the facilities to make this a reality.[41] Although decades of sustained advocacy has been directed towards improving the experiences of vulnerable crime victims in the pursuit of criminal justice, very few improvements are visible. A community activist who worked closely with victims of violence through her church observed:

[40] Interview. Anathi, Counsellor. South Africa, March 15, 2013.
[41] Interview. Dale, Prosecutor. South Africa, March 12, 2013.

When there are new laws, police do not know about them. We have to tell them they cannot ask girls what they [were] wearing. It's not laziness but lack of training. Prosecutors also don't know the law, and don't care about protecting rape victims. Believe it or not, even prosecutors share the same views as the police.[42]

The Treatment of Gender Violence by DR Congo's Eastern Courts

In stark contrast to South Africa, courts across DR Congo's eastern provinces have ruled surprisingly responsively on a range of sexual and gender-based offenses. Despite all of the challenges associated with weakened state infrastructure and an under-resourced judiciary, sexual and gender-based violence cases have been prioritized at various stages of the legal process. Victim-centered processes for rape and sexual assault are surprisingly common, especially given the relative material deprivation of the legal system. Provisions from the 2006 Sexual Offences Law and the 2009 Child Protection Law are invoked and applied widely, with many judges demonstrating intimate understanding and familiarity with the content of the laws, and with newly introduced definitions. While there are certainly still a great many shortcomings, and many rulings and processes that do not remain faithful to the law, Congolese courts have made good use of the legal reforms discussed in the previous chapter, defying scholarly expectations with regard to the decoupling of law and practice in weaker state environments. Courts are also known to employ innovative protections for victims of sexual assault, which is notable given the state's overwhelmingly weak capacity. Judges have drawn from international human rights instruments when domestic protections are found to be insufficient, to ensure attention to retraumatization in victim questioning and to attempt to ensure the victim's identity and security is protected during the process, despite logistical challenges.

Congolese legal practice is by no means exemplary in every case. Indeed, a number of legal problems persist and variation is evident from case to case. This variation and some of the common challenges faced are discussed at greater length in Part II. Yet, in light of the country's overall poor human rights record, the local-level implementation of international human rights protections and domestic legal reforms by courts across the east offers compelling evidence of diffusion. Human rights actors, gender violence advocates, and rule of law projects have utilized opportunities created by state weakness to exert direct influence over aspects of the legal

---

[42] Interview. Nikelwa, Community Activist. South Africa, March 6, 2013.

process, resulting in demonstrable advancements in the way that sexual and gender-based violence claims are handled in local courts.

In general, the military courts demonstrate greater compliance with gender protections in sexual violence cases than do the civilian courts, although evidence of gender-sensitive legal practices can be found in both systems. Poor record keeping makes comprehensive analysis challenging, and necessitated extended in-person observation and analysis. For the months of June and July 2012, I therefore monitored and observed judicial proceedings at the juvenile court in Goma, a division of the TGI housed at the time at the Munzenze prison. In this period, the Juvenile Court had ninety-seven open cases on record, of which seventy-eight pertained to sexual violence. During this period, prison records and interviews with prison personnel, police, and detainees, suggested that approximately sixty percent to seventy percent of all those detained at Munzenze were alleged sexual offenders (although not all were yet charged with crimes). While this period only offered one snapshot in time, sexual offenses comprised a high proportion of the juvenile court's workload, a trend that continued throughout my research.

The non-juvenile caseload of the TGI in Goma was more varied. Court statistics indicate that the court heard 145 new sexual offenses cases in 2012, as compared to 37 cases of robbery, 39 cases of aggravated robbery, 39 cases of theft, and 32 cases of destruction of property (Tribunal de Grande Instance 2012).[43] Rapes have received striking levels of attention when compared to other crimes, such as robbery or assault. In the provincial capitals of Goma and Bukavu, increased attention to gender violence from the civilian courts and by NGOs has also led to a heightened public awareness of the possibility of facing criminal charges for rape. One colleague in North Kivu joked – in a refrain I heard many times over the course of my research – that he was afraid to spend any time alone with the women he knew after the passage of the law, because [women] were now ready to bring rape charges against anyone they could.[44] Such commentary was born out of the widespread perception that courts easily rendered guilty verdicts.

In 2010–2011, the United Nations Development Program monitored 5,042 gender violence cases reported to the police across the North Kivu,

---

[43] Note that, due to lost or destroyed court records and discrepancies resulting from switching to an online system, many cases were not recorded in the TGI's official record book. While there is some reason to believe that sexual assault cases may have been recorded more meticulously than other cases, given that NGOs were collecting data on these cases, interviews with prosecutors and clerks in Goma and Bukavu indicated that approximately sixty-five percent of their workload was spent on sexual and gender-based offenses. Many jokingly reported that "rape was the only crime that NGOs cared about." Field notes, DR Congo, June 28, 2012.

[44] Field notes, DR Congo, January 21, 2013.

South Kivu, and Ituri provinces. Of these 5,042 reported cases, 3,866 were transferred to the prosecutors' office – a full 76.6 percent – which is high compared to attrition rates at this stage of the legal process elsewhere. Yet these successes are not uniform and do not always result in resolved cases. For example, between 2008 and 2011, the American Bar Association (ABA) assisted with 2,800 complaints involving rape or gender violence. Only 645 of these (twenty-three percent) went to trial, and these are cases that received support from an NGO throughout the process. Of those that went to trial, however, 434 (67.2 percent) resulted in convictions (American Bar Association 2011), suggesting that the American Bar Association and its partners are effective at supporting the prosecution in the cases it selects.

In addition to frequent court visits, trial observations, and observing the work of police, prosecutors, legal aid clinics, medical centers, and NGOs, I also collected as many written decisions as I could from across North and South Kivu. As discussed in Chapter 2, this proved challenging, given that many courts lacked record-keeping capabilities, could not locate or produce written decisions, or produced case files that were part destroyed, part missing, or illegible. Most of the judgments I procured from the civilian courts were handwritten. Ultimately, I managed to collate a sample of 149 complete and legible files (included written judgments) from between 2007 and 2013. Thirty-three of these were from military courts, and 116 from civilian courts. The vast majority were cases tried in the provincial capitals; however, a small number were from elsewhere, including thirteen from Uvira.

Of the case files I analyzed, forty percent resulted in acquittals. Typically, cases supported by NGOs were more likely to be resolved in favor of the victim than those where the civil party received no external assistance. However, many cases that were pursued without NGO support exhibited similar patterns, suggesting that practices promoted by legal capacity-building NGOs generated some spillover effects in other cases.

Sentencing guidelines for rape and sexual assault are generally broader under Congolese law than South African law (with penalties ranging from five to twenty years for rape in DR Congo, and from ten years to life in South Africa, depending on the circumstances). Indecent assault in DR Congo is punishable by six months to five years' penal servitude. Indecent assault against a minor is punishable by five to fifteen years, and if the victim is under ten, five to twenty years (DR Congo 2006). Anyone found guilty of rape receives between five and twenty years, and a fine of at least 100,000 Congolese francs;the minimum penalty is doubled if: the defendant wields a position of authority over the victim; the defendant is a public figure; the victim suffers from any disability; the victim suffers physical or mental ill health as a result of the incident; the victim is threatened with the use of force; or various other conditions. If the rape or indecent assault causes the death of the person against whom it was committed, the perpetrator shall be sentenced to life imprisonment.

While sentences were longer, on average, in South Africa, therefore, those awarded by Congolese courts were more likely to remain within the legally mandated guidelines. This was especially true in the military courts, where only three judgments analyzed awarded sentences of less than ten years, and the majority fell between fifteen years and life imprisonment.

In the civilian courts, convictions resulted in sentences ranging from twelve months to ten years for civilian rapes, and twelve months to five years for other sexual offenses. In 19 of the 116 civilian case files, judges reduced rape sentences on the basis of extenuating circumstances. Many of these were statutory rape cases, in which the judges were convinced that intercourse occurred within the context of a relationship or without the accused knowing the civil party's true age.[45] In one case, involving the nonconsensual rape of a minor, the court awarded only a three-year sentence on the basis that it was the accused's first offense. This judgment was problematic in various other ways that were uncharacteristic of the majority of decisions.[46]

In many cases, judges treated the question of consent with extreme caution, using the provisions of the law to reason that a victim's professed consent cannot be taken at face value. Characteristic of the many decisions exemplifying such logic, in a case of statutory rape involving an eighteen-year-old defendant and a fourteen-year-old victim, the TGI in Bukavu noted:

Under Article 171 of the Law on the Protection of Children, if a defendant commits the rape of a child, either by means of violence or by serious threat or coercion against a child, either directly or through a third party, either by surprise,

---

[45] In these cases, judges reduced sentences from the seven years required by law to between twelve to thirty-six months.

[46] The judgment misquoted the Sexual Offences Act and the Child Protection Law to read: "The analysis of this article shows that for a child to have been raped, the following elements must each be present: the minor age of the victim, the exercise of violence, serious threats, coercion, psychological pressure, abuse, ... and introduction of a sexual organ" (RP 21716, September 14, 2011). In fact, the correct article reads: "Rape of a minor is committed if violence, serious threats or coercion are used against a child, directly or through a third party, or through the use of surprise, psychological pressure, or abuse of a child who, by reason of illness, impairment of his faculties or any other accidental cause, has lost the use of his senses" (DR Congo 2009. Loi n° 09/001 du 10 janvier 2009 portant protection de l'enfant, Article 171). It is not the case, as the judge inferred in the decision, that each of these elements must be present. The judge also failed to provide reasoning for the reduced sentence beyond the fact that it was the accused's first offense.

by using psychological pressure, or in the context of an otherwise coercive environment, or by abusing a child who, due to illness, an alteration of his mental faculties, or who, by any other accidental cause, has lost the use of his senses, any man who penetrates the anus, the mouth, or any other orifice of the body of a child, using a sexual organ, an object, or any other part of the body, or any woman who obliges an infant to expose his or her sexual organ and then touches it with any part of his or her body, or by any object whatsoever . . .

. . . The material elements of [child] rape comprise: 1) A material act of penetration; however superficial, of the vagina, the anus or the mouth, or any other orifice of the body by a woman or a man, with a sexual organ, with any other part of the body, or with any object whatsoever; 2) The victim must be a human being under the age of 18; and 3) Lack of consent results in the case of an underage individual, given that a person under the age of eighteen-years cannot give free and voluntary consent. In such a case, lack of consent is absolute. The moral element with regard to the accused resides with his intent to take possession of the body of the victim of less than eighteen-years . . .

. . . Since in the case under examination, the accused admitted the fact that he had penetrated the victim anally using his penis, and the fact that the latter was under the age of eighteen-years . . . the court establishes a violation of the law in the case of child rape.[47]

The court used the 2006 Sexual Violence Law to sentence the defendant to seven years' penal servitude and a fine of 800,000 Congolese francs (approximately $500 USD) in damages, on the basis that the defendant penetrated the victim anally in a context in which her genuine consent could not be granted. Similar reasoning characterized many of the decisions analyzed. In one case involving the rape of a fifteen-year-old girl in Rutshuru, the defendant acknowledged having sexual intercourse three times, but claimed that he had been in a relationship with the plaintiff for three weeks and that she told him she was seventeen-years-old. The court found in favor of the prosecution, sentencing the defendant to ten years in prison and a fine of 2000,000 Congolese francs. The court noted:

Any act of sexual penetration of any kind committed by one person against another using violence, coercion, threat, or surprise, constitutes rape. A rape requires the material act and a lack of consent on the part of the victim. Since the accused does not deny that the material act took place, lack of consent must be established. Lack of consent can result from violence, coercion, or from the age of the victim. Since in this case the victim was fifteen years-old at the time of the offence, there is no need to establish any further lack of consent.[48]

In many cases, judges remained faithful to the intent of the law, carefully approaching the question of consent, and particularly the sentiment

[47] Tribunal de Grande Instance de Bukavu 2052/PR/021/RMP5743/BKM/SEC/012; South Kivu, DR Congo. October 31, 2012.
[48] Tribunal de Grande Instance de Goma, RP 23473. March 12, 2014.

that genuine consent could not be granted by minors or in the case of psychological pressure or an imbalance in power. Every civilian court ruling I procured quoted the complete 2006 Sexual Offences Act definition of rape in full. I include the text earlier as representative of the language utilized in the decisions analyzed, demonstrating that judges typically employ an expansive definition of rape in compliance with the 2006 law, making explicit reference to penetration, however slight, of any orifice by any object or any part of the body. The hostility toward victims of sexual and gender-based assaults, the caution with which their testimony is often treated, and the questioning that victims and witnesses frequently endure in South Africa, has become increasingly rare (although certainly not non-existent) in North and South Kivu.

Moreover, despite logistical challenges, in many locations – particularly in urban centers – routine processes are in place to support and protect victims and witnesses. In the majority of sexual violence trials I observed in the military courts, and in around half of those I observed in civilian courts, victims of sexual assault were offered the services of a counselor or psychologist. In the civilian courts, this was most often true where cases were supported by an NGO or legal aid clinic. Such support services were also generally not availed in statutory rape cases where the victim and the accused were romantically involved. In military cases, victims and witnesses were often given the opportunity to testify using a microphone from an adjoining area or room in order to prevent the retraumatization associated with recounting personal events in front of a busy courtroom. They may be given robes, masks, or veils to conceal their identities in the courtroom.

In civilian cases, the practice of concealing victims' identities was less common, although the TGI in Goma on occasion made some effort to offer similar protections. Given that the vast majority of gender violence trials takes place in courtrooms lacking electricity, and many more are held in courthouses in remote rural locations, generators and other innovative technological solutions are necessary in order to make these legal protections a reality. Providing the facilities for victims to testify in private thus requires a great deal of effort, creativity, and coordination among multiple actors. These kinds of accommodations for victims are rare even in high rule-of-law countries around the world.

The diffusion of innovative and gender-sensitive legal practice was most evident in rape and sexual assault heard by DR Congo's military courts in the east, and in war crimes and crimes against humanity trials in particular. Indeed, many of the gender-progressive policies and practices promoted by gender rights advocates were pioneered in trials involving international crimes.

The Congolese courts were among the first domestic courts in the world to invoke the Rome Statute of the ICC to convict soldiers implicated in war crimes and crimes against humanity in 2005. Since this landmark decision, the Rome Statute has been readily invoked to sentence soldiers for a variety of sexual offenses. In the case of *Songo Mboyo*, the court cited Rule 70(a) of the ICC's Rules of Procedure and Evidence (RPE) in its judgment, which provides that: "consent cannot be inferred from the victim's silence, lack of resistance, words or conduct, where that victim's ability to give free and genuine consent has been undermined through coercion, threat or use of force".[49] The court also drew on Rule 70(b) of the Rome Statute's Rules and Procedures of Evidence to argue that the credibility, character, or "predisposition to sexual availability" of a victim cannot be inferred from prior or subsequent sexual conduct. The Rome Statute provisions were used in this case to sentence seven defendants to life imprisonment for the systematic rape of thirty-one women. The court also referred directly to the Rome Statute in its order that the defendants pay damages of $5,000 USD to surviving rape victims, and $10,000 USD to the families of those who were deceased.[50] This approach to consent stands in stark contrast to the approach to consent employed even in the most high-profile cases in South Africa.

In trials across the east, judges have frequently drawn on the Rome Statute's RPE in order to recognize and uphold the rights of victims. The RPE has been cited directly to justify the presence of an interpreter, the use of a translator, the frequent breaks afforded to the interviewees under cross-examination, the right to wear clothing to conceal the victims' identity from the gallery, and the right to testify from an adjoining area.

In a crimes against humanity trial in Walungu, South Kivu, in 2013, the judge ruled that:

In accordance with Article 68 of the Rome Statute of the ICC and Article 74 of the Criminal Procedure Code, civil parties appearing before the court should be identified and referred to by all parties at the trial as "F1" in the case of females and "M1" in the case of males to protect their identities. All civil parties appearing before the court, and especially rape victims, must be veiled and wear sunglasses.[51]

---

[49] Tribunal Militaire de Garnison Mbandaka. 2005. RP N°084/2005. DR Congo. April 12, 2006. See also: ASF 2007: 38.

[50] Tribunal Militaire de Garnison Mbandaka. RP N°084/2005. DR Congo. April 12, 2006. Cour Militaire de   l'Equateur. RMP N°154/PEN/SHOF/05. RPA 014/2006. DR Congo. June 7, 2006. See also: International Bar Association 2009: 38; Baylis 2008: 35; Avocats Sans Frontiéres 2007.

[51] Tribunal Militaire de Garnison de Bukavu. Case involving Kabala Mandumba Mundaune and three others, Walungu, RP N°708/12; RMP N°1868/TBK/KMC/10–12. DR Congo. May 20, 2013.

Figure 3 Witness testifying in the Minova rape trial wearing a mask and robes to conceal her identity while giving evidence in court.
© Diana Zeyneb Alhindawi

This practice – dressing victims and witnesses head to toe in cloth, with veils or sometimes sunshades to conceal their identities – has been employed in many trials, often with explicit reference to the Rome Statute.

In addition to victim-sensitive legal protections in court, the spirit of the 2007 reforms has been reflected in legal practice more broadly. In cases I observed, victims of violence were rarely questioned about their prior sexual conduct. Questioning was also often careful to avoid potential retraumatization, embarrassment, or discomfort. One prosecutor told me that, like the practices employed for the international criminal tribunals, victims of sexual assault should be asked whether and when an assault occurred, and should be subject to no further questioning. He noted: "If the victim says she did not give consent, then she did not give consent. All other evidence can be drawn from the medical reports."[52]

When penetration has been established by a medical report or by testimony from the defendant and prosecutors seek to establish non-consent, the victim may be asked if s/he felt coerced into the sexual encounter. In such cases, even if s/he gave verbal consent at the time, some judges and prosecutors declined to interpret that consent as genuine. In contrast to the

[52] Interview, Katindo, Prosecutor. DR Congo, August 5, 2009.

dominant societal norms that have shaped attitudes toward consent in the past, the Rome Statute Elements of Crimes upholds that consent "cannot be inferred by reason of any words or conduct of a victim where force, threat of force, coercion or taking advantage of a coercive environment undermined the victim's ability to give voluntary and genuine consent." Consent cannot either "be inferred by reason of any words or conduct of a victim where the victim is incapable of giving genuine consent (International Criminal Court 2002b)." Mirrored in the 2006 and 2009 laws, the broad wording of these clauses has provided opportunities for legal practitioners to call into question claims that consent was granted, even in cases when the victim indicated verbal consent.

For instance, in the appeal of the case of Albati Ali in the military court of South Kivu, the judgment upheld the prior conviction of the Tribunal Garnison d'Uvira.[53] The garrison court had sentenced Albati Ali to twenty years' imprisonment, the maximum sentence recommended for the crime of rape. The appeal court upheld the conviction and granted the victim an additional $1,000 USD in damages on the basis that psychological pressure had been applied and genuine consent could not be granted due to the coercive environment in which the incident took place. The judgment noted:

Under the terms of this provision, the accused must have: "committed a rape, using violence or serious threats of coercion against a person, either directly, or through a third party. Coercion can be construed as surprise, psychological pressure, taking advantage of a coercive environment, or the abuse of power against a person incapable of giving genuine consent.

In this case, the defendant imposed the physical act of sexual union on the victim, [name omitted]. The Court does not uphold the defense of the accused, on the grounds that he changed his story at multiple stages of the legal process. After initially trying to justify his actions by claiming that he engaged in sexual relations with [victim] after negotiating an agreement with her, he did an about face before the trial judge to declare that he had never known the victim. The Court also notes that the accused had tried again to justify his act before the prosecutor, this time by claiming that because of drunkenness he could not remember the events of that day. The Court finds the story of the accused implausible, because a woman married to an officer would be unlikely to consent to sexual relations with a subordinate officer, particularly in the bush within earshot of houses ... The absence of consent from the victim can be established from the fact that she cried out in such a way that would alert others to come to save her.[54]

---

[53] Cour Militaire du Sud-Kivu. 2009. RPA 098/RMP n°0567/BMN/09. On appeal from the Tribunal Militaire de Garnison d'Uvira. DR Congo. April 21, 2009.

[54] Ibid.

The skepticism with which the court treated the defendant's claims that consent was granted, even in the absence of corroborative testimony, is fairly representative. In the case of Mupoke, the court noted that consent was impossible by virtue of the coercive and threatening nature of the environment in which intercourse occurred: "In this case, none of the victims of rape who went before the judge have testified that they gave consent to the act committed by her attacker . . . Finding themselves before gunmen shooting in all directions, the Court notes that their consent has been torn by violence, constraint, psychological pressure, and a coercive environment of fear".[55] Many convictions from the military courts involving ordinary crimes referred to the position of power held by soldiers in military uniform to discredit the defendants' claims that genuine consent could be granted.

Lower and higher courts have also used an expansive definition of rape (as any form of penetration of any orifice, however slight, with any object or part of the body of the perpetrator), allowing for more victim-centered court processes. In the case of Mbenza Maganya, a police officer from the Police Nationale Congolaise, the lower court handed down a twenty-year prison sentence and $1,000 USD in damages for rape of a minor, for having inserted his fingers into the vagina of a six-year-old girl. The girl was on her way to the market with her older sister when the policeman invited the two girls into his home and abused them. On April 21, 2009, the Tribunal Militaire de Garnison d'Uvira ruled that Mbenza Maganya was "convicted of rape with violence and sentenced to twenty years of penal servitude for rape." The conviction was upheld on appeal on the basis that:

The material act [of rape] consists of introducing any part of the body into the vagina of the victim. In this case, the accused, Mbenza Maganya, introduced his finger, which is a part of his body . . . into the sexual organs [of his victim], constituting rape.[56]

Since under Congolese law victims can file civil claims for damages in sexual assault cases, in questioning the victim, judges often take into consideration the physical, moral (such as harm to honor or reputation), and material damage incurred, particularly in cases involving pregnancy or sexually transmitted diseases or loss of work due to trauma or depression. The decision to award compensation is decided somewhat arbitrarily by judges, and varies dramatically from case to case. However, in cases in which the defendant is found guilty, the compensation awarded

[55] Tribunal Militaire Garnison de Bukavu. 2012. RMP 1868/TBKKMC/1012. Judgment of October 15, 2012; Cour Militaire de Sud Kivu. RMP 1868/KMC/ 11. Appeal Judgment of October 20, 2013.
[56] Tribunal Militaire de Garnison d'Uvira. 2009. RP101. DR Congo. April 21, 2009.

to victims is high. In the case of Albati Ali (RMP No. 0567/BMN/08) in Uvira, the judge noted that: "The said act caused a damage that must be repaired fairly. In fact, the woman . . . mother of five children, was humiliated and dishonored throughout the city of Luvungi by the sergeant who sexually abused her." The court found the defendant guilty and awarded the plaintiff $1,000 USD in damages. In the case of Ngoy Kambi (RMP N°0509/BMN/08) the court similarly recognized that:

Certain physical, moral and material damage was suffered by the victim. That damage is the consequence of the act committed by the accused. In addition to the beating that injured the victim, the rape has exposed her to dishonor and stigma in our society. It is this despicable act that will likely scar the victim psychologically for the rest of her days. In the absence of objective criteria for assessing the injury, the Court considers that an amount equivalent to $1,000 USD can be allocated. All conditions of liability are met, and the accused must compensate the plaintiff to this amount.[57]

Civilian decisions are usually more lenient, with reparations ranging from a few hundred dollars to $1,000 USD. The defendant is responsible for paying damages directly to the victim. In cases where the defendant cannot pay, the state is theoretically supposed to assume responsibility; however, in practice this rarely occurs.

Although the types of protections discussed in this section are not uniformly applied, their prevalence is informative. The (albeit spotty) foregrounding of human rights protections for victims in cases involving sexual and gender-based violence, and the frequent incorporation of newly introduced definitions of rape and consent, is puzzling. How have local courts produced these types of innovative and victim-sensitive human rights rulings given an environment of ongoing state fragility and weakness, particularly when victim-centered processes have proved so elusive in South Africa's courts?

Explaining Divergent Treatment in South African and Congolese Gender Violence Cases

State Fragility and Opportunity Structures in Local Justice Sector Institutions

With a few exceptions, much of the political science scholarship on human rights advocacy has taken policy reform at the level of the central state as its primary unit of analysis. In Keck and Sikkink's famous

---

[57] Tribunal Militaire d"Uvira. 2008. RP 09; RMP N°0509/BMN/08. DR Congo. October 19, 2009.

boomerang model, local actors are vital. However, they are ultimately important for the role they play in shaping the policies and practices of the central government. The central state is responsible for respecting, upholding, or abusing the human rights of its citizens. However, the Congolese and South African examples illustrate that, in order to understand divergent local outcomes, we need to look not only at the activities of the central government, but at the activities of stakeholders working within local courts and rule-of-law institutions – actors who are sometimes far removed from the legislative and policy reforms unfolding in the capital.

Rather than a decoupling between law and practice as World Society scholars have predicted, evidence from these two cases demonstrates that state fragility in eastern DR Congo has, in fact, created openings for NGOs and other non-state actors to exert considerable influence over judicial processes in ways that prove impossible in stronger state environments. State fragility has facilitated victim-sensitive human rights practices in local courts in two ways. First, when states are described as weak or fragile, that description often reflects an empirical reality in which armed actors, NGOs, international organizations, religious groups, and/ or civil society organizations have already assumed responsibility over many governance functions in certain parts of the country. Because the central state appears absent, it is widely accepted that other non-state actors will step in to perform regulatory tasks. The empirical realities of weak statehood in eastern DR Congo have thus meant that domestic and international NGOs and UN agencies have assumed responsibility for maintaining public order, paying fees to public officials in lieu of salaries from the state, and providing health and education services. International agencies, sometimes in partnership with domestic human rights actors, have also assumed responsibility for activities such as legal training, and funding and coordinating trials. Human rights actors have taken advantage of these entry points to direct legal attention toward an issue of considerable concern to the international community that was previously neglected by DR Congo's courts, namely, the prosecution of sexual and gender-based violence. These types of activities have simply not been possible in contexts like South Africa, where the state has greater bureaucratic capacity, reach, oversight, and assumes responsibility for its own governance activities.

In addition to the de facto assumption of power by non-state actors, certain discursive or "juridical" dimensions of state fragility have also created opportunities for domestic and international human rights organizations to involve themselves in the activities of local courts. In addition to the roles they play in generating funding and directing the attention of donors toward issues involving rule of law and governance, terms such as "fragile," "(post)-conflict," or "failed" statehood have served to justify continued intrusions on Kinshasa's sovereignty. In countries such as Somalia, Haiti, and Afghanistan, state weakness has been invoked by the international community to provide moral or legal justifications for interventions in the domestic authority structures of states through UN peacekeeping missions or international occupations, or to participate in other governance activities (Krasner 1999, 2004; Keohane 2002). In DR Congo, the UN Security Council has used its formal recognition of the state's inability to engage in basic governance activities to establish a United Nations Peacekeeping Mission, which has assumed responsibility over various governance activities, including aspects of judicial administration.

On the other hand, since the South African state is internationally regarded as a regional leader on a range of human rights issues, local and external stakeholders' efforts to influence aspects of judicial administration have been routinely obstructed. There are limited openings for activists to promote change within and throughout law enforcement hierarchies. Due to the fact that the vast majority of justice sector activities, including judicial training, managing caseloads, and setting judicial priorities, are overseen by the democratically elected South African government, NGOs have not benefited from the same openings and opportunities structures that make the kind of work they carry out in eastern DR Congo possible.

In addition, South African NGOs, civil society activists, and elites have expressed staunch resistance to the types of activities carried out by non-state actors in eastern DR Congo. Many activists look to the central government as the appropriate institution to remedy governance failures. The idea that NGOs – especially foreign NGOs – should assume responsibility in areas where the government is seen to be failing was seen by many to resemble a flagrant violation of South African sovereignty. Moreover, such actions would be seen to let the government "off the hook" for its basic responsibilities to its citizens. Therefore, the increasing hostility towards gender-based violence exhibited by the South African government presents a significant barrier to the practical implementation of gender-based legal reform. The following sections evidence the obstructions and opportunities encountered by gender activists in each case.

Evidence from DR Congo

This research demonstrates that, in order to understand DR Congo courts' sensitive treatment of the issue of sexual and gender-based violence, it is necessary to look not to laws and policies passed by the central government, but to *local* justice sector institutions as critical entry points through which non-state actors have shaped criminal justice processes. State fragility in eastern DR Congo has allowed for the direct implementation of reforms by external actors at the level of local justice sector institutions. Interventions at the local level can be understood in terms of two key types of activities: the provision of training and resources to existing institutions and personnel (as discussed in other contexts by Cichowski 2007; Hilson 2002; McCarthy and Zald 1977; Wilson and Cordero 2006), and the direct coordination and implementation of judicial activities by external stakeholders.

Legal Training and Gender Sensitivity

In addition to the disproportionate number of gender violence investigations pursued compared to other categories of offenses, the practices of courts and legal practitioners have been responsive to victims' needs. Evidence of this can be found in the sensitivity displayed toward victims giving testimony, and the language and reparations awarded in judicial decisions. A number of judgments invoke international human rights instruments to uphold the legal rights and protection of victims and witnesses in court. It is noteworthy that internationally recognized best practices are often absent from judicial proceedings in many Western legal systems.

The legal reasoning underpinning these protections requires sophisticated training in a complex area of international human rights law. Moreover, it requires an intimate understanding of the hierarchies and sources of domestic and international law, and knowledge of the legal framework governing the prosecution of sexual offenses, neither of which is necessarily covered in formal legal curricula. The judge in the *Walungu* case cited the Congolese Constitution (which states that duly ratified treaties have a value superior to domestic laws) as a basis to invoke the Rome Statute.[58] This provision of the Constitution has been interpreted by many Congolese lawyers and judges to mean that Congolese courts must take up the *exact* definitions of war crimes and crimes against humanity and genocide, and respect the rights of victims and witnesses, as protected by the Rome Statute. The judge in the *Walungu* case thus upheld: "In view of the above listed texts, and the failures of the Military Penal Code, the Court will apply the Rome Statute of the ICC because, since its ratification, it forms an integral part of our national legal system. Yet this legal instrument [the Rome Statute] is more explicit in its

---

[58] Tribunal Militaire de Garnison de Bukavu. 2012. RP 708/12; RMP 1868/TBK/KMC/ 10-12. DR Congo. October 15, 2012: 29

definition of concepts, and is better suited [than our national laws] in that it provides clear mechanisms for the protection of victims' rights."[59]

In the absence of any formal or institutionalized training in international human rights law, where did Congolese judges inherit their detailed knowledge of the Rome Statute and its applicability in the Congolese legal system? And how did they become so well acquainted with the content of the 2006 Sexual Violence Law and the 2009 Law on the Protection of Children, whose provisions are cited in full in nearly every judgment? Evidence from South Africa suggests that, despite the passage of the 2007 Sexual Offences Act and accompanying legislative amendments, many legal practitioners still demonstrate limited knowledge of its content, particularly concerning the definition of rape and permissible questioning and treatment of victims and witnesses. Yet, compared to DR Congo, South Africa's infrastructure for disseminating new legal knowledge is far more institutionalized. What, then, leads to such strikingly different implementation of newly passed laws by Congolese and South African courts?

The answers to these questions can be found in part to the extraordinary determination of a number dedicated Congolese judges and lawyers, and in part to the extensive training offered to legal practitioners across the east. These were often pioneered by non-state legal capacity-building organizations and funded by global donors. Many lawyers, magistrates, and other legal practitioners participating in sexual violence cases were initially trained in workshops organized by domestic and international NGOs dedicated to combating impunity for sexual and gender-based violence through rule of law development. Those who attended sessions organized by NGOs or UN agencies received extensive training in human rights and international criminal law from leading domestic and international experts. Many lawyers, prosecutors, judges, magistrates, and even police officers attend multiple trainings over a period of years. Participants study the statutes and jurisprudence of the ICC, the International Criminal Tribunals for Rwanda and the former Yugoslavia, and other relevant national and regional courts. Trainers also familiarize participants with the Geneva Conventions, other international human rights treaties, and new legislation and legislative amendments. Participants receive extensive training, including in the form of roleplaying exercises, in how to apply international human rights instruments, as well as relevant provisions from the Congolese military and penal codes, in practice. Participants often receive stipends or per diems to attend these training courses to incentivize their attendance.

---

[59] Ibid.

In addition to intensive training courses, many NGOs have pioneered programs to ensure that hard copies of relevant Congolese laws are distributed among lawyers and magistrates. For example, an American Bar Association Rule of Law Initiative (ABA ROLI) project, which operates in partnership with local NGOs, has disseminated thousands of copies of the country's 2006 Sexual Violence Law across DR Congo's eastern provinces. The law is printed in both French and Swahili in a short, colorful booklet designed to be easily accessible for those with limited literacy or legal training. International and domestic NGOs also organize periodic workshops in which lawyers and magistrates discuss and practice the application of the 2006 Sexual Violence Law, as well as other relevant laws, in mock cases. Every single one of the lawyers, prosecutors, and judges I interviewed had participated in at least one of these trainings, and normally two to three. Many police in the provincial capitals, although very few that I encountered in rural locations, had attended similar. As a result, large numbers of Congolese practitioners have developed a sophisticated understanding of complex international legal principles pertaining to gender, and how they should be implemented according to evolving international best practices, at multiple stages of the legal process, from reporting to investigation and trial.

In a country such as DR Congo, with weak judicial infrastructure, high levels of corruption, and ongoing conflict, legislative reform would be meaningless if lawyers and judges lacked the knowledge or will to invoke new laws in their arguments and procedures. These types of training activities, initially pioneered and funded almost exclusively by organizations such as the United Nations Development Program, the UN Joint Human Rights Office (UNJHRO), the American Bar Association, REJUSCO, Open Society, USAID, Avocats Sans Frontières, and others, ensure that practitioners across the east are well acquainted with emerging human rights instruments and best practices. In addition, the Prosecution Support Cells (CAP) within the UN Joint Human Rights Office advise prosecutors on legal strategy for high profile prosecutions. While international organizations continue to offer legal advice, many Congolese lawyers, judges and magistrates have accumulated a level of expertise that rivals global experts.

The Mobile Court Program and External Coordination of Justice Sector Activities

Weak statehood in DR Congo has meant that a variety of domestic and international actors have assumed direct responsibility over activities that would normally fall to the sovereign government. The priorities of the justice sector have resultingly shifted toward activities emphasized by these stakeholders and their donors – namely, the prosecution of sexual and gender-based violence.[60]

The recognition of the Congolese state's need for urgent infrastructural assistance encapsulated in the UN Security Council resolutions, combined with DR Congo's consistent rankings at the bottom of development and state failure indices, has prompted development aid from a variety of major donors (including the EU and the Belgian, German, and British governments, among others). This aid has been pledged to support various aspects of state development, such as the implementation of the 2007 Action Plan. The scale of international intervention in tasks normally reserved for domestic governments (such as control over budgets and development of policy priorities), as well as the money poured into these enterprises, were justified and enabled by the formal and informal recognition of the institutional challenges faced by the Congolese state and justice system, and the fact that the Congolese state had consistently proved itself unable to manage and oversee the activities of its own justice sector.

International actors have thus directly intervened in the management of national budgets and the structuring of governmental priorities in ways that would be impossible if the state were stronger. Under the umbrella of the UN Mission, international funds have been earmarked in the national budget to pay salaries to justice sector personnel and to develop legal infrastructure at the provincial, district, and municipal levels. Moreover, international actors such as the European Commission have played critical roles in contributing to decisions about where specific funds are directed. For example, when MONUC established its Rule of Law Section it emphasized supporting the legislative and executive branches in coordinating strategic plans to build judicial capacity through legislation and judicial restructuring, as well as providing direct support and resources to courts themselves. The UN Joint Human Rights Office oversees the implementation of many country-wide strategies. Over the years, offices such as the Sexual Violence Unit; the Gender Affairs Section; the Women's Protection Advisors; and other gender representatives across the Mission, have worked to systematize aspects of the country's gender-based policy implementation and sexual violence response.

In addition to shaping national policy, therefore, international organizations have directly involved themselves in the work of prisons, police units, and courts, providing critical support to criminal investigations and

---

[60] See Donais (2009) and Zaum (2006) for a discussion of norms promoted by influential Western governments in post-conflict states.

trials. Without this financial and logistical support, the gender violence trials analyzed in this book would not exist.

As part of the justice sector reforms, for example, le Groupe Mixte de Réflexion sur la Réforme et la Réorganisation de la Police produced a 2006 report on the weaknesses and shortcomings of the PNC. The "Police de Proximité" initiative, supported by donors such as UNDP and DFID, was subsequently created to close the gap in trust between the police and the population, and resulted in parallel outreach and sensitization activities. In North Kivu, the reorganization led to the creation of a Special Police Unit for the Protection of Women and Children (PSPEF), and in South Kivu, the Police de la Protection de l'Enfant et Lutte Contre Violence Sexuelle (PELVS). The PSPEF is supported by a coalition of actors known as Ushindi (USAID, IMA World Health, the American Bar Association, Care International, Heal Africa, and Save the Children). Ushindi funded the building of a police station in Goma to house the special unit and provided resources such as computers, vehicles for conducting investigations, desks, and filing systems. Importantly, Ushindi also provided gender sensitivity training and logistical support to police officers and administrative personnel in collaboration with local partners. The project supported efforts to recruit women into the police force. Police officers are trained in international best practices with regard to collecting evidence in sensitive and complex gender violence cases, as well as taking testimony from vulnerable and traumatized individuals. As a result of its focused mandate, gender violence victims who report cases to PELVS or the PSPEF do not typically encounter the same hostility or accusatory questioning about their prior sexual conduct that is common outside of the Kivus, in rural areas, or in the police stations in Khayelitsha and Gugulethu. Because PELVS and the PSPEF works closely with the American Bar Association, Avocats Sans Frontières, and United Nations Development Program lawyers, these stakeholders monitor compliance with international standards and ensure that police meet their obligations under the gender-based legal reforms promoted in the capital. More generally, in 2006, the Ecole de Formation de la Police Judiciaire began rolling out trainings for police across the country, with support from MONUC, EUPOL, GIZ and other donors. Without these interventions, the work of the national police vis-à-vis gender violence reporting would likely look very different.

Another crucial component of legal capacity building that has proved central to the gender violence decisions analyzed has been the establishment of legal aid clinics providing free legal representation to victims of gender-based offenses. Legal aid clinics run by international organizations have often been accompanied by large outreach programs designed to encourage victims of violence to pursue legal avenues of redress. Many of these clinics are attached to medical facilities. After they receive medical attention, victims of sexual assault may be accompanied to the legal aid clinics by doctors and nurses. In these visits, lawyers and psychologists typically discuss the case with the victim and, if the victim wishes to move forward with legal proceedings, she or he is escorted to the police station by a lawyer to formally report the incident. All medical costs incurred by the victim associated with the case will typically be borne by the clinic for the duration of legal proceedings, and clinics play a crucial role in ensuring compliance with the law.

In addition to bringing cases into the criminal justice system, legal aid clinics will typically track cases of their clients through each stage of the legal process, ensuring that cases are not dropped or corrupted. One interviewee, Jani, explained how she ended up bringing a case to trial after she was raped by three men who broke into her house in Uvira, South Kivu:

When they left the house, we started crying and my neighbors came to help. Some others close by woke up and ran after the people who did this, and they caught one of them. He was immediately arrested and obliged to denounce the others ... When we arrived at the police station, there was somebody there working on sexual violence whose job was to monitor sexual violence cases at judicial institutions. His name was Allain and he was working for an NGO, monitoring all those cases of rape. He was there to see if a woman had been raped and to help her to access justice. Our neighbor knew that Allain always helped survivors to access justice so she told us about him. The case was transferred from the police to the court and eventually the perpetrators were sentenced to twenty years of jail.[61]

Clinics like those run by the American Bar Association will usually fund all costs associated with the case, including transportation for police officers to conduct interviews, collect evidence, or visit the crime scene; travel for all relevant parties to and from the courtroom (including defense counsel, the victim, prosecutors, etc.); and transportation to take the accused into custody. They will also check on the case periodically to make sure it is progressing.

With material and logistical assistance from MONUC and the European Commission, the Comité Mixte de la Justice, discussed in the previous chapter, played an important role in supporting a mobile justice initiative that has been critical to the fast-tracking of a number of sexual and gender-based violence cases. The mobile court program was introduced into law under Article 67 of the 1982 Code d'Organisation et de Competence Judiciaire, with the intention of "bringing the state's

---

[61] Interview. Jani, Civil Party. DR Congo. January 11, 2013.

presence to remote areas of the country."[62] The first mobile court initiative was commenced by NGO Avocats Sans Frontières (ASF) in 2003, and similar programs have since been undertaken by organizations including the American Bar Association Rule of Law Initiative (ABA ROLI), the United Nations Development Program, the UN Joint Human Rights Office, and others. Funding and logistical support is provided by the UN, the European Union, the Open Society Initiative, and various foreign governments through aid demarcated to develop infrastructure in fragile states and prevent the resurgence of conflict. Mobile courts work within both the military and civilian justice systems.

The mobile court programs have been critical to the production of gender violence decisions in eastern DR Congo, and especially to investigations into crimes committed by soldiers, police, military personnel, and rebel combatants. While prosecutors are free to embark on mobile hearings of their own accord, in reality mobile court activities heavily rely on coordination by a coalition of external stakeholders. In both the civilian and military justice systems, cases typically come to the attention of donors and NGOs through specialized police units or the NGO legal aid clinics. Impetus thus lies with the victim to initially report a case to the police, a medical professional, or an NGO in order to begin an investigation. However, for military cases that involve mass violence or international crimes, NGOs are most commonly alerted through their own networks: through personal contacts, rapid response units, partner NGOs in remote areas, or the United Nations Office for Humanitarian Affairs (UN-OCHA). When organizations involved in administering mobile courts (such as ABA ROLI) learn of such incidents, they work with Congolese justice authorities, MONUSCO, and other donors and organizations to provide a legal response. In both the civilian and military systems, mobile court programs work with relevant justice sector personnel to conduct preliminary investigations, issue charges, collect evidence, secure witnesses, and organize trials. NGOs involved in mobile courts processes will often provide psycho-social and medical support to affected victims and witnesses, and conduct outreach activities in the location the trials will take place.

Once arrests have been made and evidence collected, external actors assist in transplanting the relevant justice sector institutions and personnel from the provincial capitals to remote locations that have had little prior exposure to the formal justice sector. Legal representatives or outreach coordinators from domestic and international partner organizations

---

[62] DR Congo 1982. Ordonnance Loi No 82–020 portant code de l'organisation et de la compétence judiciaires. March 31, 1982

travel with Congolese jurists to the trial location ahead of time to publicize the court, explain its purpose and mandate, socialize local communities to the objectives of criminal justice, and compile evidence on behalf of the civil parties. NGOs, lawyers and UN agencies assist civilian or military jurists (depending on the nature of the crime) in identifying and detaining indictees, facilitating trial logistics, and recruiting witnesses. Once all witnesses and evidence have been procured, trials begin. Trials can last anywhere from one day to many weeks depending on the complexities of the alleged crimes. Congolese authorities retain exclusive jurisdiction over sentencing and enforcement. At the time of writing, NGOs and international organizations working on mobile court programs focused predominantly on sexual and gender-based crimes, which donors identified as core priorities for the justice system.

In one sense, the legal authority for the mobile courts derives from legislation introduced as part of the justice sector reforms described in the previous section. However, because the state has historically had only very limited reach over its provinces, in reality the courts function with little input from Kinshasa. Instead, the empirical realities of state fragility have meant that the mobile courts exist as partnerships between local Congolese jurists and foreign stakeholders, with non-state actors assisting in the coordination of court schedules, as well as with collecting evidence and performing other tasks that would normally fall under the jurisdiction of different arms of the state.

Mobile courts are not the only ways in which non-state actors influence legal proceedings. Due to DR Congo's civil law system, victims can file for damages as civil parties in criminal cases. A large number of NGOs are dedicated to supporting civil parties in such claims, including providing free legal representation and assisting the prosecution in collecting evidence. Given that NGO lawyers are sometimes funded and paid by international organizations like the American Bar Association, and often have specialized training in the 2006 Sexual Violence Law, such cases often disproportionately favor the prosecution. The mere presence of NGO lawyers participating in the case ensures a greater likelihood of victim-sensitive practices from all stakeholders. Moreover, the JHRO's Judicial Protection Unit offers protection to victims, witnesses and judicial officers involved in criminal trials, ensuring legal processes are compliant with the 2006 reforms. The Judicial Protection scheme assists victims and witnesses when they are called to testify, including facilitating infrastructure and technology such as screens and microphones, as well as protective clothing for witnesses to conceal their identities. Non-state actors will also provide protective transport and accommodation for witnesses participating in legal process.

Formal and informal recognition of DR Congo's weak statehood has underpinned the efforts of external actors to support and direct the work of local justice institutions. Under Resolution 1279, UN representatives are authorized to build infrastructure and provide technical assistance, providing a justification grounded in international law for intervention into matters normally restricted to the jurisdiction of the sovereign government. The mobile court initiative, as well as the training provided to Congolese legal practitioners and other interventions, such as the creation of PELVS and the PSPEF, provides a dramatic example of external actors "substituting" for the state in a context of weak empirical and juridical statehood. These activities have each served to divert judicial attention toward an issue the Congolese legal system previously neglected.

Due to the international resources devoted to justice sector reform in recent years, many courts across DR Congo's eastern provinces are better equipped than before to support victims and witnesses, investigate alleged crimes, and collect and assess evidence. The evidence herein demonstrates that legislative reform alone would have been insufficient to produce the kinds of decisions discussed earlier in this chapter. Instead, lawyers, prosecutors, police, judges, and magistrates have relied heavily on training, resources, support, and other incentives pioneered at the local level by non-state actors, in order to ensure sexual and gender-based violence cases are treated as serious criminal offenses.

Evidence from South Africa

Activities by NGOs, advocacy organizations, and human rights coalitions in South Africa have differed significantly from those carried out in DR Congo. Rather than directly intervening in training practitioners and coordinating justice sector activities, advocacy efforts in South Africa have largely been directed towards influencing national policy and discourse at the level of the central state. There is a strong perception among the human rights community that progress toward implementation of the 2007 legal reforms should come from the top down in order to be sustainable (a point discussed at length later in this chapter). Many NGOs believe that if enforcement and implementation efforts do not have the support of legislative and executive elites, they are unlikely to have lasting effects.

In eastern DR Congo, this chapter identified two core activities taken up by non-state actors that have strengthened the treatment of sexual and gender-based violence in the country's legal system: the provision of gender sensitivity training to legal practitioners, and coordination and material support provided to investigations and to the organization of criminal trials. In what follows, I explore the work of stakeholders engaged in similar activities in South Africa, identifying why their experiences with legal reform have been so different. Subsequently, I analyze other activities taken up by NGOs, civil society organizations, and state officials, to examine why their work has not resulted in the types of outcomes observed in DR Congo's eastern courts.

Legal Training

The majority of training for legal practitioners involved in sexual and gender-based violence cases in eastern DR Congo has been funded by international organizations and delivered by domestic and international law and gender experts. In South Africa, legal training is organized and coordinated by the Department of Justice through the Justice College.[63] Funded by the Department of Justice and Constitutional Development, the Justice College trains the vast majority of South Africa's justice sector employees, including state attorneys and support staff, family advocates, family counselors, legal aid professionals, legal advisors to the Department of Justice, clerks, legislative drafters, interpreters, registrars of high courts and appellate courts, traditional leaders, district court prosecutors, regional court prosecutors, chief prosecutors, and directors of public prosecution. Despite rising crime levels and extensive media coverage of South Africa's "rape crisis," priorities established by the Justice College, and training programs from 2013 to 2015, included no mention of gender violence or the Sexual Offences Act. The Justice College ran trainings in a category entitled "residential robberies, vehicle hijackings, business robberies, and other serious violent crimes".[64] Among the Justice College activities, this is the category that came closest to dealing with sexual offenses; however, in spite of widespread media attention to the issue, the training program falls short of making direct mention of rape or sexual assault. Interviewees confirmed that while certain isolated trainings had been organized in earlier years to familiarize practitioners with the 2007 Sexual Offences Act, the Justice College has not systematically incorporated gender-based crimes into its general curriculum. One magistrate who had worked with South Africa's Domestic Violence Act for four years was interviewed by a research team at the University of Cape Town. He described the limited training he received on the Domestic Violence Act:

---

[63] See Justice College of South Africa - www.justice.gov.za/juscol/index.htm for further information on the activities of the Justice College.

[64] Justice College of South Africa. 2016. www.justice.gov.za/juscol/index.htm.

What can I say about training? I was trained second-hand – by a colleague who went to Justice College to be trained specifically on the Act. After presiding over domestic violence cases for a few years, I have realized that the Act is open to wide interpretation and that I fundamentally disagree with my colleagues' approach to this Act. I can confidently state that whatever training took place was given to the wrong people, and that whoever did the training has never presided over a domestic violence case before, or has done little to understand the ins-and-outs of the Act. (Artz 2003)

With the exception of the Wynberg Sexual Offenses Court, none of my interviewees could recall dedicated training in the new law for judges or magistrates. Without specific training, it is unrealistic to expect legal personnel across the country to have the knowledge and legal tools needed to ensure adequate enforcement and implementation of legal reforms. Many legal practitioners who are not gender experts, therefore, especially outside of urban centers, have limited knowledge of the provisions of the 2007 Sexual Offences Act. This is particularly true for those trained before its passage.

On rare occasions, the Justice College recruits NGO representatives to participate in training magistrates in specialized areas such as gender or diversity as part of ongoing professional development activities. The Law, Race and Gender Research Unit (LRG) at the University of Cape Town has contributed most frequently to training of magistrates in national and regional workshops. In such sessions, instructors have drawn from international sources, instruments, debates, and best practices; however, these trainings and workshops have largely been restricted to definitional changes in the law itself. Moreover, trainings have been ad hoc. The majority of interviewees was unaware of any such trainings or any efforts to involve NGOs or other gender experts in professional development activities at any level. In 2012, the Department for Justice & Constitutional Development established the Ministerial Advisory Task Team on the Adjudication of Sexual Offences Matters (MATTSO). MATTSO has devoted a significant proportion of its time so far to coordinating the work of the sexual offences courts.

More importantly, after they assume their positions in the judiciary, judges receive very little continuing formal education. In 2008, the South African Judicial Training Institute was established by law to formalize what was perceived at the time to be much-needed continuing legal education for judges.[65] This law was passed with the motivation that most judges in South Africa had received their legal training before the advent of the new constitution, and thus were not well versed in

---

[65] South Africa 2008. Judicial Education Institute Act.

constitutional jurisprudence or laws passed in the postapartheid era. The main objectives of the South African Judicial Education Institute Act of 2008 were:

To establish a national education and training institution for the judiciary so as to enhance judicial accountability and the transformation of the judiciary, in order to promote the implementation of the values mentioned in Section 1 of the Constitution, and for that purpose to provide proper, appropriate and transformational judicial education and training, having due regard to both our inherited legacy and our new constitutional dispensation; and offer judicial education and training to aspiring and newly appointed judicial officers as well as continued training for experienced judicial officers.

By 2010, no South African judges had yet received any of the training legislated for under the new Act (De Vos 2010). Since 2010, training has been rare. Substantive focus has not touched on gender-based crimes, despite calls by advocacy organizations to do so. Many interviewees commented on the fact that South African judges are confident in their abilities and proud of their education and expertise, and thus do not see the need for further training. A 2010 news article captured a sentiment expressed by many interviewees:

Many South African judges are notoriously prickly about the need to undergo further judicial education. Despite the fact that Parliament passed the South African Judicial Education Institute Act in 2008, the Institute has not yet trained any judges or aspirant judges and it is unclear when it will start its work in earnest. (De Vos 2010)

Interviewees also mentioned that South African judges are proud of the democratic values enshrined within their constitution. The idea that South African judges, considered pioneers of human rights and democracy on the international stage, would need further training in human rights, from either Western or other African jurists, was found both preposterous and offensive. Reflecting on this sentiment, one practitioner lamented: "New laws pass in parliament, but then no one ever reads them again."[66] Similar issues were raised with regard to prosecutors. The National Prosecuting Authority organizes periodic trainings, but these are few and far between, and do not tend to focus on areas of legal reform (Center for Applied Legal Studies, Cornell Law School's Avon Global Center for Women and Justice, and International Human Rights Clinic 2014).

[66] Interview. Dale, Prosecutor. South Africa. March 12, 2013.

Coordinating Justice Sector Activities and Setting Judicial Priorities

Unlike in DR Congo, where sexual and gender-based violence investigations in the eastern provinces have largely been coordinated by a coalition of NGOs and international organizations, South Africa's justice system more closely resembles the justice systems of Western Europe. Rather than relying heavily on foreign aid, justice sector funding is allocated through the budgets of the Department of Justice and Constitutional Development or the Department of Home Affairs. The priorities and activities of these arms of government have been managed at a central level, and reflect the priorities of the democratically elected government rather than those of NGOs, foreign donors, and transnational advocacy networks.

In 1999, under immense pressure from the Western Cape sexual violence coalition and other civil society activists, the Department of Justice and Constitutional Development (DOJ&CA) established the Sexual Offenses and Community Affairs Unit (SOCA) under the National Prosecuting Authority. The SOCA was intended to improve conviction rates for sexual offenders. Following this, the DOJ&CA introduced sixty-seven specialized Sexual Offenses Courts throughout the country to focus on the unique challenges faced by victims of gender violence seeking formal legal remedy. The Sexual Offenses Courts were somewhat successful. While lawyers, magistrates, judges, and prosecutors never received specialized training as such, they were provided with some resources that allowed them to do their work more effectively: special waiting rooms and bathroom facilities for victims and their families, so that victims did not need to come face to face with their alleged perpetrator; separate cross-examination rooms that allowed children and vulnerable individuals to give testimony in private; and a lower caseload focused exclusively on gender-related issues, so that practitioners could develop expertise and so that sexual offenses were not systematically deprioritized by prosecutors in favor of "easier" cases. These courts, although geographically dispersed, were somewhat effective in improving accountability for sexual and gender-based violence. Compared with the approximately thirty percent conviction rate for sexual offense cases that make it to trial in the regular criminal justice system, by 2006, the specialized courts were recording conviction rates of more than eighty percent (Davis 2013; see also Sadan, Dikweni, and Cassiem 2001 for further discussion of the specialized courts).[67]

---

[67] Higher conviction rates do not necessarily equate to a higher quality of justice, and higher incarceration rates are certainly not always beneficial for reducing crime. However, given the accountability gap in the context of sexual and gender-based violence specifically, higher conviction rates in such cases signal that courts and law enforcement agencies

However, seven years later, almost all of these courts closed down or were stalled in their activities. Commentators have hotly debated the reasons for the closures. Many report budgetary constraints. The specialized courts are estimated to cost approximately R3,654,883 ($340,000 USD) each to establish and run for one year of existence (Gender Links 2015; South Africa Department of Justice and Constitutional Development 2016). Interviewees also cited magistrates' ongoing exposure to traumatic testimony as a key reason for why the courts were unsustainable.[68] However, in May 2005, just prior to the closure of the specialized courts, then Justice Minister Brigitte Mabandla noted that:

The fact that the sexual offenses courts were better resourced than other courts was a serious violation of the constitutional right of other victims of crimes to equal protection and benefit of the law. (Davis 2013)

This was a popular opinion. However, South Africa's political elite, as well as members of the ordinary public, also expressed the opinion that rape and sexual assault were private or family matters that should not be disproportionately privileged in the criminal justice system[69] As such, despite the pressing need for the types of specialized skills, equipment, and resources granted to the Sexual Offenses Courts to improve rape and sexual assault investigations, attention to these crimes in South Africa's regular courts has been consistently deprioritized. Lacking the entry points to influence the work of local courts directly, gender rights organizations have been ineffective at shaping legal practice in areas where NGOs, practitioners and other

were beginning to take sexual violence more seriously, and overcome some of the structural barriers to justice. See Smith (2018) for a discussion of societal responses to convictions and acquittals.

[68] Interview. Pieter, Judge. South Africa. March 15, 2013.

[69] In response to the domestic and international outrage at the brutal rape and murder of Anene Booysen, discussions to reestablish the Sexual Offenses Courts were reignited. Booysen's murder created a media storm, highlighting the plight of women and girls in South Africa. The attention to this particular case can most likely be attributed to the brutality of the assault and the graphic detail in which the press reported the case. Dr. Elizabeth De Kock, the doctor who attended to Booysen when she was brought into the hospital, said her injuries were the worst she had ever seen and that she could not have been saved due to the massive injuries sustained to her intestines. Dr. De Kock claimed that Booysen was "covered from head to toe in sand and blood and had bruises all over her body. A sharp object had been used to mutilate her genitalia and her intestines may have been pulled from her vagina by hand." See the report in the *International Business Times* at: www.ibtimes.co.uk/anene-booysen-rape-murder-trial-johannes-kana-514685. For more details on the reopening of the specialized courts, see the Department of Justice and Constitutional Developments report, "Report on the Re-establishment of Sexual Offenses Courts, Ministerial Advisory Task Team on the Adjudication of Sexual Offence Matters," at: www.justice.gov.za/reportfiles/other/2013-sxo-courts-report-aug2013.pdf (South Africa Department of Justice and Constitutional Development 2013).

non-state actors in eastern DR Congo succeeded. As a result, victims of violence in South Africa have been left with few avenues of recourse.

There have been some limited avenues through which NGOs and human rights groups have succeeded in exerting influence over criminal justice processes in ways that mirror the activities of groups in eastern DR Congo. However, rather than evidencing a general pattern, in South Africa, these activities have been carried out informally and on a small scale, with few resources and fewer formal institutionalized ties to criminal justice reform.

One centralized initiative that has contributed significantly to gender justice improvements in the Western Cape and elsewhere has been the Thuthuzela Care Centres, which somewhat resemble the activities undertaken by eastern DR Congo's legal aid clinics supported by the American Bar Association. Under pressure from the Working Group on Gender Violence discussed in Chapter 2, the National Prosecuting Authority took various steps to address widespread sexual and gender-based violence and bring national policy into line with the scale of the problem. In 1999, with funding from international donors, the Thuthuzela Care Centres became institutionalized, of which there were fifty-one across the country at the time this research was undertaken. The Thuthuzela Care Centres (*thuthuzela* means "comfort" in Xhosa) are one-stop facilities aimed at reducing secondary trauma for victims and improving reporting and conviction rates within the criminal justice system. The centers have been one of the government's core strategies to address rising levels of gender violence in the country, and have been one positive outcome of gender advocacy in this area.

The Thuthuzela project was initiated by the National Prosecuting Authority's SOCA, in partnership with a number of foreign and domestic donors. Key donors include PEPFAR, USAID, and UNICEF, among others. Donors and advocacy organizations had lobbied the National Prosecuting Authority with regard to the urgent need for an integrated strategy for "prevention, response and support" for rape victims.[70] The Thuthuzela Care Centres are usually attached to public hospitals in communities with high crime rates. At their inception, the centers were also linked to the Sexual Offenses Courts, so that prosecutors, social workers, investigating officers, magistrates, health professionals, and police could develop close working relationships in order to improve the overall experiences of victims traveling through the criminal justice process. However, since the Sexual Offenses Courts were rolled back, the

---

[70] See the website for the Thuthuzela Care Centres: www.npa.gov.za/UploadedFiles/ THUTHUZELA%20Brochure%20New.pdf.

centers have devoted most of their attention to primary care, victim support, and rehabilitation.

Due to logistical and budgetary constraints, over the years clinicians have devoted less attention to criminal trials. On arrival at the facility, victims receive medical care, crisis counseling, and detailed information on the criminal justice process and what would happen if he or she wished to report the case to the police. Thuthuzela employees, like the grassroots coalitions doing similar work, are the primary point of contact between the victim and the justice system, keeping him or her informed of any developments with regard to the case. Ruth, a program lawyer, noted that one area where NGOs and activists can make a considerable difference is in ensuring that crime scene evidence is not lost. Because police are often ineffective and poorly trained at collecting evidence in delicate sexual assault cases, civil society organizations can step in to fill this gap and ensure evidence is properly collected. But Ruth added: "This really isn't a long-term fix. Not only is it unsustainable, but if NGOs are doing it for them, it means that police will never be equipped to do their jobs properly."[71]

Unfortunately, in an inquiry by Justice Minister Jeff Radebe, in 2013 only thirty-five of the fifty-one centers were found to be functioning at full capacity. The centers remain notoriously underfunded, which compromises their ability to positively influence judicial processes for victims. Moreover, in his comments on the study, Minister Radebe refers to a critical need for counseling for rape survivors, neglecting to recognize the important role such centers play in providing just this (Radebe 2013).

Other organizations such as the Tshwaranang Legal Advocacy Centre to End Violence against Women (TLAC), the Shukumisa Campaign, and Rape Crisis were established in similar periods to support victims of gender violence and to lobby for more effective national policy. These organizations conduct research, engage in litigation and policy development, lobby government, raise public awareness, provide free legal support to victims of violence, educate citizens about their rights, and analyze existing policy. The impact of these organizations has been invaluable in certain discrete areas, and particularly in keeping up pressure on the national government. But ultimately the movement has been unable to contribute to much more than incremental and episodic change.

Other than pressure applied by activists and staff at the dedicated health clinics and one-stop shops, police and prosecutors face few incentives to devote any attention to rape and sexual violence cases. On this point, one interviewee stated: "Police will take seriously armed robbery at

---

[71] Interview. Ruth, Program Lawyer. South Africa. March 15, 2013.

Pick and Pay because they don't want investors to leave. But a rape case. They see that as a matter between families."[72] Finally, and in stark contrast to the incentives in eastern DR Congo, because police in Khayelitsha are notoriously overworked, it is widely acknowledged that they will look for any excuse to drop a case. If an accused offers the victim or her family financial compensation, the police see no further need to intervene. The same civil society activist added: "If there are any gangsters involved, the police don't want to touch the case. They are afraid."[73]

The sentiments Ruth expressed echo some of the sentiments and reflections of South African gender activists more broadly. NGOs and civil society coalitions in South Africa do not typically perceive their role as "substituting" for the state or filling in where it has failed. Instead, their work is directed toward holding the government to account for its actions. On this point, Ruth added: "civil society often struggles in its relationship with government. On the one hand, it wants to support the government in a collaborative way, but more often, it wants to hold the government to account."[74] This is a fundamentally different form of gender advocacy. NGOs in South Africa have consequently been hesitant to fill the gaps left by the state's failures; a point reiterated again and again was that the solution to South Africa's "rape crisis" needed to be state-led. Even with sufficient funding and access, most interviewees saw little possibility – or value – in non-state actors "taking over" criminal prosecutions in the way that similarly situated actors have done in eastern DR Congo.

As such, the vast majority of gender advocacy in South Africa has been geared toward influencing state policy and practice. Activists have adopted different strategies at different moments in history, sometimes entering into an adversarial and oppositional relationship with the state, and on other occasions, pursuing cooperation and behind-the-scenes persuasion. After the failed 2003 Sexual Assault Bill, a number of leading members of the coalition grew so frustrated with the government's hostility toward new legislation that their tactics changed entirely, to focus on monitoring and exposing the government's lack of progress. Consequently, many members with strong connections to key legislative figures left the coalition, and its ability to influence the content of legislation through "backstage" politics was curtailed, forcing coalition members to adopt even more adversarial approaches and further alienate political elites (Hodes 2011: 14). This led to a backlash from politicians,

---

[72] Interview. Dyoli, Community Activist. South Africa, March 6, 2013.
[73] Ibid.
[74] Interview. Ruth, Program Lawyer. South Africa. March 15, 2013.

who began to engage in efforts to discredit, rather than appease, gender advocates.

There has also been criticism of the movement on the grounds that its key weakness remains that it was largely perceived as a coalition of white, middle-class, urban elites. Many interviewees pointed out that greater diversity within the coalition, and greater sensitivity toward the racial and socioeconomic disparities that influenced whose voices were heard, would have expanded the movement's profile and public support base. A greater sensitivity to racial politics may, in turn, have allowed activists greater access to and influence over the work of local justice institutions. Because the movement consistently failed over time to establish a strong regional support base, its activities were, by design, restricted to lobbying national elites in urban centers. Some politicians, frustrated at adversarial tactics employed by the Western Cape coalition and other urban feminist elites, were effective in invoking anticolonial rhetoric to discredit the movement's work. As a result, its ability to affect change in local courts waned significantly as it lost legitimacy in the eyes of key political stakeholders.

Conclusion

The fact that activists and NGOs have not been able to influence the treatment of gender violence by courts and police in South Africa in the ways their counterparts have in eastern DR Congo can be attributed to the fact that the South African state has both the resources and the capacity to oversee the activities of its own justice sector. Confronted with apathy and disinterest from political elites, South African activists have limited recourse. While gender advocates have made notable attempts to provide services and support local justice processes, their main entry point to the legal system has been through the central state, leaving them beholden to the whims and priorities of politicians. Rather than assuming direct responsibility over criminal trials, legal curriculums, or judicial budgets, as have non-state actors in eastern DR Congo, gender activists in South Africa have channeled their efforts towards influencing national policy.

This advocacy has prompted incremental change. However, given that legislative and executive elites have shown only minimal interest in engaging with the issue of gender violence, NGO pressure has resulted in little more than token gestures in the form of speeches, laws, and policies that have never been fully implemented. The creation of the Sexual Offenses Courts and the Thuthuzela Care Centres constituted important victories. Yet the state has failed to commit resources toward these institutions' effective functioning on a sustained basis. As a result, many Sexual Offenses Courts were abandoned, and the Thuthuzela Care Centres remain underfunded, leaving them impotent, and their fates uncertain.

Underscoring the dramatic contrast between the two cases, the opportunities created by state fragility and, importantly, the UN Mission in DR Congo have enabled human rights NGOs and other non-state actors to exert direct influence over criminal trials, legal training, establishing judicial priorities, and other critical activities. The work of these non-state actors has culminated directly in the gender-progressive rulings we observe. Further, the decision by global donors to prioritize gender justice has allowed for victims' rights to be foregrounded and institutionalized in criminal justice processes.

The following chapter turns to a discussion of the ways in which victims of violence – as well as the local communities in which they are embedded – have responded to NGO-led legal outreach and advocacy. It explores and documents how and why victims involved in legal processes in eastern DR Congo have been motivated to turn to the law to redress their grievances, whereas the hostility encountered by many victims of violence in South Africa has discouraged them from pursuing legal remedy.

5   Ordinary Women in Court
Socialization and Outreach from the Ground Up

Fez, seventeen years old, Kibari, North Kivu, January 11, 2012:

It was in 2010 and I was fifteen years old. One day, after I came back from school, I decided to join some others at the farm so we could get some food to eat in the afternoon. I was alone. On the way I met some soldiers ... They asked me where I was going, so I told them that I was going to meet my uncle ... They took me and put me on a mango tree and tied me there. When I started to cry, another one held my mouth. Their intention was to kill me, but after a short discussion they decided just to rape me so they started opening my legs. They kept me glued to the mango tree while they did it ... I was rescued by a neighbor [who] took me to the hospital and to the Mai Mai chief [who controlled the local area]. The Mai Mai weren't happy with what had happened. The Mai Mai commander went with my uncle to the [FARDC] commander to ask if he could do something to the soldiers who raped me. There was a long discussion and the commander was obliged to give the two soldiers who did this over to the Mai Mai. The soldiers were sent to Munzenze [prison]. They started an audience [hearing] with the parquet at the TGI [Tribunal de Grande Instance] ... Due to the M23 occupation of Goma, the soldiers who raped me escaped and there was no way to continue the trial. Their commander was also bringing money to the court, while we had empty hands. I believe the commander was corrupting the judges so the process wouldn't go through. I was expecting compensation, especially for medical treatment. It would have been good for me if the ones who did this stayed in the prison so they wouldn't do this to anyone else ... That is the most important for me. [1]

Introduction

Despite the many and varied challenges facing victims of sexual and gender-based violence in eastern DR Congo, increasing numbers of victims of violence are turning to formal legal processes to resolve sexual and gender-based grievances. Why would women in Fez's position turn to institutions of the state in moments of crisis when the legal system is notoriously corrupt, when they have little prior experience of doing so, and when the state has so consistently failed to provide even the most basic goods and services to its citizens?

---

[1] Edited, transcribed, and translated from Fez's interview testimony on January 11, 2012. DR Congo.

152

Understanding how vulnerable individuals come to see their struggles as legal violations has been a critical question for those interested in building the rule of law (Merry 2003b). Without victims and witnesses willing to report crimes, provide testimony, and generally participate in legal processes, none of the trials described in the previous chapters would have been possible. Many human rights movements, as well as organizations and institutions concerned with building legal infrastructures in weak state contexts, thus depend on buy-in and participation from those most affected by violence. To understand why legal capacity building and access to justice initiatives are successful or unsuccessful, it is critical to understand how communities come to utilize the legal processes available to them.

This chapter, therefore, explores the barriers and motivations to justice facing victims of violence in South Africa's Western Cape and DR Congo's eastern provinces, respectively. Primarily, it explores how and why women and girls in eastern DR Congo have begun to turn to the law in the aftermath of violence in increasing numbers, and why they might select formal legal mechanisms to resolve gender-based grievances that have historically been stigmatized. While men and boys are also victims of sexual and gender-based violence in both contexts, this chapter focuses predominantly on opportunities available to women and girls. Men and boys in both countries face different challenges, many of which are beyond the scope of this study.

This chapter further examines the role that rights-based outreach and socialization has played in both contexts. Beginning with the Congolese case, I present some background on the history of dispute resolution concerning sexual and gender-based violence. I move on to document the work carried out by legal aid and outreach initiatives in eastern DR Congo from the perspectives of potential claimants, analyzing how victims of violence conceptualize the range of options available to them. This chapter shows that NGOs in North and South Kivu have transformed the landscape of dispute resolution for many victims of violence, providing individuals new entry points and opportunities to access the formal justice system, as well as a number of material incentives to do so. It should be noted that, despite these efforts, many victims of violence in eastern DR Congo continue to find themselves unable to access legal aid, either because they are out of the geographical reach of access to justice programs, or because they remain uninformed or otherwise unable to access NGO support. This chapter compares outreach and advocacy work in eastern DR Congo with similar programs in South Africa's Western Cape. Although grassroots movements, as well as state-based clinics and one-stop shops, have been set up to support South African victims of gender-based violence, very few comparable opportunities exist to seek formal legal justice.

Governance and Dispute Resolution in Eastern DR Congo: Constructing the Boundaries of Illegal Violence

Options available to women and girls affected by gender-based violence in parts of the Kivus have changed significantly over the past decade. During the colonial era, Belgian authorities, missionaries, and other European actors introduced various initiatives to shape and define the boundaries of legitimate violence. These efforts frequently met limited successes. While missionaries, or organizations such as the Ligue pour la Protection de l'Enfance Noire, succeeded in influencing certain practices (from breast-feeding to postnatal sexual relationships, Hunt 1988), until very recently, formal changes to the law rarely had a decisive impact on the ways in which Congolese women assessed the options available to them in the aftermath of violence. Throughout the colonial and early postcolonial eras, most gender-related issues continued to be resolved within the family or through local chiefs or customary institutions. Victims of gen-der-based violence found few practical avenues through which to seek assistance, remedy, or recognition outside of their familial or kinship structures.

Colonial and Precolonial Governance

Any form of sexualized violence within marriage has historically been considered a private matter that should be dealt with in the home, usually at the discretion of the (male) head of the household. When families faced extreme instances of violence that could not be resolved in the home, they may have sought support and advice from the village chief (the *mwami,* or the *chef du village*), or from a local council of elders (the *baraza* or *conseil des sages*). These local authorities advised families and individuals on resolving disputes both within and outside of the family, as well as on issues of violent rape or assault, perpetrated inside or outside of marriage.

Under colonial rule, Belgian administrators formalized existing struc-tures of governance and introduced a centralized bureaucracy to facilitate communication between the administrative capital and the periphery. In the early colonial period, Congo's four (later six) provinces were divided into a number of districts and territories. Each territory was managed by a single administrator and divided into numerous *chefferies,* some of whose boundaries are still intact today. Each *chefferie* was managed by a *chef coutumier* (customary chief), who was assisted by his *chefs du villages* (village chiefs, referred to locally as the *mwami*). According to colonial law, the *mwami* and the *chef coutumier* reported directly to the colonial administrator and his assistants. However, these figures also continued to report to their traditional hierarchies, overseen by the head *mwami* – the highest traditional authority of a given collectivity in the country. This hierarchical structure was paralleled in urban areas where, instead of a *chef de village*, a *chef de quartier* was designated responsibility for a certain neighborhood. The *chef de quartier* reported to the *bourgmestre* and finally to the *maire de la ville* (the town mayor).[2]

This formalization and bureaucratization of existing hierarchies allowed colonial authorities some degree of oversight over village activity, as well as over how disputes were governed at a local level. Additionally, new reporting structures meant – theoretically, at least – that the colonial administration could promote new law and policy through its locally appointed representatives.[3]

Although customary practices regarding the governance of familial and sexual relationships remained largely intact throughout the colonial period, in 1926, a dual legal system was formally established. It comprised a European-style justice system presided over by European judges, and parallel *tribunaux indigènes* (customary or indigenous courts), presided over by the *chefs coutumiers*. Prior to that, most laws were imported directly from Belgium (Belgian Congo 1954).

Throughout the 1920s and 1930s, colonial administrators issued a number of decrees outlining the jurisdiction of the courts. These decrees were formalized in 1934 into a legal code, specifying that most serious criminal matters – and any civil matter involving European parties – would be governed by the *tribunaux européens*. Any civil matter, or minor criminal matters involving Congolese subjects, would fall under the competence of the *tribunaux indigènes*. For any criminal offense likely

---

[2] See Dembour (2000) for a detailed discussion of colonial administration in the Belgian Congo. See Mamdani (1996, 2001) and Spear (2003) for a discussion of the creation and instrumentalization of the "traditional" or the "customary" by colonial authorities across Africa more generally. My discussion of the organization of the legal system draws from original colonial-era legal codes (Belgian Congo 1954). My discussion of customary authorities derives from a combination of secondary sources and qualitative interviews in the field. Throughout this chapter, I draw from the historical memories of interlocutors from North and South Kivu to illustrate the practices and customs governing norms of appropriate behavior following incidents of gender-based violence. These reflections are not intended to offer a comprehensive history of colonial-era dispute resolution, but are simply intended to illuminate the perceived distinctions between the customs of the past and recent legal innovations.

[3] See Chanock (1985), Mamdani (1996), Massoud (2013), and Merry (2003a) for discussions of this practice in other contexts.

to warrant a sentence longer than one month, a case would be transferred from the *tribunal indigène* to a *tribunal européen*. Thus, rather than relying on conventional distinctions between formal/customary, or civil/criminal, the courts were established with broad competence over a range of *contestations* (disputes), incorporating both civil and criminal law (Dembour 2000).[4]

The *tribunaux indigènes* were organized into four tiers of authority: the *tribunal de territoire, tribunal de chefferie, tribunal de secteur/collectivité*, and *tribunal de centre (zone urbaine et rurale)*.[5] These tiers corresponded to the respective levels of traditional administration – the territory, the chiefdom, the sector, and the town/village. While under the general authority of the *chef coutumier*, the courts were comprised of panels of *assesseurs indigènes* (customary judges) responsible for deciding individual cases. These *assesseurs indigènes* were usually chosen from the existing *conseil des sages*, affording them formal legitimacy in the eyes of their colonizers by virtue of having been "selected" by the Belgians, while retaining the local authority they derived from their existing roles. While the *tribunaux indigènes* were granted formal authority over all familial disputes involving Congolese subjects (including issues of gender violence), in practice most disputes of this nature were informally resolved at the village or family level without ever going to a tribunal.

Defining Illegitimate Violence

In addition to the establishment of formal hierarchies of governance, various other colonial-era institutions and associations, including those affiliated with the Catholic Church, sought to regulate aspects of family life, intervening in the governance of sexual relationships in particular. Belgian administrators introduced new laws concerning marriage, sexual relations, consent, and other aspects of family life that had previously been left to custom. The first civil code of the Belgian Congo in 1885 fixed the minimum age of marriage for girls at twelve years old. Touro (2013: 39) discusses how discourses of civilization, morality, and "proper" conduct shaped processes of legal reforms, documenting the medicalized language used to justify far-reaching interventions into sexual relationships. Amidst the barbaric violence of the colonial regime (Dunn 2003; Ewans 2002; Mertens 2016; Nzongola-Ntalaja 2002), missionaries were also eager to promote European norms and patterns of behavior, which

[4] After independence, the dual legal system was abolished and amalgamated into one court system. The *chefs coutumiers* retain informal authority over a number of civil matters.
[5] See Dembour (2000) and Kamwimbi et al. (2008) for descriptions of customary justice in colonial and precolonial DR Congo.

their advocates presumed were superior to local practices. While inter-ventions by the Catholic Church and other European missions certainly influenced the evolution of particular social and cultural norms, custom-ary authorities retained almost exclusive jurisdiction over family law and gender violence from the perspective of both local communities and colonial officials.

Throughout the colonial era, the dissolution of marital relationships or family units remained fairly uncommon. Many interviewees, reflecting on the traditions of the past, noted that problems between a husband and wife should be solved together in the home.[6] If an agreeable resolution could not be reached at home, the couple could decide together to visit the *mwami*. Only in extreme cases of abuse, adultery, wrongdoing, or neglect would a woman have left her partner to return to her parents. Fatuma and her husband, Leonard, an elderly couple from South Kivu, explained how this worked in their memories of the colonial era and beyond:

The *mwami* knows everyone in his village, and everyone knows him. Anyone can go to talk with him – man or woman. There are people working below him, so when you go to him you bring your concerns to these people. They then inform the *mwami*. The *mwami* will call the involved parties back at a later date to discuss the problem. [For married couples] there are problems to bring to him, and problems to resolve at home. First, a couple must agree that their problem cannot be resolved between the two of them – they must agree together to seek the *mwami*'s help. Both parties have to be willing to seek his counsel; one cannot run out on the other to report a wrongdoing or crime. The *mwami* cannot change a person's character; some people have bad characters that the *mwami* cannot fix – he cannot force someone to listen to him. Therefore, the husband and wife have to agree that they have a problem that is too much for them to resolve alone. [They must decide that] they want to seek the *mwami*'s counsel, and are willing to listen to his teachings and work to change their actions. If there is a problem in marriage that can't be resolved alone, the first step is to go to a couple's parents. If that doesn't work, the *mwami*. Then the *chef de groupement, chef de localité*, and *chef de zone*. If a husband who is beating a wife refuses to admit there is a problem or refuses to seek help from the *mwami*, then the woman would just leave him and return to her parents. However, most likely she will be met with resistance by her parents, who would tell her that they already sold her. She must go back to her *bwana*, otherwise they have to return the money. But, if she returns home to parents with physical wounds from her husband's beatings, they will probably take the issue to the *baraza* themselves – the *mwami* could advise them what to do

---

[6] Sally Merry (2002) discusses how courts in colonial Hawai'i shifted from their initial efforts to preserve the sanctity of the family unit by encouraging the peaceful resolution of disputes within marriages, to adopting a protectionist and "rights-oriented" stance toward women in abusive relationships.

to make the separation more acceptable in the village, or help negotiate so they don't have to return the *dôte* [dowry] to his family.[7]

As Leonard and Fatuma described, in most such cases, dispute resolution processes remained predominantly male-led. For cases of domestic violence, for example, if a woman decided to seek help, she would go first to her parents and, if they agreed, they would go to the *mwami* and negotiate with the husband and his family on her behalf. The family would follow a similar process in cases of rape. If a married woman was raped, she may have kept it hidden for fear of being rejected by her husband or family. However, if she was unable to keep the secret, she would report the crime either to her parents or to her husband. Fatuma added:

The husband would confront the other man and fine him a goat. He had to pay. If things couldn't be resolved this way, the man could be imprisoned. Another solution is, if the man and woman were not married, he could marry her.

Some interviewees mentioned that in cases involving female adultery, which many understood to include instances where a woman was raped by a man other than her husband, a married man was permitted to take another wife. Nevertheless, the first wife would remain living with him as his property.[8] Others told me that the husband could leave his wife if she "cheats," which again included an act of rape, or her husband could simply make the offender compensate through payment in the form of a goat, for example. Alternatively, the offender and the husband or father of the victim might come together over *bugali ya muhogo* – a type of cassava soup shared between the two men in an act of reconciliation. If a couple was unsure of how to proceed in such circumstances, cases of rape or adultery could be taken to the *mwami*, who would provide guidance on the specific laws and practices of that culture. Only if the disagreement escalated considerably would any party think to turn to the *tribunaux*.

In 1940, the colonial administration introduced a formal distinction between criminal law and civil law with the creation of the Code Pénal Congolais. The criminal code explicitly defined rape as a criminal offense for the first time.[9] However, while jurisdiction over the criminal code fell

---

[7] Interview with Leonard and Fatuma, DR Congo. Conducted and translated by Julie Norman in the United States, February 12, 2013.

[8] Interview. Jean-Luc, NGO Director, DR Congo. October 17, 2013. This idea was grounded in the custom that, if a woman had been unfaithful to her husband, then he was permitted to take another wife. If a woman was raped by a man other than her husband, this would also be considered adultery and the husband would, therefore, also be permitted to take another wife.

[9] The 1940 Criminal Code criminalized indecent assault and established rape as a criminal offense punishable by five to twenty years in prison. See Articles 167–171 (Code Pénal Congolais, Décret du 30 janvier 1940).

to the *tribunaux européens*, most interviewees agreed that, despite the explicit criminalization of rape in 1940, any form of sexualized violence involving Congolese rather than European subjects was unlikely to be heard by the *tribunaux européens*. While there were some exceptions, most sexual crimes committed against Congolese women and girls continued to be considered by colonial authorities as "tribal" matters that must be informally resolved or dealt with through customary mechanisms, not by courts of law.

Governing the Family in an Independent Zaire

Deference to customary authorities on a variety of gender issues continued long into the postcolonial period, despite additional legislative changes. Belgium granted independence to the Congo on June 30, 1960. After a brief period of democratic rule under the presidency of Joseph Kasavubu, Colonel Mobutu Sese Seko seized power in a military coup in 1965. The dual legal system remained intact until 1958, when an ordinance subsumed custom into national law and created the *tribunaux de paix*. In the new court structure, professional magistrates replaced customary authorities in local courts (Dembour 2000; Kamwimbi et al. 2008).

The Criminal Code of 1940 remained largely intact following independence, with just a few legislative amendments. In 1972, Mobutu introduced the Code Pénal Militaire (Military Penal Code), and in 1987, the Code Zaïrois de la Famille (Zaire Family Code, now simply called the Code de la Famille). The Code de la Famille established the legal framework governing familial relationships in a single comprehensive document, formalizing state regulation over issues pertaining to marriage, separation, and divorce for the first time.[10] At the time of my research, the 1987 Code de la Famille remained the principal instrument governing family law in DR Congo. The Code de la Famille made it legal for either a man or a woman to seek a divorce (Art. 549) and formalized the practice of bridewealth (*dôte*). The Code also introduced certain new protections for women, strictly prohibiting marriage for women and girls under the age of fifteen (Article 419), outlawing polygamy (Art. 354 and 411), and stipulating that a marriage entered into without the full consent of both parties should be considered void by law (Art. 402).

[10] DR Congo 1987. See Ilunga (1974) and Pauwels (1970, 1973) for a discussion of its content. The new Family Code was introduced in 2015, after the research for this book concluded.

On the question of divorce, the Family Code affirmed that a woman
was entitled to pursue a divorce against her husband through the courts
without first seeking his permission (Art. 451). However, the process to
obtain a divorce is fairly complex and the law outlines a series of conditions that must be met to ensure grounds for separation. The law confirmed that a divorce granted by customary officials was not legally
binding (Art. 547). The divorce process begins with a hearing led by the
president of the *tribunal de paix* in an effort to reconcile the two parties.
Only if this fails will the court grant permission to initiate divorce proceedings. Interestingly, the Family Code was fairly thorough in its treatment of the management of finances within a household during and after
the dissolution of marriage, recognizing some gender balance by requiring men and women to contribute to the financial well-being of the family
according to his or her ability and status (Art. 447).

In the case of a divorce, the law states that the question of whether the
dôte must be returned to the husband's family should be decided according to the custom of both families (Art. 579).[11] The Code explicitly
affirmed that customary law is legally binding on such questions (Articles
361–369), noting that if there is a conflict in customs between two
families, the custom of the bride's family shall apply. On other issues,
the law simply states that cases must be decided by justices of the peace,
but offers little substantive guidance on how they should rule.

In reality, however, the protections and innovations afforded to women
through various legal reforms were rarely available in practice. Despite
a legal right to divorce, in practice women were unable to seek the support
of the law except in cases of extreme abuse (Badibanga 1980; Mianda
1995). Furthermore, the law outlines a series of conditions that must be
met to ensure grounds for separation, and courts have historically applied
these conditions more conservatively when a woman initiates the divorce.
Legal sanctions, including jail time, may be imposed if either party has
broken the law on marriage, including committing adultery or otherwise
violating the provisions of the Family Code (Art. 458–472).

The obstacles for women using the Family Code in court are reinforced
by a series of contradictory provisions within the law. These challenges
are further exacerbated when women are granted new rights under international law, such as the protections afforded by instruments such as DR

---

[11] "Le remboursement de la dôte se fera conformément à la coutume des parties; toutefois,
le mari peut toujours renoncer à demander le remboursement de la dote". Where the
customs are in conflict, the law privileges the traditions of the wife's family (La
célébration du mariage en famille se déroule conformément aux coutumes des parties
pour autant que ces coutumes soient conformes à l'ordre public. En cas de conflit des
coutumes, la coutume de la femme sera d'application, Art. 369).

Congo's ratification of the Convention on the Elimination of All Forms of Discrimination against Women (CEDAW), many of whose provisions clash with the law at home. Most significantly, Article 448 of the Family Code stipulated that married women could not engage in judicial activity without the consent of their husbands.[12] Since there was little socio-cultural support for women acting independently of their husbands, very few women had the opportunity to take advantage of the limited legal protections that were afforded to them. This tension between law and practice has led Mianda (1995: 52) to refer to the reforms of this era as "the illusion of emancipation," which, she argues, only led to the further deterioration of the status and rights of women in public life. Other contradictions also persisted. Until 2016, the Code permitted women to marry at age fifteen, yet the 2006 Law on Sexual Violence clearly states that sexual intercourse involving women or girls under the age of eighteen constitutes statutory rape. This introduced confusion for some practitioners as to whether sex with a minor within a marital relationship was a criminal offense.[13]

Reforms to the Family Code in 2016 redressed some of these contradictions, for example, by removing the need for marital consent to engage in legal action and establishing the need to consider injury to both parties in cases of adultery (DR Congo 2016). However, since these reforms were not enacted until 2016, the contradictions and inconsistencies discussed herein persisted throughout the period of my research.

No form of sexualized violence was mentioned in the 1987 Family Code, because sexual violence was not considered a family matter, but a criminal matter that should be dealt with by a criminal court. Yet, given that rape and partner violence were historically resolved within traditional familial structures, its absence in the Family Code left many with the impression that it fell outside the purview of national law, and that marital rape was an issue on which the legal system continued to defer to local custom. Other aspects of the family law reinforced the idea

---

[12] Art. 448 of the Family Code (1987) reads: "La femme doit obtenir l'autorisation de son mari pour tous les actes juridiques dans lesquels elle s'oblige à une prestation qu'elle doit effectuer en personne." The Labor Code of 1962 further states that, while women can seek employment, employers must seek the authorization of their husbands before commencing the employment (Mianda 1995).

[13] "Est puni des peines prévues à l'article 395 alinéa 1er de la présente loi, l'officier de l'état civil qui aura célébré ou enregistré le mariage d'un homme et d'une femme âgés de moins de dix-huit ans s'il connaissait ou devait connaître cette circonstance. Sont également punis des mêmes peines, le conjoint majeur du mineur, les personnes qui auront consenti au mariage des mineurs et celles qui en auront été les témoins" (Art. 407: Loi n° 16/008 du 15 juillet 2016 modifient et complètent la Loi n°87–010 du 1er août 1987 portant Code de la Famille.)

that customary authorities remained the appropriate arbiters of gender-related disputes.

Deference to local and customary authorities was characteristic of Mobutu's general approach to government, which tended toward allowing the provinces to take care of themselves. Mobutu intentionally left his country's institutions severely lacking in funds or basic infrastructure. His tenure was characterized by the popular phrase *débrouillez-vous*, which roughly translates as "fend for yourselves." This phrase is widely referred to in DR Congo as the "fifteenth article" of the country's constitution, under which, citizens are effectively expected to govern their own affairs.[14]

Following Mobutu's overthrow in the First Congo War of 1996, his successor, Laurent Désiré Kabila, implemented a number of reforms that dramatically diverged from the hands-off approach of the Mobutu government. Among Kabila's reforms was the introduction of the *nyumbakumi*, or the "representative in charge of ten houses," which was an institution imported from Tanzania's *ujamaa* that intended to bring the administration of governance closer to the people. Somewhat reminiscent of Belgian policy, the *nyumbakumi*, responsible for the affairs and security of ten houses, must report any activity, movement, or conflict within the ten houses to his superior and register any guests who arrive or leave. The *nyumbakumi* reports to the *chef du village* or the *chef du quartier* and, in some locales, has served as the first port of call for victims of gender-based violence.

In 1997, Laurent Kabila created the Commission de Pacification et de Concorde (CPC), which established "peace cells" in each region. In the context of the war, this was part of a government-wide effort aimed at resolving interethnic disputes before they became violent. The peace cells were comprised of important local elites working at the grassroots level. Much like the *conseil des sages* of earlier periods, leaders of different ethnic groups and parties to land disputes would meet in an effort to reach mutually agreeable resolutions to local conflicts (Clark 2008; Tull 2005). While the CPC was a government-run initiative, it inspired the revival of a number of traditional justice mechanisms, the most successful of which has been the *Baraza Inter-Communautaire*.

---

[14] See Vlassenroot and Raeymaekers (2004: 170) for an excellent discussion of this philosophy. They write: "The Mobutu regime was characterized by a double nature: on the one hand the state arrogated to itself the monopoly of violence, exerting it fiercely in every situation where its authority was threatened; on the other hand, the citizen was totally neglected and left to the mercy of the overbearing action of soldiers and state bureaucratic parasitic apparatus. In such a context ... a social behavior, commonly shared, asserted itself; a behavior perfectly summarized by the formula of Art. 15: *débrouillez-vous*."

Reintroduced in roughly the same period, *baraza*, meaning "meeting place" in Swahili, was revived in the 1990s to resolve interethnic conflict and other disputes within the community. The reintroduction of *baraza* has been both a top-down and a bottom-up initiative, supported by the government, NGOs, and local communities, and it has taken on different forms in different locations. In some locations in North Kivu, *Baraza Inter-Communautaire* builds directly on the structure of the CPC, although its proponents always describe it as nonpartisan and independent of the government (Clark 2008). In other areas, community justice prevails more informally under the *mwami* or village chief. Still others use colonial-era terms such as *bureau de mediation* to refer to new local offices that NGOs have built to house customary authorities and encourage traditional mediation.

The *Baraza Inter-Communautaire* and its parallel initiatives offer a forum for mediators to listen to the stories of disputants and seek mutually agreeable solutions. Although it works differently in different villages, if the *baraza* is unable to reach an agreement between the two parties, the dispute can be referred to the *arbre de paix* and finally to the *cour de paix* (distinct from the *tribunaux de paix* that forms part of the formal justice system). There, another group of mediators hears both sides and issues a binding decision. At the final stage, the *cour de paix*, the community is invited to agree or disagree with the arbitrators' decision and engages in a public display of reconciliation between the victim, the aggressor, and the community (Dunn 2013).

Where cases involving sexual violence have been brought to the *baraza*, they have traditionally been addressed through compensation – cash or livestock paid to the victim's family – regardless of the law's prohibition. This type of compensation is referred to colloquially as an *arrangement à l'amiable* (amicable arrangement or settlement). While the law is clear that customary divorce is not legally binding, the *baraza* may permit a woman who seeks a separation from a violent husband to leave after the return of the *dôte* to the husband's family. One interviewee noted that the man can demand the return of the *dôte* even if he is the one leaving his wife.[15] The result is that local justice mechanisms have tended to look to the traditions of the past to resolve disputes despite the introduction of new laws. Victims of violence remained largely unaware that courts could offer them legal protections until fairly recently.

Without training, resources, or clear substantive guidance on either the content or practical implementation of legislative reform, therefore, local customs and the legacies of colonial bureaucracy have tended to prevail

[15] Interview. Leonard. DR Congo. February 12, 2014.

on many matters, even when local custom contradicts newly introduced legal frameworks. However, more recently, judges have more readily seized on changes to the law to implement gender-sensitive provisions in local courts. Interestingly, contradictions in the law have enabled judges to more readily invoke international instruments to uphold rights where Congolese law is weak or unclear.

NGOs as Mediators: Connecting Victims to the Law

While prior legal reforms provided victims of gender violence with only limited opportunity to have crimes committed against them formally recognized, NGO advocacy in recent years has supported victims of gender violence in participating in being able to access new opportunities and participate in legal processes. Following extensive human rights outreach, education, and sensitization, victims of gendered harms have increasingly turned to the language of punitive justice to reject preexisting practices they found discriminatory. In addition, NGOs and legal aid programs have provided a range of material, social, and psychological incentives to victims of violence who participate in legal proceedings, including access to free medical care and a variety of otherwise unavailable social benefits. Serving as mediators connecting victims of violence to the law, by offering new tools, opportunities, and entry points through which to access the legal system, NGOs and international organizations have significantly contributed to a changing legal climate in eastern DR Congo.

NGOs, Advocacy, and Legal Aid

The prior section demonstrated that earlier legal reforms failed to significantly transform the attitudes of local populations toward matters of gender violence. However, in recent years, formal legal mechanisms have begun to replace traditional approaches to dealing with gender-based crime for certain communities and individuals. NGOs and gender advocates have played a crucial role in this transition.

Gender outreach has taken numerous forms, and has grown exponentially in recent years. Building on United Nations Security Council Resolution (UNSCR) 1325, which recognizes that women are disproportionately affected by conflict and emphasizes the importance of women in conflict prevention; UNSCR 1380, which reaffirms the importance of involving women in peace and security issues; and the Convention for the Elimination of All Forms of Discrimination against Women (CEDAW), humanitarian stakeholders in DR Congo have increasingly prioritized the specific needs of women and girls in peacebuilding and development efforts. Many internationally led programs and initiatives, such as the 2006 Pooled Fund on Sexual Violence, the Stabilization and Recovery Funding Facility, MONUSCO's Comprehensive Strategy on Combating Sexual Violence, and others, have directed focused and targeted attention toward gender issues.

In their study of sexual violence aid in DR Congo, Douma and Hilhorst (2012) identified thirty-five international organizations, nine UN agencies, and thirty-seven Congolese NGOs working on sexual and gender-based violence. In reality, there are many more.

Resulting from the international community's decision to prioritize this issue, stakeholders working in this area have increasingly framed the fight against sexual violence as a broad-based social problem that cannot be solved through a single approach, but instead requires a holistic, multifaceted, and coordinated response that engages multiple stakeholders. As such, domestic and international NGOs pursue increasingly diverse activities, incorporating medical assistance, legal assistance, psychosocial support, socioeconomic support, education, outreach, rehabilitation, and more.

International NGOs (35)	Netherlands: ICCO / CORDAID / MensenMet eenMissie / StichtingVluchteling / Oxfam Novib/ ZOA refugee care / Warchild / United States of America: IRC / Eastern Congo Initiative / V-day / Hope in Action / AVSI / IMC / SFCG / American Bar Association / Human Rights Watch / Women for Women /United Kingdom: Oxfam-UK / Merlin / Save the Children / Tearfund (Ireland) / SCIAF (Scotland) / Avocats Sans Frontières (Belgium) / Oxfam-Quebec (Canada) / VSF-Suisse (Switzerland) / COOPI (Italy) / Oxfam Solidarité (Spain) / AMI (France) / Fin Church Aid (Finland) / Norwegian Church Aid (Norway) / Norwegian Refugee Council (Norway) / Médicins du Monde (multiple) / Médicins Sans Frontières (multiple) / CICR (multiple) / CARE (multiple)
UN	UNIFEM-UNWOMEN / UNDP / MONUSCO-JHRO / UNHCR / UNFPA / UNICEF / UN OCHA
Congolese NGOs (37)	Caritas Congo / Centre de Recherche sur l'Environnement la Démocratie et les Droits de l'Homme, CREDDHO / Arche d'Alliance / Caucus de Femmes / Caritas / Commission Diocésaine Justice et Paix, CDJP / Cadre Permanent de Concertation de la Femme Congolaise, CAFCO / Dynamique des Femmes Juristes, DFJ / Synergie des Femmes pour les Violences Sexuelles, SFVS / Action Sociale pour la Paix et le Développement, ASPD / Synergie de l'Assistance Juridique, SAJ / Heal Africa / Fondation Femme Plus / Parzi Hospital, Panzi Foundation / Réseau des Femmes pour le Développement et la Paix, RFDP / Centre Olame / Association des Femmes ce Médias, AFEM / Bureau pour le Volontariat au Service de l'Enfance, BVES / Conseil des Organisations ces Femmes Agissant en Synergie, COFAS / Laissez l'Afrique Vivre, LAV / Village de Cobaille, VICO / Action Communautaire pour la Défense et le Progrès des Agriculteurs, ACODEPA / Action pour la Promotion et la Défense des Droits des Personne Défavorisés, APRODEPED / Association des Femmes Juristes au Congo, AFEJUCO / Réseau Vision Myriam / Œuvre Communautaire pour l'Education de Tous, OCET / Pole Institute / Collectif des Organisations de Jeunes, COJESKI / Centre d'Assistance Médico Psychosociale, CAMPS / Solidarité Paysanne / Service d'Accompagnement et de Renforcement des Capacités d'Auto Promotion de la Femme au Suc-Kivu, SARCAF / Héritiers de la Justice / Solidarité des Femmes de Fizi pour le Bien Être Familial, SOFIBEF / Réseau des Activistes des Droits Humaines de Fizi, RADHF / Action Contre l'Abolition de la Torture, ACAT / Solidarité pour la Promotion sociale et la Paix, SOPROP / Observatoire Congolaise des Prisons, OCP

Table created by Thea Hilhorst and Nynke Douma, and printed in "Fond de Commerce? Sexual Violence Assistance in the Democratic Republic of Congo" (2012). The table depicts organisations working on sexual violence in North and South Kivu that were known to the authors at the time of writing. Reproduced with permission from the authors.

Victims of gender-based violence are frequently invited to participate in microloan projects or are provided with material support and training in agriculture, clothes-making, or some other valuable life skill. Because the NGO networks in North and South Kivu are fairly tightknit and often partner with one another or share information, victims may participate in multiple initiatives at once. They may receive medical or psychosocial support from one organization, legal assistance from another, and social rehabilitation and microcredit from another.

In some cases, programs may be entirely separate, and it is purely incidental that beneficiaries overlap. In others, however, conditions may be imposed, or direct material incentives might be provided to victims who participate in multiple programs. HEAL Africa, a Congolese NGO that houses one of the biggest hospitals in Goma, has a dedicated gender justice program devoted to rehabilitating rape victims, while also conducting legal education, human rights advocacy, and grassroots capacity building with Congolese courts and legal practitioners. This work, which is part of HEAL Africa's "holistic and multipronged approach to peace-building, development and post-conflict reconstruction," has attracted a considerable amount of international funding.[16] HEAL Africa and similar organizations like the Panzi Hospital Foundation in Bukavu, SOFAD, and PAIF have established safe houses, legal aid clinics, and counseling services on their premises in the provincial capitals as well as in conflict-ridden areas. Through these services, legal personnel can easily interact with victims of violence and recruit them to participate in trials. In these ways, NGOs act as "translators" of law and human rights (Englund 2006), providing victims with emotional and economic support throughout the legal process.

Moreover, medical staff members from NGO hospitals will often travel together with legal investigators to provide counseling and other support to survivors of sexual violence participating in legal processes. Through such programs, victims may be invited to participate in workshops and trainings, where they are educated in human rights and where they meet others who have suffered similar atrocities. Within these settings, victims may be introduced to yet other partner organizations offering additional social or economic support. A program coordinator with one partner organization responsible for sensitization and community outreach told me:

It used to be the case that when a woman was raped she was expelled from her community. In eighty percent of cases, this does not happen anymore. This is a result of community sensitization. But some villages do not access these

[16] See HEAL Africa: www.healafrica.org/empowering-women/.

resources and sensitization programs. There is a big difference between villages that have received training and those that have not.[17]

In some cases, the willingness of victims of violence to participate in legal processes has been facilitated by another unfortunate feature of weak empirical statehood. The widespread displacement of civilian populations has meant that many victims of sexual and gender-based violence (albeit a small minority in total) end up in internally displaced persons (IDP) camps or safe houses far from home. These environments can serve as recruitment sites for NGOs conducting human rights workshops. If women are separated from their families and therefore have no income, they may feel fewer sociocultural constraints and be more open to opportunities NGOs present to them. When I asked Agathe from rural South Kivu why she had decided to go to the police and continue with a trial, she told me:

First of all my husband was already away, so he could not stop me. Also, I was expecting some compensation. With my husband gone, I couldn't cover most of the costs for my children, so I needed help.[18]

Moreover, being around others who have experienced similar crimes may help reduce some of the stigma or shame felt by victims of gender violence that often provide barriers to reporting. These dynamics have meant that individuals residing in emergency accommodation are exposed to new ideas about legal accountability and human rights promoted by aid agencies working within the camps, and embedded in networks that facilitate engagement with those ideas once they arrive.

Material Incentives to Report

In addition to partner referrals and other outreach and recruitment efforts that have helped socialize victims of violence toward new frames of legal accountability, NGOs have also offered direct material compensation to support victims of violence while they are participating in legal proceedings. For instance, in addition to providing free legal representation, the American Bar Association Rule of Law Initiative (ABA ROLI) covers all medical expenses for victims of sexual and gender-based violence involved in its cases for the duration of the investigation and trial. This provides significant incentives for victims to participate in legal cases, especially given the high costs of decent quality medical care. The emphasis by NGOs on the need for a holistic response to gender

[17] Interview. Michel, Program Coordinator. DR Congo. June 20, 2012.
[18] Interview. Agathe, Civil Party. DR Congo. January 23, 2013.

violence has meant that legal aid organizations also provide allowances to victims of violence participating in criminal cases so that they can feed and clothe their children. Participating in criminal cases with ABA ROLI is usually a precondition for receiving these other benefits.

Étienne, the brother of Divine, a fourteen-year-old girl from North Kivu, emphasized this point when he spoke about accompanying his sister to the ABA to report a rape. He had heard that the ABA could provide compensation. The ABA lawyer gave Divine and Étienne $20 USD for food, clothes, and shelter, and accompanied them to the police station to file a report. The lawyer also assured Divine that they would assist with her pregnancy at the local hospital. However, since neither Étienne nor Divine could identify or recognize the perpetrator of the attack, and the attacker had already fled the village in which they lived, the police were unable to move forward with the case. Étienne informed us that, once the police no longer had a file open, the ABA could no longer assist them. Étienne and Divine reported that the medical services to assist with the pregnancy were only available to those participating in criminal cases, and thus they could not qualify unless they could identify the perpetrators.

Étienne and Divine's story illustrates the fact that, whether intentional or not, many victims of sexual assault have a hard time understanding which aid organization is responsible for providing which service. For many, access to free medical care appears to depend on their participation in a criminal trial.

Others may not have felt that the decision to participate in a legal process was a choice. Analine, a fifty-two-year-old woman living in North Kivu, was raped by soldiers in her house and left badly injured. When asked how she came to be involved in a court case, she said:

There were doctors at my bed in the hospital going to every bed and asking our stories and if we want to make a case. They told us our life was nothing, and we should go to court to get reparations. They told us we would be compensated with money. The lawyers proposed an amount that would help me restart my business. And also to compensate me [for] the damages I got from being hurt – I could not do hard work. It was something like $400 USD. They had most of the process in the hospital because we were too sick to go to court. They brought a big lorry with all the prisoners, and the proceedings took place at the beds of the hospital.[19]

In other cases, material support offered by legal aid clinics either added incentives to seek justice or outweighed the emotional costs of participating in a trial. When asked why she pursued legal remedy, Francine commented: "The ABA gave me money and some baby clothes."[20] Mupenda

[19] Interview. Analine. DR Congo. January 11, 2013.
[20] Interview. Francine. DR Congo. April 26, 2013.

explained her motivations for going to the ABA and what happened when she got there:

I thought that I could get some help to look after the baby. When I went to the office they appointed someone to follow the case, and he took me to HEAL Africa for medical assistance. They were really very nice with me. The first time I went to meet [the lawyer] she gave me $5 USD for transport, but then I stayed home because I was waiting for the birth. Then when the baby was born, I went to see her again and she gave me clothes for the baby and $20 USD.[21]

Douma and Hilhurst (2012) argue that the majority of rape cases that travel through the Congolese courts do so because litigants feel they may benefit financially from pursuing a rape claim. Indeed, in contrast to prior decades when family members were rejected after they had been raped, partners or parents may now encourage – or even pressure – victims to report a case to the police or an NGO, thinking they will receive financial compensation as a result. Charlene echoed this point:

The most important thing for me was that they were in prison: justice. I want them to be punished because I don't want them to do it to other people. I wanted the chief to arrest him, but my husband wanted only money from the case.[22]

Marie, twenty-one, recounted the story of how she was raped by bandits in the bush. She similarly explains that her husband supported her in reporting the case to the police, predominantly because he wanted financial compensation.

My husband [did not throw me out] and instead reported this to the police. He wanted those people to get punished, and he wanted to get compensation. We went together. I chose to go [with him] because otherwise, if I refused, my husband could say that I was an accomplice. I had to go. I also wanted punishment for those people, and reparations for what they did.[23]

Francine described her pursuit of criminal justice as a pursuit of alimony or material support. She did not frame her grievance in terms of a criminal claim, but rather the need for child support for her pregnancy.

Can you tell me about why you went to the police, what happened to you? I realized that I was pregnant and my boyfriend disappeared. We were not engaged for marriage, but I was getting promises from him, that he was going to buy me clothes and shoes. That was my motivation for staying with him. He was nice, but he lied to me every day. I went there [to the police] because I . . . thought that I could get some reparations to look after the baby. I was thinking that I could get some assistance just to help me, in daily life, like a small business. His [the boyfriend's]

---

[21] Interview. Mupenda. DR Congo. April 26, 2013.
[22] Interview. Charlene. DR Congo. January 14, 2013.
[23] Interview. Marie. DR Congo. January 11, 2013.

friend's brother is supporting me. *He paid for the birth. Do you know what crime they charged him with?* The only thing I know is that his fault is only because he left me pregnant and went away, but otherwise I don't know. *Was your priority the criminal case, or the civil case of reparations?* I realized that it was rape because if it wasn't, he wouldn't have moved away; he could stay with me.[24]

My interviewees expressed continued confusion over the difference between ideas of financial compensation awarded as the result of a legal dispute, and funds given by legal aid organizations directly to victims in cash to assist them with childcare and medical expenses. However, despite this confusion, many of the victims interviewed saw their participation in a criminal case as an avenue – sometimes the only viable one – to access social, medical, and economic support. Despite a stark absence of choice or opportunity for many of my interviewees, some of the voices presented earlier in this chapter hint at a strategic adoption of the language of law and criminal justice in order to access non-legal benefits or support networks (Lake, Muthaka, and Walker 2016).[25] The fact that many women did not foreground the language of rights and justice when speaking about their involvement in criminal cases, but instead discussed their concrete material needs when asked why they pursued legal remedy, suggests that legal outreach NGOs have tapped into a variety of different motivations for local communities to engage in legal processes (Carlin, Howard, and Messinger 1966).

Victim-Centered Processes: Bringing Victims to Court by Redefining Consent

At the time of writing, rumors in and around Goma suggested that allegations of rape always resulted in successful convictions. Growing attention to sexual and gender-based violence has given victims a (sometimes misplaced) confidence that formal legal mechanisms will result in remedy and redress. While conviction rates are still low, it is certainly the case that judges have used Congolese and international law to tip the burden of proof ever so slightly toward the accused rather than the victim. This represents a stark break from the past and a significant contrast from other legal systems, where rape victims are often disinclined to report cases for fear their testimonies will be disbelieved. A growing perception that the justice system can support victims of violence plays a role in encouraging reporting.

[24] Interview. Francine. DR Congo. April 26, 2013.
[25] See Utas (2005) for a compelling description of the ways in which women in humanitarian environments might navigate victimcy in order to be perceived as legitimate recipients of aid.

Successful criminal indictments result from various factors, including disproportionate resources available to the prosecution. The prosecution team is frequently supported, assisted, and financially compensated by local NGOs or international organizations. By contrast, defense counsel may be appointed pro bono by local bar associations or must be hired by the defendant. Defense attorneys vary significantly in their expertise, skill, training, and knowledge of the law. Some are highly skilled or devote their time voluntarily because they are committed to the principle of impartial justice and the presumption of innocence. Others have little interest in or knowledge of the issues at hand. Resources and support for the defense stand in contrast to the legal representatives of the civil parties, who face highly competitive hiring procedures and whose salaries are often paid by international organizations.

The evolving treatment of sexual consent in eastern DR Congo's courts similarly facilitates prosecutions. In writing about the treatment of rape in the US legal system, Kristen Bumiller points out that American legal culture employs "a definition of rape that forces the prosecution to show non-consent in order to prove that a sexual assault has been committed" (Bumiller 1990: 102). This is true in many legal systems. Even where there is evidence that intercourse, penetration, or another sexual act took place, unless a minor is involved, the burden of proof lies squarely with the prosecution – and by implication, with the victim – to show that she or he did not provide consent.

The Congolese courts have often approached this principle with creativity and innovation. In a sociocultural environment that has not typically foregrounded the concept of sexual consent, particularly in relationships between a husband and wife, lawyers have been able to utilize a lack of knowledge of the law to easily prove the absence of legal consent. As discussed in Chapter 2, many Congolese communities have approached sexual consent in general terms. Men and women sometimes assume that sexual consent is granted simply through the act of accepting a gift, entering into a romantic relationship, or being alone in a room with a man. There is little cultural precedent for explicitly obtaining verbal consent before a sexual encounter, particularly in the context of a marital relationship. As such, many accused sexual offenders have heavily relied on their own (broad) interpretations of consent in their defense. These arguments are rarely legally admissible. Lawyers, judges and magistrates well trained in the law can exploit these gaps in legal knowledge. One especially common defense – heard frequently in both DR Congo and South Africa – relies on the ease with which penetration occurred, captured in phrases such as: "Her body accepted me to enter so I knew she accepted me."[26] Other common arguments include: "When a girl is asking for water in such a way, she wants sex" (Sonke Gender Justice Network 2012); "I could tell in her eyes that she wanted sex"; and "When she closed the door and touched her leg, it was she who committed rape against me because she was the one who wanted sex."[27]

Many accused individuals genuinely interpret these types of interactions as consensual. Moreover, until recently, given prevailing social norms surrounding sexual consent, many legal practitioners might have shared this broad definition of consent. However, over the past decade, the Congolese legal system and the practitioners working within it have applied strict legal standards to sexual consent. A large number of education and outreach programs have been implemented to educate legal practitioners and law enforcement officers, as well as the general public, about the legal definition of consent. According to Congolese law, consent cannot "under any circumstances be inferred from the silence of – or lack of resistance by – a victim to the alleged sexual violence" (DR Congo 2006b and 2006c; International Criminal Court 2002b). The law expands on this language to uphold that "consent cannot, under any circumstances, be inferred by the words or conduct of a victim where the ability of the latter to give genuine voluntary consent has been compromised by the use of force, deceit, alcohol, threat, coercion, or by taking advantage of a generally coercive environment" (Art. 14, DR Congo 2006c)."

As discussed in Chapter 4, legal practitioners have used these provisions to overturn dominant sociocultural scripts of rape. When defense counsel invokes the kinds of justifications outlined earlier, well-trained prosecutors, investigators, and legal representatives can easily demonstrate that the legal definition of consent has not been met. And whereas South African courts have concluded that mistaking a victim's consent as genuine warrants the benefit of the doubt (see the discussion in Chapter 4), courts in the Kivus have used the lack of explicit consent to establish guilt under the law. Congolese legal practitioners have thus moved toward redressing a legal culture that has historically privileged the testimony of the accused in sexual assault cases through the presumption of innocence (MacKinnon 2005, 2006).

This victim-sensitive approach has fundamentally turned on its head the approach of many modern legal systems toward rape, simplifying and facilitating conviction for a category of crime that has been notoriously difficult to prosecute in other legal cultures. Legal aid and NGO outreach serve to connect victims to the law, bringing victims of violence to court, and

[26] Case notes, field notes. DR Congo. August and September, 2012.
[27] Case notes, field notes. DR Congo. August and September, 2012.

incentivizing them to turn to legal institutions where they may otherwise have lacked the confidence, legal knowledge, awareness or resources to do so.

South Africa: Presumed Consent and Other Barriers to Legal Remedy

Advocacy around sexual and gender-based violence in eastern DR Congo has transformed the ways in which the legal system approaches the burden of proof around sexual consent. Even more importantly, it has begun to alter how victims of gender violence are treated at their first point of entry to the legal system. These changes, combined with extensive community outreach and material incentives to encourage women to participate in civil and criminal proceedings, have motivated victims of violence to cooperate with legal aid programs and pursue justice through formal legal avenues.

Advocacy around gender violence in South Africa's Western Cape has not met the same types of success. While many organizations do crucial work connecting victims of gender violence to the law, and supporting them against a system that denies them justice, activists and NGOs have struggled to significantly shift the legal culture around rape in South African courts and police stations. Law enforcement officers continue to engage in dismissive behavior and subscribe to old-fashioned beliefs about what constitutes "real" rape. Thus, not only have courts continued to define sexual consent conservatively – creating significant barriers to guilty verdicts in cases decided on the basis of victim testimony – but police fail to treat rape or sexual violence cases as seriously as other criminal offenses when they are first reported. This is particularly true in cases where the victim has not suffered serious physical injury, if she has been drinking or partying, or if she is in a relationship with the accused. The notoriously hostile treatment of rape by law enforcement personnel reduces incentives for victims to overcome the stigma associated with sexual assault and discourages them from reporting cases of gender-based violence.

Regulating Familial and Sexual Relationships

Like DR Congo, South Africa has had a long and complicated history of attempting to reconcile customary practices with evolving laws protecting the newly recognized human rights of groups and individuals. Under British rule, the colonial administration divided South Africa into a number of Scheduled Native Areas, which were governed by customary authorities deemed to represent existing local hierarchies. These authorities were granted immense power and influence and retained jurisdiction over almost all matters relating to the indigenous populations of

South Africa (Herbst 1930; Mamdani 1996; Simons 1968). The introduction of the Native Land Act in 1913 further formalized the authority of customary chiefs, introducing a formal centralized bureaucracy to local governance that had not existed previously.

Prior to the formalization of customary law in South Africa, local disputes – especially those involving issues such as marital violence and other familial or gender-related matters – would have been settled by lineage members and family elders, rather than customary village-level chiefs (Mamdani 1996). The current scope and power of customary authorities, therefore, derives from a mélange of long-standing traditional practices, and structures introduced under British and Dutch rule. Under British rule, for example, colonial administrators left some issues entirely to custom, while heavily regulating others through their own customary appointees. Colonial authorities often failed to recognize marriages conferred by African churches or Hindu and Muslim authorities, creating a regime in which "the family" was strictly defined in terms of monogamous Judeo-Christian European values (Comaroff and Roberts 1986; Yarbrough 2013: 52). The British also attempted to outlaw certain practices deemed "repugnant to civilized social order" (Chanock 2006), including polygamy and *lobola* (bridewealth). However, in the face of local resistance, many of these reforms failed, and the colonial administration was forced to relax its policies to permit select local practices to continue unobstructed.[28] Although polygamy was eventually outlawed in South Africa, other practices, including *lobola* and the practice of *ukuthwala* (bride capture), remain common (Cole and Thomas 2009; Hunter 2010; Yarbrough 2013). Such practices have proved extremely relevant to contemporary debates around gender violence and the governance of marriage, family, and sexual life; they are often invoked by perpetrators of gender violence, as well as influential customary authorities and prominent political elites, in order to reject formal legal governance over a variety of gender-related issues.

Throughout the apartheid regime, the customary governance of sexual and familial relationships within the homelands strongly resembled that of the colonial era. Under apartheid, South Africa's indigenous populations were heavily restricted by the government in their ability to live, travel, and work freely. However, the regulation of family life was left under the jurisdiction of customary governance structures whose powers had been strictly established, defined, and consolidated by the British (Mamdani 1996).

---

[28] See Mutongi (2007) and Thomas (2003) for a discussion of similar patterns in colonial Kenya. Many others have discussed the ways in which the empowerment of customary authorities by colonial officials was a method to ensure cooperation from local elites and avoid an uprising. See Chanock (2006) and Mamdani (1996).

After the end of apartheid, South Africa's governing elite embraced an inclusive human rights agenda that offered considerable protections to previously disenfranchised communities. However, this process gave birth to a growing tension between protecting the rights of women and sexual minorities according to international standards, and protecting indigenous South African practices, cultures and traditions. In 1996, South Africa's new constitution introduced certain formal protections for customary practices, in an effort to reverse the racial oppression of the apartheid government and create space for local customs. Postapartheid figures identified the nonrecognition of African and non-white marriages as a legacy of the prior regime's racial imperialism. As a result, "cultural rights" were explicitly protected in Sections 30 and 31 of the constitution, and Section 185 provides for the creation of a Commission for the Promotion and Protection of the Rights of Cultural, Religious, and Linguistic Communities. Section 211 explicitly provides for the application of customary law by the courts, under the logic that the right to culture implies the right to the recognition of customary law (Mubangizi 2013). In 1998, the parliament passed the Recognition of Customary Marriages Act, granting recognition to all preexisting and future customary marriages that were not previously recognized by the state.

These attempts to reconcile respect for traditional South African practices with new human rights protections have met some challenges. Whereas the customary practice of *lobola* is formally recognized as legitimate under the law, its practical implementation has proved more challenging, particularly in the context of the criminalization of all forms of gender discrimination and violence. In cases of marital violence, some women feel compelled to remain with an abusive partner because her family cannot afford to repay the *lobola*. Although South African law (which permits the exchange of *lobola*, but prohibits the requirement that it is returned upon separation) emphasizes that she is not required to pay back the *lobola* in order to divorce, many South African communities continue to subscribe to the custom in full. Indeed, even some of South Africa's most influential politicians have mis-invoked the constitutional protections for customary law to defend illegal practices. When Jacob Zuma was accused of raping Fezeka Kuzwayo in 2006, for example, he offered to pay *lobola* to her family in an effort to resolve the matter between the two families (Hunter 2010: 2).

Practices such as *ukuthwala* – the ceremonial kidnapping of the bride by a group of men including the groom – have proved equally challenging to legislate. Given that *ukuthwala* is sometimes practiced without the consent of the bride, some argue that, under certain circumstances, it meets the legal definition of forced marriage and forced sex. As such, the practice comes into direct conflict with South Africa's laws on sexual violence, the rights of the child, and the rights of women. However, despite a legislative framework that imposes new restrictions on these practices, they prevail with relative frequency, and have been protected and justified through a defense of culture and traditional authority.

The anticolonial sentiments that prompted a defense of customary law in the postapartheid period inspired the proposal of the Traditional Courts Bill. This Bill has received widespread support, as well as extensive criticism, from different stakeholders, communities, and interest groups. It was first proposed in 2003 and sought to devolve jurisdiction over a number of issues to traditional leaders. This Bill is representative of the growing tension between the rights enshrined in the constitution and the beliefs held by a large proportion of South Africans. While previous versions of the Traditional Courts Bill were rejected by the parliament, at the time of writing the latest iteration (2017) was still under discussion. Critics of the Bill have compared it to the 1927 Black Administration Act. The Traditional Courts Bill entrenches controversial tribal boundaries created under apartheid, and would grant the traditional courts sole jurisdiction over a range of civil and criminal matters within these areas. The Bill has been proposed under the premise that traditional leaders hold a great deal of influence within local communities and have the power and respect needed to resolve disputes using traditional means before they become conflictual. If passed, the Bill would effectively create a parallel justice system, akin to the customary courts of the colonial era, which would have almost exclusive jurisdiction in certain parts of the country. While the latest iteration gives parties the opportunity to "opt out" of traditional jurisdiction, many fear it compromises the constitutional rights of women, and their access to equal protections before the law (Gqirana 2017).

Stakeholders have expressed concern over the contents of the Traditional Courts Bill for a variety of reasons; one prominent concern is that it would serve to further marginalize women and vulnerable populations, such as sexual minorities. The traditional courts do not permit lawyers to represent any party to the case; instead, individuals would be represented by family members "according to customary law." This clause explicitly denies South Africans of their constitutional right to legal representation. Additionally, while the Bill does not exclude women outright, the language of prior iterations suggests that it would be appropriate for female parties to be represented by a male family member, which is customary practice. Moreover, under the pre-2017 iteration, the 17 million people living within the areas under the jurisdiction of the proposed courts would be subject to social pressures that offer them little choice as to whether they wished their cases to be heard by a civil/criminal or a customary court, thus alienating a great many South Africans from the formal legal system.

If the Bill is passed, the traditional courts would likely further entrench the exclusion of women and discourage them from seeking judicial remedy for gender-related issues. Even under the latest version, participants would only have the chance to opt out at the outset of the process, thus removing themselves from the jurisdiction of the courts if they are treated unfairly at later stages. Lauren, the executive director of a prominent gender and law center in Cape Town, explained some of the potential repercussions of the law. She gave the example of a case involving Mathilda, a fourteen-year-old girl who was married to an older man. Because her husband lived with a girlfriend in Johannesburg, Mathilda was compelled to live with his family and work for them instead of attending school. She was dissatisfied with this arrangement and thus fled home, at which point her husband brought legal action against her to demand her return, as well as the return of the *lobola* he paid for her. Through free representation provided by the Women's Legal Centre, Mathilda eventually won the case in her local magistrates' court. However, the director of the Women's Legal Centre, Jennifer Williams, publicly acknowledged that Mathilda's situation would have been very different at a customary court, which would likely have demanded her return to the husband's family and the repayment of *lobola*. Williams explained: "Firstly, under Xhosa customary law, when a wife separates from her husband and returns to her father, the husband is required to fetch her. The father and husband may then also negotiate the terms of the wife's return without consulting the wife" (quoted in Clappaert 2012).

Widespread support for the Traditional Courts Bill – from both urban and rural communities and elites – has left many South African women and sexual minorities feeling that the state does not support them. The current political debates around the Bill and the role of customary law in contemporary South Africa illustrate the striking tension between the gender-sensitive legal framework of the postapartheid era and the patriarchal values that many are still committed to. As illustrated by the case of Mathilda, these two frameworks for governing familial and sexual relationships – both of which emerged as a response to the apartheid-era repression of various groups – directly conflict with one another on a variety of gender-based issues. Because many South African police, lawyers, magistrates and judges are drawn from diverse backgrounds and communities, they can hold fairly conservative ideas with regard to gender violence, customary dispute resolution, and related issues. Given that police already encourage private resolution on a fairly frequent basis, the formalization of customary law would likely make it more difficult for women to seek recourse from the state in the aftermath of a gendered crime.

The Reporting Stage

The tension between customary and contemporary-legal approaches toward regulating rape and gender violence serves to systematically deter many victims of violence from seeking protection from the law at every stage of the legal process. Victims of sexual and gender-based violence can be deterred from seeking legal protections in the aftermath of a sexual assault if their immediate family may believe such matters should be resolved at the community level or by customary authorities. Many ordinary South Africans also continue to reject the concept of marital rape. In addition to being widespread among the general public, these types of beliefs are shared by police officers, law enforcement personnel, and even legal practitioners. Thus, those victims who do attempt to seek protections from the law are frequently confronted by the assumption that no crime occurred, or that they must have provoked the incident in question. This reception by law enforcement officers disincentivizes victims of violence seeking legal remedy as, upon deciding to report an incident, they rarely receive any validation that they are entitled to protection. In contrast to the experiences of legal claimants in eastern DR Congo, victims of violence who report cases of sexual assault in South Africa's Western Cape are often challenged by police and family members for their decision to do so, and can be told even by those in positions of authority that they have no legitimate grievance or complaint.

Furthermore, unlike in DR Congo, due to the fact that free medical care is available to all South Africans, victims of violence do not feel compelled to participate in the pursuit of legal remedy in order to access critical medical services or socioeconomic support. This makes one of the primary incentives identified in the Kivus irrelevant in the South African context.

A number of population-based surveys across South Africa have attempted to uncover contemporary attitudes of victims of violence toward law enforcement and rape reporting. A 2015 population-based survey in the Western Cape revealed that only 1.6 percent of all self-identified rape victims had reported the incident to the police (Gender Links 2015: 54). Vetten (2012) identifies approximately fourteen common barriers mentioned by victims of gender-based violence that have prevented them from turning to the law. The most common of these were the fear of being accused of lying and feelings of shame, guilt, fault, humiliation, or embarrassment. Furthermore, there was a prevailing sense among all victims that police did not take rape or gender violence "seriously" as a crime.

Many interviewees, from a variety of different demographic backgrounds, explicitly noted that police in South Africa still subscribe to a set of "rape myths" that influences their behavior and interactions. These common myths pervade many legal systems, such that when police are faced with dockets on a range of offenses, they consistently fail to prioritize those involving rape or other forms of gender violence. Rape myths identified throughout the South African Police Service and at other stages of the legal process include the expectation that a victim must be lying if s/he does not come forward to report the crime right away; that if s/he does not show physical injuries, then the incident cannot have been forced; that women often have sex with men and then regret it the next day and accuse the man of rape; that rape can only be perpetrated by an attacker unknown to the victim; that rape can only be perpetrated by a man against a woman; that rape must involve penile to vaginal penetration; as well as many other incorrect – and illegal – assumptions.

Many police, as well as a surprisingly diverse pool of the general public, share the belief that girls usually provoke sexual assaults by their behavior and dress. This attitude emerged in a number of interviews and has been confirmed in other research. For instance, Lesedi, from KwaZulu-Natal, told Human Rights Watch that when she went to report a rape to the police, they said: "Why are you running away from men? They were only giving you what you wanted" (Human Rights Watch 2011: 46). Zebo had a similar experience when attempting to register complaints against a man who was threatening to rape her and her girlfriend:

The policeman said: "They are raping you because you act as a man." They said to me, "Okay, we hear your story, but why are you dressing like a man?" They were laughing at me as they said this. They threatened to kick my ass in the police station. I felt stupid. They didn't write anything down. (Human Rights Watch 2011: 47)

Khosi, quoted in Chapter 2, worked in a logistical role for a local human rights organization focusing on gender violence in the Western Cape. He explained to me the need to distinguish between "real" rape and false claims. He told me that girls often go out to parties dressed in short skirts and un-African attire; these girls, he explained, are usually looking for sex. Khosi couldn't understand why girls would go out looking for sex and then report a rape to the police the next day. Although he worked, albeit in a technical role, for an organization devoted to combating gender violence, he nevertheless assumed that if a girl dressed in a particular way, she was inviting men to have sex with her. "Why then," he asked, "would they report this to the police as a crime?"[29]

The psychologists and counselors with whom I spoke corroborated the fact that fears of not being believed or of being mocked by police were widespread among the victims of violence they interacted with in their professional capacities. Another prominent concern that served as a strong barrier to reporting were feelings of shame that the victim had somehow provoked the attack by behaving promiscuously. The counselors with whom I spoke were attached to medical facilities, so they most frequently encountered victims who required medical attention because they had been physically injured, because they had contracted a sexually transmitted disease, or because they were pregnant. Phumzile, a counselor in a medical facility, explained:

Victims are often ashamed after they are raped. Not everyone accepts that [if you are a girl who was raped] you didn't ask to be raped. Many believe that your attire or your clothes indicate that you want to be raped. Girls aren't scared to wear these clothes. They wear whatever they like because they are not afraid. Girls are aware of rape as a societal problem, but they never think it will happen to them. And when it does, they think it is their fault because they didn't listen to those who told them not to go out, or not to wear those clothes. They think it was because of the way they dressed or behaved. They think that they have been warned and they chose to ignore that and wear those clothes anyway, so it must be their fault. [30]

Phumzile added that, in most of these types of cases, the perpetrator is known to the victim. Often, she met him at a party or might have flirted with him, which compounds her feelings of guilt about the attack. She explained: "Because they so often think it was their fault, when these girls come in, they do not think what happened to them was actually a crime. It is our job to educate them about their rights."[31]

Thembela, a community activist who supports victims of gender violence, described how police often question victims about what they were wearing, whether they enjoyed the sexual experience, and whether the person who attacked them was a boyfriend. In these lines of questions, the police insinuate – and in some cases directly assert – that the victim must have provoked the incident. Thembela, who was from the high-crime

---

[29] Informal Conversation. Khosi, Technician. South Africa, March 17, 2013.
[30] Interview. Phumzile, Program Officer. South Africa, March 15, 2013.
[31] Interview. Phumzile, Program Officer. South Africa. March 15, 2013.

urban neighborhood of Khayelitsha, also noted that police often laugh at the victim while she is telling her story or make fun of her experience.[32] Human Rights Watch reported similar interactions from its interviews with lesbian and transgender communities. For example, Manashe found out that her friends had been raped and beaten in a tavern. On reporting the incident to the police, Manashe recounted:

We said to the police that we had been attacked [for being lesbians] and beaten up. The police told us, "You are crazy. Just go sleep. There's nothing like that. There's no woman who will sleep with another woman." The next day they went to Ramokonopi police station, close to Katlehong. One policeman said he didn't know how to take the statement because he didn't know where the penis entered. They were all laughing and asking, "How do you have sex?" To my friend's girlfriend [who was raped], they said, "How do you feel after sleeping with guys, to sleep with lesbians again?" (Human Rights Watch 2011: 48)

Thembela observed that this type of response from the police made victims she had worked with feel extremely uncomfortable. Often, after these types of interactions, victims try to retract their stories or drop the case; they see little point in moving forward without any positive reinforcement from law enforcement authorities. Although, technically, Family Violence, Child Protection and Sexual Offenses (FCS) Units are attached to each court and police station to take victim statements and collect forensic and medical evidence at the stage of first reporting, in practice this does not often happen. Reportedly, the capacity of the FCS had improved by 2017, but, over the course this research was carried out, counselors, psychologists, and medical practitioners in Khayelitsha described many similarly troubling interactions between their clients and the police. Phumzile told me that she has often pushed victims to continue with their cases even after experiencing abuse from police. She said that she has to tell them: "It is not about you. It is about our government knowing that crime is rising in this area and knowing what happens to our people."[33]

These problems are compounded by underfunding and a lack of basic skills and resources that police need to do their jobs properly. Heavy workloads and insufficient resources, particularly in high-crime neighborhoods, mean that police dockets are often lost and police often fail to follow up on cases even where the security of the victim is in jeopardy. Moreover, police themselves are frequently implicated in violence. In the Western Cape alone, twelve police officers were investigated on allegations of rape in 2013.[34] Human Rights Watch has reported on the ways in

---

[32] Field notes. Thembela. Community Activist. South Africa. March 26, 2013
[33] Interview. Phumzile, Program Officer. South Africa. March 15, 2013.
[34] See IRIN News (2013), Wort (2013).

which the failure of the police to do their jobs properly has disproportionately affected victims of gender violence. Doris, for example, was raped
by a close family friend and on reporting the incident to the police, she
told them: "If he is set free, he's going to come for me" (Human Rights
Watch 2011: 50). Although the accused was initially arrested, he was
released on bail on the condition that he would not make contact with
Doris. However, this was not upheld. Doris said:

> The day he was released I was walking home. I saw him hiding behind a container
> with two friends. He was waiting for me. It was exactly on my way home. I turned
> away and started to walk in the other direction. One of them chased me. But
> I went into a shopping center. I called the investigating officer. He said he didn't
> have transport to get to me (Human Rights Watch 2011: 51).

Dyoli, the community activist quoted in Chapter 2, also spoke about
a lack of transport as a serious problem impeding the ability of police
officers to carry out their duties. Given that police do not always take
seriously gender violence offenses, they are unlikely to devote scarce time
or resources to cases that they do not feel are valid or legitimate crimes, or
to cases that are unlikely to resolve quickly. Where the case involves
ambiguities over consent, a preexisting relationship, alcohol, etc., police
may think it will ultimately be withdrawn or thrown out of court, and is
thus simply not worth their time in pursuing.

Other reasons victims of violence had for not going to the police
included feelings of pity and love toward the person responsible for the
abuse or fear of intimidation or retaliation by the person responsible.
Anathi, a counselor and medical practitioner, informed me that most of
the victims of violence she interacts with in her job are young girls,
normally teenagers, who have been raped by someone known to them.
Assaults normally took place at or after a social occasion, such as a party
or at a bar, at school, or on the way home from school. Anathi confirmed
that the majority of girls who came into the center were brought by their
parents or other family members who had encouraged them to seek
assistance. She explained that, in addition to feelings of shame or embarrassment, many of the girls she interacted with were reluctant to report
cases to the police because they were in love with the one who violated
them. This poses a problem because they do not want to see legal
ramifications. If they do end up reporting cases to the police, this can
sometimes lead victims of violence to change their stories multiple times,
which compounds doubt and skepticism among police officers that the
victim might be lying or may have "wanted" to be raped.[35]

---

[35] Field notes. Anathi, Counsellor. Field notes. South Africa. March 15, 2013.

Other barriers to reporting brought up by interviewees or identified in prior studies include: a lack of physical access to police or social workers; a lack of confidence that the legal process will result in a conviction; a fear of experiencing rudeness or poor treatment by the police; a fear of having to relive the trauma in court and during the investigation; a fear of upsetting family stability; a fear of losing economic support provided by the abuser; a preference for informal dispute resolution (such as the payment of damages by the abuser); a fear of ostracism or ridicule by peers; and, finally, wanting to avoid the stigma attached to being raped by being labeled as "damaged" (Vetten 2013). Due to the stigma associated with sexual assault, and probable feelings of guilt or fear associated with being ostracized or upsetting their families, it is often extremely painful for victims to speak out about an assault, even to a family member or medical professional. After taking the difficult decision to report a case, if a victim of violence then encounters skepticism or ill-treatment, they may conclude that their initial intuition to keep the issue secret was the correct one.

However, some women seek the support of the law in spite of these obstacles, and are confident and determined in their right to do so. In her 2013 study, Lisa Vetten identified a number of factors that have motivated victims of gender violence in South Africa to turn to formal legal processes. These include the belief that the violence is serious and that it should be reported and the desire to ensure personal safety and future protection from the offender, to prevent the offense from being repeated or the offender harming others, to make the offender take responsibility for his/her actions, to ensure the offender is brought to justice and punished, to regain a sense of control, and to gain some form of compensation.

There are also significant demographic trends in violence reporting. Survey research and police statistics in South Africa have revealed that younger women, especially teenagers, have been by far the most likely age group to report sexual offenses or other gender-based crimes. This fact was corroborated by almost everyone I spoke to. Older women, as well as men, have been extremely unlikely to report incidents of violence, unless they are so physically injured that they have little choice but to visit a medical facility. The majority of cases that travel through the criminal justice system involves young girls under the age of eighteen.[36] Other studies have found that white women are eighty percent more likely to report gender-based violence than black or colored women, and Indian women are fifty percent more likely than black or colored women (Vetten 2013). Women with university-level education are traditionally eight

[36] Interview. Zakhele, South African Police Service. South Africa. March 11, 2013.

times more likely to report gender crimes than women without higher education (Department of Health 1999: 93).

Nikelwe, a community activist and support worker, had accompanied countless victims to the police station in Khayelitsha. She pointed out racial and class-based disparities in how cases are received by the police at their first point of entry to the legal system. She told me that, in Khayelitsha, if you are white and you are raped, your case would probably be heard in one year. The police would also listen and investigate when you told your story. But, if you were black, your case would take five years at least, if the police would even agree to write it down. Many others shared this sentiment, observing that you have to really show the police you are serious for them to listen to you. A number of interviewees noted that the police judge you as soon as you arrive in the police station, and if you don't know your rights, they will just send you away. Nikelwe recalled the first time she went to the police station in Khayelitsha to report a rape:

I went to the station in Site B with a girl who was attacked by a stranger on her way to use the public toilet. The police called me a bitch. They said: "You need to open a case? Get lost, bitch." The police know whether you know your rights or not, and if they see that you don't know, they will rubbish you. If you are not a girlfriend of a policeman, your case will just always be undermined.[37]

As noted, part of the problem is that police are notoriously overworked. In their study of attrition in Gugulethu, Khayelitsha, and Manenberg in 2004, Artz, Smythe, and Leggett (2004) found that police were carrying anything between 27 and 300 dockets each. This led one researcher to conclude that detectives appeared caught up in "perpetual crisis management, responding to whoever yells the loudest ... The women who get their cases attended to are the ones who show up at the station and demand it" (Artz, Smythe, and Leggett 2004: 72).

Finally, customary beliefs have also influenced the ways in which police handle cases in their files. Dyoli reflected on a case he had been involved in, in which the accused had admitted to the police that he committed a rape. In a meeting at the police station, in which the police officers, the accused, and the victim were all present, the accused asked to talk to the victim's family about what he could "do for her" in terms of compensation. Like in the case of Zuma discussed in the previous chapter, the accused was willing to accept what he had done and pay a material price in the form of *lobola*. The police were keen to embrace this perceived solution. Because they are overworked, they welcome excuses to drop cases from their dockets. If an accused admits his mistake and asks to privately

---

[37] Interview. Nikelwe, Community Activist, South Africa. March 6, 2013.

resolve the matter, the police often see no further need to intervene. In a case investigated by Human Rights Watch in 2010, Mosa was raped by a neighbor, Judas. The police arrested the rapist, but, despite police assurances that Judas would not be released, he was freed on bail while Mosa was in hospital. When she returned home, Judas continued intimidating her. Fearing for her daughter's life, Mosa's mother sought help again from the police; they simply told her: "What's happened has happened. Judas is sorry. Here's 10,000 Rand. You should take it because you also don't want your daughter dead" (Human Rights Watch 2011: 51).

Each of these factors contributes to an environment that is incredibly hostile to victims of gender-based violence and that systematically discourages them from pursuing legal action in the aftermath of an assault. When victims of violence are laughed at or turned away from police stations, when they are questioned on what they were wearing or what they might have done to provoke or encourage an incident, when they are presumed to have "enjoyed" the sexual interaction, or when they are disbelieved, they are unlikely to view law enforcement agencies as viable or desirable avenues for redress.

The key determinants of violence reporting identified by Vetten mirror some of the reasons given by those victims of violence I interviewed in eastern DR Congo. However, there are some important differences. Rather than any possibility of positive reinforcement or social and material benefits as a result of reporting a case to the police, victims of violence in South Africa commonly received little support. Moreover, they rarely received information or assistance claiming compensation for damages. Their claims were instead dismissed altogether or they were abused or mocked by police officers. Given that it takes courage and persistence on the part of victims to report a case in the first place, and even greater perseverance to ensure that police dockets are not "lost," when those in positions of authority inform sexual assault victims that there is no case to answer, most are likely to give up. Absent any of the medical or material motivations offered by legal clinics in eastern DR Congo, victims of violence, on average, are presented with few incentives to pursue a criminal case through the legal system absent a personal motivation to do so.

The Trial Stage

As discussed in Chapter 4, the hostility of the criminal justice system toward victims of gender-based crimes is by no means restricted to the reporting stage. While very few cases ever make it from the police to prosecutors, those that do are rarely met with greater sensitivity.

Chapter 4 outlined some of the ways in which dominant sociocultural narratives around rape characterize sentencing and jury deliberations. Judges frequently invoke the prior sexual conduct of the victim, what s/he may have been wearing, and other factors as mitigating circumstances in assessing a case's severity.

Moreover, in stark contrast to eastern DR Congo, the interpretation of sexual consent has been problematically broad in a number of decisions. Evidence of this can be found in the case of *The State* v. *Zuma* and other cases discussed in Chapter 4. Because the prosecution was unable to prove beyond reasonable doubt that Mr. Zuma had *intended* to commit an act of rape, Justice Van der Merwe of the Witwatersrand High Court concluded that Mr. Zuma could not be convicted for the crime. Unlike the Congolese decisions in which the defendant had to convincingly demonstrate that genuine consent was granted, the prosecution successfully argued that Mr. Zuma misconstrued the victim's behavior as consent. Because *he* understood the act to be consensual, he did not intend to commit rape and could not be convicted of a criminal offense.

Other cases have been fraught with similarly problematic logic. Based on the set of rape myths outlined earlier, prosecutors and judges have often inferred from the victim's behavior at the time of the alleged assault that consent was tacitly given to the accused. In the cases of *Jackson* and *Ngada* discussed in Chapter 4, the courts implied that consent may have been given on the basis that the victim did not show serious enough injuries to prove that penetration resulted from force. Similarly, in the case of Van der Watt, the appeal court assumed consent on the basis that the victim had not immediately reported the case to the police. This type of reasoning was present in a variety of lower and higher court cases.

In addition to the rape myths that pervade criminal trials and deter victims of violence from feeling that the law takes them seriously even when they are in court, Phumzile, the counselor at the medical facility discussed in the previous section, pointed to barriers involving witness protection. She explained that, because she is often the first point of contact for a victim of sexual assault, she is often called to court to testify in rape cases. But, she explained, "if we are called to testify against a gang member on behalf of a client, we often don't know which gang. This is very dangerous for me. After court, I have to walk to a car or a taxi, but this is very risky, and there's no protection at all. But the law forces me to go to court, and I want to support the victim." She went on to tell me about witnesses who had been attacked, killed, or raped in these kinds of cases. And then she added:

I am very scared for my family after this. I don't trust anyone. If anyone wants to go out, I simply don't let them. After hearing all these horrible stories I just don't trust anyone.[38]

The ongoing security threat seriously reduces incentives for non-state actors – and even police – to get involved in criminal cases involving gang members.

Even if they overcome the barriers associated with reporting a case to the police, when faced with this type of logic and reasoning at the trial stage, as well as ongoing security risks, it takes a great deal of confidence and knowledge of one's rights to continue with the legal process.

In eastern DR Congo, legal outreach and NGO advocacy has provided openings and opportunities for victims of violence to identify as "rights-bearing subjects," while similarly situated victims in South Africa's Western Cape continue to be systematically shut out of the legal system. This is especially true for those who have received few educational or economic opportunities. White and black women, on aggregate, have very different experiences of the law and of having their grievances heard, recognized, and taken seriously by the state. Legal remedy is particularly elusive for those otherwise economically, socially, or educationally disadvantaged, with have no prior experiences of navigating hostile and complex legal bureaucracies. In this sense, the experiences of poor or working-class black and colored women – particularly in rural areas or high-crime townships – tend to be among the worst. These communities are those most likely to be unfamiliar with their rights and have the worst experiences with hostile and male-dominated state structures. Indeed, given that the vast majority of gender violence victims consists of poor black women, this dynamic has created a feedback loop in which the increased marginalization of gender violence within legal structures has further discouraged victims of these types of crimes from thinking about their grievances as legal violations deserving of remedy.

NGO Support Services: Connecting Victims of Violence to the Law

The South African government has, in recent years, committed additional resources to improving the Family Violence, Child Protection, and Sexual Offences (FCS) Units attached to police stations and courts. These units have made great strides in improving the collection of medical evidence in sexual assault cases at the time of first reporting. However, the effectiveness of the FCS can depend heavily on the whims, sensitivities, and experience of particular officers, who are not

[38] Interview. Phumzile, Community Support Worker. South Africa. March 15, 2013.

always inclined to behave in victim-supportive ways.[39] In addition to state-led initiatives, some South African activists, organizations, and NGOs have partnered with government initiatives or assumed roles within state-run medical facilities in order to improve state services and enhance the experiences of victims of gender violence with the criminal justice system. Other similarly situated organizations and individuals have established support services and facilities that remain independent of government-run institutions and are designed to provide extra support for victims of violence not well served by formal legal channels. These organizations and coalitions often provide an initial point of contact between the legal system and communities otherwise cut off from it. Like similarly situated organizations in eastern DR Congo, these organizations often also educate victims and the broader communities in which they are embedded about their rights vis-à-vis the law.

However, as discussed in prior chapters, these NGOs and coalitions function very differently to the activities of organizations in eastern DR Congo. Rather than engaging in direct service provision, NGOs have predominantly focused on advocacy and state development, emphasizing the need for the central state to respond more effectively to widespread gender violence. With some notable exceptions, they are not engaged in capacity building at the margins. They do not seek to systematically "recruit" victims or provide them with incentives to participate in legal proceedings. Where smaller grassroots coalitions like those described in previous sections work directly with victims, they typically provide responsive support in the form of accompanying victims to the police station and monitoring their cases as they move through the legal system, rather than entering communities and hospitals in search of cases. These activities are undertaken on a limited scale and often on an ad hoc basis. Ruth, a legal expert based in Cape Town, commented: "Civil society can monitor trials and this can drive up performance, but it's really hard to say how much impact this actually has in the long term."[40]

Some grassroots coalitions have sought to complement initiatives such as the Thuthuzela Care Centres, which were created through national policy at the behest of civil society pressure. A few small-scale collectives in Khayelitsha and Gugulethu seek to fill some of the holes left by the state's neglect of gender violence issues in ways that resemble the activities of NGOs in eastern DR Congo. For example, organizations like the Social Justice Coalition in the Western Cape offer assistance to victims of gender

---

[39] Interview. Siseko, Family Violence, Child Protection and Sexual Offences Unit. South Africa. June 8, 2017.
[40] Interview. Ruth, Program Lawyer. South Africa. March 15, 2013.

violence in some of the high-crime townships around Cape Town. The Social Justice Coalition and members of its Criminal Justice Task Force, along with other similar church groups and grassroots organizations, attempt to bridge some of the mammoth gaps between victims of violence and the justice system (Super 2016). They educate local communities and provide critical assistance to vulnerable victims of sexual assault. This may include accompanying them to report cases to the police, as well as monitoring cases as they travel through the system. Like eastern DR Congo, local initiatives like these devote considerable effort to following up with police officers so that dockets do not get "lost" or dropped.

In the few cases where organizations like the Social Justice Coalition support victims and witnesses, their work makes a monumental difference to the fate of the cases. However, these efforts are usually pioneered by small, local, often church-based NGOs or community organizations that lack the resources or capacity to carry out activities on a large scale. Many of the grassroots activists I spoke to in such roles could count the cases they had assisted with on one hand.

Given that the South African justice system is overworked and under-resourced, without careful monitoring and oversight a great many cases simply fall through the cracks. Victims often do not even get a phone call to tell them to come to court to testify. It is even more rare for them to be informed of a trial's outcome. While most of my research pertained to the urban townships of Khayelitsha and Gugulethu, one interviewee noted that problems associated with police capacity were further exacerbated in rural locations. She observed: "There are only two police vans in rural areas and the Magistrates Court is very, very far. From here it is 6 Rand to go to court by bus. In rural areas it is 40 Rand. When you call the police it might take them four to five hours to arrive if they arrive at all."[41] Where members of local community task forces monitor cases, they play an important role in encouraging victims to take cases to the police and in keeping victims and witnesses up to date with information and developments about the case's progress.

Commenting on the shortcomings of local police in the high-crime townships of Khayelitsha and Gugulethu, Dyoli, a civil society activist, commented:

Police will not make an effort with cases. If a case is going to be an effort, it will not go through. A case has to seek them out and present itself to them if it is to ever progress to the next stage. If we did not follow these cases, the police would not be interested.[42]

---

[41] Field notes. Esperance, Health Clinic. South Africa. March 14, 2013.
[42] Interview. Dyoli, Community Activist. South Africa. March 6, 2013.

A member of a self-appointed criminal justice task force claimed:

> I go with victims to the police sometimes – I have been about five times. If you don't know your rights, the police will rubbish you and send you away. But if you go, and tell them what they need to do, and watch them, and don't go away, the docket won't be lost.[43]

She added:

> If you go to the police with [our organization], the police will react much better and more professional[ly] than if you go alone. This shows that they know how to behave; they just don't feel pressure to behave well most of the time.

Because police in Khayelitsha also frequently advise victims of violence that cases should be solved within or between the implicated families, NGOs and community-based organizations can – and do – play an important role in educating victims of violence about their rights. Nikelwa, a civil society activist who had accompanied victims to the police recounted her experiences on this topic:

> On the 23rd June I dealt with a case. We arrived to the police with the victim and the accused was arrested. He [the accused] accepted that he raped her, so he said that they could talk as families and he would pay what she wanted. The police encouraged this resolution. But her sister didn't allow it. She said no – that she would go to the magistrates' court and the case would continue. Only empowered people would do this. Most people would take the money.[44]

In this sense, grassroots human rights organizations perceive part of their responsibility to be educating citizens about the law and encouraging them to seek a judicial response even in cases where the perpetrator (or the victim) prefers to settle the matter privately.

While the support provided by organizations like this undoubtedly has a powerful impact on the lives of the victims these organizations serve, these types of activities have not operated on a scale large enough to have any systemic effect on the administration of justice as a whole. The important work carried out by grassroots activists and organizations in Khayelitsha undoubtedly increases the likelihood that certain cases are taken seriously by law enforcement personnel and are propelled through the criminal justice system. Yet the work of small grassroots civil society coalitions can in no way compare to the resources, expertise, and scale of the legal aid programs deployed in North and South Kivu that fulfill the specific function of "substituting" for the state where it is weak or absent. Legal aid clinics in eastern DR Congo operate with large budgets across

---

[43] Interview. Thembela, Community Activist. South Africa. March 6, 2013.
[44] Interview. Nikelwa, Community Activist. South Africa. March 6, 2013.

the eastern provinces, sometimes employing scores of trained lawyers to seek out and assist with cases and represent victims in court. Although legal aid programs in eastern DR Congo tend to restrict their work to targeted areas– and thus the fruits of their labor are not widely accessible – they nevertheless have greater reach than those playing similar roles in South Africa. Civil society groups engaged in judicial monitoring in South Africa, for instance, simply have not had the infrastructural capacity, resources, or authority to transform the relationship between victims of violence and the law.

Conclusion

This chapter examined why increasing numbers of women in eastern DR Congo have turned to formal institutional processes in the aftermath of gender violence, despite the fact that they have little prior experience of doing so and the state has consistently failed to provide basic goods and services to its population. It compared the experiences of victims of gender violence in eastern DR Congo with similarly situated victims of violence in South Africa's Western Cape. It evidences some of the incentives and support structures that have been made available to victims of violence in eastern DR Congo in the aftermath of gendered crimes, that have been missing in South Africa's Western Cape.

Research in eastern DR Congo revealed that NGOs have acted as important mediators, connecting victims of violence with the law and providing them with powerful new tools to reject discriminatory and abusive practices. Many victims of violence who have been effective in pursuing cases through the early stages of the legal process have been guided by NGOs and legal aid clinics, even when they have little awareness that they are participating in a criminal case. Some have been provided with free medical care or other socioeconomic or material benefits to incentivize their participation.

Research in the Western Cape revealed that few of these structural incentives and entry points to participate in legal proceedings exist.[45] While some organizations have encouraged victims of gender violence to pursue cases in South Africa's courts, the support rolled out has been fairly ad hoc. The FSC and the Thuthuzela Care Centers are notoriously overworked and under-resourced. Thus, rather than directly engaging in service provision, or assuming responsibility for tasks normally carried out by police or prosecutors, as has been the case in eastern DR Congo,

---

[45] See Epp (1998), Galanter (1994), and Rubbers and Gallez (2012) for a discussion of the importance of material resources in motivating participation in legal processes.

NGOs and advocacy organizations in South Africa have been more inclined to focus on lobbying the state to improve services and holding the government accountable for its actions. And given that the South African government already provides fairly comprehensive health care and medical benefits to its citizens, victims of violence have not faced the same pressures to seek creative alternatives to accessing medical assistance. In short, victims of gender violence do not need to turn to legal aid clinics to assist them in paying medical bills, accessing healthcare or securing prenatal support.

Finally, whereas in eastern DR Congo many police face structural incentives to prioritize gender-based crimes and treat victims reporting such crimes respectfully, police in South Africa face few such incentives. On the contrary, many are incentivized to deprioritze sexual assaults due to these cases' complexity and the difficulties of securing a victim-favorable resolution. While there are certainly some victims of violence in South Africa's Western Cape who would report more positive experiences with the criminal justice system, and many in the Kivus whose experiences mirror those typical in South Africa, the perspectives represented here are illuminating. The fact that opportunities and entry points exist in any systematic form for Congolese victims of violence (albeit a small minority overall) sets its legal landscape apart. The uneven spatial dispersion of entry points for victims, however, as well as the complexities and challenges that accompany this type of access, are the subject of Part II.

Part II

Introduction to Part II

In the preface to this manuscript, I described a small human rights work-shop I attended in North Kivu in 2009, on the International Criminal Tribunal for Rwanda (ICTR). Over the course of the workshop, an uncomfortable truth emerged: the workshop's participants had been invited to learn about law and human rights in a country that is home to one of the most dilapidated legal infrastructures in the world. Even in the unlikely event that participants could access the legal system, they would need to seek out and formally identify those who had harmed them, relive the traumas they had experienced, and place their faith in lawyers and police. In doing so, they may risk retaliation or jeopardize relationships with their families over the shame of having been subjected to sexual abuse. A best-case outcome would require victims to come face to face with their perpetrators and risk their lives again by publicly testifying against husbands, partners, or other individuals in positions of relative power. All the while, criminal justice rarely provides clothes, food, or education for victims' families. Guilty verdicts do not promise medical care. And even successful convictions do not always mean prison time. No matter the ruling, powerful men with guns or money are skilled at evading justice.

Yet, despite all of these obstacles, Chapter 5 demonstrated, many victims of violence have turned to the Kivus' courts to seek formal legal remedy for crimes committed against them, and continue to do so in greater numbers than ever before. In contrast to South Africa, sexual and gender-based crimes fill the court registers in both the military and civilian justice systems, and courts increasingly rule in favor of victims. Yet we know little of the broader repercussions of these cases. How does an increased focus on gender-based crimes in local courts affect victims of violence and the communities in which they are embedded? How (if at all) do they shape or transform legal culture and landscapes of insecurity? What do legal gains in court mean in a context of otherwise dilapidated state infrastructure?

Many of these questions lie beyond the scope of this project. Yet it is important to situate the legal advancements discussed here within the broader contexts from which they emerge. In particular, it is important to weigh the gains wrought by gender activists in eastern DR Congo against the myriad harms, injustices, and obstacles that prevail.

Thus, while state fragility has created episodic opportunities for external actors to promote gender justice through the courts, developments in eastern DR Congo and South Africa's Western Cape present practitioners, donors, and policy makers with a difficult dilemma. On the one hand, many victims of violence have reported receiving tangible benefits, both psychological and material, as a direct result of legal capacity-building interventions. For many, the criminalization of gender violence and the formal recognition by the country's courts of systematic gender abuses validate and empower individuals whose specific forms of victimization had previously gone unrecognized. On the other hand, capitalizing on state fragility to advance a singular human rights agenda has created a set of problematic dynamics that call into question the channels through which these victories were won. These dynamics may even undermine the anticipated benefits of accountability over the longer term. Despite the successes of legal/gender activists in eastern DR Congo, should the strategies and interventions of external actors at the peripheries of statehood ever serve as a model for human rights advocacy elsewhere, and what factors should scholars and practitioners consider in exploring this question?

The chapters in Part II draw together some of the many tensions and challenges that gender activists and human rights practitioners have faced in their activities in eastern DR Congo. These tensions force scholars and policy makers – in sub-Saharan Africa and beyond – to confront a set of normative questions that weigh various types of human rights gains against one another. Because Part II focuses on rights at the peripheries of statehood, it draws predominantly from the experiences of the Kivus. Chapter 6 presents reflections expressed by a broad spectrum of Congolese women, most of whom sought protections from the law in the aftermath of violence. The chapter considers the very immediate ways that some of the intended beneficiaries of legal aid programs have responded to opportunities to participate in prosecutions for sexual and gender-based crimes. It also examines the material, social, and psychological support that has resulted, as well as the shortcomings and disappointments of the legal process that interviewees identified.

Chapter 7 widens the lens. It considers some of the broader repercussions and unintended consequences – both positive and negative – that emerge from the pursuit of a fairly singular human rights goal (in this case, legal justice for gender-based crimes) in an environment of ongoing state fragility. The chapter highlights a number of the trade-offs and contradictions that were revealed in the course of this research, including a reluctance for donors and NGOs to direct resources toward enforcing criminal sentences, as well as the continued marginalization of other pressing human rights issues. While some of the trade-offs identified were the direct result of shortsighted policy decisions that could have potentially been overcome with more careful and reflective program implementation, others prove far less easily resolved. The Janus-faced nature of gender justice victories in eastern DR Congo forces us to revisit old debates about the messy politics of external intervention and human rights advocacy in transitional, post-conflict, and postcolonial contexts.

6 Hard-Fought Victories
Assessing the Human Rights Benefits Felt by Victims of Violence in DR Congo

Introduction

One evening, Mayifa came home to find her daughter hurt.[1] On questioning her, Mayifa learned her daughter had been raped by a neighbor while she was preparing dinner in her home. Mayifa and her brother drove the girl to Goma for treatment and to report the incident to the police. The neighbor responsible was arrested and taken to Munzenze. Mayifa and her daughter went to the court every day for a month to provide information and to wait for the trial. After some time, however, the perpetrator escaped from prison, and there was never any resolution to the case. I asked Mayifa how she felt about the process of testifying in court, which had been time-consuming and ultimately unsuccessful. Mayifa told me: "I was glad, first because now the government knows my daughter was raped, and secondly because we received free medical treatment from HEAL Africa."[2]

Chapter 5 showed that domestic and international NGOs in the Kivus have transformed the landscape of dispute resolution by providing many Congolese women with opportunities and incentives to seek formal legal accountability for gender-based violence. NGOs have improved access to justice through engaging in outreach with local communities and providing material, social, and psychological support to those wishing to pursue legal remedy. Yet, in order to understand and assess the broader repercussions of increased legal accountability for gender-based crimes, it is important to examine how affected individuals have responded, as well as how these individuals reflect on their interactions with state law. It is also necessary to consider who, specifically, is situated to take advantage of new opportunities.

---

[1] Parts of this chapter are adapted from the article "Gendering Justice in Humanitarian Spaces: Opportunity and (Dis)empowerment through Gender-Based Legal Development Outreach in the Eastern Democratic Republic of Congo," published in *Law and Society Review* (2016) and coauthored with Ilot Muthaka and Gabriella Walker.

[2] Interview. Mayifa. DR Congo. January 11, 2013.

This chapter draws from interviews with differently situated Congolese women, aiming to understand how the immediate repercussions of gender justice interventions are felt by those intended to benefit from them. My interviews revealed that, in spite of dramatically different motivations for seeking legal remedy, NGO outreach and support has allowed many victims of gender-based crimes to exert new forms of agency over the paths taken in the aftermath of violence. New entry points into the legal system have allowed victims of violence to access social, ideological, and sometimes material benefits that were not previously accessible. Many have adopted the language of legal remedy and punitive justice to reject customary practices that they found abusive, disempowering, or dehumanizing. For these individuals, legal outreach initiatives have provided a new vocabulary for demanding formal recognition that a violation or wrong occurred (Ellickson 1986; Merry 1994; Rubbers and Gallez 2012). The pursuit of recognition is not the only new form of agency that legal outreach initiatives have offered. Other victims of violence have instrumentally adopted the language of the law to access social or material benefits, such as antiretroviral treatment or prenatal care. Rather than being "socialized" into new frames of legal consciousness as legal outreach NGOs intended, legal aid has served as a vehicle to access other avenues of support.

This chapter opens with a discussion of how differently situated victims of violence have conceptualized the options available to them in the aftermath of violence, and concludes with their post hoc reflections on their experiences as legal subjects.[3] Many of those I spoke to were let down by what the law promised. Some were denied compensation that lawyers, NGOs, or acquaintances led them to expect. Others were asked to pay bribes or were never informed of the outcome of their case. While these experiences point to serious problems in the implementation of legal support programs, a surprising number of interviewees nevertheless continued to find value in the process, if not the outcome, of their cases, which offered them newfound validation and recognition as rights-bearing citizens entitled to justice (Merry 2002b). Given that legal outreach programs cannot successfully strengthen justice systems without engaging local communities in their work, the perspectives of the intended beneficiaries of legal aid programs allow us crucial insight into legal capacity-building projects from the ground up.

---

[3] Appendix B offers a detailed discussion of the interviews, including how interviewees were contacted.

Adopting the Language of Punitive Justice

One sentiment that repeatedly surfaced in my interviews with victims of gender-based crimes was the idea that the criminalization of rape and sexual assault – and its associated convictions – permitted women to vocally reject practices that they had previously felt compelled to tolerate.

During the Mobutu era, no victim of violence would be inclined to seek assistance from the formal justice system unless he or she had reason to believe that representatives of the state would treat their case favorably. The legacies of *débrouillez-vous* meant that courts were widely recognized as corrupt, characterized by networks of nepotism and patronage. Thus, many victims of violence saw informal settlements with offenders' families as their only opportunity for recourse. This skepticism toward the legal system still permeates many communities, particularly in remote locations with limited NGO presence. Daní, seventeen, was raped by six FARDC soldiers in a town in North Kivu. When asked about the police, she claimed:

We just wanted drugs and medicine. We never thought about going to the police. Only God can punish him, so I wouldn't want to do a trial.[4]

Other victims of violence I interviewed were prepared to sacrifice any notion of formal justice for some basic material wants and needs. For instance, Aisha, thirty-four, was raped by FDLR combatants in South Kivu. She said:

I wanted money to cover the expenses. I can't choose him staying in prison because that doesn't benefit me. If he can accept what he's done and come out of prison, and carry on paying the charges, that would be better. Now I just have a big debt. If he stays out of prison but pays all the charges for the baby, that is no problem.[5]

Asante added: "I just need compensation now, because I don't know how to survive."[6]

However, these girls, who each came from remote rural locations rarely visited by international NGOs or legal advocacy organizations, were in the minority among those I interviewed. For many, "justice" was expressed as an end in itself. Moreover, representing a stark break from the past, a surprising number of the women I interviewed strongly rejected traditional leaders as the appropriate forum for resolving gender-

[4] Interview. Daní. DR Congo. May 15, 2013.
[5] Interview. Aisha. DR Congo. January 14, 2013.
[6] Interview. Asante. DR Congo. January 11, 2013.

based grievances. Instead, many perceived courts as the appropriate arbiters for these types of crimes, in spite of their many demonstrated failings (see also Ewick and Silbey 1998; Mayhew and Reiss 1969; Miller and Sarat 1980; Rubbers and Gallez 2012). A deeply held belief in the inherent value of the legal process fundamentally shaped my interviewees' reflections on whether their hopes for justice had been met.

As discussed in the previous chapters, the *baraza*, the *nyumbakumi*, and the *chef de village* still exist as the first point of dispute resolution for many Congolese citizens, particularly in rural areas. However, in the past five to ten years, some married and unmarried victims of gender violence have embraced formal legal avenues. When the new Sexual Violence Law was introduced in 2006, the practice of *arrangement à l'amiable* was strictly outlawed in cases of sexual violence. Furthermore, under new laws, customary authorities are prohibited from intervening in disputes involving rape or gender-based crimes. Although the Family Code of 1987 had also altered the legal framework on this issue, the 2006 reforms have had a far greater impact on how local stakeholders approach gender violence. My interviews suggest that increasing numbers of victims exposed to legal and human rights outreach programs are rejecting customary practices and turning to formal legal mechanisms in their place.

Émilie, a forty-two-year-old woman from North Kivu, was raped in her home by two colleagues of her husband. After she confronted the perpetrators in a police interview, she explained: "They agreed to pay us two cows, but the police said no. Even still he must be sentenced."[7] Marie, twenty-one, shared a similar sentiment, reinforcing Émilie's experience that formal legal justice was the only appropriate response to a sexual assault:

In most cases, people will try to find common ground before they go to the police. I think for most things traditional leaders are better [for resolving disputes]. When a problem is solved by a traditional leader it is well managed. If there is a problem between a man and his wife, or farm limits, or if people in the village are fighting, then the chief is good to solve these. But in the case of rape it is such a big issue it can't be dealt with by the traditional leaders.[8]

The idea that rape should not be dealt with by traditional leaders was shared by a large number of the victims of violence I spoke to, as well as the vast majority of local NGOs and civil society representatives.

---

[7] Interview. Émilie. DR Congo. January 23, 2013. It is not uncommon for the victim and members of her family to participate in meetings in which the police confront and interview the alleged perpetrators about their actions and take their statements.
[8] Interview. Marie. DR Congo. January 11, 2013.

Moreover, a number of interviewees strongly rejected the idea of *arrangement amiable* in cases involving sexual violence. When asked how she felt when the family of the man who raped her offered her money as compensation, Joellie, seventeen, from a village in South Kivu said:

They must take this man and punish him for what he did, and he should know he is the father of this child and do his responsibilities with this child. He has destroyed my life, and giving me money would not be the solution. He should be arrested.[9]

Many others echoed Joellie's desire for punishment for what they did. Rachelle, a seventeen-year-old raped by a soldier in North Kivu, told me:

I was expecting compensation, especially for medical treatment. But the most important [thing] for me is that he stays in prison so he won't do it to anyone else.[10]

Charlene, forty, added:

The most important thing for me was that they were in prison – justice. I want them to be punished because I don't want them to do it again to other people. I want them to spend twenty years or the rest of their lives inside so they don't do it to anyone else.[11]

Naema, an eighteen-year-old from South Kivu who was raped by a boy she knew from school, said:

I don't want to take their money and I don't want to take them to court because I am afraid. The parents of the perpetrators said they would pay a dowry to me, and they would look after the child, but I don't want them to take the child. They have offered me money, but I don't want to marry the attacker because he has ruined my life. I don't even want their money.[12]

And Mashika, a seventeen-year-old raped by soldiers, claimed:

I want him to be punished. I want justice. What I expect is only punishment. Money, no. Compensation, no. Only punishment.[13]

Mupenda, another seventeen-year-old raped by soldiers in North Kivu, added:

I am ready to go to court and tell my case. Because when people commit mistakes, they must go to prison.[14]

[9] Interview. Joellie. DR Congo. May 6, 2013.
[10] Interview. Rachelle. DR Congo. May 15, 2013.
[11] Interview. Charlene. DR Congo. January 14, 2013.
[12] Interview. Naema. DR Congo. May 6, 2013.
[13] Interview. Mashika. DR Congo. January 23, 2013.
[14] Interview. Mupenda. DR Congo. April 26, 2013.

While it is impossible to know whether the attitudes of Naema, Mashika, Charlene, and Mupenda have been shaped by shifting societal norms, or simply represent their own very personal preferences, some interviewees – like Marie – explicitly linked their rejection of *arrangement à l'amiable* to a declining cultural tolerance of rape. Année Joyeuse was raped by a group of Mai Mai soldiers when she was traveling from Maniema to North Kivu. She explained:

> Here in our Congo, you have to pay. Even if you are stolen from, if you go to the police, it is you who will have to pay, instead of the one who stole from you. But now it's very strict. Now, the police, they are serious. If you rape and you are arrested, you have to spend twenty-five years in prison, because rape is serious now.[15]

Luce, a forty-five-year-old woman living in North Kivu, spoke about her disappointment at having to marry the man who caused her such physical and emotional harm. But she similarly observed that things were very different now than when she was raped in 1995:

> It was 1995, under Mobutu's regime. The man with whom I'm living now, with whom I have children, we got to know each other and after we met he asked me to come and see where he was staying, where he was living. I refused. There were two men and I was with another woman. I was still a girl. Then I went and the woman asked me to go with them. When I went to his house, we sat up talking. It was around 6:30 PM and he was joking with me. Then he forced me, and he raped me. That is the way that he raped me. At the time, rape was not known as a problem; it was not known in the same context. I stayed there, and after three days I escaped and ran away and went to stay at my friend's, and I explained what happened and she told me that I was already a woman. She said that I should go back home because this was a problem so there was nothing to do. It's in those circumstances that I started my household ... it's not that way that someone should marry a girl ... But since then it is in that way that I am living with him, but I am always a victim of violence. Every time, torture, beating, and everything. It is part of my life. I am violated in all ways. I take charge of the children myself, I have to pay school fees and food and everything, and I always speak loudly and I feel bad for the trauma for my daughter. At that moment I didn't report the case to the justice system because rape was not then a priority for justice ... Today it is quite different; if you have raped, justice is formed and you shall be punished.[16]

As Luce demonstrates, in the past two decades, the landscape of options available to victims of rape or sexual assault has dramatically changed. Rather than turning to a trusted male elder, victims of violence have recently been introduced – in some cases for very the first time – to courts and police as possible venues for resolving these types of grievances.

[15] Interview. Année Joyeuse. DR Congo. January 23, 2013.
[16] Interview. Luce. DR Congo. January 23, 2013.

Despite their imperfections, for Marie, Année, and Luce, the police now represent the *only* appropriate venue for crimes of this nature. Grâce captured this sentiment, expressed by many of my interviewees, very simply: "If something bad happens to you, then you go to the police. That is what you should do."[17]

The idea that rape is "too serious" of a crime to be dealt with by customary authorities is a very recent development. While many victims of violence may have always felt repulsed at being compelled to marry or accept money from a man who caused them such harm, the quotes just cited demonstrate that legal outreach and changing societal attitudes toward rape have enabled them to frame and express these opinions in the language of law, punishment, and criminal justice. Domestic and international advocacy has made it culturally acceptable for some women to speak out about gendered crimes. The opportunity to adopt the language of law, punishment, and criminal justice in the aftermath of gendered violence, whether motivated by a heartfelt desire for criminal justice or otherwise, has given many women the confidence and authority to reject and condemn assaults they had previously been expected to tolerate.

Experiencing the Law

My interviewees in North and South Kivu expressed a wide variety of motivations for turning to formal legal remedies in the aftermath of a sexual assault, which included material, social, and ideological factors. After initiating legal proceedings, their experiences with the justice system also varied considerably.

Many of those I interviewed who had turned to formal legal mechanisms affirmed and validated their decision to do so, even after reporting largely negative experiences. When asked about whether or not they were glad that they had reported a crime to the police, or whether they were likely to pursue a similar course of action again in the future, many individuals reaffirmed their desire for justice as the reason why they felt validated in taking the action they did. The vast majority of interviewees who had participated in a court case shared this sentiment, regardless of their initial reasons for going to court, or of their own positive or negative experiences. For instance, many of my interviewees referred to the various failings of the legal system when talking about their own experiences. Of thirty-seven women I interviewed who had attempted to initiate criminal proceedings, eighteen reported having to pay a bribe at some stage of

[17] Interview. Grâce. DR Congo. January 23, 2013.

the process. Some mentioned that the accused was released after he payed a bribe to the police or offered financial compensation to the victim's family. Others reported that the accused evaded justice after the main prison in North Kivu was liberated in a rebel occupation in 2012. Thus, very few victims of violence saw their perpetrators held legally accountable. Yet, in spite of these seemingly insurmountable obstacles, most still confirmed that they would follow a similar course of action in the future. After never having been informed of the verdict of her case or receiving any of the compensation she was promised, Mayifa's comment in the introduction to this chapter is particularly illuminating. Noting that she was glad that she took the action she did because the government now "knew that her daughter had been raped" demonstrates that, in spite of the legal system's failings, she valued the formal, institutional recognition that a crime had been committed.

Aisha told a similar story that captures the complex and sometimes contradictory emotions interviewees expressed toward the police. Aisha was raped on two separate occasions: the first involved unknown FDLR bandits, and the second involved the FARDC as she was on her way to buy charcoal near her home in rural North Kivu. Aisha recognized the FARDC soldiers who raped her, so she reported the case to the police, and those responsible were arrested and tried in a military court. After they were found guilty, they were sent to Munzenze, but later escaped when the prison was liberated in the occupation of Goma. Aisha told me:

Before I was living with my uncle but when I was pregnant I was cast away from the house ... I went to the police because I expected support from him. Because I was pregnant, I expected I would get it. I was thinking that if I was pregnant, or infected with any disease, he would be responsible. The police know that when someone is in trouble they can go to the government to get help, so I knew they would help. I knew that when I had a problem, I should go to the police, but when I was raped I spoke to my friends and family and they also said I should go to the police. I knew that the police and the whole government like money. I knew that they will ask for money, but I arrived there crying and no one asked me for anything. I was surprised. I went for support. I didn't have any money so I believed that if they refused I would go back home ... We would only go to a pastor for help with prayers, but for a real problem you can't go to a pastor. From the case in the military court I was expecting that I would get some help to take care of the baby; M23 controlled the town when I was in the hospital, so I went to the military court to get help before the trial was over. They told me they would force him to accept [what he had done] because he was the one responsible ... The judges told me that. They said that the money would come from the perpetrator. The court was trying to decide how he would [agree to] pay the money. He has not yet accepted. I am really disappointed about the court, because they did well in arresting him, but now I still have nothing. We can solve most things with ease at the family level, but if it is something like rape, you don't have to solve it at the family level. You must go to the police. If someone has been punished for that, when he is released, he won't do the same thing again.[18]

In this interview, Aisha went back and forth, at times commenting on her grave disappointment with the justice system, and at other times affirming the value of the legal process. Aisha expressed similar ambivalence with regard to her treatment by the police and the military courts. Earlier in the interview, Aisha had told me that the military court had requested a fee of $10 USD, but she later confirms that she wasn't asked for any bribe. In rural areas, many of the victims that I spoke to went – like Aisha – directly to the police after they were attacked, rather than to an NGO or a legal aid clinic. At this point, they were often asked for money by the officers on duty. Yet, interestingly, like Aisha, most of the interviewees did not speak about these demands as bribery or corruption – instead, they interpreted these requests as part of a necessary fee they were required to pay for reporting the crime. In their reflections, informal fees did not detract from whether or not they considered the police to have been helpful, sympathetic, "good," or effective in their jobs. Moreover, thirteen of the thirty-seven interviewees who went to the police explicitly noted that the police had been nice, helpful, or effective. This was in spite of the fact that eight of these individuals had paid a bribe themselves, and in seven of these cases, the perpetrator either escaped or was released after paying a bribe. Grâce, whose husband was killed by rebels when she was raped, reflected:

I always went to the TGI to give my testimony. I knew the police could help if something bad happens to you ... If something bad happens to you, then you go to the police. That is what you do. I know they ask for money, but they are not bad.[19]

It is difficult to know whether this (often ill-founded) confidence in the police was the result of outreach efforts by NGOs to improve the image of the police among local communities, or whether it was part of some more deeply held belief that the police are the appropriate arbiters of disputes, despite the fact that they are embedded within corrupt and inefficient bureaucracies. The contradictions inherent in many interviewee testimonies, particularly in interviewees' descriptions of their interactions with and attitudes toward police, exemplify the deep ambivalence that characterizes ordinary citizens' experiences with state law.

[18] Interview. Aisha. DR Congo. January 14, DR Congo.
[19] Interview. Grâce. DR Congo. January 23, 2013.

Even in cases where international NGOs had supported them, interviewees often recalled extremely negative experiences with the legal system. Victims were often cast aside after their role in giving testimony was over. They were rarely kept informed of the outcome or progress of the trial, by their legal representatives, NGOs, courts, or police. Agathe from South Kivu, the same interviewee who had explained to me that she was assisted by Allain in Chapter 5, told me that she never received the compensation she had been promised.[20] After she was raped, she described how neighbors chased after her attackers and captured one of them, who was immediately arrested.

MILLI: *Did you receive any compensation from your attackers after the court case?*

AGATHE: No, I didn't receive anything because it was Allain who was following everything.

MILLI: *Did Allain receive the compensation?*

AGATHE: No, Allain didn't receive it. The one who did this accepted that he was going to pay and he wrote down and signed, but he didn't pay already.

MILLI: *And how did you feel after the judgment?*

AGATHE: The first thing bad was that after that action my husband decided to divorce, so I took the charges myself. But after the judgment and the trial, and [the one who did this] having been sentenced for twenty years, I felt really satisfied because I saw him in jail.

MILLI: *Did you expect that the attacker would be convicted? Did you expect that you would win the case?*

AGATHE: Yes, I knew that I would win.

MILLI: *How did you know?*

AGATHE: The man who was involved – Allain – I knew that he would defend my case very well.

MILLI: *And did you ever have to pay any money to the court?*

AGATHE: I paid only $20 USD when the police came to look for them.

MILLI: *And so what motivated you at the very beginning to go forward with the case?*

AGATHE: First of all, my husband had already left me. I was expecting some compensation, as I couldn't cover most of the costs for my children.

MILLI: *If your husband hadn't divorced you, do you think it would have been more difficult to proceed with the court case?*

AGATHE: Yes, but even so, I would continue with the case.

MILLI: *So was it mainly the compensations that motivated you?*

AGATHE: Yes, I wanted to be compensated because my reputation was now dirty.

MILLI: *Do you mean compensated financially?*

AGATHE: Yes.

MILLI: *So had you heard of other people where you were who had also had successful cases with Allain?*

AGATHE: Yes, up to ten. They were all successful.

MILLI: *And are you still in touch with Allain now?*

AGATHE: Nowadays, no.

[20] Interview. Grâce. DR Congo. January 23, 2013.

MILLI: *So if you had a problem again or knew someone else who experienced something like what happened to you, do you think you would do the same this time?*

AGATHE: I could help him or her – I could guide that person so that he may report the case to the justice.

MILLI: *Do you think that would be better than going to a* chef coutumier?

AGATHE: Yes, because the local chief can be corrupted. The police can be corrupted, but not a lot.

Agathe's story – that she had been assisted by an NGO; been promised compensation; decided to participate in a trial and give evidence, but then never heard anything more of the case; never received compensation; and never learned of the verdict – was a common one. Of those I spoke to, rarely did anyone receive the compensation they were awarded. Of the thirty-seven victims of violence who had attempted to initiate legal proceedings, only four received any form of monetary compensation, yet twenty-three still reported that they would take a similar course of action again.

For many, by the time we spoke, the compensation was simply not the main point of the case. When asked about their overall feelings toward the justice system in light of their negative experiences, interviewees spoke about how it felt to see their perpetrators arrested and to have their crimes acknowledged, rather than about the lack of remuneration or other failings they encountered.

Agathe, for example, followed up her story by telling me that she was forced to leave her hometown after the case because the family of the accused was threatening her. "But," she repeated, "I felt really satisfied because he was sentenced to twenty years in jail. The perpetrator wrote down that he was going to pay, but Allain was taking care of that. I'm not in touch with Allain anymore. The compensation would be good, but I am satisfied because [the perpetrator] is in prison." Similarly, after paying out large sums in legal "fees" and receiving nothing back, Grâce told me: "I was surprised, because I thought he wouldn't be arrested. But when the people called the police, they came with a car and put him inside and put him in the prison ... I was satisfied because, right now, the one who did this to me is in jail."

In spite of its imperfections, formal recognition of the violations committed and an acknowledgment that perpetrators of these types of assaults *should* be jailed is perhaps what has driven a number of Congolese women to attribute value to the formal institutional mechanisms of the state, even when those institutions have failed to live up to their promises. Merry (2003b) notes that, in turning to formal legal mechanisms for the first time, some women undergo a change in self-perception. Rather than perceiving themselves as defined (and protected) by the same patriarchal familial structures within which they have been violated, the process of turning to the law allows them to take on a new and more autonomous self: one entitled to and deserving of protection outside of the family. While none of the women I spoke to explicitly articulated this idea, it is plausible that some shared this sentiment.

Backlash, Retribution, and Resistance to Law

In order to understand the potential value of legal processes for victims of gender-based violence and their communities, it is necessary to also understand the difficult social realities that many women must confront or overcome in order to consider pursuing legal remedy. It is also necessary to consider which women are able to take advantage of new opportunities for justice, and which women continue to be excluded. As in many parts of the world, the decision to turn to state institutions, rather than family or community-based remedies in the aftermath of violence, represents a stark challenge to societal gender norms. For some, this challenge can be empowering and emancipatory. For others, it has disrupted existing structures of power and patterns of behavior in unanticipated and sometimes uncomfortable ways. Agathe reported that she had been driven out of her hometown after threats against her from her attacker's family. Alika, eighteen, from South Kivu expressed a similar experience:

Men are very bad people. I wanted to go to the court so he could know what he did and be punished. My mother was very, very angry ... but many people, they are taken to the court, or they are arrested, but they are not going to spend much time there. Someone is taken to the court, and then tomorrow he is released. So if you make someone arrested, and then tomorrow he is released, then this person is going to do very bad things against you. Some neighbors encouraged us about the opinion of taking him to court, but others did not. They said: "Don't jeopardize the life of your daughter. You can take him to the court, but tomorrow this man can jeopardize her life by killing her or bringing gunmen to the house to do bad things against her.[21]

Estelle, who was raped and impregnated by her former boyfriend, noted:

Our police are very weak. Being that weak, if you take the case there, for example, if I take my case to them, I remember how my former boyfriend promised that he would kill me if anything bad happened against him. Promising to kill me made

[21] Interview. Alika. DR Congo. May 6, 2013.

me very afraid of what happened, which is why I didn't take the case to the police.[22]

Naema also expressed fear of retaliation or revenge. When asked about her decision not to report a case of rape to the police, Naema said:

One of my neighbors tried to report a case like that, and they came one night to burn her, to burn down the house. Take him to the police and he will come back to burn down your house.[23]

While these types of repercussions have clearly not deterred every aggrieved individual from seeking legal remedy, they serve to illustrate the complex decisions, negotiations, and trade-offs that many women in vulnerable positions are forced to address when considering their options in the aftermath of sexual assault. Although the choice to pursue legal remedy may exist on paper, for many, fear of retribution means it is not a practical reality in their day-to-day lives. Furthermore, the fact that so many women indicated that their attackers had escaped or evaded justice underscores that these fears are not unfounded.

In addition to their fears of retribution from perpetrators of sexual violations, women may also be vulnerable to backlash or retribution from their partners. Sally Merry, in her powerful 2003 study of gender violence in Hawai'i, has written about how the adoption of new "rights-bearing" identities by victims of gender violence can lead to backlash and new forms of violence from male partners (Merry 2003b). She follows Butler (1990) in observing that, by going to court, women are often challenging their "received" gender identities, as well as challenging the hegemonic masculinity of their partners (Merry 2003b: 351). Merry notes that gender is continually transformed through its performance in legally regulated contexts:

As women victimized by violence call the police, walk into courtrooms, fill out forms requesting restraining orders, tell their stories of violence and victimization in forms and in response to official queries, they enact a different self. Such performances reshape the way these women think about themselves and the relationship between their intimate social worlds and the law. Turning to the courts for help in incidents of violence by partners represents a disembedding of the individual in the structure of kin, neighbors, friends, and churches in favor of a new relationship to the state ... Categories such as the private domain of the family, insulated from state supervision by the patriarchal authority of the husband, although at the same time fully constituted by the state in its capacity to marry and divorce, may exist at the level of the unrecognized, the taken for granted, the hegemonic. It is these categories that are challenged by contemporary

---

[22] Interview. Estelle. DR Congo. May 6, 2013.
[23] Interview. Naema. Dr Congo. May, 2013.

feminist movements about violence against women. The promise of rights and the penetration of law into the patriarchal sphere of the family represent a radical transformation in gender and the family.

When women in eastern DR Congo threaten go to court in the context of a physically or emotionally abusive relationship, or assume new empowered identities that do not easily conform to the narrowly constructed image of the submissive or subservient female, they may make themselves increasingly vulnerable to those who do not share or acknowledge their new empowered identities. In addition, when woman turn to the law to pursue gender-accountability, her actions potentially undermine traditional understandings about her place within the home, her male family members may interpret this as a direct assault on their authority or masculinity. This may be especially true in cases in which the wife is victimized by her partner and seeks state support. Yet it may also be true in cases in which a woman has been victimized outside the home and, rather than turning to her husband to resolve the issue privately, she instead seeks support from the legal system.

A number of excellent studies have examined how men's perceived social or economic marginalization has led to feelings of humiliation and vulnerability (see Baaz et al. 2010; Lwambo 2013; Merry 1994, 2003b; Sonke Gender Justice Network 2012).[24] These studies concur that, when men feel disempowered or that their sense of masculinity is under attack, they may resort to violence and aggression to reassert their sense of place within the household or community (Merry 1994; Wood 2005). Indeed, in this vein, many commentators have drawn a direct link between the high levels of domestic violence in South Africa to precisely these forms of oppression and marginalization (Wood 2005). Gender outreach programs and related development initiatives may lead to very real improvements in the lives of some individual women and communities. Yet, when human rights outreach addresses only the symptoms and not the underlying causes of widespread societal violence, thus failing to engage legacies of oppression or to confront dominant representations of masculinity and femininity, then the rule of law-based efforts of human rights practitioners may fall short of disrupting the underlying gender inequities from which that violence stems. Instead, such efforts may result in increased insecurity for women and a complex set of constraints facing victims of gendered abuses when they are considering whether or not to turn to legal institutions.

---

[24] See also Rahman (1999) and Schuler, Hashemi, and Badal (1998) for a discussion of increases in domestic violence following female empowerment programs in other contexts.

The extent to which NGOs have focused on women rather than men in their programing has potentially exacerbated this response. Not only have gender violence programs often overlooked the specific concerns of male victims of sexual and gender-based violence, but they have also reinforced binary representations of women as victims and men as perpetrators (Lewis 2018). In doing so, the vast majority of attention and support has been directed toward supporting and empowering women, rather than engaging men or addressing root causes of violence. Typically, gender violence programming has been reactive, offering victims of violence economic opportunities, access to microcredit programs, and opportunities to learn about their basic gender rights. Excluding perpetrator – or potential perpetrator – communities from their work has important implications for the ability of these programs to deter violence over the long term.

Although there is a broad-based consensus among donors and service providers that combating mass violence requires a holistic and multipronged response, where men have been included in post-conflict gender development programming, it has tended to occur in sectors like security sector reform, disarmament, and demobilization. With some (increasing) exceptions, men are rarely incorporated into broader discussions of matters such as gender equality in the household or children's education, which, by implication, continue to be framed as "women's problems." As a result, women may receive microloans, rights-based education, and skills-training, yet continue to return home to abusive relationships or other highly gendered household conflicts. Moreover, the explicit exclusion of men from many development initiatives can foster further resentment and antagonism, leading some men to perceive advocacy on gender violence as "just for women" and thus irrelevant to their behavior. Many male interlocutors in the Kivus spoke about a perceived NGO "war" on men that may be detrimental to longer-term program goals if not tackled head on.[25] Furthermore, an emphasis on military reform and demobilization as the primary areas in which the international community works with men in eastern DR Congo sends a signal that violence and the military continues to remain a "male" domain, whereas other development issues are somehow feminized (Cronin-Furman and Gowrinathan 2015; Lewis 2018; Mackenzie 2009). This binary approach presents development work as inherently gendered and reinforces the popular perception that violence is inextricably bound up with masculinity.

---

[25] Informal conversations about men's perceptions of gender advocacy. Field notes, DR Congo, April 2013.

Although organizations like HEAL Africa have for a long time worked with the families of rape victims in order to diffuse and confront the stigma and shame felt by victims of gender violence and foster local support for a rule of law-based response, at the time at which this research was carried out very little work had sought to directly and explicitly engage with men concerning issues of pervasive violence. Over the past two years, this practice has been changing. Programs have begun to emerge that work with samples of the male population on gendered attitudes and behaviors that affect the propensity toward violence. The International Rescue Committee (IRC), for instance, has begun organizing outreach and gender socialization courses for men across North and South Kivu, engaging participants in discussions about gender inequity, household division of labor, sexual consent, positive masculinity, and other such topics (World Bank 2016). Local organizations like Congo Men's Network (Men Engage), partnered with Sonke Gender Justice, have been undertaking similar activities on a smaller scale for some time. Congo Men's Network has pioneered a number of incredibly powerful programs designed to combat and overturn "negative masculinities" and raise awareness and facilitate dialogue among men around issues of violence. Their focus on male and societal responses to gender violence, rather than on women or victims, represents a promising step toward challenging and redefining gendered behavior. Yet these programs have historically been notable outliers. It is interesting – and perhaps troubling – that, until very recently, support programs and advocacy efforts aimed at combating gender violence have been focused almost exclusively on women as victims (Berry and Lake 2017a).

Conclusion

Even in the context of ongoing institutional failings and the emotional trauma and stigmatization that follows sexual assault, it is evident that legal outreach has provided some victims of gender-based violence with new avenues and opportunities, and even new feelings of closure and resolution, that were previously unavailable to them. Legal outreach and gender-based *sensibilisation* has encouraged victims of violence to view a variety of gender-based harms as *legal* violations that can be interpreted within a criminal justice framework. The language of punitive justice and legal remedy has thus given some victims crucial new tools to reject customary responses to gender violence that they found disempowering or unjust. In such cases, the language of the law has been critically important in enabling victims of violence to assume, adopt, and assert new identities deserving of protection from the state, regardless of whether or not legal proceedings were resolved in their favor.

For others, the interviews revealed that some victims of violence have been able to make use of various "extralegal" programs, opportunities, and support networks provided by legal aid clinics that move beyond criminal justice into other socioeconomic realms. Given that the internationally funded legal aid programs operating in eastern DR Congo have recognized that legal support alone is insufficient, they have offered medical care, as well as other social benefits, to both encourage and support civil parties and witnesses participating in trials or pursuing legal remedy. Some individuals have thus adopted the language of legal accountability to exert increased agency over their fate in the aftermath of gender violence and to access a range of socioeconomic benefits and support services that would otherwise be inaccessible.

Yet the stories of Divine, Analine, and Mupenda in the previous chapter illustrate that certain types of medical or socioeconomic support can be conditional upon participating in criminal case. Divine and her brother Étienne commented that support for their medical care was canceled when they failed to identify the perpetrators of violence and their case was terminated. While donor decisions to provide material, medical, and social support alongside legal aid to victims of gender-based violence is commendable, the landscape of legal development aid can perpetuate dynamics wherein victims of violence feel compelled to turn to legal aid organizations to access assistance, even if they have little interest in legal remedy. By earmarking certain provisions and social benefits for a subset of the population deemed to be "most" in need (in this case, victims of conflict-related gender violence), and by compelling vulnerable individuals to present themselves as victims of particular types of harms in search of a very specific form of remedy in order to access these services and support structures, human rights programs have contributed to the construction of a hierarchy of harm. The unintended consequence of this well-intentioned approach is that only certain forms of violence are perceived as worthy of aid and assistance.

The interviews discussed in this chapter undoubtedly draw from a limited sample. The majority of victims of violence interviewed for this project had chosen to report instances of gendered violence to NGOs or law enforcement agencies, which automatically sets them apart from the vast majority of gender violence victims. For a great many other women, particularly those living in rural locations, legal remedy in any form was simply not an option for consideration. Thus, while this chapter does not suggest that victims of gender-based violence in eastern DR Congo are universally exposed to opportunities for legal remedy, it highlights the paradox of opportunity and disempowerment (Lake, Muthaka, and Walker 2016) that can emerge from a disproportionate emphasis on one particular form of violence.

Even though Congolese women living throughout the Kivus are not equally privy to legal outreach, and even though many of the most successful claimants still encounter deeply disappointing outcomes in their cases, participants in legal processes have nevertheless expressed feelings of validation and recognition that derive from adopting an identity as a rights-bearing subject before the law. When comparing experiences across the South African and Congolese contexts, therefore, it is important to weigh two counterveiling forces against one another. First, the opportunities that NGO-led legal aid processes offer for limited forms of agency and empowerment in the aftermath of violence in parts of eastern DR Congo are rarely accessible to South African victims of gendered harms (nor to those outside of the Kivus). Second, however, these limited gains for some women cannot be considered in the absence of the practical obstacles that many Congolese victims of gender violence continue to confront in accessing legal support. The fact that even those participants in successful cases rarely receive the compensation, support, or remedy promised by the legal system exposes the precarity of rights gains procured amidst an environment of volatility and state collapse. While it is important not to dismiss or undermine the episodic experiences of empowerment that gender-based legal aid has afforded to some Congolese victims of violence, scholars and practitioners should be wary of divorcing these victories from the broader context of state retrenchment from which they emerged.

7 Justice for Whom?
The Unintended Consequences of Hard-Fought Victories

Introduction

The most striking difference between the Congolese and South African experiences of pursuing accountability for gender violence is the institutional context that has shaped the outcomes of respective NGO interventions. In Part I, I showed that state fragility in DR Congo created opportunities for human rights actors to bypass existing state infrastructure and circumvent obstructive elites who did not always share the commitments to gender justice promoted by domestic and international human rights organizations. While these dynamics permitted gender rights advocates in eastern DR Congo to promote gender-sensitive treatment of sexual violence cases in local courts, similarly situated organizations in South Africa were constrained by a comparatively cohesive state apparatus that demonstrated itself to be broadly hostile to gender advocacy. As a result, victims of gender-based crimes in South Africa have encountered fewer opportunities to enter the legal system or have their cases heard sympathetically in court.

Yet, while state fragility in DR Congo has created a number of opportunities for the local diffusion of international human rights practices, these gains in local courts have come at a price. Indeed, capitalizing on openings created by state fragility to advance a singular human rights agenda has given rise to a number of unintended consequences. The previous chapter summarized how increased judicial attention to gender violence has offered victims of violence new language and tools for rejecting practices that were previously widely tolerated. The chapter also highlighted the support networks that many victims of violence in eastern DR Congo have been able to access, which do not typically exist for similarly situated victims of violence in South Africa. Yet a disproportionate focus on gender-based crimes by donors and NGOs, as well as the tendency for legal aid organizations to overlook existing inequalities and local dynamics of power in the pursuit of criminal convictions, has the potential to undermine rights in other areas.

This chapter explores some of the broader challenges and repercussions, both positive and negative, that have accompanied the pursuit of gender justice in a context of state fragility and weakness. It begins with a discussion of donor-driven incentives to foreground particular issues and activities and de-emphasize others. It proceeds to reflect on the dangers of building legal capacity amidst pervasive corruption, and the potential for criminal justice processes to be coopted by local power brokers, or for the justice system to disproportionately target political, ethnic, or economic outsiders. Third, it questions the long-term ramifications of international organizations "substituting" for the state where it is weak or absent. Finally, it weighs the perils and pitfalls of advocacy at the peripheries of statehood against some of the longer-term positive externalities that may result from increased legal attention to gender-based violence.

This book does not, and cannot, offer evidence of the long-term value of criminal prosecutions. It is simply too soon to tell whether the rights gains that gender advocates have won in Congolese courts can withstand the accompanying challenges brought about by state fragility. However, exploring how and why the efforts of activists in eastern DR Congo and South Africa's Western Cape have reaped such different results forces us to also consider how the respective *contexts* in which these outcomes were produced shapes their long-term impacts. When we look beyond narrow legal gains to the broader sociopolitical landscape in both countries, the "successes" and "failures" of advocacy and intervention do not look as clear-cut. When engaging in program design, policy makers and practitioners need to evaluate the benefits of short-term human rights gains against their potential limitations.

A Top-Down Agenda: Issue Displacement

External interventions of the type observed in eastern DR Congo have been driven by top-down agendas. As discussed in Chapter 3, in the mid-1990s, a number of influential international decision-makers chose to prioritize gender-based violence in global policy instruments, resolutions, and organizational mandates. Around the same time, international courts, such as the International Criminal Tribunal for Rwanda (ICTR), highlighted the unique ways that women have been victimized by conflict and violence. While many human rights advocates have applauded the attention donors have given to the issue of gender violence, the top-down nature of this attention has meant that a handful of powerful Western donors and organizations has almost entirely determined which issues are spotlighted and which projects receive funding (Carpenter 2003, 2007). This narrow approach has created dynamics that may hinder the anticipated overall benefits of gender-based legal development.

At first glance, it is easy to interpret the attention devoted to gender-based violence in eastern DR Congo's courts as a success story for gender activists. Yet the disproportionate focus on sexual and gender-based crimes in eastern DR Congo versus other categories of crime raises alarm bells for some human rights practitioners.

Importantly, the prioritization of sexual and gender-based violence by international donors has created a series of perverse incentives for local service providers and human rights organizations. Rather than addressing the broad range of problems facing individuals and communities in eastern DR Congo, organizations have sometimes felt pressured to focus on gender to the exclusion of other issues of concern. For instance, until fairly recently, there was a common perception among human rights and development organizations in eastern DR Congo that, in order to receive international funding, programs must have a gender component to their work. In some instances, this has led organizations to abandon other important policy objectives. Autesserre (2012) and D'Errico and colleagues (2013) report that many public health organizations and local medical centers have a surplus of funds to treat sexual violence victims, yet insufficient funds to respond to other grave health-related issues. In survey interviews with 121 participants across the provinces of North and South Kivu, Maniema, and Orientale, D'Errico and colleagues (2013) found that eighty-two percent of respondents identified food insecurity as one of the most pressing health-related concerns. Urban and rural respondents also highlighted hospital infrastructure as an important impediment to positive or improved health outcomes. Yet the vast majority of humanitarian funding was directed toward serving female victims of sexual violence. Although a number of respondents mentioned gender violence as a crucial issue facing Congolese women, many expressed disquiet at the disproportionate attention the issue received compared to other pressing concerns. D'Errico and colleagues quote one survey respondent who articulated this sentiment: "You say rape, I say hospitals, but whose voice is louder?" (D'Errico et al. 2013: 63).

In their interviews with local human rights organizations in the Kivus, Baaz and Stern (2008) similarly highlight the difficulties Congolese human rights organizations confront when trying to access funding from global donors, particularly when focusing on issues other than rape. They quote one NGO representative on this point (Baaz et al. 2010: 55):

There are so many different aspects of it [violence against women]. There is domestic violence; that is a very big problem that we have not yet started to address. Women's rights are violated on a massive scale in this country. Also a huge problem if you talk to women in the villages is all the problems connected to inheritance and property rights. But there are some ... problems with different views between us and the donors. They are mostly interested just in sexual violence, especially the ways in which it is used as a weapon of war and all that. And it is. But sexual violence is also committed by civilians, and in our very houses. But it is difficult to get money for other projects. So there is a certain difference in views between us and the donors. But if you discuss too much, and try to get in other things that they don't think are important, you might miss the funding [laughing]. So you avoid discussing too much with them.

While my interviews for this project did not explore this issue directly, I repeatedly heard similar commentary from local partners, informants, and organizations, particularly those with experience of fundraising and grant writing. Memorably, the director of one local NGO noted: "It is very hard for organizations working on issues that do not involve women and gender. Even for me, working with men. It was hard to get funding. But before, at least, funders wanted to work on gender. Now the situation has changed again. Donors now only want to fund work on climate change."[1] In other informal conversations, local NGO staff members noted that much-needed maternal mortality programming and access to health care initiatives lost momentum in the mid- to late 2000s, as organizations working on these issues felt compelled to divert their efforts and resources to exclusively work on gender in order to access international funding. Thus, as Autesserre (2012) articulates, rather than address the root causes of conflict and violence, local organizations have been increasingly incentivized to focus on one of its many symptoms.

Perhaps the most damaging outcome of this dynamic is that the emphasis of the legal system on one *type* of crime (gender violence) has undermined broader efforts to combat the embedded culture of impunity that persists elsewhere. Issues such as theft, grievous bodily harm, murder, aggravated assault, perjury, etc. rarely receive adequate attention or investigation from the legal system. By way of illustration, a 2014 United Nations Development Program evaluation of its support for legal programs across eastern DR Congo notes that in order for a mobile court initiative to receive support from United Nations Development Program, it must hear "a minimum number of cases that pertain to sexual and gender-based violence." The report also states that the United Nations Development Program will prioritize cases involving criminal offenses over non-criminal gendered harms (United Nations Development Program 2014: 9).

[1] Gilbert, DR Congo, August 2, 2014. Paraphrased from an informal conversation.

In areas with a proliferation of NGOs working on gender-based legal capacity building, police, prosecutors, or investigators faced with a choice over whether to prioritize a case involving a sexual offense or one involving another type of crime will almost certainly elect to pursue the case that falls under the NGOs' purview. A law clerk at the TGI in Goma told me: "I have a busy workload, but the lawyers at the ABA come to check on these [sexual violence] cases, so we can't move slowly with these ones."[2] A policeman from the PSPEF echoed the sentiment: "We don't have any money to take motorbikes to investigate cases. I have to walk. So if the victim or her lawyers come and give me fare for a moto-taxi, I can go to do my job. I am able to question the perpetrator or arrest him, or locate the medical report. Otherwise I have to stay here. We don't have the money to do anything else."[3]

Because gender investigations are subsidized and supported by international organizations, other cases struggle to make it to the parquet at the same rate. As discussed in Chapter 4, at the time this research was conducted, the American Bar Association covered costs directly for police officers investigating gender violence cases, to facilitate their transportation to conduct interviews, collect evidence, transmit information, and travel to and from work. Although police officers must account for the dollars spent, program lawyers will advance these funds – in cash – to pay for moto-taxis, cellphone credit, and other crucial resources police and investigators need to advance a case. Whenever I accompanied legal aid representatives to local police stations, I observed these types of interactions. Often, lawyers would bring with them a checklist of open cases in order to question the investigating officers about their progress. They would typically also bring envelopes of small bills and a receipt book. When asking about a dossier's progress, the lawyer would reimburse the officer in question for trips taken pertaining to the case, or front cash for planned excursions. Officers are far more likely to devote their time to the cases for which they can receive financial support, fronted in cash, to interview a potential witness, victim, or accused perpetrator, rather than spend their time investigating other reported crimes. This creates an imbalance in the attention investigators and prosecutors are willing to spend on non-gender cases. Further, when NGO or legal aid representatives later check up on whether particular interviews or tasks related to their cases were completed, they introduce an additional layer of accountability that is not present for other offenses.

[2] Interview. Vitale, Law Clerk. DR Congo, November 29, 2012.
[3] Interview. Danny, Police Officer. DR Congo, May 11, 2013. This sentiment was expressed by many police officers I interviewed over the course of my research.

Special police units that focus on gender-based crimes serve to compound some of these tensions. While specialized gender units trained in collecting evidence in sexual assault cases have proved crucial to improving police capacity to respond sensitively and appropriately to gender-based crimes, in the Kivus these units are often better trained and disproportionately resourced compared to other police agencies.

Similar problems arose in South Africa, such that the specialized Sexual Offenses Courts were attacked for their constitutionality. Particularly during the periods when the specialized courts and police units were most effective in their work, critics felt that they unfairly privileged victims of sexual assaults over victims of other types of crimes, thus undermining victims' rights to equal treatment before the law. These assaults on constitutional grounds have considerably disrupted the work of gender activists, leading to cuts in funding and programming, and, for a number of courts, to their dissolution altogether (South Africa Department of Justice and Constitutional Development 2013). Gender activists maintain that specialized courts and police units are necessary to redress the historical marginalization and deprioritization of gender offenses in the legal system and fill the gaps left by a lack of specialized skills in this area. Yet critics perceive that resources channeled into bolstering the capacity of specialized sexual offenses units diminish resources that should be devoted to improving the experiences of all victims of crime. When the South African Sexual Offenses Courts were reintroduced in 2013 and 2014, the Minister of Justice noted that they did not need to be exclusive to sexual offenses. In 2017, discussions were ongoing as to whether the specialized courts should be mandated to focus at least thirty percent of their time on nonsexual offenses in order to maintain a sense of balance.[4] Responding to similar critiques, donors, practitioners, and organizations in eastern DR Congo have also recently begun to focus their attention beyond sexual offenses.

In addition to creating a vivid distinction between gendered and nongendered forms of violence, the targeted attention from international donors to conflict-related sexual violence has also obscured other types of gendered harms. Evidence suggests that a large number of rapes across DR Congo are likely committed in the context of intimate partner relationships. However, the international response to the issue has focused almost exclusively on rape as an instrument of war (Freedman 2015). The attention to conflict-related sexual violence obscures the many pressing issues, challenges, and hardships faced by individuals who are not

---

[4] Interview. Liza, Court Registrar. South Africa, June 17, 2017.

victims of conflict-related rape, but may be victims of other forms of gendered harm (Heaton 2013; Hoover Green, Parkinson, and Crawford 2014).

An exclusive focus on a single category of violence can thus lead to poor data, ill-informed policy, and misdirected programming. When international attention and outreach are singularly directed toward preventing rape as a weapon of war, without taking into account potentially more prevalent forms of gender injustices, such programs are unlikely to tackle the underlying gender inequities that make ordinary gendered harms and conflict-related sexual violence more likely. Since gender inequality and violence affect sexual relationships across DR Congo in ways that predate the conflict, the failure to attend to these dynamics suggests that they may continue to prevail after the conflict ends.

A final consideration that emerges from prioritizing services for victims of conflict rape, however well intentioned, is the resultant effect of restricting treatment and services for other victims of injustice or violence, making access to those services fraught and contested. Earlier work has argued that the social and material incentives provided by legal outreach organizations to encourage victims of gender-based violence in DR Congo to participate in legal processes has encouraged a pattern of "false claiming" by those seeking to access social or material benefits that would not otherwise be available to them (Autesserre 2012; Baaz et al. 2010; Douma and Hilhorst 2012; Heaton 2013).[5] Evidence from the previous chapters clearly demonstrates that many victims of violence turn to the legal system not for abstract notions of justice or recognition, but because they believe they will be able to access social, economic or medical assistance. It follows, therefore, that opportunists, or those facing desperation or vulnerability resulting from other forms of harm or injustice, may similarly perceive the legal system as a vehicle through which to access aid.

This tension plays out on an institutional as well as an individual level. Service providers face similar incentives to overlook patterns of misidentification among beneficiaries and service recipients. Baaz and Stern (2008) describe a frequently referenced example concerning fistula repair. They note that, contrary to popular belief, the vast majority of fistula cases is not rape-related, but stems from complications during childbirth. In fact, only 0.8 percent of fistula cases in DR Congo are believed to be related to rape (Onsrud et al. 2008). Yet, due to the extensive attention received by rape-related fistula (Bhatia 2009; Nolen

[5] See Utas (2005) for a discussion of navigating victimcy in war in Liberia.

2005), a great deal of international funding and support has been channeled toward hospital fistula repair services under sexual violence programming. Indeed, media and NGO coverage of fistula in DR Congo rarely acknowledges the most common cause of the condition – tearing after poor C-sections or childbirth complications. Instead, reporting typically emphasizes rape as the primary cause. In a report on the fistula repair program at Panzi Hospital in Bukavu, for example, CNN notes: "At [Panzi] hospital, women are treated for vaginal fistula – a muscular tear caused by violent rape" (Perraudin and Busari 2010). Baaz and Stern point to the perverse incentives this creates for hospital staff and organizational grant writers, as well as for victims of violence. If donor-allocated funds are directed explicitly toward fistula for victims of rape, then when a woman arrives at a hospital in need of fistula surgery for other health complications, it can be easier to treat her as a rape victim (thus covered under sexual violence programming) than to have her document alternative sources of harm. Baaz and Stern note that this creates a situation in which "destitute women and girls who are not rape survivors ... for example, women with fistulas related to childbirth, sometimes present themselves as rape survivors to get access to surgery and other medical treatment" (Baaz et al. 2010: 51).

Service recipients may be unaware of these dynamics. In Luvungi, after mass rapes against a number of civilians by a coalition of armed groups in North Kivu, Laura Heaton observed, medical centers and other humanitarian response teams are not in the business of "forensically verifying" the sources of harm reported by the victims they provide assistance to (Heaton, interviewed by Stearns 2013). Thus, International Medical Corps (IMC), the group on the ground responsible for offering first response support, had reportedly treated upward of 60 to 100 victims of rape during the July 2010 mass rape. Yet further investigations and interviews by Heaton revealed that, during the time that rebels had been in the area pillaging houses and harassing people, and in the days immediately following, the IMC appeared to have treated only six patients who had been raped – not hundreds (Heaton 2013). Heaton notes that, of the 100 or so patients seen by the IMC doctor between July 30 and August 6, most needed treatment for maladies common to the region – malaria and diarrhea – or for injuries sustained while fleeing to the bush during the occupation. The disparities between the 337 rape victims cited in the UN investigative report and the far lower numbers that Heaton reports can be explained by both individual and organizational incentives to categorize the need for treatment as pertaining to rape. For individuals, women may learn that they will be less likely to be denied particular services, ranging from free medical care to school fees for their children, if they identify directly – or refrain from correcting assumptions – that they have been victims of mass rape. For organizations, Heaton notes, increases in funding for sexual violence programming may result from having treated large numbers of sensationalist crimes that garner horrified attention from international audiences. Thus, language such as "the IMC health center received 100 patients following rapes committed by armed groups in Luvungi" may not be factually incorrect, but certainly creates the impression that treatment pertained to victims of rape where, in fact, those patients may have been receiving other services. In July 2010, the IMC was awarded a $16 million USD grant from USAID to treat victims of sexual violence in eastern DR Congo that coincided directly with the Luvungi rapes (International Medical Corps 2010). While the timing of the grant makes it unlikely that it was a direct consequence of the Luvungi incident, Heaton argues that the attention the IMC received from providing support to the 337 reported rape victims demonstrated the centrality and impact of IMC programming, potentially serving to build confidence in the importance of the IMC's role in the context of such violence and to direct additional future funding to similar programs. Thus, even where official IMC records diverge from the statistics reported by the media, there are few institutional incentives to correct contradictions or draw attention to misreporting.

When social services designed to redress historical imbalances are offered exclusively to victims of particular harms, other forms of victimhood are necessarily sidelined. The impression that certain types of violence are more or less worthy of attention may lead to a system in which "need" or "harm" must be framed in terms donor communities will respond to. In eastern DR Congo, this has led to a widespread perception that sexual violence against women is uniquely deserving of attention and remedy. This marginalizes victims of other forms of injustice and discredits the testimonies of genuine victims of sexual assault. The belief that non-gendered harms are simply unimportant to international donors and organizations not only creates a hierarchy in which certain needs appear unworthy of help or attention, but it also potentially contributes to further misinformed or misguided policy. These perils, as well as the opportunities that emerge from state fragility in eastern DR Congo may serve to inform activists working elsewhere at the peripheries of the state.

An Unbalanced System: Goal Displacement

An additional challenge that results from donors' attention to combating impunity for gender-based crimes is that certain types of activities – such as criminal trials – have been prioritized over other critical aspects of legal capacity building or justice reform. Goal displacement refers to a situation in which "the major goals claimed by an organization are neglected in favor of goals associated with building or maintaining the organization" (Warner and Havens 1968). This critique, developed within organizational theory, has a great deal of relevance in the Congolese justice sector, where organizations engaged in judicial reform are frequently incentivized to overlook their overarching goals in favor of meeting specific, short-term program objectives that donors require as a condition for future funding. The structure of NGO funding has meant that activities with quantifiable outcomes – such as the numbers of cases reported to the police, judgments delivered and processed, police or lawyers trained, or convictions reached – have been prioritized over activities that may lead to more incremental change.

Historically, the public has overwhelmingly lacked faith in the Congolese justice system. Despite some recent improvements, many judges and law enforcement officials remain susceptible to bribes. Even in the area of gender justice, more than two thirds of my interviewees who had sought support through legal avenues reported having paid a bribe or fee of some form to courts or police in order to further their case. Interviewees were asked for money at multiple stages of the legal process, but most commonly by police. Others reported large sums demanded from judges and prosecutors. In most cases, if the victim could not pay, the case was terminated. Alika, eighteen, raped by a stranger on the road to school in South Kivu, told me:

[I was not] able to take the case [to the police] for lack of money ... [In DR Congo], many people, they are taken to court, or arrested, but they are not going to spend much time there.[6]

When cases are not closely monitored by an NGO or an international organization, it is not uncommon for verdicts of guilt and innocence simply to be auctioned to the highest bidder, either at the trial stage or during the course of investigations.

In spite of pervasive dynamics of corruption in the Congolese justice system, the American Bar Association (ABA) reports steady improvement in the capacity of the justice system in the east, noting in a 2012 report that more than seventy percent of gender violence trials processed in eastern DR Congo since its program began have resulted in convictions (Open Society Foundation 2013). In such reports, organizations clearly emphasize activities that move them closer to being able to report "success stories" to their donors. Figures that allow donors to easily quantify the successes of

---

[6] Interview. Alika. DR Congo. May 6, 2013.

their programs prove helpful in renewing existing funding or securing new grants, regardless of other factors. Thus, organizations are by and large more inclined to work on projects whose successes can be easily measured, rather than programs that require sustained attention over long periods of time and fail to generate immediately visible results.

As a result, at the time the research was carried out, there were few incentives for international organizations and NGOs to focus their attention on enforcing judicial decisions once judgments were handed down. Processing trials and securing convictions immediately signal success to donors as well as media outlets and advocacy organizations. A United Nations Development Program monitoring report in 2014 highlighted the weak execution of court decisions and a lack of reparations for victims of serious crimes as two of four primary challenges legal aid programs in eastern DR Congo continue to confront (United Nations Development Program 2014). Apparently, the enforcement of decisions already rendered is not especially newsworthy or attention-grabbing for the major global contributors of legal development aid.

Enforcement problems in eastern DR Congo are rife. This is partly due to the poor quality of local prisons, which remain characterized by petty corruption and patronage. Prison guards and police officers stationed in DR Congo's prisons are rarely and poorly paid. When they receive salaries, they are insufficient to meet their basic needs. Thus, guards and police can be very susceptible to even the smallest of bribes. When friends, family members, or colleagues of defendants make threats or offer money, food, cigarettes, or other goods to local officials themselves living below the poverty line, indictees may be released without question. Sentence enforcement varies greatly depending on the prison and the case. The larger prisons in the provincial capitals of Goma and Bukavu (which hold upward of 1,000 prisoners each) are typically better administered than smaller or more rural police stations, prisons, and detention centers. Yet the prisons in Goma and Bukavu are by no means immune from corruption. And when indicted individuals have powerful political connections, it is unlikely that they will remain in prison for long, no matter the sentence or the location.

In cases involving important or well-connected defendants, therefore, military, political, or business allies of the accused can more effectively subvert the justice process after a sentence has been handed down, rather than intervening in the trial itself. Officers might ensure that their colleagues "escape" after sentencing, once attention to the case wanes. Following the country's first domestic trial for international crimes (the case of Songo Mboyo discussed in the opening of this book), six of the seven indictees escaped from prison soon after their sentences were handed down.[7] It is not entirely uncommon for allies or superiors to either break colleagues out of prison using force or by ambushing convoys transporting prisoners, or to exert political leverage to ensure defendants are liberated. In 2017 alone, there were five high-profile prison breaks (Reuters 2017). For this reason, influential or high-profile indictees such as Lieutenant Colonel Kibibi, who was convicted for his role in the mass rape in Minova in 2011, and Balumisa Manase, who was indicted for the mass rape of civilians in Katasomwa in 2009, have been sent to Kinshasa to serve out their prison sentences, thereby reducing the risk of being broken out of jail by accomplices or allies.

Many of the victims of violence interviewed for this project who had participated in a court case informed me that their attackers had been "released" even after being handed down a sentence at trial. Étienne, who described the attack in which his twelve-year-old sister was raped in his house by four men, reported that after he paid $70 USD in bribes to ensure that the perpetrators remained in custody, his sister's attackers paid an even greater sum to secure the perpetrators' release. Similarly, Analine, whose case was discussed in the previous chapter, was obliged to pay large sums of money to prosecutors to investigate her case. Even with the help of a local NGO, she reported that her perpetrators, who were her neighbors, had been very rich. They gifted cows to the relevant authorities and were immediately released, despite a strong case against them. Analine reported that those same perpetrators tried to kill her in retaliation after they were released. They were arrested once again, but escaped after the M23 attack on Goma in 2012. In only three cases could the interviewee definitively report that those who attacked her remained in prison. The frequency with which indictees are liberated from prisons or police detention indicates a troubling pattern of sentence non-enforcement that pervades military and civilian dossiers.

It is not only prison sentences that are poorly enforced. Relatedly, the infrequent payment of reparations awarded to victims compromises the pursuit of justice. While judges frequently hand down generous compensation packages to civil parties in gender violence cases, these are rarely ever paid to the victims involved. The state has no means to deliver compensation to civil parties, and those indicted can rarely afford to pay. Even when indictees can afford the damages awarded, there are no mechanisms to follow up and ensure they are paid. Such follow up is left to individuals and NGOs, if it is to take place at all.

The reality is that, as evidenced in Chapter 6, once judgments are handed down, courts, police, and even the legal aid organizations involved in cases

---

[7] Tribunal Militaire de Garnison Mbandaka. 2005. RP N°084/2005. DR Congo. April 12, 2006.

typically have no further interest or involvement. Only a handful of those I interviewed received any form of compensation, and even those who were awarded reparations in court received a final sum that amounted to less than they had paid out in bribes to advance the process. In an especially extreme case, and in the most resounding legal success story of those I interviewed, Virginie reported receiving $5,000 USD in compensation from her attacker following the judgment. This was overshadowed, however, by the $8,000 USD she claimed to have paid in legal fees. Virginie described how her family had sold all their land, including her brothers' farms, in order to hire the best lawyers and motivate the relevant legal practitioners to take the case seriously. When asked how she felt afterward, Virginie noted, "It was not worth it because the money I received was not a lot ... Maybe next time it could be a higher amount than what I received ... these perpetrators, they came from poor families."[8] Similarly, Noelle, who was awarded and received $1,500 USD in compensation, informed me:

I was obliged to sell all my farms, and give my money to my family so they could go and continue the trial and the process at the parquet, because the case was successfully transferred from Minova to Bukavu ... He paid $1,500 USD. It was his family who was giving the money [he died in prison]. They were also selling their farms. I had to pay a lot of money. I don't remember how much.[9]

Far more common were those who saw nothing at all of the sums they were awarded. The case of Agathe in Chapter 6 demonstrated the ways in which victims are often cast aside after their role in the process is over. Shani commented:

The TGI [was] always asking for money, and ... as a result, always postponing the hearings ... The lawyers were asking for money, and the judges, each one his own amount. Some $100 USD, others $50 ... At the beginning, the TGI told me that [it] would pay the charges for the baby when I gave birth, but I always go there and there is no money for me.[10]

Motivated by these troubling outcomes, some NGOs, led by the American Bar Association Rule of Law Initiative, are working with government agencies to establish a trust fund that would ensure that the Congolese state has sufficient funds to pay damages awarded to victims by the state in gender violence cases. However, at the time of writing, the fund was still in early developmental stages.

NGOs and international organizations have not always been convincing in their rejection of patronage and corruption. Since international

---

[8] Interview. Virginie. DR Congo, January 23, 2014.
[9] Interview. Noelle. DR Congo, January 23, 2014.
[10] Interview. Shani. DR Congo. January 11, 2013.

stakeholders in DR Congo prioritize trials and convictions over other slower-burning capacity-building activities, staff and practitioners may face pressure to move cases through the legal system. As a result, they may not have the luxury of being attentive to the micro-processes determining *which* cases end up in court. In summer 2012, Celéne, a program lawyer with a legal aid organization in Goma, described one of her recent cases in which an influential pastor was implicated in the rape and sexual assault of a number of small girls. Once sufficient evidence had been collected, parents of the children, as well as investigative police officers and an important local politician, each received threats to drop the case. While, initially, the legal aid organization was determined to continue, with waning political support, prosecutors were compelled to abandon the case and focus their energy elsewhere.[11] Those with money, power, or influence are rarely compelled to face the full force of the law, and even under NGO supervision, judges and police can be convinced to lose dockets for the right price.

An eagerness to secure convictions has led some NGOs providing legal support to be less concerned with the rights of the defendants than with the rights of victims and witnesses. The American Bar Association, for instance, does not provide free legal counsel to defendants – only to the civil party. Dynamique des Femmes Juristes similarly offers free legal representation to victims of gender violence but not to defendants. Free legal counsel is, in theory, provided to defendants pro bono by local bar associations; however, it can be of varying quality if provided at all. In mobile court cases, the American Bar Association will pay costs associated with travel for the defense counsel (including transport, accommodation, and possibly a per diem). However, defendants are unlikely to receive the same level of support, expertise, and financial compensation as the prosecution or any civil parties.

While prosecutors in South Africa are paid through state budgets, and thus face similar constraints as state-appointed defense attorneys (in the form of high caseloads and limited resources), prosecutors in gender violence cases in the Kivus are often heavily supported by international organizations. For many sexual and gender-based violence cases in eastern DR Congo, therefore, the legal system disproportionately privileges the prosecution to the point where equality of arms is a mirage. Although some international trainings have been directed toward defense attorneys, in general, they lack the resources, support, and training afforded to prosecutors and civil parties. Many defense attorneys interviewed for this project reported that they are frequently not kept up to date on cases, not given sufficient time to prepare their cases, miss hearings

---

[11] Interview. Celéne, Lawyer. DR Congo, June 27, 2012.

because of a lack of communication, and are not provided with case briefs or other critical information. One interviewee noted that, in a fairly high-profile case, he was appointed to represent the accused just three days prior to the initial hearing, at which point he was given more than 6,000 documents to consult.[12] Prior to this, the defendants had no representation. Representatives of civil parties, on the other hand, had been preparing the case for months; they were provided with resources to make copies of case files and transport them to their offices, and they were able to solicit assistance to locate evidence and build an impressive and effective case (Human Rights Watch 2015). For the three days leading to the trial, the defense counsel had to remain in the clerk's office to view the case documents, and could not remain there once the clerk had departed for the day. These problems were cited frequently by defense attorneys in civilian as well as military cases. One Congolese program lawyer employed by an international organization and with extensive experience representing civil parties in sexual violence cases commented that judges even take NGO lawyers more seriously. He observed: "Judges weigh different pieces of evidence differently. For example, if there is conflict between the evidence presented by the Parquet and that presented by the [defense] lawyer, the judge will always believe the prosecutor's evidence over that of the lawyer."[13] In an evaluation of its support for criminal trials in the Kivus, the United Nations Development Program highlighted the lack of an adequate defense as one of the major obstacles to the long-term successes of its rule of law programs. The UNDP report attributed this "to the fact that victims receive more effective representation by lawyers" (United Nations Development Program 2014: 11).

Motivated by the need to demonstrate quantifiable successes in court, legal aid organizations may not always be sufficiently attentive to possibilities of false accusations. This issue is exacerbated by the fact that convictions can be reached with fairly minimal evidence. Cases are frequently decided on the basis of a single medical report confirming that the victim was raped. While many of the reports are genuine, others would not hold up to close scrutiny in other legal systems, since they can be as minimal as stamped statements from the hospital stating the victim received treatment for sexual assault, without including any further medical proof. Whereas poor-quality medical reports are frequently grounds for delaying or throwing out cases altogether in the Western Cape, they are often admitted without question in the Kivus. Moreover, doctors are rarely brought to testify at trial. Some interviewees noted that these

---

[12] Interview. Calliste, Defense Counsel. DR Congo. August 12, 2014.
[13] Interview. Felicién, Program Lawyer. DR Congo, August 12, 2014.

medical reports can be purchased at low cost from medical practitioners, and thus were meaningless as evidence.[14] Yet, in many cases, vague or incomplete medical reports constitute the only piece of evidence beyond the witnesses' testimony, fueling serious concerns about the quality of evidence on which otherwise innovative judgments are produced.[15]

Scholars have thus made the critique that families may take advantage of the ease with which a conviction can be obtained by levying false charges against neighbors or acquaintances who appear unable to pay for qualified legal representation or unable to subvert the legal process in other ways. Baaz and Stern (2010: 52) observe that "[male] family members accuse other young men, often the boyfriends of their daughters, of raping their daughters/sisters in order to press the men for money." Baaz and Stern quote a soldier they interviewed making a similar point about the ease and frequency with which false claims are made, adding that human rights defenders and the military justice profit as well:

You cannot trust them [prostitutes]! You agree to give them money, but then they want more. And if they don't get what they want they accuse you of rape. You know, they [women and civilians] have their defenders, the human rights defenders and the military justice. And they eat too. (Quoted in Baaz and Stern 2010: 52)

According to these commentators, rape cases have become an "industry," perceived by some families as a means to secure reparations or compensation from neighbors they have felt wronged by, or for parents to punish young boys of whom they do not approve who are romantically involved with their daughters. Due to the glaring inequality of arms and a newly entrenched legal culture that prioritizes the rights of victims, such accusations can result in fairly easy convictions when levied against those without the means to secure experienced or well-trained legal representation.

Short-term funding cycles are generally not equipped to address (or measure) systemic or long-term change. Slow-burning activities, such as developing communication infrastructures, overcoming systemic corruption, ensuring adequately guarded prisons, or monitoring the enforcement of compensation awarded or sentences handed down, are inevitably relegated to low priority or neglected in favor of other activities. Yet, without these types of activities, which require far deeper structural capacity building and a long-term vision toward developing the rule of law, recorded successes could be short-lived. If potential offenders observe criminal trials as no more than a minor inconvenience that

---

[14] Florine, NGO Employee. August 14, 2014. Author's fieldnotes, April 2013.
[15] See Seelinger (2015) for a discussion of the medical evidence used in DR Congo's courts.

sufficient funds, connections, power, or influence can resolve, then increased criminal accountability for certain types of crimes is unlikely to have the intended deterrent effects that rule of law architects anticipate. Rather than promoting a system of impartial justice, such programs demonstrate that patronage, power, and political influence continue to reign.

Local NGOs as well as UN agencies and large international donors are frequently all too aware of problems of enforcement, manipulation, corruption, and inequality of arms. However, they are working within structures that constrain systemic organizational or behavioral change. In 2006, the Canadian government became one of the first major donors in the fight against sexual violence in eastern DR Congo, having contributed more than $15 million USD to these efforts. In 2008, an internal Canadian International Development Agency (CIDA) report reflecting on the successes and failures of the various gender violence initiatives noted that the CIDA's efforts had been "weak" in preventing further acts of sexual violence (York 2010). The report criticized the CIDA for spending too much money on awareness-raising (in the form of T-shirts and vests intended to educate Congolese people about sexual violence) and on "relatively minor activities such as thousands of dollars planned for meetings" (York 2010). Even as early as 2008, coordinators of global and international programs recognized the irony of spending funds on services for victims without attending to broader landscapes of violence and rule of law. In concrete terms, despite the fact that donors, practitioners, and NGOs working on the ground recognize an urgent need for longer-running development activities unconstrained by short-term funding objectives, the structure of international development aid allows for little of this work to be carried out.[16] Instead, organizations applying for grants are forced to return to the same sets of activities that have a "proven" track record of success, rather than tasks whose goals are elusive and difficult to obtain.

Hollowing out the State

The private compensation introduced to the justice sector also introduces challenges to state authority. Many scholars have highlighted the threats posed to local economies by creating dependency on external resources (Easterly 2007; Moyo 2010). Others have pointed to the unintended consequences of relying too heavily on NGOs and non-state actors to assume responsibility over activities that normally fall under the authority

---

[16] For further discussion of this phenomenon in other contexts, see Birdsall (2004), Bob (2002), Cooley and Ron (2002), Morfit (2011), and Prakash and Gugerty (2010).

of the central state (Bratton 1987; Ferguson 2006; Hanlon 1991, 2000; Hanlon, Barrientos, and Hulme 2010; Jeater 2011; Petras 1999; Van de Walle 2005; Vogel 2012). Bayart and colleagues (1999), Clapham (1996), and Reno (1999) have each noted that the rolling back of the state pioneered under structural adjustment and pursued to the present day has led to a "criminalization" of the African state, in which state officials lack resources and are paid inadequate salaries, and thus look elsewhere for rents, often to illicit sources of income. Ferguson writes:

As more and more of the functions of the state have been effectively outsourced to NGOs, state capacity has deteriorated rapidly – unsurprisingly, as Joseph Hanlon has pointed out, since the higher salaries and better terms of employment offered by NGOs quickly decapitated governments by luring all the best civil servants out of the government ministries. Those who remained were often paid less than subsistence salaries, with the inevitable consequences of corruption and an explosion of "parallel businesses." (Ferguson 2006: 38)

As Ferguson and many others have observed, local individuals employed by international organizations are often well compensated for their work. In the case of DR Congo, this raises a number of questions about the short-term motivations of local stakeholders, not only for participating in legal capacity-building activities in the first place, but also with regard to ultimately returning to state employment. Evidence of these trends can be observed in eastern DR Congo. For example, many lawyers demand greater and greater financial compensation from international organizations in exchange for their participation in such activities, and internationally supported criminal trials are already extraordinarily expensive. The United Nations Development Program notes that its support for a single mobile court hearing, involving a trial and setup of approximately fifteen days, can cost upward of $25,000 USD, not including the transportation and pretrial costs paid by MONUSCO and the American Bar Association. More than than seventy percent of this figure is normally spent on per diems for judges and prosecutors (United Nations Development Program 2014: 10). Since international agencies heavily rely on cooperation with local stakeholders for legitimacy, they often use financial and material support to encourage the cooperation of various individuals and government agencies. The United Nations Development Program itself acknowledges that this potentially undermines the long-term impact of its work, raising questions about the sustainability of these types of initiatives once funds from global donors are no longer available. The United Nations Development Program report notes:

The high costs – approximately $25,000 for a 15-day [mobile court hearing] – and the fact that these are provided in full by the international community are hampering the sustainability of the mobile court system. Similarly the lack of a national strategy for mobile justice, and the ad hoc approach adopted for the implementation of mobile courts, raises concerns in terms of how the initiative will continue without donor support. (United Nations Development Program 2014: 11)

To support the justice process, international agencies provide stipends, per diems, or transportation costs to Congolese nationals and justice sector employees who participate in trials and outreach. As mentioned, organizations like the American Bar Association pay police directly for their transportation and any other incidental costs associated with investigating sexual violence cases. However, while such programs could not run without this kind of financial support, justice sector employees, military personnel, and police directly benefit, both personally and professionally, from these arrangements. Given the fact that government resources are extremely limited, and the state has a poor track record of paying salaries, few stand to benefit from withdrawing international intervention from the Congolese justice sector and shifting responsibility over the criminal justice system back to the state.[17]

Besides supporting, overseeing, and subsidizing the monitoring and disbursement of salaries to police, military, prosecutors, judges, and other state employees engaged directly or indirectly in justice sector work, international aid heavily benefits national budgets. Specific individuals involved in the administration of justice as well as government ministries and national institutions gain from external involvement. If these programs were to disappear, there is no certainty that the state would resume responsibility over these tasks, that salaries would continue to be paid, or that the justice sector would continue to function. In 2009, in the early years of legal capacity building, only 58 of the 180 *tribunaux du paix* established by law were actually in existence, and only forty-five of those were found to function to any capacity. Furthermore, only 0.03 percent of the country's annual budget was allocated to the justice sector; this figure ($1.2 million USD) was insufficient to pay salaries to Congolese judges for even one month of the year and, thus, many individuals had not received a salary from the state in nearly two decades (International Bar Association 2009: 18). Individually and institutionally, many individuals are incentivized to maintain strong relationships with international organizations and to continue sharing responsibility for justice sector administration.

---

[17] For a discussion of spoilers in state-building efforts in other contexts, see Menkhaus (2007).

234 Justice for Whom?

In addition to the lack of structural incentives to shift judicial administration back to the Congolese state, it is well known that there are also considerable financial incentives for the most qualified Congolese practitioners to seek employment with international agencies, rather than work for the the Ministry of Justice, or other arms of the state that continue to be plagued by limited resources. Qualified lawyers, technicians, administrators, and program managers often seek the prestige of employment within international organizations, where they will receive a regular and generous salary. While salaries for national staff are far lower than those of their international counterparts, they typically still exceed the inadequate compensation employees would otherwise receive from the state. Moreover, they are granted access to new career trajectories, opportunities for promotion and professional development, and other benefits, such as use of NGO cars, and sometimes health coverage or security in the event of renewed conflict. In addition, they may receive promotion opportunities abroad, promising even higher remuneration. Although there are exceptions, this means that state institutions continue to be dominated by individuals who have either chosen not to pursue opportunities with international organizations for personal reasons, or those who are not afforded the opportunity.

Finally, legal and human rights developments that appear to constitute a radical break from the past must be understood in the context of a long historical trajectory of external actors defining and redefining the boundaries of legitimate violence across sub-Saharan Africa. While for some victims of violence new opportunities offered by foreign NGOs represent considerable emancipatory potential, offering a departure from potentially damaging traditions of the past, for others, NGO activities are reminiscent of colonial-era interventions that similarly sought to codify and criminalize certain behaviors and build new institutions through which to regulate social and sexual interactions. This history led many of my interviewees to question the legitimacy of external intervention in DR Congo's justice sector. One prosecutor explained:

I will tell you the truth about our relationship with the NGOs. As a Congolese, it disturbs me that they are here. We need to go through NGOs to get everything. These chairs that are badly made [gestures at a wooden chair], these shelves. NGOs are not working for us. They send the money and they take the money. And as a result, they control everything we do. They built the court. Euros 240,000, to build the parquet. This building could have cost less than $20,000 USD ... It is us who do our work. But how can we be independent from someone who provides the means for us to do our work? Indirectly, we are under the NGOs. This is not normal, because justice is a part of sovereignty. We are no longer independent.[18]

[18] Interview. Bahati, Prosecutor. DR Congo, May 10, 2013.

Hoffman and Verweijen have described how rebel groups everywhere appropriate state performance and symbolism by mimicking government command structures and establishing parallel systems of bureaucracy and governance. In doing so, they argue, such groups reproduce the myth of the state, while simultaneously *undermining* its legitimacy by challenging its right to govern. When NGOs and development practitioners mimic the institutions of the state by setting judicial priorities, pioneering criminal trials, and creating makeshift courthouses, they similarly deploy the language of "stateness" to legitimize their interventions into state bureaucracies. As a number of South African activists noted, the idea of foreign non-state actors "substituting" for the state where it has failed to provide basic goods and services can be deeply problematic. Indeed, this type of state mimicry may contribute to similar processes of state "making" and "unmaking" simultaneously, recalling the very practices employed by the fragmented authority structures that new legal institutions intend to hold accountable. In this way, the practice of state-building by non-state actors can be understood to contribute to precisely the fragmentation and fragility it was designed to overcome.

As discussed elsewhere in the text, for reasons often beyond their control, the approaches adopted by practitioners and human rights activists in South Africa have been almost entirely opposite to those adopted in eastern DR Congo. A point reiterated again and again by interviewees in South Africa was that the solution to South Africa's "rape crisis" must be state-led. Even if they were granted sufficient funding and access, most of the practitioners I interviewed in South Africa saw little value in non-state actors assuming direct responsibility over criminal prosecutions in the ways they have done in DR Congo. As such, the vast majority of advocacy on this issue in South Africa, led by domestic experts, has been geared toward influencing state policy and practice. Activists have adopted different strategies at different moments in history, sometimes entering into an adversarial and oppositional relationship with the state, and on other occasions pursuing cooperation and behind-the-scenes persuasion. After the failed 2003 Sexual Assault Bill, a number of leading members of the coalition grew so frustrated with the government's hostility toward new legislation that their tactics changed entirely to focus on monitoring and exposing the government's lack of progress on various issues. As a result, many members with strong connections to key legislative figures left the coalition, curtailing its ability to influence the content of legislation through "backstage" politics and forcing coalition members to adopt even more adversarial approaches.

However, despite the many shortcomings of advocacy efforts in DR Congo, the emphasis on state-led reform in South Africa has meant that the status quo for victims of gender violence, and their ability to seek remedy and redress through formal avenues, remains in dire shape. For all the advocacy of the past two decades, at the time of writing, victims of gender violence in South Africa appeared little closer to having their concerns taken seriously by the state, by law enforcement officers, or by local courts. Moreover, courts have failed to keep step with legislative amendments, continuing to reproduce gender-conservative practices and reasoning, and thereby rendering justice illusory for the majority of gender violence victims. While there are certainly myriad problems that arise from the Congolese response, individuals affected by gender-based violence in eastern DR Congo may encounter a more favorable legal response than are their counterparts in South Africa, by virtue of newly institutionalized protections. What this means for the future of gender justice depends very much on the value onlookers attribute to incremental gains in court.

Deterrence and Socialization

The extent to which policy makers will interpret developments in eastern DR Congo and South Africa as human rights successes or failures relies heavily on their perspectives toward the relationship between law and social change. While many scholars have adopted the position that selective implementation or imperfect compliance with a state's legal obligations serves as nothing more than a political lion skin that serves to impede full access to newly granted rights, others subscribe to ideas of socialization, habituation, and incremental change. For socialization scholars, human rights reform occurs gradually, requiring states to achieve compliance before individuals within the relevant bureaucracies become gradually habituated toward new behaviors and ultimately internalize new human rights norms (Finnemore and Sikkink 1998; Risse-Kappen, Ropp, and Sikkink 1999a). For critics, the spotty or selective granting of rights promises emancipation through human rights victories that only serve to mask and further entrench underlying power inequities (Goluboff 2007; Marx 2012; McCann 2006, 2014)

We know little about the extent to which increased judicial attention to sexual and gender-based violence has deterred gendered crimes. Reported incidents of gender-based crimes have actually increased over the past six years. A United Nations Development Program monitoring report of cases of sexual and gender-based violence brought to the police between 2010 and 2011 observed that gender violence cases reported to the police increased by sixteen percent in North Kivu and twenty percent in South Kivu (United Nations Development Program 2012: 23, Table 1). Similarly, the Demographics and Health Survey found a significant increase in reported incidents of sexual violence between 2007 and 2014 (Demographic and Health Survey 2007, 2014).

Table 1 *UNDP Figures Documenting Sexual and
Gender-Based Violence Cases Reported to the Police
(United Nations Development Program 2012: 23).*

	Ituri	Nord Kivu	Sud Kivu	Total
2010	867	1,353	859	3,079
2011	875	1,573	1,027	3,475
Total	1,742	2,926	1,886	6,554

However, this increase can almost certainly be attributed to an increase in reporting, rather than an increase in violence, due to previously non-existent support services for victims. Lower levels of stigma around rape, resulting from extensive outreach and sensitization carried out by NGOs, have also lowered reporting barriers. And indeed, the Special Advisor to the President on Conflict Related Sexual Violence and Child Recruitment, Jeanine Mabunda Lioko, in 2016 claimed a dramatic decrease in conflict-related sexual violence in the years since the Congolese Government implemented the Sexual Violence in Conflict Action Plan.[19]

There are, too, other indicators of changed societal attitudes toward sexual and gender-based violence. Over the past decade, for example, combatant groups have transformed the ways in which they have engaged with issues involving conflict-related violence. Although rape has been employed widely by different armed groups in eastern DR Congo as a deliberate tactic to undermine social cohesion and punish members of specific communities (Cohen 2013; Farr 2009; Green 2006), there are hints that combatant approaches to gender issues may be evolving in response to mounting global pressure and attention. Evidence of such trends can be gleaned from the M23 movement. After the mass defection of ex-CNDP troops from the national army, the M23 leadership immediately set up the Commission for Gender Equality (CGE) and a Special Police Unit for the Protection of Women and Children (PSPEF) in the territories under its control. This move should be treated with extreme caution. M23 was some-what atypical in that it was unusually concerned with projecting an image of good governance to the international community in order to strengthen its claims for legitimacy as a political movement. Thus, the creation of the CGE and the PSPEF did not likely reflect a changing culture of gender norms within the group's command structure; rather, these bodies largely served

[19] See All Africa "UN Recognizes the DRC as 'Most Successful Experience' in Countering Sexual Violence." November 3, 2016. http://allafrica.com/stories/201611031004.html.

purely symbolic purposes, aiming to signal to external actors that the group constituted a credible alternative to the existing political regime.

Regardless, M23's leadership appeared increasingly concerned at the idea of being associated with problematic gender practices and consequently took far-reaching measures to remedy this perception. One interviewee from the M23 rebel movement assured me: "I have never seen a case of military rape in M23. The M23 is very strict on this."[20] Although Human Rights Watch (2012) has, in fact, documented a great many rapes and other gender-based assaults carried out by M23 troops in areas under its control, the fact that my interviewees among the M23 movement were so concerned with assuring me that the group takes gender issues seriously evidenced their own perceptions vis-à-vis the extent to which the international community cared about this issue, and the extent to which they were concerned with representing their practices in a particular light.

In addition to creating the CGE and the PSPEF, the M23 movement also replicated many of the governance structures, policies, and procedures of the national government and the NGOs working to support them in the territories under its control. For instance, the M23 created an independent branch of the Police National Congolaise (the national police service) and a parallel legal system. Within this parallel governance structure, the M23 replicated DR Congo's criminal justice processes. It professed to strictly apply Congolese national law, and when its officers or employees were found to have violated the law, they faced the full force of the parallel legal system. A high-ranking member of M23's command structure informed me: "If there is anyone who deviates from normal procedure, we discipline him according to the Loi Registrant La Police National ... [Under our regime,] people are afraid to commit rape and sexual violence."[21] As with the implementation of the 2006 sexual violence law by local authorities discussed in Chapters 3 and 4, M23's police officers explained to me: "If it is a case of rape, it cannot be resolved by local chiefs. They can't have anything to do with it. For rape cases, they must go straight to the [M23's] police and we make sure they [the victims] can access medical services. All cases involving rape must be transferred to the PSP. There was even one police officer that asked a victim for money when she reported the case. He was immediately arrested when we found out, and transferred to the central prison."[22]

This description of how the police are required to handle rape cases (including refusing to permit private settlements or informal resolutions)

---

[20] Interview. Pepé, M23 Police Unit for the Protection of Women and Children. DR Congo, January 25, 2013.

[21] Interview. Vaincouer, M23 Prosecutor. DR Congo, January 25, 2013.

[22] Interview. Vaincouer, M23 Prosecutor. DR Congo, January 25, 2013.

closely resembles the practices of the Congolese police force discussed in Chapter 4. Interviews in M23 territory in 2013 revealed that national policy on this issue had become so deeply institutionalized before the defection that newly established procedures for dealing with sexual and gender-based violence through the criminal justice system were immediately implemented in the group's parallel governance structure once the group established its own territorial control. Josephat, a junior police officer employed by M23 in Rutshuru territory, confirmed that the information given to me by the M23 elites had indeed made its way into the training and work of the movement's junior officers. Josephat told me about the gender training he had received from M23 before assuming his post. He went on to explain: "Two weeks ago we had a case of a two-year-old girl raped by a fourteen-year-old boy. We tried to find proof and obtain medical statements, but the family would not provide this. I am not allowed to release someone who has committed a rape, so I transferred the file to the Parquet [the prosecutor's office]."[23] Another officer, Antoine, added: "We go into the communities and sensitize the population about sexual violence. We do this through activities with local chiefs, but also with the population. We educate them about sexual violence using positive and negative examples."[24] While these interviews with individual officers by no means offer conclusive evidence of a genuine commitment to reducing gender violence and, much less, of changing battlefield behavior, they do indicate that the M23 hierarchy was concerned with portraying itself as a movement that takes gender issues seriously.

Autesserre (2012) suggests that rather than leading to a declining tolerance of rape among armed groups, increased international attention to gender issues has in fact made gender violence *more* likely. Autesserre notes that the singular attention to sexual and gender-based crimes signals that this form of abuse is uniquely forbidden and punishable, thus creating incentives for various groups to exploit it (Autesserre 2012: 16). She points to the example of the Mai Mai Sheka group, implicated in the mass rapes in Walikale territory in 2010, noting that Sheka ordered his soldiers to engage in systematic rape because he wanted to draw attention to his group and to be invited to the negotiating table, which, she observes, is exactly what happened (Autesserre 2012: 16). It is certainly possible that armed groups have employed this as a strategy, as Autesserre suggests. However, as time goes on, combatants, officers, and administrative personnel from across armed groups seem hesitant to be associated with conflict-related gender violence. M23 has responded defensively to

---

[23] Interview. Josephat, M23 Police Officer. DR Congo, January 25, 2013.
[24] Interview. Antoine, M23 Officer. DR Congo, January 25, 2013.

Human Rights Watch's 2012 allegations documenting the continued prevalence of rape perpetrated by M23 combatants, signifying that it is deeply uncomfortable with being associated with problematic gender practices. In contrast to Autesserre's assertions that international attention increases the likelihood of rape, therefore, commanders seem less inclined than they were previously to explicitly order the use of sexual violence as a military strategy.

Groups other than the M23 have similarly shied away from being associated with wartime rape. While anecdotal evidence suggests that opportunistic rape remains as prevalent as ever, groups that previously employed rape as a targeted military strategy – such as the Democratic Forces for the Liberation of Rwanda (FDLR) – have done so less frequently in recent years (UN Group of Experts 2013). In his interviews with FARDC officers in North Kivu, Michael Broache (2013) found that soldiers of all ranks in the national army were aware of indictments, arrest warrants, and trials in Congolese domestic courts and at the International Criminal Court (ICC) in The Hague. Some believed that the threat of these trials had influenced their superiors' behaviors and strategic calculations. Broache quotes one soldier who acknowledged: "Of course they [his commanders] are afraid of the ICC, because they know if they make crimes, they will be arrested." Another noted: "The high commanders are now afraid; they know they will be held responsible if they order their subordinates to commit crimes" (27).

Of course, none of this offers any certainty that increased legal accountability for sexual and gender-based violence has any genuinely deterrent effect on combatant behavior.[25] Human Rights Watch strongly professes that M23's gender practices are as abhorrent as they have always been (Human Rights Watch 2012). However, these examples illustrate that prosecutions, combined with international attention to the issue, have fundamentally altered how military units and strategists engage and associate with gender violence. Rather than treating rape unquestioningly as a spoil of war as groups have done in the past, some commanders appear to be rethinking the consequences of rape in their ranks, displaying an awareness of the threat of prosecution as well as a wariness of damage to their public image. These factors are only likely to play out among armed groups explicitly engaged in the pursuit of external legitimacy (Huang 2012, 2016; Jo 2015).

---

[25] See Cronin-Furman (2013) for a compelling critique of the expectation that criminal trials will have any deterrent effect on battlefield behavior.

Conclusion

Many argue that, over time, increased legal accountability will lead to fewer human rights violations and more peaceful, stable, and prosperous political environments (Sikkink 2011). For those subscribing to this view, legal practitioners in eastern DR Congo have undoubtedly proved incredibly effective in directing legal attention to a previously overlooked crime, in ways that could have long-term spill-over effects for other human rights outcomes. Yet, if we scrutinize the repercussions of devoting such targeted attention to a single crime without considering the broader landscape of violence and law, the picture becomes far murkier. Looking beyond gains won in court, this chapter demonstrated that an emphasis by NGOs in eastern DR Congo on activities like criminal trials, which can demonstrate quantifiable successes by meeting specific program objectives, has displaced other slower-burning activities that may have greater potential to contribute to long-term, sustained change. Moreover, since foreign NGOs and other external actors are often unfamiliar with the political terrain in which they are working, and are under pressure to quickly demonstrate evidence that programs are being successfully implemented, those engaged in rule of law activities can be incentivized to turn a blind eye to the ways in which local dynamics of conflict and power overshadow and influence the activities they are able to pursue. It will be the job of future work, and possibly the passage of time, to weigh the many different repercussions of these interventions against one another. More research is needed – in DR Congo, South Africa, and elsewhere – to evaluate the extent to which increasing numbers of criminal trials in fragile state contexts can generate lasting positive externalities for victims of violence, in spite of their visible limitations.

8   Conclusion
NGOs and State (Un)Making

This book explored why courts in eastern DR Congo have offered a robust judicial response to gender-based violence, prioritizing gendered crimes despite considerable logistical challenges, while gender activists in South Africa, home to a far stronger legal infrastructure and a friendlier human rights regime, have struggled to shape the work of local courts. The institutional response in the two countries has been puzzling. For the past few decades, South Africa has been home to a well-organized and internationally renowned feminist movement, which has heavily influenced global discourse surrounding the criminalization of gender violence. Yet, despite the notable successes of South Africa's women's rights movement in shaping the country's legislative framework, NGOs and gender activists have failed to significantly alter the treatment of sexual and gender-based violence by the country's domestic courts. In contrast, domestic and international NGOs in eastern DR Congo have dramatically transformed how local courts have approached gender violence, providing new protections for victims that are frequently invoked in local justice sector institutions.

These divergent institutional responses are surprising for a number of reasons. Hafner-Burton and Tsutsui (2005), Neumayer (2005), and Simmons (2009) have each found evidence to suggest that a proliferation of NGOs or international organizations in a given country should increase the likelihood that legislative human rights commitments will improve domestic human rights practices. Others have analyzed the powerful role played by transnational advocacy networks in influencing domestic human rights outcomes. Keck and Sikkink (1998) famously argued that strong links between local and transnational organizations lead to increased pressure on offending regimes to improve policies and practices: where transnational activist networks are present, pressure can be simultaneously levied by domestic actors and those from abroad, leading to the increased likelihood that domestic law reform will result in compliance and local implementation. Murdie and Peksen (2014) provide further evidence of these claims. Sally Merry (2006) similarly demonstrated that advocacy around emerging international human rights norms should be more effective when it is supported by a robust home-grown domestic human rights movement, arguing that domestic actors are well positioned to "translate" international human rights norms into local practice. Yet none of these expectations bore out in the cases of DR Congo and South Africa.

In addition to bucking scholarly expectations about the strength of local advocacy movements, the experiences of South Africa and DR Congo also cast doubt on what state strength and weakness might mean for the diffusion of international human rights norms. Scholars in the World Society school highlight the importance of state capacity for the local adoption and implementation of new human rights laws. In their seminal work on the spread of emerging global norms, Meyer and colleagues (1997) predicted a decoupling of law and practice in weak state environments. Börzel and Risse (2013) and Krasner and Risse (2014) have also made important contributions to this debate, outlining how "degrees" of statehood shape the potential for advocates and NGOs to influence domestic human rights developments, and anticipating that weak state capacity would ultimately impede the implementation of human rights law and policy. By virtue of its dilapidated judicial infra-structure and ongoing insecurity, DR Congo remained a least likely case for diffusion and local implementation.

Through an in-depth analysis of two key cases, this book augments our knowledge of how human rights organizations operate in strong and weak states alike. It reveals that, under certain circumstances, state fragility creates opportunity structures that enable domestic and international NGOs and human rights activists to exert influence over local governance (in this case, the justice sector), in ways that are not possible where the state is stronger. The institutional configurations of state fragility in east-ern DR Congo created openings for non-state actors – including NGOs, foreign governments, and international organizations – to influence the setting of national policy agendas with regard to gender violence, as well as their implementation in local courts and police stations. In South Africa, despite a regime historically supportive of human rights, and a robust and well-organized gender rights movement, stronger and more centralized state capacity has served to curtail the influence gender advocates are able to exert over legal processes.

In the same way that Jackson and Rosberg (1982) have argued that statehood exists both in juridical form (as the *recognition* of state sovereignty by other states and international institutions) and as an empirical reality (in which the state can enforce laws and control populations within its terri-tory), I show that state weakness also possesses empirical and juridical qualities. Precisely *because* the Congolese state is removed from the organization and regulation of local communities, domestic and international non-state actors have stepped in to perform these tasks. This de facto assumption of power has created opportunities for NGOs and human rights practitioners to enter and influence the legal system in ways that prove impossible where the state has greater reach and autonomy.

Juridical dimensions of state fragility also present new opportunities. Jackson and Rosberg (1982) use the idea of juridical statehood to suggest that the formal recognition of the sovereign state facilitates actions and resource flows from other states and members of the international community. I show that state fragility can also be recognized both formally (for instance, by UN Security Council Resolutions), and informally, through development indices and the discursive frames employed by development practitioners. When ascribed by international representatives, terms such as "fragile," "(post-)conflict," or "failed" statehood have channeled international funding toward specific aspects of state development, and justified continued external intrusions into domestic governance activities. These actions and resource flows are not forthcoming in contexts of better-established and respected state sovereignty.

Interventions by external human rights actors have shaped legal practice in eastern DR Congo in a variety of consequential ways. First, state fragility has enabled organizations working on sexual and gender-based violence to intervene more directly in setting law and policy at the national level in ways that were only evident in South Africa in the earlier stages of the country's transition to democracy. Second, a general lack of oversight and capacity on the part of the Congolese state has meant that well-resourced international organizations in partnership with local human rights NGOs have, in effect, been able to assume direct responsibility over aspects of the administration of justice in the provinces. While non-state actors work in partnership with the Congolese government to coordinate local justice sector activities, the reality is that, by virtue of the structure of development aid, international partners have assumed de facto control over setting judicial priorities.[1] Third, empirical and juridical dimensions of state fragility have allowed non-state actors to integrate fairly extensive community-based outreach with formal legal structures. This has included providing material incentives to encourage local communities and individuals to participate in legal processes. While similar outreach activities have been attempted in South Africa, the institutional landscape differs so greatly that these efforts tend to be less integrated and less well

---

[1] See Donais (2009) for a discussion of the disproportionate influence of international stakeholders over peacebuilding initiatives that espouse local ownership.

funded. A relatively strong central state and a well-functioning judiciary in South Africa has meant that activists and gender violence practitioners have struggled to overcome the deeply institutionalized conservative attitudes toward gender that permeate the legal system, and generate resistance from policy makers in the capital to police, judges, and prosecutors in court.

In addition to identifying the openings and opportunities created by weak empirical statehood, however, the research also reveals the precarity of human rights gains that circumvent the state. When human rights and rule of law practitioners use opportunities presented by state fragility to advance a singular human rights agenda, their successes are inevitably accompanied by a host of new challenges. Weak rule of law undermines the durability of newly introduced gender protections. Ongoing corruption and unchecked patronage limit the extent to which intended beneficiaries of legal aid can take advantage of the protections they are afforded in court. NGOs and international organizations substituting for the state in the areas it is perceived to be failing may serve to weaken state institutions and retrench state capacity over the long term. Given that the Congolese state has such a poor track record of paying public employee salaries and investing in state infrastructure, there are few incentives for domestic stakeholders to shift sole responsibility over the administration of justice back to the central government. And NGOs, constrained in their ability to act outside of the strict funding priorities established by donors, prove unable to advocate for more broad-based legal reform. The ways in which external actors circumvented state authority in eastern DR Congo, and even coopted the work of local justice sector institutions, were considered deeply problematic by South African activists, who emphasized the paramount importance of strong state involvement even in the face of hostility and resistance.

Looking Further Afield: Beyond DR Congo and South Africa

Organizations like the American Bar Association (ABA), the United Nations Development Program (UNDP), the European Union, Avocats Sans Frontières, and others are engaged in promoting human rights and building legal capacity all over the world. While eastern DR Congo and South Africa's Western Cape represent two very different experiences, dynamics present in each case look familiar to practitioners from across institutional settings, and working in different issue areas. Afghanistan, Armenia, Belarus, Georgia, Haiti, Liberia, Mexico, Pakistan, Peru, the Philippines, Sierra Leone, Somalia, South Sudan,

Sri Lanka, and Timor Leste are just a few of the countries, for instance, in which very similar coalitions of stakeholders have engaged in rule of law promotion and development. With some notable exceptions, the weaker the state apparatus, the more far-reaching the program. This is because fragile or volatile states are typically those whose legal systems are most urgently in need of support and resources, thus constituting priorities for the international community. It is also because organizations working in aid-dependent countries characterized by climates of weak regulatory authority can engage in interventions that government actors might reject or resist elsewhere.

Timor Leste

Timor Leste offers one such example. In 1975, the country declared its independence from Portugal, but was occupied again by Indonesia mere days later. After a brutal period of Indonesian occupation, a UN-supported referendum in 1999 resulted in a clear vote for Timor's independence. Pro-Indonesia militias engaged in widespread retributive violence following the results of the referendum, and an Australian-led peacekeeping force, followed closely by the United Nations Mission in East Timor (UNTAET), assumed control of the country.

UNTAET assumed full legal sovereignty over the territory until the country's formal independence in 2002. The conditions of the post-conflict landscape were such that non-state actors could exert unparalleled influence over human rights and governance activities in this period. NGOs, in partnership with UNTAET and other international stakeholders, were at the forefront of rebuilding the country's health infrastructure after the civil war. NGOs provided direct emergency relief to the population throughout the occupation, as well as in the post-2002 period. External actors entirely restructured the Ministry of Health and put in place policies and regulations to ensure the long-term functioning of health services across the country. The European Commission Humanitarian Office (ECHO), in collaboration with the World Bank, the Asian Development Bank (ADB), and others, established processes for the recruitment of physicians and specialists through internationally competitive procurement procedures. They allocated cars and motorcycles to each district and facility, trained ambulance drivers and nurses, introduced policies and procedures governing the effective distribution of essential medicines, and established a radio network linking all district and subdistrict facilities, ambulances, referral hospitals, central medical stores, and Ministry of Health offices (Alonso and Brugha 2006). The result was the emergence of an effective and steadily improving health system that outperformed others in the region. Timor Leste was one of the few countries in the world to approach the Millennium Development Goal of reducing maternal and child mortality by half (Asian Development Bank 2015).

Similar efforts were undertaken in other sectors. Akin to efforts in eastern DR Congo, UNTAET was instrumental in building a competent national police force in order to provide protection to civilian populations and investigate and respond to a broad range of violent and nonviolent criminal offenses. Like in DR Congo, international stakeholders were involved in recruiting, training, equipping, and resourcing the new police force, as well as educating its members in international human rights principles and best practices (United Nations Security Council Resolutions UNSC-S/1999/1024: 57 -59; UNSC-R 1272). New police units received specialized training in responding to the needs of vulnerable populations and, specifically, in questioning victims of domestic violence, collecting evidence in sexual assault cases, and responding to allegations of intimate partner violence (Grenfell 2013; Radin 2012).

In tandem, the Australian Agency for International Development (AUSAID), in partnership with United Nations Development Program (UNDP) and other major donors, engaged in sweeping efforts at legal reform. International judges and trainee lawyers were recruited to participate in domestic trials, train local practitioners, and even hear cases. Timor's domestic courts developed the capacity to hear complex war crimes and crimes against humanity cases (Cohen 2002). UNSC-R 1272 set up a system of district courts and gave the Dili District Court exclusive jurisdiction over international crimes, including genocide, war crimes, crimes against humanity, murder, sexual offenses, and torture committed between January 1 and October 25, 1999. Extensive international involvement enabled approximately fifty militia members to be taken into UN custody, many of whom were indicted for crimes against humanity. The UN Security Council dedicated upward of $6 million USD toward the specialized district courts, which, for all their shortcomings, transformed the country's capacity to prosecute international crimes. With support from global donors, international judges also sat in ordinary district courts. Under the jurisdiction of the UN Mission, international judges and lawyers participated in criminal cases and mobile court hearings in multiple locations for the District Court of Suai (United Nations Development Programme 2014b). To support these activities, the UNDP's Justice System Program (JSP) in Timor Leste benefited from $13 million USD in in-kind contributions from Australia, Brazil, Japan, Norway, and Portugal, and a further $9 million USD from the UN budget

(United Nations Development Programme 2014a). A number of parallels can be drawn with interventions in the Congolese case. Nevertheless, like in the DR Congo, interventions have been criticized for their limitations and, in particular, for their extreme shortsightedness. The involvement of international practitioners in Timor Leste's international crimes cases meant that few local judges developed the experience or training to pick up human rights cases once international practitioners left. Others dismiss international involvement as "international justice on the cheap," doing little to improve opportunities for criminal accountability beyond a select number of cases involving international crimes (Cohen 2002).

Liberia

Since Liberia's Second Civil War ended in 2003, international organizations have engaged in systematic rule of law reform, as well as a host of other state-building activities. Donors have identified preventing violence against women, improving access to justice, and strengthening the capacity of police and courts as core rule of law priorities. In rural areas especially, the immediate postwar era saw considerable confusion over relevant sources of law and the appropriate jurisdictional authority of courts. Moreover, local justice sector institutions, including police stations and lower courts, severely lacked basic infrastructure, including access to vehicles to carry out investigations, copies of relevant laws, and even pens and paper to take notes or record judicial decisions (Carter 2008). Until fairly recently, legal practitioners also lacked any formalized training through state channels.

Since the end of the war in 2003, many non-state actors have been involved in reforming the justice sector. With support from international partners, one of the postwar government's first acts was to pass new sexual violence legislation, introducing life sentences for rape, criminalizing other forms of sexual violence, and narrowing the definition of legal consent.[2] Similar to the PSPEF in DR Congo, UNICEF has supported the establishment of the Women and Children Protection Section (WCPS) within Liberia's national police force, specifically to investigate and respond to sexual abuses and other violent gendered offenses committed against women (IRIN News 2016). This was followed by the introduction of a small number of specialized sexual offenses courts (Association of Female Lawyers of Liberia, AFELL 2014; Buss et al. 2014). Thus, various UN agencies, as well as the American Bar Association, the Carter Center, the

---

[2] Gender activists were unsuccessful in lobbying the government to explicitly criminalize marital rape in the 2005 law.

Catholic Justice and Peace Commission, Médecin Sans Frontières, the American Refugee Council, USAID, and a host of other transnational organizations, have engaged in activities following Liberia's civil conflict that closely parallel the initiatives undertaken in eastern DR Congo. In addition to the efforts around sexual and gender-based offenses, interventions have included pressing for the introduction and dissemination of a law protecting women's property rights, establishing and appointing community legal advisors who can provide counsel and mediation services, supporting police in monitoring and investigating cases, and introducing a rural paralegal program (Carter 2008; Timap for Justice: Liberia 2014). The American Bar Association advised the Ministry of Labor in the drafting of the 2013 Decent Work Act that set the country's minimum wage at $6 USD per day (American Bar Association Rule of Law Initiative 2012; Johnson 2013). This broad coalition of actors has also offered socio-material support similar to the types provided in the Kivus, in order to encourage community participation in legal processes and support rehabilitation and reintegration into the community for victims of stigmatized crimes.

Finally, the American Bar Association has been closely involved in training judges, magistrates, and public defenders in the country. As part of this work, the American Bar Association supported the establishment of the James A. A. Pierre Judicial Institute (JAAPJI) as a sustainable, Liberian-led training institution equipped to identify and address local justice needs. In a country whose legal system was almost entirely decimated after the civil war, key activities have included the recruitment and training from scratch of qualified legal practitioners to oversee judicial administration and law enforcement, and a sustainable system of legal education that would increase the numbers of qualified practitioners over time. The American Bar Association has also established a law school in Monrovia and a legal information institute, as well as worked with Liberian lawyers to create and disseminate the country's first bench books, which systematized, publicized, and distributed criminal procedure and other relevant laws across the country. The bench books now serve as the JAAPJI's prime teaching resource, and are increasingly cited as the predominant courtroom reference material for local judges (American Bar Association 2012).[3] As in DR Congo, the American Bar Association and similar stakeholders have established legal aid clinics across the country, offered free legal representation to victims of sexual and gender-based assaults, and provided legal aid services to detainees and those at risk of prolonged pretrial detention. Despite the usual challenges, as well as some local resistance to certain

---

[3] See Liberlii: www.liberlii.org/.

efforts, activities have resulted in increasingly more progressive human rights decisions and stronger human rights practices employed by courts and legal institutions.

Applications Elsewhere

Liberia and Timor Leste are not the only sites of expansive rule of law reform by external actors, although they are among the most far-reaching. Since the end of Sierra Leone's civil war, the United Kingdom's Department for International Development (DfID), in partnership with the United Nations Development Program and GIZ, has supported legal capacity through training, legal outreach, and direct intervention – including a mobile court program that closely resembles the mobile courts in eastern DR Congo. The three global donors have assumed direct responsibility over the coordination of mobile circuit courts in Sierra Leone, as well as provided financial support directly to the central government in order to sponsor judicial salaries, legal education, and clerical resources to support courts, trials, and investigations. Mobile circuit courts provide an opportunity to transfer cases involving sexual and gender-based violence from existing first-instance courts (which were traditionally part of the country's customary legal system and no longer have jurisdiction over gender violence offenses) to magistrates' courts. Previously, customary courts would continue to hear sexual assault cases despite changes to the law, since access to higher courts was severely restricted by money and geography. With international support, this is no longer the case. International donors cover approximately eighty percent of the circuit courts' budget (United Nations Development Programme 2014b) and have been fairly effective at increasing access to justice in rural areas. They provide transportation to victims, witnesses, and their legal representatives, bolster the capacity of select magistrates' courts, and direct legal attention toward previously marginalized crimes (Timap for Justice: Sierra Leone 2014). While activities in Sierra Leone have not been as expansive as those in Liberia, the mobile courts have nevertheless transformed access to the formal justice system in many locations.

In Somaliland, the United Nations Development Program has sought to displace local reliance on customary mechanisms in order to increase the capacity and reach of the formal legal system. To this end, support has been provided to mobile courts on an ad hoc basis. Yet, due to challenges of local legitimacy, the United Nations Development Program's mobile court program must be explicitly requested by local judicial staff, police officers, traditional elders, or victims of crimes (United Nations Development Programme 2014b). The United Nations Development

Program states that its efforts to incorporate female prosecutors, lawyers, registrars, and paralegals are gradually changing cultural norms that restrict Somali women's participation in public life and decision-making , as well as providing women with an alternative to traditional justice mechanisms that may discriminate against them, such as the Xeer system. Yet, since the UNDP is the only major partner to the legal system in Somalia, its work and impact have been limited.

In the Central African Republic (CAR), the American Bar Association and the United Nations Development Program have partnered to support rule of law outreach and legal capacity building since 2009. In dialogue with international program officers, judicial authorities prepare lists of cases eligible for mobile court sessions and the Ministry of Justice (MOJ) submits an official request for support to United Nations Development Program. Much like in DR Congo, the United Nations Development Program supports per diem and fuel for legal practitioners and other relevant personnel, and the American Bar Association supports state prosecutors in their investigations and provides legal representation to civil parties. International stakeholders are heavily engaged in monitoring the activities of the legal system and conducting outreach, publicity, rights trainings, and legal education, yet ongoing security issues and the lack of a stable political administration means that activities are frequently halted and programs have been implemented fairly sporadically.

Even in Pakistan, home to a comparatively robust state apparatus, the United Nations Development Program has engaged in fairly expansive access to justice initiatives. A 2015 United Nations Development Program report opens:

In a remote village in the outskirts of Peshawar, Pakistan, court is in session. The stenographer is typing away, the judge is listening intently and the air conditioner strains to keep the room cool as two property dealers from Hayatabad argue over USD $6,000. But this is no ordinary courtroom. This trial is taking place in a big green bus. (United Nations Development Program 2015)

Building on its successes in DR Congo and Liberia, the United Nations Development Program has begun to deploy mobile court programs in a wide range of countries with varying institutional capacity, including, since 2013, Peshawar Province in Pakistan (United Nations Development Program 2015). Although the justice sector was already under-resourced across much of the country, the 2007 to 2009 conflict exacerbated these challenges, decimating the country's legal infrastructure and seriously impeding its law enforcement capacity outside of the capital. As in eastern DR Congo, mobile courts in Pakistan bring well-trained judges, lawyers, and prosecutors to remote areas, aiming to dramatically reduce judicial delays and encourage local participation in formal legal processes. Legal representation is offered free of charge, but, unlike DR Congo, mobile courts in Pakistan also offer possibilities for mediation. Courts cut caseloads by hearing six to seven civil or criminal cases per day. The United Nations Development Program mobile courts in Peshawar courts operate under the authority of the Peshawar High Court, but other United Nations Development Program activities across the country, supported financially by the Dutch and Swiss governments, include bolstering police capacity by providing resources, funding, and logistical assistance; as well as resources and direct support to local government agencies; training prosecutors, investigators, police, and judges; and supporting bar associations and civil society organizations.

In countries that boast stronger state infrastructure and bureaucracy rule of law advocacy has proved more challenging. This is particularly true in regimes vocally hostile to human rights. While the American Bar Association has provided support to Addis Ababa University's law faculty in Ethiopia in partnership with USAID (USAID 2012), other activities have proved unworkable. Since the passage of Ethiopia's 2009 Proclamation for the Registration and Regulation of Charities and Societies, most international organizations have been required to cease programs altogether or, at the very least, significantly curtail their work. The 2009 Proclamation divides NGOs and civil society organizations working in Ethiopia into three categories: Ethiopian organizations, Ethiopian resident organizations, and foreign organizations (Brechenmacher 2017). Under the Proclamation, only Ethiopian organizations (those that receive ninety percent of their funding from domestic sources) are permitted to work on justice and law enforcement activities or other rights-based programs, meaning that international influence is muzzled.

Following Rwanda's genocide and civil war, international organizations were integral to rebuilding government infrastructure. By 2003, the United States and the United Kingdom were providing almost $100 million USD between them per year in bilateral development aid to the Rwandan government, with this figure followed closely by Canada, Germany, Belgium, and Norway (OECD 2005). These funds were predominantly directed toward budget support dispersed to government ministries, but also included funds for direct program implementation. Because state infrastructure and capacity was decimated after the war, even state-led projects were typically collaborations with international partners. Donor priorities included rebuilding justice and health systems, reconstructing government infrastructure, building roads and communication networks, and training government practitioners, bureaucrats, and technicians (USAID 2016). Technical consultants were placed within a number of government ministries and agencies (such as the Ministries for Health, Education, Gender, and Land), with technical assistance in general comprising a full twenty percent of all Rwanda's foreign aid (Hayman 2006). In the aftermath of the genocide and civil war, external actors contributed significantly to aspects of law reform. In-kind contributions were also paid directly to domestic and international NGOs to facilitate service provision, support victims of violence, and build aspects of civil society.

Yet, as the Rwandan government strengthened and stabilized opportunities for non-state actors to shape Rwanda's legal and human rights landscape closed. In recent years, a smaller proportion of the country's foreign aid has been spent on training and technical assistance, and funds have instead been redirected toward initiatives encompassing women's empowerment, malaria prevention, AIDS relief, poverty reduction, maternal health, and other Millennium Development Goals and Sustainable Development Goals targets (USAID 2016). The strength and authority of the Rwandan state has made the far-reaching governance interventions employed by international stakeholders in the early post-conflict period less necessary from a technical capacity-building perspective. But far reaching interventions – especially those focused on human rights – have also been less appealing to President Paul Kagame, in the context of an increasingly authoritarian political apparatus. Whereas in the early years of the postwar transition, international actors exerted considerable influence over state policy and in Rwanda, in recent years, interventions have been subject to increased governmental monitoring, scrutiny, and regulation. Human rights advocacy and democracy promotion in particular have been criticized by Kagame as inappropriate or "un-African" (Freedom House 2015; Rundell 2010; Stubbs 2016).

Tunisia, Egypt, Hungary, and Zimbabwe are similarly home to governments that have invoked the rhetoric of state sovereignty to curb the influence of international organizations. In many cases, governments have introduced legislation similar to Ethiopia's 2009 Proclamation in an effort to regulate the activities and influence of NGOs and foreign funding. This has been particularly true in the areas of human rights and democracy promotion (Bratton 1987; Dupuy, Ron, and Prakash 2015; Jalali 2008). Given the fairly hefty restrictions many governments place on foreign NGOs, some external actors have commented, formally and informally, that they find it easier to operate where the state is weak, as they can cut bureaucratic corners, bypass formal arrangements, and avoid complex regulation (Dupuy et al. 2015: 421). Liberia and Timor Leste demonstrate how low state capacity can facilitate external actors' abilities to meet fairly sweeping policy objectives. However, the immediacy of human rights gains won in environments that lack robust infrastructure means that outputs can be fleeting and may be vulnerable to displacement or distortion as donor priorities or institutional landscapes shift.

Scope Conditions

In his influential body of work, Stephen Krasner observes that the norm of state sovereignty dominates in the international system but is consistently violated in practice (Krasner 1999). The states that are home to the most sweeping and far-reaching interventions tend to be those that have "collapsed" altogether, affording them designations as weak, failed, or trusteeship states.[4] However, Krasner famously purports that international intervention into states' domestic affairs occurs far more commonly than prevailing norms of sovereignty would dictate. Interventions can involve naming and shaming a country's human rights practices, attaching governance conditions to loans and other international financial transactions, offering formal or informal incentives for legislative or policy changes, or demanding policy concessions in exchange for trade or investment.

The foregoing examples illustrate a range of such intrusions that differ in form and reach. Even in the comparably strong state of Pakistan, ongoing civil unrest has created *some* empirical and juridical opportunities that have served to justify and facilitate otherwise inconceivable levels of international intervention in local justice administration. In none of these cases, however, do we see the dramatic strides in a single issue area that we observe in the prosecution of gender violence in eastern DR Congo. This is because, in most of these cases, international intervention has focused on a broad repertoire of human rights and legal capacity-building initiatives. Even in Liberia, where advocacy around sexual and gender-based violence has been fairly targeted, a range of other program activities

---

[4] Keohane (2002), Krasner (2004a), and Lake and Fariss (2014) define "international trusteeships" as states that have lost or given up their ability to exercise authority within their own territory (Lake and Farris 2014: 571). Examples include UNTAET, which had full sovereign control from 1999 to 2002, after which the UN Mission retained varying executive powers in the security sector. In Kosovo, UNMIK retained executive control even though Yugoslavia retained sovereignty over the territory. See Radin (2012), UNSC-R 1272 (1999) and 1704 (2006), and S/1999/779 (July 12, 1999: 35). Chesterman (2005: 5) defines this category of weak states as "transitional administrations" whereby international actors assume "some or all of the powers of the state on a temporary basis." Radin (2012: 22) defines "transitional" or "international" administrations as emerging from civil wars, created by the international community (meaning they must have buy-in and participation by major Western states and international organizations), with international actors having assumed executive authority therein and established a legalized authority to rule, and governing with mandate to pursue state-building.

has accompanied this work. The almost exclusive donor interest in sexual and gender-based violence in eastern DR Congo, which has emerged from a rather singular narrative of the conflict (Autesserre 2012), has been at the heart of the movement's expansive influence. The convergence of a weak and fragmented state and an extraordinarily coordinated international effort to address one *particular* policy problem has led to the striking outcomes wrought in local courtrooms.

Conclusion

This book does not seek to suggest that the absence of state authority is beneficial for human rights advocacy. Indeed, despite the implementation of gender-progressive practices in local courts and police stations, the lack of reliable transportation and communication infrastructure, ongoing corruption, pervasive security challenges, issues of program sustainability, and coordination problems between development agencies and local partners, all serve to stifle and undermine rights protections more broadly. In demonstrating the surprisingly effective diffusion of internationally promoted human rights norms in areas of state weakness, therefore, this book warns against interpreting rights gains won in court as emblematic of broader human rights victories. Indeed, whether the language of punitive justice proves personally relevant to victims of gendered crimes is not the only measure of its value; these gains cannot be understood in isolation from the broader landscape of violence and insecurity that made them possible. To begin to comprehend the long-term legacies of victories won by gender advocates and NGOs, scholars and practitioners need to be attentive to the myriad externalities – positive and negative – that accompany human rights developments at the peripheries of consolidated statehood.

Part II of this book thus considered how new opportunities for legal remedy affected the lives of those most directly intended to benefit, while also considering their repercussions in other areas. For instance, in spite of the myriad challenges that have resulted, legal outreach has resulted in tangible and observable gains for some victims of violence. Luce expressed disgust and regret at having to spend her life with a man who violated her trust by sexually assaulting her and applauded a changing legal culture that criminalized rape rather than socially sanctioning it. The language of law gave Luce a powerful tool to reject a customary response to rape that she found unjust. Others, however, expressed frustration or disinterest at having to respond and readjust to new externally imposed systems regulating and governing their responses to violence, when they felt that real justice could not be found through law. Although many of those interviewed expressed a genuine desire to see those who had hurt them incarcerated or punished, others were unable to see how legal accountability could be relevant to the lived hardships of their day to day lives.

Socio-legal scholars have long questioned the idea that legal remedy can serve genuinely emancipatory purposes for marginalized or under-represented communities (Englund 2006; Massoud 2011, 2013; McCann 2006). Galanter (1994), Epp (1990), and others have shown that a reliance on legal avenues to remedy past injustices serves only to alienate those who are most disadvantaged. Studies in the United States and elsewhere have shown that education, race, and socioeconomic status are powerful predictors of the extent to which individuals can take advantage of new rights granted by law (Bumiller 1990; Ewick and Silbey 1998; Rubbers and Gallez 2012). Those with low levels of education, or who are disadvantaged in other ways, remain disenfranchised, while only their already more privileged counterparts are able to realize their rights through the legal system (Berry 2015; Berry and Lake 2017a, 2017b). Moreover, since human rights movements based around legal remedy and rights-claiming in court often turn collective grievances into individualized disputes (Goluboff 2007; McCann 1994, 2014), legal avenues may impede more far-reaching, systemic, or broad-based possibilities for social change. "Rights"-based remedies are, by nature, reactive, focusing on redress (often through financial compensation) for individual claimants, rather than addressing underlying problems associated with violent crime or socioeconomic disparity.[5]

Colonial and postcolonial trajectories of legal reform provide necessary context for the ways in which international actors have sought to reshape, redefine, and regulate violence in DR Congo and South Africa. Scholars of colonialism have explored how new legal frameworks and the formalization of existing regulatory structures served supposedly emancipatory purposes – to free colonial subjects from the shackles of their "uncivilized" pasts – while at once subjugating them within newly formalized hierarchies of governance in which their behaviors in public and private spheres were tightly regulated and controlled by colonial

---

[5] These critiques of rights-based mobilization stand in contrast to positions adopted by socialization scholars. The socialization literature asserts that once human rights practices become normalized and habituated in daily life, new norms will eventually be internalized (Finnemore and Sikkink 1998; Goodman and Jinks 2004; 2013; Risse-Kappen, Ropp, and Sikkink 1999b). These differing interpretations derive from fundamentally different approaches towards mechanisms for social change.

authorities (Comaroff 2001; Fischer-Tiné and Mann 2004; McClintock 2013). New European codes of behavior – covering education, governance, worship, sanitation, and reproductive health – were presented as morally, socially, and physically superior to preexisting local practices (Brantlinger 1985; Chanock 1985; Mamdani 1996; Merry 2003a). Postcolonial aid and development work does not tend to be cloaked in the rhetoric of racial inferiority as the civilizing mission of colonialism. Yet the tactics humanitarian actors employ – to reeducate and emancipate victims of perceived injustices – certainly share some characteristics with those employed by missionaries and colonial administrators. Based on medical innovation, and couched in technocratic language, program beneficiaries are told that their practices are unsanitary, illegal, or immoral. They are expected to integrate new patterns of social behavior unquestioningly into their daily lives.

Nevertheless, my interviews demonstrated that even those who explicitly reject externally imposed norms of legal accountability have engaged with the law in a variety of innovative and dynamic ways. Some have used legal language to publicly call attention to private abuses or to reap compensation or other practical material benefits. While access to justice still heavily depends on proximity to courts and to rule of law programming, victims of various injustices are increasingly coming into contact with the discourse of legal remedy to address gender violence. In addition to creating space for women, and some men, to claim new rights, educational programs designed to promote gender equality in the household and endorse women's political participation have provoked broader conversations about entrenched gender norms that will likely have lasting impacts. While these activities have sometimes brought with them a backlash from men who feel excluded from gender and development discourse, they have strengthened and supported a growing feminist movement. Whatever else has resulted, Congolese women have used shifting legal opportunity structures to reject of practices they find to be discriminatory and unjust; to publicly identify and condemn a variety of gendered harms; and to push forward new conversations about gendered power. In sum, while individual expressions of empowerment and opportunity cannot be divorced from the broader institutional contexts from which legal developments emerged, conversations about legitimate and illegitimate violence cannot be undone. Given important questions about the legitimacy and efficacy of externally led human rights innovations, it is the dynamic local responses to gender advocacy, rather than the legal developments themselves, that are likely to determine future trajectories of violence and the rule of law.

Appendix A   Decisions in the Field

Scholars have written extensively about the ethics, strategies, and techniques employed by researchers in volatile conflict environments and dealing with sensitive subject matters (Cronin Furman and Lake 2018; Fujii 2010; Miller et al. 2012; Parkinson 2015; Schatz 2009; Soss 2006; Wedeen 2010). In Appendix B, I provide details of my research decisions involving victims of violence and trauma.

Scheduling Interviews

I knew a number of Congolese and South African legal organizations from prior work in the field, both as a researcher and as a human rights practitioner. I thus began my research with the network of contacts I already had. During the course of these early meetings, I developed a more complete lists of potential interviewees. Mutual acquaintances frequently made informal introductions, and I was able to follow up easily with relevant stakeholders after an initial exchange of names and contact details. Introductions like this greatly facilitated my research.

My interviews varied significantly in length and style. Some took place in organizational offices, and others in the homes of interviewees. Many were conversational in nature. These type of interviews lasted anywhere between one and four hours. Other interviews, in the offices of legal practitioners, in court buildings, or in police stations, were more structured and formal in nature. For these, I asked targeted and direct questions, and recorded everything that was discussed in my notebook or on my computer.

For all interviews, I employed verbal consent procedures. A number of my interviewees could not write, and I did not wish to begin my interviews with questions about their literacy. Second, given the volatile security environment, I did not wish to keep a paper trail linking interviewees with identifying information in my work. Finally, given that many of my interviewees had lived through wars, armed struggles, or repressive authoritarianism I did not feel it was appropriate to ask them to sign written documentation they did not fully understand. I simply explained in as much detail as possible the nature of my research project before the interviews began, and asked interviewees for their permission to pose questions around specific topics and write down their answers for use in my research.[1] To maintain consistency, I employed the same verbal consent procedures for all of my interviewees.

With the exception of twenty-one interviews, I conducted all the interviews myself. In twenty-one cases, I had the opportunity to interview individuals on occasions where I was unable to be present in person, and therefore I entrusted the interviews to research assistants with whom I had worked closely. In 88 of the remaining 172 interviews, I was accompanied by a research partner or a translator. These interviews were normally conducted in local languages and translated into either French or English. I conducted the remaining eighty-four interviews alone, in either French or English. In some cases, I conducted more than one interview with an individual. Given the nature of my research, and the time I spent in the field, a great deal of the data I accumulated was through participant observation, informal conversation, and traveling and spending time in court houses, police stations and legal aid clinics with practitioners. Informal interviews and conversations from my field-notes are not included in my list of interviews. When I directly reference material from informal meetings in the text, I cite these as "field notes."

Recording Stories and Citing Interviews

In order to clearly reference my interviews in the manuscript, I give each interviewee a first name pseudonym. To avoid breaking the flow of the text, whenever I quote interviewees directly or invoke their ideas in the text, I simply refer to them by their first name pseudonym, and cite the date and location of the interview in a footnote. Where clarifying information is relevant, I have also provided the age, position, or employment of the interviewee in the body of the text. I do not provide specific place names or names of organizations in order to ensure the full confidentiality of my interviewees. While many interviewees spoke freely to me in their positions as public spokespeople for their organizations, others met me in private, and disclosed highly confidential information. In order to remain consistent in the text, I have employed the same practices and procedures regarding confidentiality for all my interviewees.

[1] Study Application 42090, IRB Committee C, University of Washington Institutional Review Board 2012; Study Application 00004368, Arizona State University Institutional Review Board 2016.

Where I quote the words of my interviewees in the text, I normally use my own direct translations of their words. For those interviews conducted in languages other than French or English, I use translations provided by my research partners and interpreters.

Where I have changed words or clarified concepts in my quoted interviews, I use square brackets to identify my insertions. For some of the longer quotes, I have omitted clarifying questions asked by the interviewer in order to avoid disrupting the flow of the text or obscuring the key point.

Appendix B   Interviews with Victims of Gender Violence

In Appendix A, I discussed the general interview techniques I employed during the course of this research. In addition to the ethnographic field-work conducted for this research project as a whole, my discussion of DR Congo also draws from a subset of fifty interviews with recent self-reported victims of gender-based violence conducted in one urban and two rural locations in North and South Kivu. Given that legal outreach programs cannot successfully strengthen justice systems without engaging local communities in their work, these interviews were designed in order to assess the ways in which victims of violence in eastern DR Congo engaged with the justice system, and how they experienced and interpreted the various avenues available to them in the aftermath of violence.

For the subset of interviews discussed in Chapters 5 and 6, respondents were selected in three overarching categories: those who had experienced crimes of a sexual nature and had successfully initiated legal proceedings (twenty-seven); those who had experienced crimes of a sexual nature and had attempted to initiate legal proceedings, but failed (twelve); and those who had experienced crimes of a sexual nature and had opted against pursuing any kind of formal legal remedy (eleven).

Interviewees were all female and, with one exception, ranged between sixteen and sixty-three years of age. Interviewees came from a variety of ethnic and socioeconomic backgrounds. It is important to note that there are a number of male survivors of sexual violence in DR Congo in addition to female survivors. While I did not intend to recruit only female interviewees, none of the partner organizations with whom I worked had come across male survivors who had reported crimes or would be willing to speak to us. While I would have liked to better understand the experiences and decisions made by male victims, the sample is representative of the gender breakdown of litigants in gender violence cases, who are predominantly female. In a 2010–2011 judicial monitoring project, for instance, United Nations Development Program recorded only 35 male litigants (as compared to 4,859 females) out of a sample of 6,554 (the gender of the victim was unknown in 1,660 cases). Due to the fact that this sample included only female interviewees, the discussions presented here do not generalize to male victims of violence who face distinct forms of stigma, and different barriers to accessing the legal system.

This subset of interviews was carried out between January and June 2013, in partnership with three Congolese partner organizations, which I refer to here as "A," "B," and "C." "A" and "B" are organizations based in South Kivu working to bring peace and healing to victims of conflict: "A" houses a women's center and offers educational assistance programs to victims of conflict, and "B" provides skills-based training and material and psychological support to vulnerable women and children. "C" is based in North Kivu and provides sexual health education and gender empowerment training across the province. "C" also engages in advocacy work toward gender parity and the eradication of male violence, and works with local church groups and civil society organizations to provide a range of support services to victims of sexual abuse.

None of these organizations directly engages in legal outreach or works closely with the justice system. However, each of them works with Congolese and international organizations that provide a spectrum of medical, legal, social, and economic services. Thus, each was well positioned to assist in the recruitment of interviewees. Moreover, these local partners were familiar with the pool of potential interviewees and sensitive to the local context, and were well placed to judge who would be willing and able to talk to us about their experiences. Given the sensitive subject matter, it was crucial to work with local partners accustomed to working with vulnerable individuals. I wished to avoid contacting anyone who would be unsettled by responding to questions about their experiences with the legal system. Interviewees were thus selected by my partner organizations on the basis that they had 1) voluntarily reported having experienced a gendered crime; and 2) the partner organization felt they would feel genuinely comfortable in speaking to academic researchers.

I spent a great deal of time with representatives from "A," "B" and "C" discussing the best ways to broach and explain the research with potential interviewees, while ensuring that they in no way felt coerced into participating. Based on their own expertise, preferences and recommendations, each of these partners employed different processes. Since two of the organizations housed service recipients, either on their premises ("A") or close by ("B"), they directly approached individuals who were present or close to the premises on the days we were working. "C" provided services to the largest number of beneficiaries and hand-selected interviewees from a list of individuals they were working with.

Interview times greatly varied depending on the information provided by the interviewee, and how forthcoming she was in speaking about her experiences. The average interview time was approximately forty minutes. The majority of the interviews took place on the premises of "A," "B," or "C," or at premises used by their partner organizations. Some interviews took place in the homes of interviewees. All interview locations were chosen by the interviewee, in conversation with the facilitating partner organization, according to where would be most practical and where the interviewee would feel most comfortable and secure. Where the interviewee was required to travel to a location other than her home, she was given up to 2,000 Congolese francs (approximately $2 USD) for transport to and from the interview location. I was unable to provide any other form of financial remuneration to the interviewees by virtue of requirements imposed on this project by the ethics review board at the University of Washington.

I conducted all fifty interviews with support either from one of my Congolese research partners or from a translator used by the partner organization. Thus, all interviews were carried out in local languages (Kinyarwanda, Kiswahili, or Moshi), by two individuals, with translation into either French or English. In some cases, a friend, family member, or support worker of the interviewee was present at her request for either all or part of the interview, to ensure that she felt comfortable and at ease. Interviewees were informed that they could stop the interview at any time, or decline to answer any questions they did not wish to answer. The majority of interviewees was very forthcoming with information, and no one requested to terminate the interview or declined to answer any questions. In two cases, I decided to terminate the interview early on grounds that the interviewee appeared visibly upset by the questions. The data from these two interviews are used where available, and coded as missing where the interview was terminated before I had the chance to pose certain questions.

All interviews were semi-structured and divided into two parts. Interviewees were first asked a number of demographic questions, such as their age, place of birth, place of residence, ethnicity, education level, marital status, and number of children. In the second part of the interview, they were asked to describe the incident they had experienced, what course of action followed, what options were available to them, and how they decided what to do.

All interviews were transcribed and analyzed in July and August 2013. During the analysis, specific attention was paid to the precise words used by the interviewee, in her native language, to describe her experiences and opinions. "Justice" can be an abstract, amorphous concept, and words associated with it do not always carry the same meanings in every language and context. Thus, understanding exactly what the interviewee meant when she invoked words like "justice," "compensation," or "reparations" was critical to ensuring accuracy in the data analysis process. The data were analyzed in collaboration with my research partners, who were familiar with the native languages of the interviewees. I systematically coded interviews using key words and themes, but also took care to understand and present stories within their holistic contexts, so as not to miss meaning. The quotes presented in the chapter reflect individual reflections and experiences, as well as overarching narratives that capture key themes or ideas expressed by participants.

Appendix C   DR Congo's Criminal Justice System

DR Congo's formal justice system has its roots in French civil law, imported by Belgian colonizers in the early twentieth century. The legal system is officially divided into three distinct branches: the civilian, the military, and the administrative.

The Structure of DR Congo's Legal System

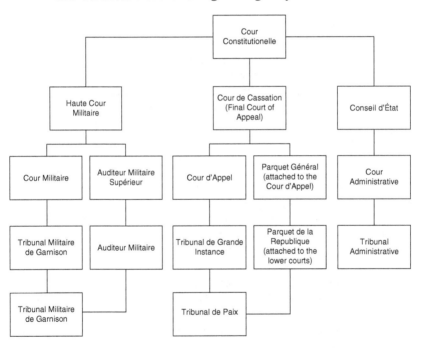

By law, civilian courts try cases in which the defendant did not commit a crime in the exercise of his duty as an employee of the Congolese armed forces or police service, and has not been charged with an international crime (in this case, crimes against humanity or war crimes). During the period of study, where the defendant was an employee of the state, where s/he was alleged to have committed a crime in the course of serving the state, where s/he was accused of committing an "international" crime (a war crime or crime against humanity), or where s/he has committed a crime using a weapon of war, the military courts retained sole jurisdiction (*Ordonnance/Loi portant institution d'un code de Justice militaire* No 72/060 du 25 septembre 1972 (Article 161)). A 2013 law revised this jurisdiction, giving civilian courts jurisdiction over international crimes (see: the *Loi organique No13/011/B portant organisation, fonctionnement et competences des juris-diction de l'ordre judiciaire*, or, in English, the Law on the Organization, Functioning and Jurisdiction of the Courts). Judges in military courts are officers of the Congolese armed forces. The military penal code stipulates that judges presiding over cases involving military personnel must be of equal or superior rank to the defendant.

The law prescribes that a Tribunal de Paix is located in each territory, and a district court (Tribunal de Grande Instance) is located in each major provincial city. In theory, lower courts may only try criminal cases in which the maximum sentence is five years. Given that most sexual violence cases hold mandatory minimum sentences of five years, such cases must theoretically be heard by the district courts, but due to the fact that many sexual violence cases are heard by traveling mobile courts (*audiences foraines*), in practice, these distinctions are somewhat blurred. Furthermore, because many courts within the eastern provinces – and, indeed, across the entire country – are not operational, many victims in gender violence cases do not have access to a competent tribunal. In such circumstances, victims of gender violence must have their cases channeled through an NGO or a legal aid clinic in order for them to reach the justice system.

Like many legal systems, in both civilian and military cases, the state prosecutor must be a party to the case; however, in both jurisdictions, victims can appear as "civil parties" to the case. In both the civilian and military justice systems, cases may be initiated in three ways: the victim may open the case directly with the prosecutor, they may report cases to the police who will refer them on to the parquet, or the prosecutor may initiate a case on his or her own accord. Once a case has been opened, it will be registered in the *Registre du Ministre Public* (RMP) and assigned a docket number (RMP number). The case may also be registered on the *Rôle Pénal* (RP) by the court's clerk at this stage and assigned an RP number in the clerk's registry. Once a dossier is formally opened, the prosecutor's office may issue a *mandate d'ammener* as part of the infor-mation-gathering phase, or a *mandate d'arret* to the Office of Judicial Police (OPJ). The Inspecteurs de Police Judiciaire (IPJ) and Officiers de Police Judiciaire (OPJ) identify, document, and investigate the alleged offense and establish potential witnesses before referring the case to the Prosecutor's Office.

When the case involves active military personnel, arrest warrants are first issued to the commander of the provincial military region and, if approved, are then issued to the implicated individual's commanding officer, who has responsibility to execute the warrant and turn the individual in question over to the military justice system. When the case involves a police officer, his/her superior must execute the warrant. When the case involves an armed actor from a non-state group, the warrant is issued directly to the commander of the provincial military region or to the judicial police to execute.

The chart that follows details the various pathways through which victims or alleged perpetrators of gender-based assaults may enter into formal legal processes and have their cases resolved.

The Justice Process

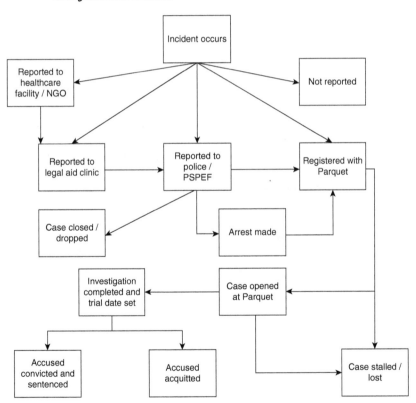

Appendix D South Africa's Criminal Justice System

South Africa's legal system is an adversarial system with its roots in Dutch-Roman law. The following pages outline some key features of the criminal justice system, highlighting the aspects of relevance to the prosecution of sexual offenses.

Like DR Congo's, South Africa's legal system is divided into multiple branches. The Constitution establishes a Constitutional Court and Supreme Court of Appeal (SCA) in Johannesburg and Bloemfontein, respectively. Below these, sit the country's high courts, magistrates' courts and other courts established by an Act of Parliament. The Supreme Court of Appeal has jurisdiction to determine appeals against any high court decision. Supreme Court of Appeal decisions are legally binding on all lower courts. High courts hear criminal matters that exceed the jurisdiction of the lower courts (such as crimes involving penalties higher than three years, or a maximum fine of R100,000 for District Courts, and fifteen years, or fines up to R300,000 for Magistrates' Courts). Except where minimum or maximum sentences are prescribed by law, the penal jurisdiction of the high courts is unlimited.

In addition, South Africa has various special courts with jurisdiction over particular crimes (such as the specialized sexual offenses courts discussed in Chapters 3 and 4). The legal system also includes income tax courts, labour courts, the Land Claims Court, the Competition Appeal Court, the Electoral Court, divorce courts, small claims courts, military courts, and equality courts.

Permanent judges in the higher courts are appointed by the President in consultation with the Judicial Service Commission. The appointment of magistrates falls under the Magistrates' Commission and the Minister of Justice.

The Structure of South Africa's Legal System

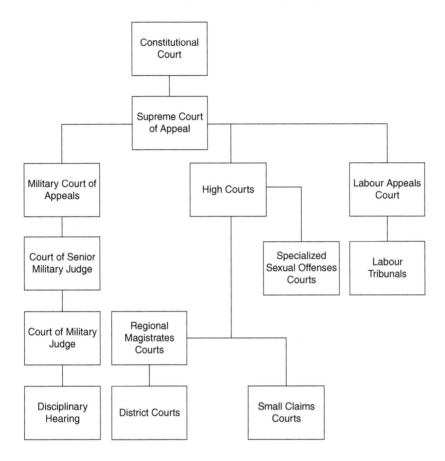

Unlike in DR Congo, the processes enshrined in South African law are strictly followed by law enforcement authorities. The criminal justice process begins when a crime is committed and is reported to the police or a charge is laid by a complainant. At this point, the South African Police Service assesses the case and decides to open a docket in preparation to forward to the National Prosecuting Authority (NPA). Once the investigating officer looks into the case and deems sufficient evidence to have been collected, the docket is sent to the prosecutor who decides whether further investigation is necessary. At this point, the National Prosecuting Authority may decline to move forward with the case because there is insufficient evidence, or because the case is not strong enough.

Once the case is sent to the prosecutor and the prosecutor is satisfied that there is sufficient evidence to prosecute, a court date is scheduled and a trial date set. In the case of a guilty verdict, on the date of sentencing, victims can request compensation for loss or damage to property, including money, as a result of a criminal offense. In cases where the criminal court fails to grant a compensation order, victims can open a civil case against the accused for psychological damages or pain and suffering. In practice, compensation orders are rarely granted and filing a civil case is costly and difficult. The chart that follows details the processes by which sexual assault cases make their way into the South African legal system and reach conclusion.

The Justice Process

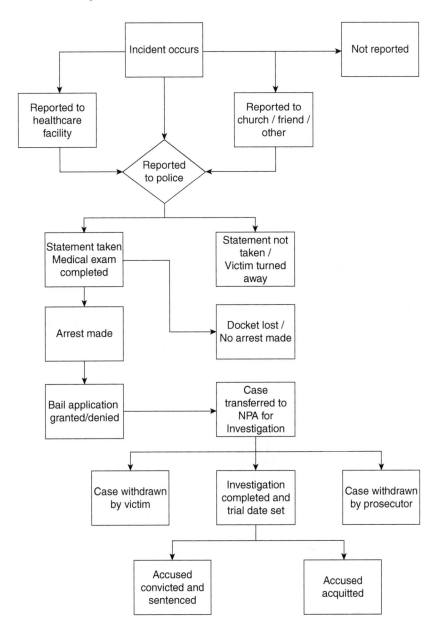

Bibliography

Abrahams, Naeemah. 2013. "SA 'a Leader' in Violence against Women." *News 24*, February 18. www.news24.com/SouthAfrica/News/SA-a-leader-in-vio lence-against-women-20130218.

Acemoglu, Daron, and James A. Robinson. 2012. *"Why Nations Fail: The Origins of Power, Prosperity, and Poverty."* New York: Crown Publishers.

AfriMap. 2010. *Democratic Republic of Congo – Military Justice and Human Rights: An Urgent Need to Complete Reforms. South Africa: A Study by AfriMAP and the Open Society Initiative for Southern Africa.* Johannesburg: AfriMap.

Alonso, Alvaro, and Ruairí Brugha. 2006. "Rehabilitating the Health System after Conflict in East Timor: A Shift from NGO to Government Leadership." *Health Policy and Planning* 21 (3): 206–216.

Alter, Karen J., and Jeannette Vargas. 2000. "Explaining Variation in the Use of European Litigation Strategies: European Community Law and British Gender Equality Policy." *Comparative Political Studies* 33 (4): 452–482.

All Africa. 2016. "UN Recognizes the DRC as 'Most Successful Experience' in Countering Sexual Violence." November 3. http://allafrica.com/stories/201 611031004.html.

American Bar Association Rule of Law Initiative. 2012. "Liberia: Rule of Law Programmes." Washington, DC. www.americanbar.org/advocacy/rule_of_ law/where_we_work/africa/liberia/background.html.

Anckar, Carsten. 2008. "On the Applicability of the Most Similar Systems Design and the Most Different Systems Design in Comparative Research." *International Journal of Social Research Methodology* 11 (5): 389–401.

Andersen, Ellen Ann. 2009. *Out of the Closets and into the Courts: Legal Opportunity Structure and Gay Rights Litigation.* Ann Arbor, MI: University of Michigan Press.

Apodaca, Clair. 2004. "The Rule of Law and Human Rights." *Judicature* 87: 292.

Artz, Lillian. 2003. "Magistrates and the Domestic Violence Act: Issues of Interpretation." Institute of Criminology, University of Cape Town, Gender Project, Community Law Centre, University of the Western Cape, Rape Crisis Cape Town, Health Sector, and Gender Violence Project.

Artz, Lillian, and Dee Smythe. 2005. "Bridges and Barriers: A Five Year Retrospective on the Domestic Violence Act." *Acta Juridica* 2005 (1): 200–226.

   2007. "Feminism vs. the State?: A Decade of Sexual Offences Law Reform in South Africa." *Agenda* 21 (74): 6–18.

2008. *Should We Consent?: Rape Law Reform in South Africa.* Juta.

Artz, Lillian, Dee Smythe, and Tina Leggett. 2004. "Reflections on Integrated Rape Case Management." Cape Town, South Africa: University of Cape Town.

Asian Development Bank. 2015. *Key Indicators for Asia and the Pacific 2015.* Asian Development Bank. www.adb.org/publications/key-indicators-asia-and-paci fic-2015.

Association of Female Lawyers of Liberia. 2014. AFELL: Monrovia, Liberia. http:// afell.org/index.php.

Autesserre, Séverine. 2009. "Hobbes and the Congo: Frames, Local Violence, and International Intervention." *International Organization* 63 (2): 249–280.

2010. *The Trouble with the Congo: Local Violence and the Failure of International Peacebuilding.* New York, NY: Cambridge University Press.

2012. "Dangerous Tales: Dominant Narratives on the Congo and Their Unintended Consequences." *African Affairs: The Journal of the Royal African Society* 111 (443): 202–222.

Avocats Sans Frontières. 2007. "The Application of the Rome Statute by the Courts of the Democratic Republic of Congo." Brussels, Belgium; Kinshasa, Congo: Avocats Sans Frontières asbl and Avocats Sans Frontières à Kinshasa.

Baaz, Maria Eriksson, Jason K. Stearns, and Judith Verweijen. 2013. "The National Army and Armed Groups in the Eastern Congo: Untangling the Gordian Knot of Insecurity." The Rift Valley Institute Usalama Project. Kampala, Uganda.

Baaz, Maria Eriksson, and Maria Stern. 2008. "Making Sense of Violence: Voices of Soldiers in the Congo (DRC)." *Journal of Modern African Studies: A Quarterly Survey of Politics, Economics and Related Topics in Contemporary Africa* 46 (1): 57–86.

2011. "Whores, Men, and Other Misfits: Undoing Feminization in the Armed Forces in the DRC." *African Affairs* 110 (441): 563–585.

Baaz, Maria Eriksson, Maria Stern, Sida, and Nordiska Afrikainstitutet. 2010. *The Complexity of Violence: A Critical Analysis of Sexual Violence in the Democratic Republic of Congo (DRC).* Stockholm; Uppsala: Sida and Nordiska Afrikainstitutet.

Badibanga, Madeleine. 1980. "La Desorganisation Familiale Au Zaire." Masters Thesis Submitted in Fulfilment of the Masters in Sociology. University of Ottawa. National Library of Canada. Collections Development Branch. Ottawa, Canada.

Baehr, Kristina Scurry. 2008. "Mandatory Minimums Making Minimal Difference: Ten Years of Sentencing Sex Offenders in South Africa." *Yale Journal of Law and Feminism* 20 (1): 212–247.

Baer, Judith A. 1999. *Our Lives before the Law: Constructing a Feminist Jurisprudence.* Princeton, NJ: Princeton University Press.

Bartels, Susan, Jennifer Scott, Jennifer Leaning, Denis Mukwege, Robert Lipton, and Michael VanRooyen. 2013. "Surviving Sexual Violence in Eastern Democratic Republic of Congo." *Journal of International Women's Studies* 11 (4): 37–49.

Bayart, Jean-François, Stephen Ellis, Béatrice Hibou, and International African Institute. 1999. *The Criminalization of the State in Africa.* London; Bloomington, IN: International African Institute in association with J. Currey, Oxford; Indiana University Press.

BBC News. 2017. "DR Congo: UN Peacekeepers Face Fresh Sexual Abuse Claims." *BBC News*, April 28, sec. Africa. www.bbc.co.uk/news/world-africa-39745357.

Belgian Congo. 1954. *Codes et Lois Du Congo Belge: Contenant Toutes Les Dispositions Législatives et Réglementaires En Vigueur, et Les Mesures Provinciales Les plus Usuelles, Annotées D'après Leur Concordance Avec La Législation Belge, Les Travaux Préparatoires, Les Circulaires et Instructions Officielles, et La Jurisprudence Des Cours et Tribunaux,* edited by Pierre Piron, Octave Louwers, and Leon Strouvens. 7th edn Brussels: F. Larcier.

Bennett, Jane. 2008. "Challenges Were Many: The One in Nine Campaign, South Africa." In *Changing Their World*, 1st edn. Building Feminist Movements and Organizations. 1–11.

Berger, Tobias and Milli Lake. 2018. "Human Rights, Rule of Law, and Democracy," in *The Oxford Handbook on Governance in Areas of Limited Statehood.* Oxford University Press.

Berry, Marie E. 2015a. "From Violence to Mobilization: War, Women, and Threat in Rwanda." *Mobilization:* An International Quarterly: June 2015, Vol. 20, No. 2. 135–156.

2015b. "When 'Bright Futures' Fade: Paradoxes of Women's Empowerment in Rwanda." *Signs* 41 (1): 1–27.

Berry, Marie E. 2018. *War, Women, and Power: From Violence to Mobilization in Rwanda and Bosnia-Herzegovina.* New York, NY: Cambridge University Press.

Berry, Marie E., and Milli Lake. 2017a. "Gender Politics after War: Mobilizing Opportunity in Post-conflict Africa." *Politics & Gender* 13 (2): 336–349.

2017b. "Women and Power after War." *Political Violence at a Glance.* June 6.

Bhatia, Juhie. 2009. "DRC: Rape Epidemic Fuels Fistula Cases." *Global Voices.* July 29. https://globalvoices.org/2009/07/29/drc-rape-epidemic-fuels-fistula-cases/.

Biddlecom, Ann E. 2007. "Prevalence and Meanings of Exchange of Money or Gifts for Sex in Unmarried Adolescent Sexual Relationships in Sub-Saharan Africa: Original Research Article." *African Journal of Reproductive Health* 11 (3): 44–61.

Birdsall, Nancy. 2004. "Seven Deadly Sins: Reflections on Donor Failings." *Center for Global Development Working Paper* 50.

Bloodgood, Elizabeth A., Joannie Tremblay-Boire, and Aseem Prakash. 2013. "National Styles of NGO Regulation." *Nonprofit and Voluntary Sector Quarterly*, 43: 4. 716–736.

Bob, Clifford. 2002. "Merchants of Morality." *Foreign Policy*, 36–45.

Bois, François du, and Antje du Bois-Pedain. 2008. *Justice and Reconciliation in Post-apartheid South Africa.* Cambridge: Cambridge University Press.

Börzel, Tanja, and Thomas Risse. 2011. In *Governance without a State?: Policies and Politics in Areas of Limited Statehood*, edited by Thomas Risse. New York, NY: Columbia University Press.

Bouka, Yolande. 2015. "Researcher Positionality." *Conflict Field Research*. www.conflictfieldresearch.colgate.edu/working-papers/researcher-positionality/.

Bourdieu, Pierre. 1994. "Rethinking the State: Genesis and Structure of the Bureaucratic Field." *Sociological Theory* 12 (1): 1.

Bourgois, Philippe. 2001. "The Power of Violence in War and Peace: Post–Cold War Lessons from El Salvador." *Ethnography* 2 (1): 5–34.

Brantlinger, Patrick. 1985. "Victorians and Africans: The Genealogy of the Myth of the Dark Continent." *Critical Inquiry* 12 (1).

Bratton, Michael. 1987. *The Politics of Government–NGO Relations in Africa*. University of Nairobi, Institute for Development Studies. Working Paper 456. Nairobi.

Brechenmacher, Saskia. 2017. *Surveillance and State Control in Ethiopia – Civil Society under Assault: Repression and Responses in Russia, Egypt, and Ethiopia*. Pittsburgh, PA: Carnegie Endowment for International Peace.

Broache, Michael. 2013. "Deterrent, Instigator, or Irrelevant? International Criminal Court Prosecutions and Violence against Civilians in Armed Conflict." Paper presented at the African Studies Association Annual Conference 2013. Baltimore, MD.

Bumiller, Kristen. 1990. "Fallen Angels: The Representation of Violence against Women in Legal Culture." *International Journal of the Sociology of Law* 18: 125–42.

Bunch, Charlotte. 1990. "Women's Rights as Human Rights: Toward a Re-vision of Human Rights." *Human Rights Quarterly* 12 (4): 486.

Burgess, Ann Wolbert, William P. Fehder, and Carol R. Hartman. 1995. "Delayed Reporting of the Rape Victim." *Journal of Psychosocial Nursing and Mental Health Services* 33 (9): 21–29.

Büscher, Karen, and Koen Vlassenroot. 2010. "Humanitarian Presence and Urban Development: New Opportunities and Contrasts in Goma, DRC." *Disasters* 34: 256–73.

Buss, Doris, Joanne Lebert, Blair Rutherford, Donna Sharkey, and Obijiofor Aginam. 2014. *Sexual Violence in Conflict and Post-conflict Societies: International Agendas and African Contexts*. New York, NY: Routledge.

Butler, Judith. 1990. *Gender Trouble: Feminism and the Subversion of Identity*. New York, NY: Routledge.

Byrne, Paul. 2013. *Social Movements in Britain*. New York, NY: Routledge.

Caplan, Gerald. 2012. "Peacekeepers Gone Wild: How Much More Abuse Will the UN Ignore in Congo?" *The Globe and Mail*, August 3. www.theglobeandmail.com/news/politics/second-reading/peacekeepers-gone-wild-how-much-more-abuse-will-the-un-ignore-in-congo/article4462151/.

Caplan, Richard. 2006. *International Governance of War-Torn Territories: Rule and Reconstruction*. Oxford: Oxford University Press.

Carlin, Jerome E., Jan Howard, and Sheldon L. Messinger. 1966. "Civil Justice and the Poor: Issues for Sociological Research." *Law & Society Review* 1 (1): 9–89.

Carothers, Thomas. 2006. *Promoting the Rule of Law Abroad: In Search of Knowledge.* Washington, DC: Carnegie Endowment for International Peace.

Carpenter, R. Charli. 2003. "'Women and Children First': Gender, Norms, and Humanitarian Evacuation in the Balkans 1991–95." *International Organization* 57 (4): 661–694.

2007. "Studying Issue (Non)-Adoption in Transnational Advocacy Networks." *International Organization* 61 (3): 643–667.

Carter, Jimmy. 2008. "Reconstructing the Rule of Law: Post-conflict Liberia." *Harvard International Review* 30 (3): 14–18.

Celik Levin, Yasemin. 2004. "The Effect of CEDAW on Women's Rights." In *Human Rights in Turkey*, edited by Zehra F. Kabasakal Arat. Philadelphia: University of Pennsylvania Press. 202–216.

Center for the Study of Violence and Reconciliation. 2001. "South Africa's Equality Courts: An Early Assessment." Race and Citizenship in Transition Series. www.csvr.org.za/wits/res/pubsrctp.htm.

2014. "Sexual Violence by Educators in South African Schools: Gaps in Accountability." University of the Witwatersrand School of Law. Cornell Law School's Avon Global Center for Women and Justice, and International Human Rights Clinic.

Chanock, Martin. 1985. *Law, Custom, and Social Order: The Colonial Experience in Malawi and Zambia.* Cambridge; New York, NY: Cambridge University Press.

2006. *The Making of South African Legal Culture, 1902–1936: Fear, Favour, and Prejudice.* Cambridge: Cambridge University Press.

Chesterman, Simon. 2005. *You, the People: The United Nations, Transitional Administration, and State-Building.* Oxford: Oxford University Press.

Cichowski, Rachel. 2007. *The European Court and Civil Society: Litigation, Mobilization and Governance.* Cambridge; New York, NY: Cambridge University Press.

Clapham, Christopher S. 1996. *Africa and the International System: The Politics of State Survival.* Cambridge: Cambridge University Press.

Clappaert, Sabine. 2012. "South Africa's 'Traditional Courts Bill' Impairs Rights of 12 Million Rural Women." *Inter Press Service*, May 26. www.ipsn ews.net/2012/05/south-africas-traditional-courts-bill-impairs-rights-of-12-million-rural-women/.

Clark, Cari Jo, Susan A. Everson-Rose, Shakira Franco Suglia, Rula Btoush, Alvaro Alonso, and Muhammad M. Haj-Yahia. 2010. "Association between Exposure to Political Violence and Intimate-Partner Violence in the Occupied Palestinian Territory: A Cross-Sectional Study." *Lancet*, London 375 (9711): 310–316.

Clark, Christina R. 2007. "Understanding Vulnerability: From Categories to Experiences of Young Congolese People in Uganda." *Children & Society* 21 (4): 284–296.

Clark, Phil. 2008. "Ethnicity, Leadership and Conflict Mediation in Eastern Democratic Republic of Congo: The Case of the *Barza Inter-Communautaire*." *Journal of Eastern African Studies* 2 (1): 1–17.

Cockburn, Cynthia. 2004. "The Continuum of Violence: A Gender Perspective on War and Peace." In *Sites of Violence: Gender and Conflict Zones*, edited by Wenona Giles and Jennifer Hyndman. Berkeley and Los Angeles: University of California Press.

Coetzee, David, Katherine Hildebrand, Andrew Boulle, Gary Maartens, Francoise Louis, Veliswa Labatala, Hermann Reuter, Nonthutuzelo Ntwana, and Eric Goemaere. 2004. "Outcomes after Two Years of Providing Antiretroviral Treatment in Khayelitsha, South Africa." *AIDS* London, 18 (6): 887–895.

Coffey, Amanda. 1999. *The Ethnographic Self: Fieldwork and the Representation of Identity*. 1st edn. London; Thousand Oaks, CA: Sage Publications.

Cohen, Dara Kay. 2013. "Explaining Rape during Civil War: Cross-National Evidence (1980–2009)." *American Political Science Review* 107 (3): 461–477.
2016. *Rape during Civil War*. Ithaca, NY: Cornell University Press.

Cohen, Dara Kay, Amelia Hoover Green, and Elisabeth Jean Wood. 2013. "Wartime Sexual Violence: Misconceptions, Implications, and Ways Forward." US Institute of Peace.

Cohen, David. 2002. "Seeking Justice on the Cheap: Is the East Timor Tribunal Really a Model for the Future?" *Asia Pacific Issues: East West Center*, no. 61 August.

Cole, Jennifer, and Lynn M. Thomas. 2009. *Love in Africa*. Chicago, IL: University of Chicago Press.

Comaroff, Jean, and John L Comaroff. 2006. *Law and Disorder in the Postcolony*. Chicago, IL: University of Chicago Press.

Comaroff, John L. 2001. "Symposium Introduction: Colonialism, Culture, and the Law: A Foreword." *Law & Social Inquiry* 26 (2): 305–314.

Comaroff, John L., and Simon Roberts. 1986. *Rules and Processes: The Cultural Logic of Dispute in an African Context*. Chicago, IL: University of Chicago Press.

Cooley, Alexander, and James Ron. 2002. "The NGO Scramble: Organizational Insecurity and the Political Economy of Transnational Action." *International Security*. 27: 1. Summer, 2002. 5–39.

Cronin-Furman, Kate. 2013. "Managing Expectations: International Criminal Trials and the Prospects for Deterrence of Mass Atrocity." *International Journal of Transitional Justice* 7: 3. 434–454.

Cronin-Furman, Kate, and Nimmi Gowrinathan. 2015. "The Forever Victims: Tamil Women in Post-war Sri Lanka." The Politics of Sexual Violence Initiative, Colin Powell School for Civic and Global Leadership. www.wron gingrights.com/2015/09/the-forever-victims.html.

Cronin-Furman, Kate, and Milli Lake. 2018. "Ethics Abroad: Research and Field Methods in Areas of Limited Statehood." *Politics Science and Politics*. Forthcoming.

Daly, Kathleen, and Brigitte Bouhours. 2010. "Rape and Attrition in the Legal Process: A Comparative Analysis of Five Countries." *Crime and Justice* 39 (1): 565–650.

Davis, Rebecca. 2013. "Sexual Offences Courts Are Back." *Daily Maverick*, August 7. www.ru.ac.za/perspective/perspectivearticles/name,91622,en .html.

De Swardt, Cobus, and Chantal Uwimana. 2013. "South Africa Needs to Establish an Anti-corruption Agency." *The Mail & Guardian Online*, January 18. http://mg.co.za/article/2013–01-18–00-south-africa-needs-to-establish-an-anti-corruption-agency/.

De Vos, Pierre. 2010. "Urgently Wanted: Judicial Training Constitutionally Speaking." http://constitutionallyspeaking.co.za/urgently-wanted-judicial-tr aining/.

Dembour, Marie-Bénédicte. 2000. *Recalling the Belgian Congo: Conversations and Introspection.* New York, NY Berghahn Books.

DR Congo Ministry of Public Health. 2007. Demographic and Health Survey. Ministère du Plan et Suivi de la Mise en oeuvre de la Révolution de la Modernité, Ministère de la Santé Publique. Kinshasa, République Démocratique du Congo

2014. Demographic and Health Survey. Ministère du Plan et Suivi de la Mise en oeuvre de la Révolution de la Modernité, Ministère de la Santé Publique. Kinshasa, République Démocratique du Congo

D'Errico, Nicole C., Tshibangu Kalala, Joseph Ciza Nakamina, Luc Malemo Kalisya, Paulin Bukundika, Felicien Maisha, and Bashige Nzigire. 2013. "'You Say Rape, I Say Hospitals. But Whose Voice Is Louder?' Health, Aid and Decision Making in the Democratic Republic of Congo." *African Journal of Political Economy* 40 (135): 51–66.

Dixon, Bill, and Elrena Van der Spuy. 2004. *Justice Gained?: Crime and Crime Control in South Africa's Transition.* Cape Town; Cullompton: UCT Press; Willan.

Donais, Timothy. 2009. "Empowerment or Imposition? Dilemmas of Local Ownership in Post-conflict Peacebuilding Processes." *Peace & Change* 34 (1): 3–26.

Douma, Nynke, and Dorothea Hilhorst. 2012. "Fond de Commerce? Sexual Violence Assistance in the Democratic Republic of Congo." *Disaster Studies Occasional Paper Series* 2 (1): 1–78.

DR Congo. 1959. Décret du 6 août 1959 portant le Code de Procédure Pénale. Journal Officiel n° Spécial 20 March 2007 (Special Issue). Cabinet du Président de la République.

DR Congo. 2002a. Loi N°023/2002 du 18 novembre 2002 portant Code Judiciaire Militaire. Journal Officiel n° Spécial 20 mars 2003. Cabinet du Président de la République.

DR Congo. 2002b. Loi n° 024–2002 du 18 novembre 2002 portant Code penal militaire. Journal Officiel n° Spécial 20 mars 2003. Cabinet du Président de la République.

DR Congo. 2004. Code Penal Congolais. Décret du 30 janvier 1940 tel que modifié et complété à ce jour mis à jour au 30 novembre 2004. Journal Officiel n° Spécial 30 novembre 2004. Cabinet du Président de la République.

DR Congo. 2006a. Constitution de la République Démocratique du Congo. 2006. *Modifiée par la Loi n° 11/002 du 20 janvier 2011 portant révision de certains articles de la Constitution de la République Démocratique du Congo du 18 février 2006.* Journal Officiel de la République Démocratique du Congo. Cabinet du Président de la République.

DR Congo. 2006b. Le Loi Sur Les Violences Sexuelles Loi No 06/018 du 20 juillet 2006 modifiant et completant le Décret du 30 janvier 1940 Portant Code Penal Congolais. Journal Officiel n° Spécial 1er août 2006. Cabinet du Président de la République.

DR Congo. 2006c. Loi n° 06/019 du 20 juillet 2006 modifiant et complétant le Décret du 06 août 1959 portant Code de Procédure Pénale Congolais. Journal Officiel n° Spécial 1er août 2006. Cabinet du Président de la République.

DR Congo. 2009. Loi n° 09/001 du 10 janvier 2009 portant protection de l'enfant. Journal Officiel n° Spécial 25 mai 2009. Cabinet du Président de la République.a

DR Congo. 2013. Loi organique n°13/011-B du 11 avril 2013 portant organisation, fonctionnement et compétences des juridictions de l'ordre judiciaire. Journal Officiel n° Spécial 1er avril 2013. Cabinet du Président de la République.

DR Congo. 2015a. La Loi de Mise En Oeuvre Du Statut de Rome En RDC. Loi n° 15/022 du 31 décembre 2015 modifiant et complétant le Décret du 30 janvier 1940 portant Code pénal. Journal Officiel n° Spécial 29 février 2016. Cabinet du Président de la République.

DR Congo. 2015b. La Loi de Mise En Oeuvre Du Statut de Rome En RDC. Loi n° 15/023 du 31 décembre 2015 modifiant la Loi n° 024–2002 du 18 novembre 2002 portant Code pénal militaire. Journal Officiel n° Spécial 29 février 2016. Cabinet du Président de la République.

DR Congo. 2016. *Loi N° 16/008 du 15 juillet 2016 modifient et complètent La Loi n° 87–010 du 1er août 1987 portant Code de La Famille.* Forthcoming in the Journal Officiel de la République Démocratique du Congo.

DR Congo Ministere du genre, de la Famille et de l'enfant. 2009. "Strategie Nationale De Lutte Contre Les Violences Basées Sur Le Genre (SNVBG)." Kinshasa, DR Congo.

DR Congo Ministry of Gender (MinGenre). 2013. "Manuel des Procédures de Collecte des Données sur les Violences Sexuelles et Basées sur le Genre." Ministère du Gender, de la Famille, et de l'Enfant: Kinshasa.

Dubow, Saul. 2012. *South Africa's Struggle for Human Rights.* Athens: Ohio University Press.

Dunkle, Kristin L., Rachel K. Jewkes, Heather C. Brown, Mieko Yoshihama, Glenda E. Gray, James A. McIntyre, and Siobán D. Harlow. 2004. "Prevalence and Patterns of Gender-Based Violence and Revictimization among Women Attending Antenatal Clinics in Soweto, South Africa." *American Journal of Epidemiology* 160 (3): 230–239.

Dunn, Holly. 2013. "Customary Justice and the Rule of Law in Eastern DRC: A Case Study of Baraza." Paper presented at the African Studies Association Annual Conference 2013. Baltimore, MD.

Dunn, Kevin. 2003. *Imagining the Congo – The International Relations of Identity.* New York, NY: Palgrave Macmillan.

Dupuy, Kendra E., James Ron, and Aseem Prakash. 2015. "Who Survived? Ethiopia's Regulatory Crackdown on Foreign-Funded NGOs." *Review of International Political Economy* 22 (2): 419–456.

Easterly, William. 2007. *The White Man's Burden: Why the West's Efforts to Aid the Rest Have Done So Much Ill and So Little Good.* New York, NY: Penguin Books.

The Economist. 2014. "Nkandla in the Wind: Corruption in South Africa." *The Economist,* April 12. www.economist.com/news/middle-east-and-africa/216 00729-why-string-corruption-scandals-top-so-disquieting-nkandla.

Eisinger, Peter K. 1973. "The Conditions of Protest Behavior in American Cities." *The American Political Science Review* 67 (1): 11.

Ellickson, Robert C. 1986. "Of Coase and Cattle: Dispute Resolution among Neighbors in Shasta County." *Stanford Law Review* 38 (3): 623–687.

Englund, Harri. 2006. *Prisoners of Freedom.* California Series in Public Anthropology. Berkeley, CA: University of California Press.

Englebert, Pierre and Dennis Tull. 2008. "Postconflict Reconstruction in Africa: Flawed Ideas about Failed States." *International Security* 32 (4): 106–139.

Epp, Charles R. 1990. "Connecting Litigation Levels and Legal Mobilization: Explaining Interstate Variation in Employment Civil Rights Litigation." *Law & Society Review* 24 (1): 145–163.

  1998. *The Rights Revolution: Lawyers, Activists, and Supreme Courts in Comparative Perspective.* Chicago, IL: University of Chicago Press

Etinga, Stéphane. 2015. "Le Sénat Vote Le Projet de Loi de Mise En Œuvre Du Statut de Rome." 7sur7.cd, December 9.

Evans Case, Rhonda, and Terri E. Givens. 2010. "Re-engineering Legal Opportunity Structures in the European Union? The Starting Line Group and the Politics of the Racial Equality Directive." *Journal of Common Market Studies* 48 (2): 221–241.

Ewans, Martin. 2002. *European Atrocity, African Catastrophe: Leopold II, the Congo Free State and Its Aftermath.* London: Routledge Curzon.

Ewick, Patricia, and Susan S. Silbey. 1998. *The Common Place of Law: Stories from Everyday Life.* Chicago, IL: University of Chicago Press.

Farr, Kathryn. 2009. "Extreme War Rape in Today's Civil-War-Torn States: A Contextual and Comparative Analysis." *Gender Issues* 26 (1): 1–41.

Faul, Michelle. 2013. "3 Women Killed Each Day in South Africa, World's Worst Gender Violence." *The Toronto Star,* March 8. www.thestar.com/news/world /2013/03/08/3_women_killed_each_day_in_south_africa_worlds_worst_gen der_violence.html.

Ferguson, James. 2006. *Global Shadows: Africa in the Neoliberal World Order.* Durham, NC: Duke University Press.

  2013. "Declarations of Dependence: Labour, Personhood, and Welfare in Southern Africa." *Journal of the Royal Anthropological Institute* 19 (2): 223–242.

Ferree, Myra Marx, and Aili Mari Tripp, eds. 2006. *Global Feminism: Transnational Women's Activism, Organizing, and Human Rights*. New York, NY: New York University Press.

Finnemore, Martha, and Kathryn Sikkink. 1998. "International Norm Dynamics and Political Change." *International Organization* 52 (4): 887–917.

Fischer-Tiné, Harald, and Michael Mann. 2004. *Colonialism as Civilizing Mission: Cultural Ideology in British India*. London: Anthem Press.

Fraser, Arvonne S. 2000. "Becoming Human: The Origins and Development of Women's Human Rights." *Women's International Network News* 26 (1).

Freedman, Dr. Jane. 2015. *Gender, Violence and Politics in the Democratic Republic of Congo*. London: Ashgate Publishing, Ltd.

Freedom House. 2015. "'Game Over' for Democracy in Rwanda Freedom House." Interview with David Himbara. Washington D.C. https://freedom house.org/blog/game-over-democracy-rwanda.

Fujii, Lee Ann. 2010. "Shades of Truth and Lies: Interpreting Testimonies of War and Violence." *Journal of Peace Research* 47 (2): 231–241.

    2012. "Research Ethics 101: Dilemmas and Responsibilities." *PS: Political Science & Politics* 45 (4): 717–723.

Galanter, Marc. 1994. *Why the "Haves" Come Out Ahead: Speculations on the Limits of Legal Change*. Law & Society Review Vol. 9 (1). Litigation and Dispute Processing: Part One (Autumn, 1974), pp. 95–160.

Gary, Ian. 1996. "Confrontation, Co-operation or Co-optation: NGOs and the Ghanaian State during Structural Adjustment." *Review of African Political Economy* 23 (68): 149–168.

Gender Links. 2015. "GBV Indicators Study – Western Cape Province, SA." Johannesburg, South Africa.

George, Alexander L., and Andrew Bennett. 2005. *Case Studies and Theory Development in the Social Sciences*. Fourth printing edn. Cambridge, MA: MIT Press.

Gerring, John. 2004. "What Is a Case Study and What Is It Good For?" *American Political Science Review* 98 (2): 341–354.

Gillwald, Cheryl. 1999. "Address by the Deputy Minister of Justice and Constitutional Development, Ms Cheryl Gillwald, In The Debate On Incidence of Rape and Other Forms of Violence against Women, Parliament, 26 October 1999." Pretoria, South Africa.

Global Fund for Women. 2007. https://grants.globalfundforwomen.org

Godoy, Angelina Snodgrass. 2006. *Popular Injustice: Violence, Community, and Law in Latin America*. Palo Alto, CA: Stanford University Press.

Goldstone, Richard, J. 2006. "A South African Perspective on Social andEconomic Rights." *Human Rights Brief.* 13 : 2.

Goluboff, Risa Lauren. 2007. *The Lost Promise of Civil Rights*. Cambridge, MA: Harvard University Press.

Goodman, Ryan, and Derek Jinks. 2004. "How to Influence States: Socialization and International Human Rights Law." *Duke Law Journal* 54 (3): 621–703.

    2013. *Socializing States: Promoting Human Rights through International Law*. New York, NY: Oxford University Press.

Gqirana, Thulani. 2017. "Traditional Courts Bill: What's Changed?" *News24*, January 23. www.news24.com/SouthAfrica/News/traditional-courts-bill-wh ats-changed-20170123.

Graham, Aubrey. 2014. "One Hundred Years of Suffering? 'Humanitarian Crisis Photography' and Self-Representation in the Democratic Republic of the Congo." *Social Dynamics* 40 (1): 140–163.

Gray, Mark M., Miki Caul Kittilson, and Wayne Sandholtz. 2006. "Women and Globalization: A Study of 180 Countries, 1975–2000." *International Organization* 60 (2): 293–333.

Green, Jennifer Lynn. 2006. *Collective Rape: A Cross-National Study of the Incidence and Perpetrators of Mass Political Sexual Violence, 1980–2003.* Athens: Ohio State University.

Grenfell, Laura. 2013. *Promoting the Rule of Law in Post-conflict States.* Cambridge: Cambridge University Press.

Guardado, Jenny, Sabrina Karim, Michael Gilligan, and Bernd Beber. 2015. "U.N. Peacekeeping and Transactional Sex." *Washington Post*, June 16. www.washingtonpost.com/blogs/monkey-cage/wp/2015/06/16/u-n-peace keeping-and-transactional-sex/.

Gumede, William M. 2008. "South Africa: Jacob Zuma and the Difficulties of Consolidating South Africa's Democracy." *African Affairs* 107 (427): 261–271.

Hafner-Burton, Emilie M., and Kiyoteru Tsutsui. 2005. "Human Rights in a Globalizing World: The Paradox of Empty Promises." *American Journal of Sociology* 110 (5): 1373–1411.

Hafner-Burton, Emilie M., Kiyoteru Tsutsui, and John W. Meyer. 2008. "International Human Rights Law and the Politics of Legitimation: Repressive States and Human Rights Treaties." *International Sociology* 23 (1): 115–141.

Hanlon, Joseph. 1991. *Mozambique: Who Calls the Shots?* London; Bloomington: J. Currey; Indiana University Press.

2000. "Re-framing Development for the 21st Century [Special Topic]." *Journal of International Development* 12 (6).

Hanlon, Joseph, Armando Barrientos, and David Hulme. 2010. *Just Give Money to the Poor: The Development Revolution from the Global South.* Sterling, VA: Kumarian Press.

Hassim, Shireen. 2006. *Women's Organizations and Democracy in South Africa: Contesting Authority.* Madison, WI: University of Wisconsin Press.

Hayman, Rachel. 2006. "The Complexity of Aid: Government Strategies, Donor Agendas and the Coordination of Development Assistance in Rwanda 1994–2004." November. Centre of African Studies Thesis and Dissertation Collection. Edinburgh Research Archive.

Heaton, Laura. 2013. "What Happened in Luvungi?" *Foreign Policy*, March 4. www.foreignpolicy.com/articles/2013/03/04/what_happened_in_luvungi.

Herbst, Jeffrey F. 1930. "The Administration of Native Affairs in South Africa." *African Affairs* 29 (117): 478–489.

Herbst, Jeffrey, and Greg Mills. 2003. *The Future of Africa: A New Order in Sight?*
   Oxford; New York, NY: Oxford University Press for the International
   Institute for Strategic Studies.
   2013. "The Invisible State." *Foreign Policy*, June 24. www.foreignpolicy.com/
   articles/2013/06/24/the_invisible_state.
Hilson, Chris. 2002. "New Social Movements: The Role of Legal Opportunity."
   Journal of European Public Policy 9 (2): 238–255.
Hodes, Rebecca. 2011. "The Making of South Africa's Sexual Offences Act
   (2007): Structure and Agency in a Women's Rights Coalition." CSSR
   Working Paper No. 298. December. AIDS and Society Research Unit,
   University of Cape Town, South Africa.
Hoffman, Kasper, and Judith Verweijen. 2013. "The Strategic Reversibility of
   Stateness: Contemporary Mai-Mai Militias and Processes of State (un)
   making in South Kivu, DR Congo" Unpublished manuscript presented at
   the Conference on Armed Groups in Africa. Kampala, Uganda.
Holmstrom, L. L., and A. W. Burgess. 1980. "Sexual Behavior of Assailants
   during Reported Rapes." *Archives of Sexual Behavior* 9 (5): 427–439.
Holzgrefe, J. L., and Robert O. Keohane. 2003. *Humanitarian Intervention: Ethical,
   Legal, and Political Dilemmas.* Cambridge; New York, NY: Cambridge
   University Press.
Hoover Green, Amelia, Sarah E. Parkinson, and Kerry F. Crawford. 2014.
   "Wartime Sexual Violence Is Not Just a 'Weapon of War.'" *Washington Post:
   The Monkey Cage*, September 24.
Horn, Rebecca, Eve S. Puffer, Elisabeth Roesch, and Heidi Lehmann. 2014.
   "Women's Perceptions of Effects of War on Intimate Partner Violence and
   Gender Roles in Two Post-conflict West African Countries: Consequences
   and Unexpected Opportunities." *Conflict and Health* 8 (August): 12.
Huang, Reyko. 2012. *The Wartime Origins of Postwar Democratization: Civil War,
   Rebel Governance, and Political Regimes.* New York, NY: Cambridge
   University Press.
   2016. "Rebel Diplomacy in Civil War." *International Security* 40 (4): 89–126.
Human Rights Watch. 1995. "Violence against Women in South Africa: State
   Response to Domestic Violence and Rape." New York, NY.
   1997. "South Africa: Violence against Women and the Medico-Legal System."
   New York, NY; Washington D.C.; London, UK; Brussels, Belgium.
   2001a. "Scared at School: Sexual Violence against Girls in South African
   Schools." New York, NY; Washington D.C.; London, UK; Brussels,
   Belgium.
   2001b. "Unequal Protection: The State Response to Violent Crime on South
   African Farms." New York, NY; Washington D.C.; London, UK; Brussels,
   Belgium.
   2009. "Soldiers Who Rape, Commanders Who Condone: Sexual Violence and
   Military Reform in the Democratic Republic of Congo." New York, NY;
   Kinshasa, DR Congo; Brussels, Belgium.
   2011. "'We'll Show You You're a Woman': Violence and Discrimination
   against Black Lesbians and Transgender Men in South Africa."
   Johannesburg, South Africa; New York, NY.

2012. "DR Congo: M23 Rebels Committing War Crimes." New York, NY; Kinshasa, DR Congo; Brussels, Belgium.

2014. "134 NGOs Call on ICC Prosecutor to Continue Investigations in Congo." New York, NY; Kinshasa, DR Congo; Brussels, Belgium.

2015. "Justice on Trial: Lessons from the Minova Rape Case. New York, NY; Kinshasa, DR Congo; Brussels, Belgium.

Hunt, Nancy Rose. 1988. "'Le Bebe En Brousse': European Women, African Birth Spacing and Colonial Intervention in Breast Feeding in the Belgian Congo." *International Journal of African Historical Studies* 21 (3): 401–432.

Hunter, Mark. 2010. *Love in the Time of AIDS: Inequality, Gender, and Rights in South Africa*. Bloomington, IN: Indiana University Press.

Ilunga, Kalala. 1974. "Le Statut de La Femme Dans Le Droit de La Famille Au Zaïre." *Revue juridique et politique: Indépendance et coopération*. 28 (4): 835–45.

International Bar Association. 2009. "Rebuilding Courts and Trust: An Assessment of the Needs of the Justice System in the Democratic Republic of Congo."

2015. "Training and Capacity Building." www.ibanet.org/Human_Rights_Institute/About_the_HRI/HRI_Activities/Training-and-Capacity-Building.aspx.

International Center for Transitional Justice (ICTJ). 2010. "DRC and the Rome Statute." http://ictj.org/sites/default/files/ICTJ-DRC-Rome-Statute-2010-English.pdf.

2015. "Regions and Countries." www.ictj.org/our-work.

International Criminal Court. 2002a. The Rome Statute of the International Criminal Court.

International Criminal Court. 2002b. Elements of Crimes.

International Criminal Court. 2002c. Rules and Procedures of Evidence.

2004. "The Office of the Prosecutor of the International Criminal Court Opens Its First Investigation." Press Release, June 23. www.icc-cpi.int/en_menus/icc/press%20and%20media/press%20releases/2004/Pages/the%20office%20of%20the%20prosecutor%20of%20the%20international%20criminal% 20court%20opens%20its%20first%20investigation.aspx.

International Medical Corps. 2010. "International Medical Corps Awarded 5-Year Grant from USAID to Address Sexual and Gender-Based Violence in Democratic Republic of Congo." Los Angeles, CA, USA. https://internationalmedicalcorps.org/sslpage.aspx?pid=1726.

Institute for Security Studies. 2014. "The South African Police Service Must Renew Its Focus on Specialised Units." *ISS Africa*. March 31.

IRIN. 2008. "DRC: Rape Crisis Set to Worsen amid Kivu Chaos." *IRIN News*, November 19. www.irinnews.org/Report/81549/DRC-Rape-crisis-set-to-worsen-amid-Kivu-chaos.

2013. "A Look behind the Statistics of South Africa's Rape Epidemic." *IRINNews*, November 1. www.irinnews.org/report/99039/a-look-behind-the-statistics-of-south-africa-s-rape-epidemic.

2016. "Liberia: Special Court for Sexual Violence Underway." *IRINNews*. www.irinnews.org/report/77406/liberia-special-court-for-sexual-violence-underway.

Jackson, Robert H., and Carl G Rosberg. 1982. "Why Africa's Weak States Persist: The Empirical vs. the Juridical in Statehood." *World Politics* 35 (1): 1–24.

Jalali, Rita. 2008. "International Funding of NGOs in India: Bringing the State Back In." *VOLUNTAS: International Journal of Voluntary and Nonprofit Organizations* 19 (2): 161–188.

Jeater, Diana. 2011. "Zimbabwe: International NGOs and Aid Agencies – Parasites of the Poor?" *African Arguments*, August 8.

Jewkes, Rachel, Nicola Christofides, Lisa Vetten, Ruxana Jina, Romi Sigsworth, and Lizle Loots. 2009. "Medico-legal Findings, Legal Case Progression, and Outcomes in South African Rape Cases: Retrospective Review." *PLOS Medicine* 6 (10).

Jewkes, Rachel, and Naeemah Abrahams. 2002. "The Epidemiology of Rape and Sexual Coercion in South Africa: An Overview." *Social Science and Medicine* 55 (7).

Jewkes, Rachel, Loveday Penn-Kekana, Jonathan Levin, and Margaret Schrieber. 1999. "'He Must Give Me Money, He Mustn't Beat Me': Violence against Women in Three South African Provinces." South Africa Medical Research Council (CERSA, Women's Health).

Jewkes, Rachel, Yandisa Sikweyiya, Robert Morrell, and Kristin Dunkle. 2011. "Gender Inequitable Masculinity and Sexual Entitlement in Rape Perpetration, South Africa: Findings of a Cross-Sectional Study." *PloS One* 6 (12): 29590.

Jo, Hyeran. 2015. *Compliant Rebels.* New York, NY: Cambridge University Press, London: UK.

Johnson, Kirsten, Jennifer Scott, Bigy Rughita, Michael Kisielewski, Jana Asher, Ong Ricardo, and Lynn Lawry. 2010. "Association of Sexual Violence and Human Rights Violations with Physical and Mental Health in Territories of the Eastern Democratic Republic of the Congo." *Journal of the American Medical Association* 304 (5): 553–562.

Johnson, Obediah. 2013. "Liberia: Decent Work Bill Passed, Minimum Wage Set at $6/Day." *Africa Speaks 4 Africa.* http://africaspeaks4africa.org/liberia-dec ent-work-bill-finally-passed-with-minimum-wage-set-at-u-s-six-per-day/.

Jordan, Jan. 2004. "Beyond Belief?: Police, Rape and Women's Credibility." *Criminal Justice* 4 (1): 29–59.

Kabemba, Claude. 2001. "The Democratic Republic of Congo." In *Big African States*, edited by Jeffrey Herbst and Greg Mills. South Africa: Wits University Press. 97–122.

Kamwimbi, Theodore Kasongo, Ivo Aertsen, Jana Arsovka, Holger C. Rhone, Marta Valiñas, and Kris Vanspauwen. 2008. "Between Peace and Justice: Informal Mechanisms in the Democratic Republic of Congo." In *Restoring Justice after Large-Scale Violent Conflicts: Kosovo, DR Congo and the Israeli-Palestinian Case.* Cullompton: Willan Publishing. 359–391.

Karim, Sabrina, and Kyle Beardsley. 2016. *Equal Opportunity Peacekeeping: The Need for Gender Equality in the Search for Quality Peace.* Oxford: Oxford University Press.

Keck, Margaret, and Kathryn Sikkink. 1998. *Activists beyond Borders: Advocacy Networks in International Politics*. Ithaca, NY: Cornell University Press.

Keith, Linda Camp. 2002. "Judicial Independence and Human Rights Protection around the World." *Judicature* 85: 195.

Kelly, Liz, Jo Lovett, and Linda Regan. 2006. "Gap or a Chasm?: Attrition in Reported Rape Cases." National Criminal Justice Reference Service. Home Office Research Study 293. Child and Woman Abuse Studies Unit, London Metropolitan University. London; U.K.

Keohane, Robert Owen. 2002. *Power and Governance in a Partially Globalized World*. London: Routledge.

Kirchner, Stefan. 2007. "Hell on Earth – Systematic Rape in Eastern Congo." *Journal of Humanitarian Assistance* 6.

Kitschelt, Herbert P. 1986. "Political Opportunity Structures and Political Protest: Anti-nuclear Movements in Four Democracies." *British Journal of Political Science* 16 (1): 57–85.

Koss, Mary P., Karen J. Bachar, C. Quince Hopkins, and Carolyn Carlson. 2004. "Expanding a Community's Justice Response to Sex Crimes through Advocacy, Prosecutorial, and Public Health Collaboration Introducing the RESTORE Program." *Journal of Interpersonal Violence* 19 (12): 1435–1463.

Krasner, Stephen D. 1999. *Sovereignty: Organized Hypocrisy*. Princeton, NJ: Princeton University Press.

2004. "Sharing Sovereignty: New Institutions for Collapsed and Failing States." *International Security* 29 (2): 85–120.

Krasner, Stephen D., and Thomas Risse. 2014. "External Actors, State-Building, and Service Provision in Areas of Limited Statehood: Introduction." *Governance* 27 (4): 545–567.

Lake, David A., and Christopher J. Fariss. 2014. "Why International Trusteeship Fails: The Politics of External Authority in Areas of Limited Statehood." *Governance* 27 (4): 569–587.

Lake, Milli. 2017. "Building the Rule of War: Postconflict Institutions and the Microdynamics of Conflict in Eastern DR Congo." *International Organization* 71 (2) (Spring): 281–315.

Lake, Milli. 2014. "Organizing Hypocrisy: Providing Legal Accountability for Human Rights Violations in Areas of Limited Statehood." *International Studies Quarterly* 58 (3): 515–526.

Lake, Milli, Ilot Muthaka, and Gabriella Walker. 2016. "Gendering Justice in Humanitarian Spaces: Opportunity and (Dis)empowerment through Gender-Based Legal Development Outreach in the Eastern Democratic Republic of Congo." *Law & Society Review* 50 (3): 539–574.

Le Monde. 2010. "Des milliers de Congolaises défilent contre les violences sexuelles." *Le Monde.fr*, October 17. www.lemonde.fr/afrique/article/2010 /10/17/des-milliers-de-congolaises-defilent-contre-les-violences-sex uelles_1427478_3212.html.

Lemarchand, René. 2013. "Reflections on the Recent Historiography of Eastern Congo." *Journal of African History* 54 (3): 417–437.

Lewis, Chloé. 2018. "Gender Protection / Protecting Gender: Rethinking Responses to Sexual Violence in Conflict and its Aftermath." Dissertation Manuscript. Oxford, UK.

Lieberman, Evan S. 2009. *Boundaries of Contagion: How Ethnic Politics Have Shaped Government Responses to AIDS*. Princeton, NJ: Princeton University Press.

Lock Swarr, Amanda. 2012. "Paradoxes of Butchness: Lesbian Masculinities and Sexual Violence in Contemporary South Africa." *Signs* 37 (4): 961–986.

Lonsway, Kimberly A., and Joanne Archambault. 2012. "The 'Justice Gap' for Sexual Assault Cases: Future Directions for Research and Reform." *Violence against Women* 18 (2): 145–168.

Lorde, Audre. 1984. *Sister Outsider: Essays and Speeches*. Crossing Press. Berkeley, CA.

Lund, Christian, ed. 2006. *Twilight Institutions: Public Authority and Local Politics in Africa*. Malden, MA: Blackwell Publishing.

Lupu, Yonatan. 2013. "Best Evidence: The Role of Information in Domestic Judicial Enforcement of International Human Rights Agreements." International Organization. Vol. 67: 3 July 2013. pp. 469–503International Organization. Vol. 67: 3 July 2013. pp. 469–503.

Lwambo, Desiree. 2013. "'Before the War, I Was a Man': Men and Masculinities in the Eastern Democratic Republic of Congo." *Gender & Development* 21 (1): 47–66.

MacKenzie, Megan. 2009. "Securitization and Desecuritization: Female Soldiers and the Reconstruction of Women in Post-Conflict Sierra Leone" *Security Studies*. 18: 2.

MacKinnon, Catharine A. 2005a. *Women's Lives, Men's Laws*. Cambridge, MA: Belknap Press of Harvard University Press.

  2006b. *Are Women Human?: And Other International Dialogues*. Cambridge, MA: Belknap Press of Harvard University Press.

Mail & Guardian. 2009. "Sentencing Postponed Again in Tembisa Rape Case." *The Mail & Guardian Online*. http://mg.co.za/article/2009-08-26-senten cing-postponed-again-in-tembisa-rape-case/.

Mamdani, Mahmood. 1996. *Citizen and Subject: Contemporary Africa and the Legacy of Late Colonialism*. Princeton, NJ: Princeton University Press.

  2001. *When Victims Become Killers: Colonialism, Nativism, and the Genocide in Rwanda*. Princeton, NJ: Princeton University Press.

Mampilly, Zachariah Cherian. 2011. *Rebel Rulers: Insurgent Governance and Civilian Life during War*. Ithaca, NY: Cornell University Press.

Mangcu, Xolela. 2009. *The Democratic Moment: South Africa's Prospects under Jacob Zuma*. Aukland Park, Johannesburg: Jacana Media.

Marx, Karl. 2012. *On the Jewish Question*. CreateSpace Independent Publishing Platform. London, U.K.

Marston, Cicily. 2005. "What Is Heterosexual Coercion? Interpreting Narratives from Young People in Mexico City." *Sociology of Health and Illness* 27 (1): 68–91.

Massoud, Mark F. 2006. "Rights in a Failed State: Internally Displaced Women in Sudan and Their Lawyers." *Berkeley Journal of Gender, Law & Justice* 21.

    2011. "Do Victims of War Need International Law? Human Rights Education Programs in Authoritarian Sudan." *Law & Society Review* 45 (1).

    2013. *Law's Fragile State: Colonial, Authoritarian, and Humanitarian Legacies in Sudan.* Cambridge: Cambridge University Press.

Mayhew, Leon, and Albert J. Reiss. 1969. "The Social Organization of Legal Contacts." *American Sociological Review* 34 (3): 309–318.

McBride, Dorothy E., Amy Mazur, and Joni Lovenduski. 2010. *The Politics of State Feminism: Innovation in Comparative Research.* Philadelphia, PA: Temple University Press.

McCann, Michael W. 1994. *Rights at Work: Pay Equity Reform and the Politics of Legal Mobilization.* Chicago, IL: University of Chicago Press.

    2006. "Law and Social Movements." *Annual Review of Law and Social Science* 2: 350–52.

    2014. "The Unbearable Lightness of Rights: On Sociolegal Inquiry in the Global Era." *Law & Society Review* 48 (2): 245–273.

McCarthy, John D., and Mayer N. Zald. 1977. "Resource Mobilization and Social Movements: A Partial Theory." *American Journal of Sociology* 82 (6).

McClintock, Anne. 2013. *Imperial Leather: Race, Gender, and Sexuality in the Colonial Contest.* London: Routledge.

Meger, Sara. 2010. "Rape of the Congo: Understanding Sexual Violence in the Conflict in the Democratic Republic of Congo." *Journal of Contemporary African Studies* 28 (2): 119–135.

    2011. "Rape in Contemporary Warfare: The Role of Globalization in Wartime Sexual Violence." *African Conflict & Peacebuilding Review* 1 (1): 100–132.

Menkhaus, Kenneth John. 2007. "Governance without Government in Somalia: Spoilers, State Building, and the Politics of Coping." *International Security* 31 (3): 74–106.

Meredith, Martin. 1988. *In the Name of Apartheid: South Africa in the Postwar Era.* New York, NY: Harper Collins Publishers.

Merry, Sally Engle. 1994. "Narrating Domestic Violence: Producing the 'Truth' of Violence in 19th- and 20th-Century Hawaiian Courts." *Law & Social Inquiry* 19 (4): 967–993.

    2000. *Colonizing Hawai'i: The Cultural Power of Law.* Princeton, NJ: Princeton University Press.

    2002. "Governmentality and Gender Violence in Hawai'i in Historical Perspective." *Social & Legal Studies* 11 (1): 81–111.

    2003a. "From Law and Colonialism to Law and Globalization." *LSI Law & Social Inquiry* 28 (2): 569–590.

    2003b. "Rights Talk and the Experience of Law: Implementing Women's Human Rights to Protection from Violence." *Human Rights Quarterly* 25 (2): 343–381.

    2006. *Human Rights and Gender Violence: Translating International Law into Local Justice.* Chicago, IL: University of Chicago Press.

Mertens, Charlotte. 2016. "Sexual Violence in the Congo Free State: Archival Traces and Present Reconfigurations." *Australasian Review of African Studies* 37 (1): 6.

Meyer, John W., John Boli, George M. Thomas, and Francisco O-Ramirez. 1997. "World Society and the Nation-State." *American Journal of Sociology* 103 (1): 144.

Meyer, John W., and Brian Rowan. 1977. "Institutionalized Organizations: Formal Structure as Myth and Ceremony." *American Journal of Sociology* 83 (2): 340–363.

Mianda, Gertrude D. M. 1995. "Dans L'ombre de La 'démocratie' au Zaïre: La Remise En Question de L'émancipation Mobutiste de La Femme." *Canadian Journal of African Studies / Revue Canadienne Des Études Africaines* 29 (1): 51–78.

Migdal, Joel S. 2001. *State in Society: Studying How States and Societies Transform and Constitute One Another.* Cambridge; New York, NY: Cambridge University Press.

Miller, Richard E., and Austin Sarat. 1980. "Grievances, Claims, and Disputes: Assessing the Adversary Culture." *Law & Society Review* 15 (3/4): 525–566.

Miller, Tina, Maxine Birch, Melanie Mauthner, and Julie Jessop. 2012. *Ethics in Qualitative Research.* Thousand Oaks, CA: Sage Publications.

Mitchell, Audra. 2013. "Escaping the 'Field Trap': Exploitation and the Global Politics of Educational Fieldwork in 'Conflict Zones.'" *Third World Quarterly* 34 (7): 1247–1264.

Mitchell, Timothy. 1999. "Society, Economy, and the State Effect." *In State/Culture: State-Formation after the Cultural Turn*, edited by George Steinmetz. Ithaca, NY: Cornell University Press.

Moffett, Helen. 2006. "The Political Economy of Sexual Violence in Post-apartheid South Africa." Harold Wolpe Memorial Trust's Tenth Anniversary Colloquium, "Engaging Silences and Unresolved Issues in the Political Economy of South Africa." September 21–23, 2006, Cape Town, South Africa.

Montoya, Celeste. 2015. *From Global to Grassroots: The European Union, Transnational Advocacy, and Combating Violence against Women.* Place of publication not identified: Oxford University Press.

MONUSCO. 2014. "Project Factsheet - UNA027 OHCHR WPA in MONUSCO: Strengthening the Capacities of MONUSCO to Implement the MARA Provisional Guidance Note, through the Deployment of Women Protection Adviser (WPA)." UN Action against Sexual Violence. Kinshasa, DR Congo.

MONUSCO and UN-OHCHR. 2014. "National Guidelines for the Coordination of Action between Humanitarian Actors and the United Nations Organization Stabilization Mission in the Democratic Republic of Congo." Kinshasa, DR Congo.

Morfit, N. Simon. 2011. "'AIDS Is Money': How Donor Preferences Reconfigure Local Realities." *World Development* 39 (1): 64–76.

Motley, Kimberley. 2014. "Transcript of 'How I Defend the Rule of Law.'" TED-Global. Humboldt; Eureka, CA.

Motlhabi, Mokgethi B. G. 1988. *Challenge to Apartheid: Toward a Moral National Resistance*. Eerdmans Pub Co. Grand Rapids. MI.

Moyo, Dambisa. 2010. *Dead Aid: Why Aid Is Not Working and How There Is a Better Way for Africa*. 1 Reprint edn. New York, NY: Farrar, Straus and Giroux.

Mubangizi, John. 2013. "A South African Perspective on the Clash between Culture and Human Rights, with Particular Reference to Gender-Related Cultural Practices and Traditions." *Journal of International Women's Studies* 13 (3): 33–48.

Muehlenhard, Charlene L., and Lisa C. Hollabaugh. 1988. "Do Women Sometimes Say No When They Mean Yes? The Prevalence and Correlates of Women's Token Resistance to Sex." *Journal of Personality and Social Psychology* 54 (5): 872–879.

Murdie, Amanda, and Dursun Peksen. 2014. "Women's Rights INGO Shaming and the Government Respect for Women's Rights." *Review of International Organizations* 10 (1): 1–22.

Mutongi, Kenda. 2007. *Worries of the Heart: Widows, Family, and Community in Kenya*. Chicago, IL: University of Chicago Press.

Neumayer, Eric. 2005. "Do International Human Rights Treaties Improve Respect for Human Rights?" *Journal of Conflict Resolution* 49 (6): 925–953.

News 24. 2009. "Gang Rape Sentence Delayed." *News24*. www.news24.com/Africa/News/Gang-rape-sentence-delayed-20090728.

Nojumi, Neamat, J. Alexander Barfield, and Thomas Thier. 2008. "The Clash of Two Goods: State and Non-state Dispute Resolution in Afghanistan." *United States Institute of Peace*.

Nolen, Stephanie. 2005. "Not Women Anymore . . .." *Ms. Magazine*. www.msmagazine.com/spring2005/congo.asp.

Noonan, Rita K. 1995. "Women against the State: Political Opportunities and Collective Action Frames in Chile's Transition to Democracy." *Sociological Forum* 10 (1): 81–111.

Nzongola-Ntalaja, Georges. 2002. *The Congo: From Leopold to Kabila: A People's History*. London; New York, NY: Zed Books.

Oberschall, Anthony. 1995. *Social Movements: Ideologies, Interests, and Identities*. New Brunswick, NJ: Transaction Publishers.

Olsson, Louise, and Theodora-Ismene Gizelis. 2015. *Gender, Peace and Security: Implementing UN Security Council Resolution 1325*. London: Routledge.

One in Nine Campaign. 2007. "One in Nine Campaign: Solidarity with Women Who Speak out." Johannesburg, South Africa. www.womensnet.org.za/campaign/one-nine-campaign-solidarity-with-women-who-speak-out.html.

2009. "Timeline on Buyisiwe's Case." Internal Document. Johannesburg, South Africa.

Onsrud, Mathias, Solbjørg Sjøveian, Roger Luhiriri, and Denis Mukwege. 2008. "Sexual Violence-Related Fistulas in the Democratic Republic of Congo." *International Journal of Gynecology & Obstetrics* 103 (3): 265–269.

Open Society Foundation. 2013. *Justice in DRC: Mobile Courts Combat Rape and Impunity in Eastern Congo*. New York, NY: Open Society Justice Initiative. www.opensocietyfoundations.org/sites/default/files/justice-drc-20130114 .pdf.

Organization of Economic Cooperation and Development (OECD). 2005. "International Development Statistics: ESDS International, University of Manchester." Manchester, UK.

Oudraat, Chantal de Jonge. 2011. *Women and War: Power and Protection in the 21st Century*. Washington, DC: US Institute of Peace Press.

Parkinson, Sarah Elizabeth. 2013. "Organizing Rebellion: Rethinking High-Risk Mobilization and Social Networks in War." *American Political Science Review* 107 (3): 418–432.

Pauwels, Johan M. 1970. *Repertoire de Droit Coutumier congolais: Jurisprudence et Doctrine 1954–1967*. Office National de la Recherche et du Développment.

1973. "La Réforme Du Droit Civil Au Zaïre Comment Concilier Tradition et Développement?" *Journal of African Law* 17 (2): 216–226.

Perraudin, Frances, and Stephanie Busari. 2010. "Nobel Peace Prize: Congo Rape Trauma Surgeon among Favorites – CNN.com." *CNN*, September. www.cnn.com/2013/10/10/world/africa/nobel-prize-congo-surgeon-mukeg we/index.html.

Peterman, Amber, Tia Palermo, and Caryn Bredenkamp. 2011. "Estimates and Determinants of Sexual Violence against Women in the Democratic Republic of Congo." *American Journal of Public Health* 101 (6): 1060–1067.

Petras, James. 1999. "NGOs: In the Service of Imperialism." *Journal of Contemporary Asia* 29 (4): 429–440.

Pithey, Bronwyn, Lillian Artz, Heléne Combrinck, and Nicolette Naylor. 1999. "Legal Aspects of Rape in South Africa." Rape Crisis (Cape Town); Women & Human Rights Project Community Law Centre, and the University of Cape Town Institute of Criminology.

Prakash, Aseem, and Mary Kay Gugerty. 2010. *Advocacy Organizations and Collective Action*. Cambridge; New York, NY: Cambridge University Press.

Radebe, Jeff. 2013. "Sex Courts to Be Reinstated." *eNews Channel Africa*, August 6. www.enca.com/south-africa/sex-courts-be-reinstated.

Radebe, Jeff. 2012. "Keynote Address by Minister Jeff Radebe at the 20 Year Celebration of the Rape Crisis Centre, Port Elizabeth." Department of Justice and Constitutional Development. 16 November, 2012. Port Elizabeth, South Africa.

Radin, Andrew. 2012. *The Limits of State-Building: The Politics of War and the Ideology of Peace*. Cambridge, MA: MIT Press.

Raeymaekers, Timothy. 2005. "Collapse or Order? Questioning State Collapse in Africa." *Conflict Research Group*, Working Paper 1 (May).

Raeymaekers, Timothy, Kenneth John Menkhaus, and Koen Vlassenroot. 2008. "State and Non-state Regulation in African Protracted Crises: Governance without Government." *Afrika Focus* 21 (2): 7–21.

Ragin, Charles C. 2014. *The Comparative Method: Moving beyond Qualitative and Quantitative Strategies*. Univ of California Press.

Rahman, Aminur. 1999. "Micro-credit Initiatives for Equitable and Sustainable Development: Who Pays?" *World Development* 27 (1): 67–82.

Ramirez, Allison Marie. 2012. "Human Rights Strategies in the Context of Changing Political Opportunity Structures: The Case of Two Transnational Networks in El Salvador." May.

Reno, William. 1999. *Warlord Politics and African States*. Boulder, CO: Lynne Rienner Publishers.

Reuters. 2017. "Eleven Dead, Hundreds Escape in Congo Jail Attack." *Reuters*, June 11. www.reuters.com/article/us-congo-violence-prisonprison-idUSKBN1920Y3.

Ridde, Valéry, and Florence Morestin. 2011. "A Scoping Review of the Literature on the Abolition of User Fees in Health Care Services in Africa." *Health Policy and Planning* 26 (1): 1–11.

Risse, Thomas, ed. 2011. *Governance without a State?: Policies and Politics in Areas of Limited Statehood*. New York, NY: Columbia University Press.

Risse, Thomas, Steve C. Ropp, and Kathryn Sikkink. 2013. *The Persistent Power of Human Rights: From Commitment to Compliance*. Cambridge [u.a.]: Cambridge University Press.

Risse-Kappen, Thomas, Stephen C. Ropp, and Kathryn Sikkink. 1999a. *The Power of Human Rights: International Norms and Domestic Change*. New York, NY; Cambridge: Cambridge University Press.

1999b. *The Power of Human Rights: International Norms and Domestic Change*. New York, NY: Cambridge University Press.

Rodrik, Dani, Arvind Subramanian, and Francesco Trebbi. 2002. *Institutions Rule: The Primacy of Institutions over Integration and Geography in Economic Development*. Washington, DC: International Monetary Fund.

Rosenberg, Gerald N. 1991. *The Hollow Hope: Can Courts Bring about Social Change?* Chicago, IL: University of Chicago.

Rubbers, Benjamin, and Emilie Gallez. 2012. "Why Do Congolese People Go to Court?: A Qualitative Study of Litigants' Experiences in Two Justice of the Peace Courts in Lubumbashi." *Journal of Legal Pluralism and Unofficial Law*, no. 66: 79–108.

Rundell, Sarah. 2010. "Rwanda Is Not Ready for the Medicine of Democracy, Says Kagame." *The Independent*, May 29. www.independent.co.uk/news/world/afr ica/rwanda-is-not-ready-for-the-medicine-of-democracy-says-kagame-19862 10.html.

Sadan, Lulama, Mastoera Dikweni, and Shaamela Cassiem. 2001. "Pilot Assessment: The Sexual Offences Court in Wynberg & Cape Town and Related Services." AfriMap. Cape Town, SA.

Schatz, Edward, ed. 2009. *Political Ethnography: What Immersion Contributes to the Study of Power*. 1st edn. Chicago; London: University of Chicago Press.

Scheingold, Stuart A. 2004. *The Politics of Rights Lawyers, Public Policy, and Political Change*. Ann Arbor, MI: University of Michigan Press.

Schlichte, Klaus, and Joel Migdal. 2005. "Rethinking the State." In *The Dynamics of States: The Formation and Crises of State Domination*. Aldershot, Hants, England; Burlington, VT: Ashgate.

Schuler, Sidney Ruth, Syed M Hashemi, and Shamsul Huda Badal. 1998. "Men's Violence against Women in Rural Bangladesh: Undermined or Exacerbated by Microcredit Programmes?" *Development in Practice* 8 (2): 148–157.

Seay, Laura. 2009. *Authority at Twilight: Civil Society, Social Services, and the State in the Eastern Democratic Republic of Congo.* Austin, TX: University of Texas, Austin.

Seekings, Jeremy. 2013. "Economy, Society and Municipal Services in Khayelitsha." Centre for Social Science Research, University of Cape Town, Report Center for Social Science Research.

Seelinger, Kim Thuy. 2015. "The Long Road: Accountability for Sexual Violence in Conflict and Post-conflict Settings." The Human Rights Center at Berkeley School of Law. Berkeley, CA.

Sikkink, Kathryn. 2011. *The Justice Cascade.* London; New York, NY: W. W. Norton & Company.

Simmons, Beth A. 2009. *Mobilizing for Human Rights: International Law in Domestic Politics.* New York, NY: Cambridge University Press.

Simons, Harold Jack. 1968. *African Women: Their Legal Status in South Africa.* Evanston, IL: Northwestern University Press.

Skaar, Elin. 2011. *Judicial Independence and Human Rights in Latin America: Violations, Politics, and Prosecution.* Basingstoke, U.K.: Palgrave Macmillan.

Smith, Alex Duval. 2014. "Safe Toilets Could Prevent Sexual Assault and Sickness, Say South Africa's Poor." *The Guardian*, sec. Global Development. www.theguardian.com/global-development/2011/sep/16/safe-toilets-prevent-sickness-assault.

Smith, Nicholas Rush. 2015. "Rejecting Rights: Vigilantism and Violence in Post-apartheid South Africa." *African Affairs* 114 (456): 341–360.

2018. *Resisting Rights: Vigilantism and the Contradictions of Democratic State Formation in Post-apartheid South Africa.* Oxford: Oxford University Press.

Snodgrass, Lyn. 2015. "South Africa: A Dangerous Place to Be Poor, Black and a Woman." *Times LIVE*, September 11. www.timeslive.co.za/local/2015/09/11/South-Africa-a-dangerous-place-to-be-poor-black-and-a-woman.

Social Justice Coalition. www.sjc.org.za/.

Sonke Gender Justice Network. 2012. "Gender Relations, Sexual Violence and the Effects of Conflict on Women and Men in North Kivu, Eastern Democratic Republic of Congo: Preliminary Results from the International Men and Gender Equality Survey (IMAGES)." Washington, DC: International Center for Research on Women (ICRW) and Rio de Janeiro: Instituto Promundo.

Soss, Joe. 2006. "Talking Our Way to Meaningful Explanations: A Practice-Centered Approach to In-Depth Interviews for Interpretive Research." In *Interpretation and Method*, edited by Dvora Yanow and Peregrine Schwartz-Shea. New York, NY: M.E. Sharpe. 161–182.

South Africa 2008. Judicial Education Institute Act. 14 of 2008. Assented to September 12, 2008.

South Africa 2010. "Education and Training Unit." www.etu.org.za/toolbox/docs/government/basic.html#sanitation.

South Africa Commission for Gender Equality. 1996. "Commission for Gender Equality." Johannesburg, South Africa. www.cge.org.za/.

South Africa 1997. Criminal Law Amendment Act [No. 105 of 1997]. 105. Government Gazette. Cape Town. 19 December 1997. Vol 390. No. 18519.

2007. Criminal Law (Sexual Offenses and Related Matters) Amendment Act 32 of 2007. 32. Government Gazette. Cape Town. 14 December 2007. Vol. 1224. No. 30599.

2013. Superior Courts Act 10 of 2013 Government Gazette. Cape Town. 12 August 2013. Vol. 578. No. 36743.

South Africa Department of Health. 1998. "South Africa Demographic and Health Survey 1998". Macro International and the Government of South Africa. Pretoria, South Africa.

2017. "South Africa: DHS 2016 – Key Indicators Report (English)." Johannesburg, South Africa.

South Africa Department of Justice and Constitutional Development. 2013. "Report on the Re-establishment of Sexual Offences Courts." Ministerial Advisory Task Team on the Adjudication of Sexual Offence Matters. Johannesburg, South Africa.

South Africa Department of Justice and Constitutional Development. 2016. "Justice/Courts Organization." Government of South Africa. www.justice .gov.za/about/sa-courts.html.

South African Police Service (SAPS). 2014. "South African Police Service (SAPS) Analysis of the 2014/15 National Crime Statistics." Johannesburg, South Africa.

2015. "SAPS South African Police Service Annual Crime Statistics." Johannesburg, South Africa. www.saps.gov.za/services/crimestats.php.

South African Truth and Reconciliation Commission. 1997. "Further Submissions and Responses by the African National Congress to Questions Raised by the Commission for Truth and Reconciliation." Johannesburg, South Africa. www.justice.gov.za/trc/hrvtrans/submit/anc2.htm#Appendix.

Spear, Thomas. 2003. "Neo-traditionalism and the Limits of Invention in British Colonial Africa." *The Journal of African History* 44 (1): 3–27.

Stearns, Jason. 2013. "Interview: Is There Too Much Focus on Sexual Violence in the Congo? Interview with Laura Heaton." *Congo Siasa*. March 8.

Stubbs, Thomas. 2016. "Why Kagame's Bid to Serve a Third Term Makes Sense for Rwanda." *The Conversation*, January 27.

Super, Gail. 2016. "Volatile Sovereignty: Governing Crime through the Community in Khayelitsha." *Law & Society Review* 50 (2): 450–483.

Swart, Lu-Anne, Angela Gilchrist, Alex Butchart, Mohamed Seedat, and Lorna Martin. 2000. "Rape Surveillance through District Surgeon Offices in Johannesburg, 1996–1998: Findings, Evaluation and Prevention Implications." *South African Journal of Psychology* 30 (2): 1–10.

Thies, Cameron G. 2004. "State Building, Interstate and Intrastate Rivalry: A Study of Post-Colonial Developing Country Extractive Efforts, 1975–2000." *International Studies Quarterly*, Volume 48: 1. pp. 53–72

Thomas, Lynn M. 2003. *Politics of the Womb: Women, Reproduction, and the State in Kenya*. University of California Press.

Thomson Reuters Foundation. 2011. "The World's Most Dangerous Countries for Women 2011." www.trust.org/spotlight/the-worlds-most-dangerous-countries-for-women-2011/.

Tickner, J. Ann. 1992. *Gender in International Relations: Feminist Perspectives on Achieving Global Security*. New York, NY: Columbia University Press.

1997. "You Just Don't Understand: Troubled Engagements between Feminists and IR Theorists." *International Studies Quarterly* 41 (4): 611–32.

Tickner, J. Ann, and Laura Sjoberg. 2011. *Feminism and International Relations: Conversations about the Past, Present, and Future*. London; New York, NY: Routledge.

Timap for Justice: Liberia. 2014. "News: Timap for Justice." www.timapforjustice.org/news.

Timap for Justice: Sierra Leone. 2014. "News: Timap for Justice." www.timapforjustice.org/news.

Touro, Amadine. 2013. "De La Puberté Féminine Dans Les 'Zones Torrides' Expertise Médicale et Régulations Du Corps Des Jeunes Filles Dans Le Congo Colonial." *Sextant* 30: 33–45.

Towns, Ann E. 2010. *Women and States: Norms and Hierarchies in International Society*. Cambridge; New York, NY: Cambridge University Press.

Trefon, Theodore. 2011. *Congo Masquerade: The Political Culture of Aid Inefficiency and Reform Failure*. London; New York, NY: Zed Books.

Tripp, Aili Mari. 2010. "Legislating Gender-Based Violence in Post-conflict Africa." *Journal of Peacebuilding and Development* 5 (3): 7–20.

2013. "How African Feminism Changed the World: Think Africa Press." *Think Africa Press*. Africa Research Institute. London, U.K.

2015. *Women and Power in Postconflict Africa*. New York, NY: Cambridge University Press.

Tripp, Aili Mari, Myra Marx Ferree, and Christina Ewig. 2013. *Gender, Violence, and Human Security: Critical Feminist Perspectives*. New York, NY: New York University Press.

Trochev, Alexei. 2010. "Meddling with Justice: Competitive Politics, Impunity, and Distrusted Courts in Post-Orange Ukraine." *Demokratizatsiya* 18 (2): 122–147, Spring 2010; Indiana Legal Studies Research Paper.

Tull, Denis. 2005. *The Reconfiguration of Political Order in Africa: A Case Study of North Kivu (DR Congo)*. Hamburg: GIGA-Hamburg.

United Nations. 1993. Declaration on the Elimination of Violence against Women. www.un.org/documents/ga/res/48/a48r104.htm.

1995. Beijing Platform for Action. www.un.org/womenwatch/daw/beijing/platform/plat1.htm#statement.

UN News. 2011. "UN News – DR Congo Mass Rape Verdicts Send Strong Signal to Perpetrators – UN Envoy." *UN News Service Section*, February 21. www.un.org/apps/news/story.asp?NewsID=37580&Cr=sexua#.UuBAO43nZpk.

United Nations Children's Fund (UNICEF) and Graça Machel. 1996. "The Impact of Armed Conflict on Children." A/51/306. New York, NY: United Nations.

United Nations Development Programme (UNDP). 2012. "United Nations Development Programme, Afghanistan." www.undp.org.af/.

    2014a. "Justice System Programme: East Timor." www.undp.org/content/ti mor_leste/en/home/operations/projects/democratic_governance/TL_DG_Ju sticePgmme.html.

    2014b. "Evaluation of UNDP's Support to Mobile Courts in DRC, Sierra Leone and Somalia." www.undp.org/content/undp/en/home/librarypage/crisis-pre vention-and-recovery/evaluation-of-undp-s-support-to-mobile-courts-in-drc– sierra-leo.html.

    2015. "Mobile Courts Bring Justice to Rural Pakistan." United Nations Development Programme, Washington Representation Office. www.undp .org/content/washington/en/home/ourwork/democraticgovernance/successs tories/mobile-courts-bring-justice-to-rural-pakistan.html.

United Nations Office of Drugs and Crime. 2014. "Statistics." United Nations Office of Drugs and Crime (UNODC) Database. www.unodc.org/unodc/en/ data-and-analysis/statistics/index.html.

United Nations Population Fund (UNFPA). 2013. "Ampleur Des Violences Sexuelles En RDC et Actions de Lutte Contre Le Phénomène de 2011 À 2012." Democratic Republic of the Congo: Ministere du Genre, de la Famille et de l'Enfant.

United Nations Security Council. 1999a. United Nations Security Council Resolution 1234 on the Situation in the Democratic Republic of Congo. April 9. (S/RES/1234).

United Nations Security Council. 1999b. United Nations Security Council Resolution 1279 on the Situation in the Democratic Republic of Congo. November 30. (S/RES/1279). United Nations Security Council. 2000. United Nations Security Council Resolution 1325 on Women, Peace and Security. October 21, 2000. (S/RES/1325).

United Nations Special Representative on Sexual Violence in Conflict. 2015a. "About the Office | Office of the Special Representative of the Secretary-General on Sexual Violence in Conflict." Action against Sexual Violence in Conflict Network. www.un.org/sexualviolenceinconflict/about-us/about-the-office/.

    2015. "Democratic Republic of the Congo | Office of the Special Representative of the Secretary-General on Sexual Violence in Conflict." March. www.un.org/sexualviolenceinconflict/countries/democratic-repub lic-of-the-congo/.

US Department of State. 2009. *Country Reports on Human Rights Practices 2009.* Washington, DC: Government Printing Office.

USAID. 2012. "USAID Ethiopia Joins ABA and AAU Law School in Launching First Law Textbooks in 40 Years." *USAID Leadership*. Washington D.C.

    2016. "History of USAID/Rwanda | Rwanda | U.S. Agency for International Development." Washington, DC: US Government. www.usaid.gov/history-usaidrwanda.

Utas, Mats. 2005. "Victimcy, Girlfriending, Soldiering: Tactic Agency in a Young Woman's Social Navigation of the Liberian War Zone." *Anthropological Quarterly* 78 (2): 403–430.

Van de Walle, Nicolas. 2005. *Overcoming Stagnation in Aid-Dependent Countries.* Washington, DC: Center for Global Development.

Vanhala, Lisa. 2012. "Legal Opportunity Structures and the Paradox of Legal Mobilization by the Environmental Movement in the UK." *Law & Society Review* 46 (3): 523–556.

Vetten, Lisa. 2013. "Police Crime Statistics." Institute of Security Studies. Johannesburg, SA.

Vetten, Lisa, and Danielle Motelow. 2004. "Creating State Accountability to Rape Survivors: A Case Study of Boksburg Regional Court." *Agenda* 18 (62): 45–52.

Vetten, Lisa, Romi Sigworth, Lizle Loots, Rachel Jewkes, Olivia Dunseith, and Nicola Christofides. 2008. "Tracking Justice: The Attrition of Rape Cases through the Criminal Justice System in Gauteng." Johannesburg: Tshwaranang Legal Advocacy Centre, the South African Medical Research Counciland the Centre for the Study of Violence and Reconciliation.

Vlassenroot, Koen, and Timothy Raeymaekers. 2004. *Conflict and Social Transformation in Eastern DR Congo.* Conflict Research Group. Gent Belgium: Academia Press Scientific Publishers.

Vogel, Christoph. 2012. *Operational Stalemate or Politically Induced Failure? On the Dynamics Influencing Humanitarian Aid in the Democratic Republic of the Congo.* Marburg: Tectum-Verl.

2013. "Why Herbst and Mills Are Wrong about Congo's 'Invisible State.'" *ChristophVogel.net.* June. http://christophvogel.net/2013/06/27/why-herbst-and-mills-are-wrong-about-congos-invisible-state/.

VonDoepp, Peter. 2009. *Judicial Politics in New Democracies: Cases from Southern Africa.* Boulder, CO: Lynne Rienner Publishers.

Vos, Pierre De. 2007. "The 'Inevitability' of Same-Sex Marriage in South Africa's Post-apartheid State." *South African Journal on Human Rights* 23 (3): 432–465.

Walker, Liz. 2005. "Men Behaving Differently: South African Men since 1994." *Culture, Health & Sexuality* 7 (3): 225–238.

Warner, W. Keith, and A. Eugene Havens. 1968. "Goal Displacement and the Intangibility of Organizational Goals." *Administrative Science Quarterly* 12 (4): 539.

Wedeen, Lisa. 2010. "Reflections on Ethnographic Work in Political Science." *Annual Review of Political Science* 13 (1): 255–272.

Weingast, Barry R. 1997. "The Political Foundations of Democracy and the Rule of Law." *The American Political Science Review* 91 (2): 245.

2010. "Why Developing Countries Prove so Resistant to the Rule of Law." In *Global Perspectives on the Rule of Law*, edited by James J. Heckman, Robert L. Nelson, and Lee Cabatingan. London; New York, NY: Routledge. 28–52.

Widner, Jennifer A. 2001. *Building the Rule of Law: Francis Nyalali and the Road to Judicial Independence in Africa.* New York; London: W.W. Norton.

Wilkinson, Kate. 2014. "Africa: Why It Is Wrong to Call S. Africa or Any Country the 'Rape Capital of the World.'" *Africa Check (Johannesburg)*, January 28. http://allafrica.com/stories/201401281018.html?viewall=1.

Willett, Susan. 2010. "Introduction: Security Council Resolution 1325: Assessing the Impact on Women, Peace and Security." *International Peacekeeping* 17 (2): 142–158.

Wilson, Bruce M., and Juan Carlos Rodríguez Cordero. 2006. "Legal Opportunity Structures and Social Movements: The Effects of Institutional Change on Costa Rican Politics." *Comparative Political Studies* 39 (3): 325–351.

Witte, Eric A., 2011. "Putting Complementarity into Practice Domestic Justice for International Crimes in DRC, Uganda, and Kenya." Open Society Foundations, Open Society Initiative for East Africa, Open Society Justice Initiative, and Open Society Initiative for Southern Africa. Johannesburg, SA.

Wolfe, Lauren. 2014. "Unarmed and Dangerous." *Foreign Policy*, March 7. www .foreignpolicy.com/articles/2014/03/07/unarmed_and_dangerous_congo_rape.

Women's Legal Centre (WLC). 2012. "Rape Sentencing in South Africa 2008– 2012."

Women's Legal Centre and Rape Crisis Cape Town Trust. 2013. *Protecting Survivors of Sexual Offences: The Legal Obligations of the State with Regard to Sexual Offences in South Africa.* Cape Town, South Africa: Women's Legal Centre and Rape Crisis Cape Town Trust.

Wood, Elisabeth Jean. 2006a. "The Ethical Challenges of Field Research in Conflict Zones." *Qualitative Sociology* 29 (3): 373–386.

2006b. "Variation in Sexual Violence during War." *Politics & Society* 34 (3): 307–342.

Wood, Kate. 2005. "Contextualizing Group Rape in Post-apartheid South Africa." *Culture, Health & Sexuality* 7 (4): 303–317.

Wood, Kate, Helen Lambert, and Rachel Jewkes. 2007. "'Showing Roughness in a Beautiful Way': Talk about Love, Coercion, and Rape in South African Youth Sexual Culture." *Medical Anthropology Quarterly* 21 (3): 277–300.

Wood, Katharine, and Rachel Jewkes. 1997. "Violence, Rape, and Sexual Coercion: Every Day Love in a South African Township." *Gender & Development* 5 (2): 41–46.

1998. "'Love Is a Dangerous Thing': Micro-dynamics of Violence in Sexual Relationships of Young People in Umtata." *Medical Research Council Technical Report*, 1–48.

Woodrow Wilson Center. 2013. "The Rise of Non-consensual Bride Kidnapping in Kazakhstan: Developing a Culturally-Informed and Gender-Sensitive Response." www.wilsoncenter.org/publication/the-rise-non-consensual-bri de-kidnapping-kazakhstan-developing-culturally-informed-and.

World Bank. 2016. "Preventing Intimate-Partner Violence: Impact Evaluation of Engaging Men through Accountable Practice in Eastern DRC." *ClinicalTrials.Gov* International Rescue Committee. https://clinicaltrials.gov/ ct2/show/NCT02765139.

World Economic Forum. 2012. "What Is the State of the BRICS Economies?" *World Economic Forum.* www.weforum.org/agenda/2016/04/what-is-the-stat e-of-the-brics-economies/.

Wort, Tamsin. 2013. "Western Cape Police Rape Stats Highest in South Africa." *Eye Witness News*. http://ewn.co.za/2013/09/06/Cape-cop-rape-stats-alarming.

Yarbrough, Michael William. 2013. "'I Now Declare You': State Law and the Making of Marriage in Post-Apartheid South Africa." PhD, Yale University. Newhaven, NY.

York, Geoffrey. 2010. "Anti-rape Funds in Congo Wasted: Critics." *The Globe and Mail*, March 14. www.theglobeandmail.com/news/world/anti-rape-funds-in-congo-wasted-critics/article4192389/.

Zaum, Dominic. 2006. *The Sovereignty Paradox: The Norms and Politics of International Statebuilding*. Oxford: Oxford University Press.

Zwingel, Susanne. 2012. "How Do Norms Travel? Theorizing International Women's Rights in Transnational Perspective." *International Studies Quarterly* 56 (1): 115–129.

Index